John L. Lewis

John L. Lewis

AN UNAUTHORIZED BIOGRAPHY

by Saul Alinsky

Vintage Books

A DIVISION OF RANDOM HOUSE · NEW YORK

VINTAGE BOOKS EDITION, November 1970
First Edition

Copyright 1949 by Saul D. Alinsky
Copyright © 1970 by Saul D. Alinsky

Manufactured in the United States of America

To
DAVID *and* KATHRYN
and
to the memory of
HELENE

Contents

Introduction to the Vintage Edition

THIS is the story of a man, of a revolution and how he led it.

It is relevant to our own revolutionary times. All great social crises turn on certain common concepts. One is that progress occurs only in response to threats, and reconciliations only result when one side gets the power and the other side gets reconciled to it. Another is that the power of organized people is required to defeat the power of the establishment and its money. A third is that effective tactics means going outside the experience of the enemy, and a fourth is that all issues must be polarized. These and other revolutionary concepts hold true through all the revolutions of man, no matter in what place or time.

Today the greatest technological revolution in history finds us in a computerized, cybernetic, nuclear-powered, mass-media jet age, where we are inundated with information and know more about the happenings in the world around us, from Cambodia to

In 1940 the alliance between Lewis and Roosevelt was shaky. Roosevelt's proposed negotiator with Lewis was Daniel Tobin, then head of the Teamsters Union. Lewis rebuffed Tobin as unqualified to be a "negotiator" since he was a partisan supporter of the President. The situation steadily deteriorated, and finally the President informed Lewis that he would meet with a "negotiator" who would be acceptable to Lewis. I found myself with the late Bishop Sheil of Chicago in the role of negotiator. To me, F.D.R. and John L. were my idols (at the age of thirty-one I still had idols), and in those negotiations I saw the human weaknesses in both. Today it seems absurd that I ever thought of any man as near-perfect, but then it was an extraordinary educational experience. Subsequently, I grew to accept a man who was 50.01 on the side of the angels as a saint. It was agreed that none of the details of the negotiations would ever be divulged during Roosevelt's and Lewis' lifetime. Following the President's death, Lewis released me from his part of the agreement.

Biafra, and yet we know less. The massive deluge of information and the onrush and changing character of problems give us no time to digest and think. Thus it is especially important today to remember, as I have pointed out elsewhere, that with rare exceptions revolutionaries arise from the middle class, whose members, having a certain economic security, have time to think and develop. Today most people in western society have more time to look around, to be aware of other things and how they are related to their personal lives. Mass media have smashed their private worlds with "Look! Pollution is here and killing you!" "Look! Overpopulation is destroying the world!" "Look! We can't even get out of Vietnam and we're getting in somewhere else!" "Look! Inflation! Race Riots! Campus Riots! Police Pigs! Law and Order! The Bomb! Look! Look!"

Everything is so fractured, ever moving and changing, that it makes a kaleidoscope look static. To many the world is hellbent for hell in a hundred different ways.

But let us go back to "the good old days," three decades ago, to the time of this story. The early 1930's were days of great violence. Negroes (they are called Blacks today—but only white racists called them blacks then) were being lynched regularly in the South and rigidly segregated in the North by restrictive covenants in real estate. White civil rights agitators and labor organizers were being tarred, feathered and castrated. The Ku Klux Klan claimed in its membership nearly every southern political leader. Our corporate establishment was even more arrogant, proud and all-powerful, and profound believers in the American way of a free competitive society, free to exploit, free to crush any obstacle which blocked the road to Mammon. Labor unions were stamped as subversive. Workers who even mentioned them were fired and blacklisted by industry. None of America's corporations, from steel to oil, from auto to rubber to meat packing and everywhere else, had a labor union. The vast bulk of workers was unskilled, and were hired and fired with brutal callousness. They worked as dehumanized, animated accessories to the ever-moving assembly line. Relatively few were specially skilled. The elite of the blue-collar working class had their craft unions in the American Federation of Labor, but they differed from the corporations only in that they regretted the plight of the vast mass of the unorganized exploited workers but generally the country was all right as long as they got theirs.

Profit and patriotism went together in that order. There were no gouging stores in the ghettos of the poor, only company-owned stores in company towns which robbed you outrageously and didn't permit competition. There were no deteriorated inner cities, only stinking slums across the tracks. Upton Sinclair's *The Jungle* accurately described the living and working conditions of the times.

In foreign affairs our government was pursuing an even-handed policy of great foresight. It knew then that Russian Communism was doomed, certain that the Russian people would at any moment rise to overthrow these bloody-handed revolutionists. This we balanced off with a paranoid fear of world-wide creeping Communism. Our attorney general had a very energetic young director named J. Edgar Hoover, head of a young bustling organization called the F.B.I., who was systematically hounding, raiding and arresting all suspected agitators, subversives and reds. With this, Congress conceived a new committee called the House Un-American Affairs Committee, which was hysterically unearthing Communist revolutionary plots everywhere. The republic was in great danger!

Meanwhile we denounced the Japanese invasion of "Free" Manchuria but sold Japan the scrap iron with which to make war. We denounced Franco's fascist invasion—armed by Hitler's Panzer divisions, Nazi strike-dive bombers and Mussolini's soldiers—against the democratic republic of Spain and at the same time slapped an arms embargo on the republican government of Spain. For the first time in history a legitimate government was denied the right to purchase arms for its own defense. We sold Europe the idea of a League of Nations, the United Nations of that time, and then wouldn't join it. Very different from today, when we belong to the United Nations but pay as much attention to it as we did to the old League. Wars, tensions, resistance movements, rebellions against colonialism were all over the globe. We brought in Selective Service; strange new things sprouted, like passive resistance, and a skinny little revolutionary with a loincloth and spinning wheel showed up. Many didn't like him, but felt better when he rejoined the human race by banning non-violence and forcibly invaded Kashmir. Yes, those were the days, my friend, sane, rational, stable and secure, very different from the frenetic, mad violence of today.

We had no problem of pollution then. People were born and grew up in the overpowering stench and crapped-up air in meat-packing sections, but then you got so used to it that fresh air smelled funny and sick, only Communist agitators complained about the stink. All the workers in steel and coal-mining towns lived in an atmosphere of black-gray dust and soot but we had no words like pollution or environmental violence. They were different times. The big demand then, with crime rampant and bloody strikers, was for "Law and Order." Those were the "good old days."

Then it happened. Suddenly the bottom dropped out. The world they knew closed around them, their savings lost in closed banks, their jobs lost in closed factories; homes and farms were lost as mortgages and rent collection closed in; sharecroppers were forced off their farms. The great depression had begun. Everything went cold and lifeless, from smoke stacks to steeples. America tried to close its eyes and say, "This isn't for real—it's a nightmare and we will all wake up back in our jobs, homes, Sunday picnics, two chickens in every pot and two cars in every garage and all the other goodies." But it didn't work.

Then we tried to laugh and sing our way out, with Will Rogers leading the way and "Brother, can you spare a dime?"— but it began to hurt too much to laugh. We then turned to the ever human hope, "It can't last much longer." We were reassured by rhetoric from the White House that relief was just sixty days away, and our churches solemnly sermonized that "This, too, shall pass away," but it didn't; it got worse. We began seeing things we thought couldn't happen.

Veterans of the American army, encamped along the Potomac, petitioning for sustenance in the form of a bonus, were driven out by the bayonets of the American army. The months went by and despair set in; evictions began for non-payment of rent; youngsters left home and took to the road, either so that there would be one less mouth to feed or just to get away from what had been cheerful bustling homes but had turned into funeral parlors. Maybe "over the rainbow" there would be something better, or at least something.

Yet something was stirring in the land—a common misery began to break down the barriers between people, began to erode the good old American ways of rugged individualism, the survival of the fittest, sanctimonious charity, "The poor we shall always have with us. After all, a certain number of people are too stupid to make it, so they're poor." But now that most of us were poor—were we all stupid and incompetent? We knew this couldn't be true. All of our guide points, our values, our way of life had disintegrated and we were lost and dangling in a cold emptiness. In this void we reached out for something, anything to hang on to, and found each other. We found we needed each other. Unbelievably in this great crisis it came as a revelation that people could care about us and that we had it in us to care for others. New values began to creep in. Our literature began citing John Donne's "No man is an island, entire of itself...any man's death diminishes me, because I am involved in mankind; and therefore never send to know for whom the bell tolls; it tolls for thee." And Steinbeck's Okies suffered through *The Grapes of Wrath*. A common tragedy shattered our private worlds and we found we had much in common with our fellow man. There was a warmth in our getting together and getting out of the uncaring cold. It was a wondrous experience.

People caring for each other began to fight the evictions of others; as fast as the sheriff moved the furniture into the streets, the neighbors carried it back and then defied the police. People organized for more relief; they demanded jobs, and if industry couldn't provide them, then the government must.

The fact that many things that were talked about were no longer in the traditions of the past "American way" was just too bad. To hell with the past. The past was dead. If this meant revolution—so be it. With considerable skepticism they elected, as the lesser of two evils, Franklin D. Roosevelt and his New Deal. Desperation gave some wishful meaning to rhetoric such as "We have nothing to fear but fear itself." F.D.R. got across through radio "Fireside Chats," through manner, words and smile, that he cared, and most important, he began to be bitterly attacked by the establishment and its press. Cartoons showed a group of the rich in evening dress outside a swank city club, calling up to friends standing by in an open window, "Come along, we're on our way to the Trans-Lux to hiss Roosevelt." New Deal Democrats were being elected from everywhere, and soon the only Republicans that could be found came from under the rocks of Maine and Vermont. Massive government programs were in the air. Government agencies were popping up every other week and being identified by their letters. W.P.A.—T.V.A.—S.E.C.—N.Y.A.—and so through the alphabet.

Hope began to come, and hope begat anger, anger against the system, way of life, the establishment, call it what you will, which was held responsible for the economic disaster.

The suffering began to coagulate the unskilled unemployed poor, the unemployed artists like Ben Shahn, writers like Richard Wright and radicalized middle-class college students into a militant working class. Into all this came a man, John Lewellyn Lewis, to organize an economic revolution: to fight the entire corporate structure of the nation; occasionally with his own government, with the organized labor union establishment, with large sectors of organized religion and with the rest of the establishment. Rarely has anyone been so reviled by the nation's press. To the establishment he was Satan reincarnate. To the people he was Jefferson, Jackson, Lincoln, Lenin, Garibaldi and Napoleon rolled into one. Every radical of every suasion flocked to the banner of John L. Lewis. "A man's right to his job transcends the right of private property." "We are the workers—they are the enemy." It was war, and the Chicago police maintained their historic role, shot down peaceful pickets, shot them in the back at the infamous Memorial Day Massacre—but then you must remember those were the days of violence. Many of John L. Lewis' tactics were brilliant in conception and execution. There are important lessons here for today's battles; important warnings of mistakes not to be repeated. This is the story of John L. Lewis.

1970   S.D.A.

Foreword

THIS is an unauthorized biography. I have tried to give an honest presentation of the facts as I know them. This is always an unpopular undertaking, and usually everyone is offended. While Lewis gave me unlimited interviews as well as access to records, there were no commitments of any kind. He knew that in this study the sharp edge of criticism would cut everywhere and everybody including himself— and it has. No one, including Lewis, was permitted to read these pages before publication.

I believe that it is the right of every reader to know the prejudices of the biographer. There are still too many who talk about "objective" and "unprejudiced" writers. There is not and never has been a living person lacking prejudices. The best we can do in the striving for so-called objectivity is to be consciously aware of and on guard against these prejudices.

To me, Lewis is an extraordinary individual and certainly one of the outstanding figures of our time. As a person I like him. As a labor leader, I share the opinion of many including some of his bitterest enemies, that John Lewis is the most powerful and dramatic product of the history of American labor. I have been in violent disagreement with his position at different times and particularly on his isolationism during those critical days of 1941—again on his break with Roosevelt, which I struggled to avert. Yet Lewis will not break a relationship because of criticism if the criticism is honest and open. On the whole I have felt that his career was a great American tragedy in terms of what might have been.

One more word on my prejudices. I am pro-labor. My record as a friend of organized labor is well known in Chicago. I have fought at the side of the CIO for the past twelve years, and have earned the right to criticize as a friend.

Now a word on the extraordinary difficulties of modern biographical research. No longer can the student dig through archives for detailed written records. Today most important decisions are made over the phone or in face-to-face conversation, with little written evidence for the future historian except distorted secondhand accounts or firsthand rationalizations. Even written materials are dishonest in many cases by omission rather than commission. To the honest biographer research becomes a nightmare of garbled, tortured pieces of information that parade as fact. There are days when you are haunted by Mark Twain's rejection of history as being "written with the ink of lies." There is only one way out for the honest biographer, which is to state, wherever possible, the source of his information, leaving the reader the right to weigh its credibility.

The organized labor movement is a human institution and possessed of those virtues and vices common in mankind. Unfortunately there are labor leaders who decry even the criticism of a friend as labor baiting. This stifling of freedom of criticism with the tyranny of the smear is evil no matter what its source. Today the precious American right of dissent is in great jeopardy by pressures from the right as well as the left. To write of the human motivations, both good and bad, of leaders of labor one's eyes cannot be bound by the blinders of any doctrinaire policy or line of thought.

There are so many to whom I am indebted that it is impossible to name them. I am most grateful to John L. Lewis for the unlimited time he placed at my disposal and his releasing me from my only commitment to him dating back to 1940—that was not to reveal the events of the Roosevelt negotiations of that year. I am also grateful for the invaluable help of his loyal and devoted secretary, Elizabeth Covington. Too much cannot be said for the willingness and frank assistance of my close friend for many years, Kathryn Lewis.

I am grateful to the many labor leaders and former Government officials who gave so generously of their time both in interviews and in correspondence.

To my good friend George Bye who gently pushed me back into harness when I was discouraged.

To Herbert Hewitt of the reference department of the Chicago Public Library, who helped unearth every bit of written material on the subject, and to Sylvia Abrams who typed the long manuscript.

I will never forget the heart-stirring experience of those devoted friends of mine endlessly searching for ways to relieve me of undue domestic pressures, particularly through the months of this year. To them I owe a debt that is impossible ever to repay.

Without the selfless help of Babette Stiefel in research, editing, scolding, and cajoling, this book would certainly not have been complete at this time.

Last there are my two children, David and Kathryn, who were most patient and understanding of their father's nightly absences in the preparation of this book.

SAUL D. ALINSKY

October 1, 1949
Chicago

John L. Lewis

Chapter 1

Of Men and Coal

COAL is the prime mover of our life. In these black chunks of the earth's history is the energy that pours power into our gigantic industrial empire. Beyond the conjuring of any imagination is the awesome vastness of man's industrial procession. Just a small segment of this Gargantuan industrial scene reveals interlaced speeding railroads, giant whirring dynamos lighting up the nation, and overwhelming surges of power spun from steam. For within coal is man's industrial holy trinity of light, heat, and power.

More than half of American homes are heated by coal. Nearly ninety-five per cent of our railroad locomotives are driven by the fiery energy of coal.

Coal is essential in mass production of steel. If steel provides the skeleton for our cities and towns, then coal provides the heart. It also yields infinite products to our chemical industry. Break up this jet black nugget, and its by-products burst into more than ten thousand hues and colors, shaming the rainbow with its most delicate tints; for coal is basic to our making of dyes and colors.

This black chunk, which murders men underground, is the base for that lifesaving miracle of modern times, the sulfa drugs. From nylon to plastic, from aspirin to perfume, the list of products is as great as our supply. It is estimated that in America alone we have enough coal to last twenty-five hundred years. Contrast this with the dwindling crude-oil reserves, and coal assumes the role of not only our prime but our permanent mover. Coal is King.

It follows that he who controls coal holds within his hands the reins of our society. John Lewis, through his nearly half-million coal miners, holds that power. For the men who mine coal can always strike out the flow of this life-giving energy.

These men who mine coal are a mystery to the overwhelming majority of our nation. They are thought of as a strange, defiant, rebellious, abnormal people, peculiar just like their ruler; for Lewis, too is "strange, defiant, rebellious, and abnormal."

The miners are filled with bitterness bordering on hatred for the outside world—this outside world with its newspapers always attacking them, its politicians always intriguing against and insulting them, their union, and their leader, John L. Lewis. They bear little friendship for this strange, hostile world outside where, as the miners say, "People seem to think miners are some kind of animal—underground rats as they call us." [1] Or, "The way people outside think of us, we should be living in a zoo." One miner added bitterly, "We'd get better fed and be a hell of a lot safer in cages! Damn that outside world!" [2] And Lewis, like his miners, thinks bitterly of that outside world, feeling that every man's hand is turned against them.

Suspicion begets brooding, and many miners do brood as does their leader. Surrounded by hostility, they have suffered from fears of insecurity and have reacted with that pugnacious belligerence so typical of Lewis.

They respond to threats with that indifference of men who work down below where death never takes a holiday. Familiarity with death breeds contempt for any threatened punishment. They have that stoicism born in suffering and tragedy. Lewis, too, contemptuously rejects punitive threats and does not flinch before authority, the press, or any of the thunder or lightning of the outside world.

The men who dig coal are fiercely independent, for under the physical conditions of mining each man works as his own boss. He has learned to stand and work, and if need be, die alone down below the ground. Lewis, like his miners, is possessed of the same independence.

Just as Lewis stands aloof and apart from the life about him, so do the miners, who live in a separate world and who are a people apart unto themselves. It becomes quite clear that the

---

[1] *Fortune*, March, 1947, p 97.
[2] Statement to the writer by the miners.

key to the enigma of John L. Lewis is embedded in coal and the miners. Therefore, to know the miners is to begin to open the door on the mystery of Lewis.

While America's cities sleep, the men who mine coal are awake, moving quietly about the house trying not to disturb their sleeping children. They wash and dress by instinct in the darkness and then turn to the sudden dim light in the kitchen. There the miners' wives stand by as their husbands wolf down a massive breakfast that would be both shocking and revolting to fifty-seven per cent of America's population which lives in our cities and greets the new day with the morning ceremonial of toast and coffee. The miner's breakfast may be fried chicken or ham with potatoes, hot cakes, biscuits, and endless steaming coffee, or, as they say, "the kind of eats that sticks to a man's ribs." But the miners need all the food they can eat, for ahead of them are both backbreaking physical exhaustion and the mental fatigue of constant alertness against the danger that lies about and above them.

As the sleeping city dweller stirs restlessly at 6:30 in the morning, the miners have already checked in at the entrance, or portal, of the mine. They have received their electric cap lamps, unless they are working at the kind of mine where the price of life is low and they are given open-flame carbide lamps. Then just as the sun comes up, they go plummeting down in an elevator cage—down into the earth.

If it is a large mine, they ride a coal train, banging, grinding, bumping, constantly careening around curves, and lurching up and down through long, seemingly never level, endlessly dark, subterranean passageways. They may ride for as far as six miles on what they call the "man trip" until they come to their place to dig. Here they climb out, and the train rolls off, leaving them alone watching the fast-fading trail of trolley flashes as the darkness closes in. For a moment they stand there, ankle deep in water, surrounded by darkness so black they can feel it. It is a darkness dripping with the oily black slime of the guts of the earth.

Then they turn, and each miner sloshes off to his individual workroom. This is a space opening off the tunnel and lined on two sides by walls of solid rock or coal and slate. Directly ahead of the miner is the end wall of solid coal known as the face. This is the coal to be mined.

The miner's workroom may be only three feet high, compelling him to crawl into it and work through the day lying on his side. If it is four feet high, he will work on his knees, but if he is lucky, his workroom will be a little more than five feet high, and then he will spend his workday in a crouch.

He does not directly approach and begin to mine on the working face, for over him is the ever threatening roof. He knows what every miner knows—that above his head, like the sword of Damocles, hangs his most dangerous enemy. Falling roofs kill and maim more miners than any other single underground hazard. He knows that with the collapse of the roof his workroom will instantly become his tomb. So he begins by checking the timbers supporting the roof and goes about setting up more timbers as they are needed to give maximum support to this dangerous roof above. All the time he knows that the shoring timbers themselves will not save him, but their noise of cracking as a roof begins to cave in may give him a warning of some seconds to try to flee for his life. For him, the tearing of the timbers is the crack of doom.

Satisfied with the supports, he is ready to mine. An undercutting machine is then brought into the room and set next to the bottom of the coal face. It is started, and its whirling, tough, jagged teeth chew and rip like a buzz saw through the bottom of the coal face. The machine, moving from side to side, slices a deep groove along the bottom of this wall of coal.

When the machine's job is finished, it is removed from the workroom, and now the miner is ready for the moment of danger, the shooting of explosives to break down the coal face. He will usually have an electric drill, although in old mines hand drills are still used. Small holes are drilled of a depth and location selected by the miners with their long experience as a guide. Into these holes they slip sticks of explosives with detonators of small mercury fulminate capsules attached to wires, some more than a hundred feet long. These holes are then tamped with incombustible materials to ensure that the force of the explosion will be expended inside the wall of coal. With everything set the miner retreats outside of the room, and attaching the wires to a dry cell, he shoots off the explosives.

With a muffled roar, amid blinding dust, the wall of coal thuds to the floor. The large chunks of coal are crumbled with picks and made ready for the next stage of loading it into the railroad cars. Loading coal by hand is one of the hardest jobs known to mankind. Hour after hour the hand loader, crouched in his cramped quarters, shovels tons of coal into the small mine railroad cars. Today, with the progress of mechanization of mines, more and more loading machines are being used. With the loading machine, a miner and his buddy can load as much as ten tons of coal in just a few minutes. However, the majority of coal mines do not have machine loaders.

Once the coal is loaded into the railroad cars the cycle is repeated. Again the ripping of the undercutting machine, the whir of drills, the blast of explosives, the crash of the coal face, and the clatter of loading.

The miner is never alone, for death is all about him. It is over his head with the collapsing roof and his sudden crushing burial; it is in front of him in the pockets of invisible, odorless, tasteless, deadly methane gas released by cutting into the coal face and ignited by his explosives. Then it comes as a blinding flash and oblivion. It is behind him in the long tunnels, where it comes with the reptilian hiss of the rolling wall of smoke and flame as he shakes and screams in agony knowing that death is coming either by cremation or asphyxiation.

He knows the toll of his underground fraternity, for every morning he goes down under with the odds just a shade more than nine to one in his favor of escaping death or injury. Every day he shoots dice with death. Compare his mortality rate with that of the armed services. The miner knows that he digs death as well as coal, and the death tonnage is appalling.

He knew some of the 68,842 miners killed from 1910 through 1945, and he knew some of the 2,275,000 injured. He had stood awkward and choked with emotion before some of the 211,468 widows and orphans of these men. He contributed generously to collections for the impoverished survivors with the chilled feeling that the next collection might be for his widow and children.

And the dead were not just those entombed below or brought up as blackened, lifeless husks inside a roll of blanket. No, the dead were all about him, even next door, where as long as he could remember that miner with the broken back had been decaying in his bed inside a rotting shack. Across the road lay another, paralyzed from the hips down since the blast four years ago. They say he'll never walk again. The younger miner knows some of the 841 men killed in the ten months between June, 1946, and March, 1947. He, too, has seen the agony on those charred, suffocated, smashed faces.

But he goes on, undercutting, drilling, blasting, and loading until his workday is ended. Then the elevator whisks him up to the surface, and the miner is homeward bound.

But even with the ground below him, he still cannot escape, for the miner's life is the daily living of "dust to dust." It is a life of dirt below and above, a life of coal blacks and dark grays as he comes up from the blackness below to the gray shroud above. For here, safe in his home, he is surrounded by the coal dust from the tipple, the bitter pungent stench of the burning slag heaps, and the dust clouds of dirt roads—all sinking together into a suffocating gray blight streaked with the black soot from the railroad tracks. It covers everything, and once settled, seems to creep inside every corner of the village and of the miners. It gets into the nostrils, and many miners say, "into our insides." It is that melancholy gray so somberly suited to the grim stark tragedy that hangs over the lives of these—God's forgotten people, the men who mine coal.

Here, too, the grim struggle for survival goes on as the miners wage their fight for the bread and the means, not for life, but for abysmal existence.

It is no exaggeration to describe the past life of the miners as one of serfdom. The shack a miner's family lived in, miserable as it was, did not belong to him—it was owned by the Company. The food he bought came from stores—owned by the Company. The clothes he bought came from a store—owned by the Company. When illness struck, his family called the doctor —owned by the Company. His shoes came from a store—owned by the Company; and the road they walked on was—owned by the Company. The stinking air of soot and coal dust was—owned by the Company. His children, condemned by family need of food, entered the mines, and they, too, were—owned by the Company. The miners buried their dead, and the companies buried their living in a present and future as black as the coal pits below. The Company owned everything, everything but the spirit of the miners—that they owned themselves.

And so it was a saga, not of a war of the miners against the coal companies or operators, but of an insurrection. In a revolution there is none of the mercy of war, for there are no prisoners taken alive and mercy is a synonym for weakness. The only rule was no rule. The price of coal, always cheap, was for years higher than the price of human life. The story of coal and the miners is a saga of brutality and blood.

The miners tried for years to mobilize an army in the form of a union. It was to be a torturous blood-soaked trail bending downward into the black hell of Ludlow.

In the entire death-ridden history of the struggle between the miners and the operators, the Ludlow Massacre will always be remembered as one of the few upheavals in our history when class war broke out in full violence in the United States.

Ludlow, Colorado, was the site of the mines of the Rockefeller-owned Colorado Fuel and Iron Company. The latter had been struck by the mine workers union. The management of the company was implacably hostile and extraordinarily intransigent on the subject of organized labor. They fought the union in every conceivable way, importing the Baldwin-Felts Detective Agency, which rode around in an armored car shooting down strikers on sight. They got injunctions and indictments against labor organizers. They evicted miners and their families from company homes into the freezing temperatures of a Colorado winter. To meet this forced exodus, the union set up tents, where soon hundreds of miners and their families were sheltered.

The tension increased, and the militia was called in under the command of a Major Patrick Hamrock. Early on the morning of April 20, 1914, just as this tent community was preparing for breakfast, the state militia attacked. *The New York Times* reported: "The Ludlow Camp is a mass of charred debris and buried beneath is a story of horror unparalleled in the history of industrial warfare. In holes that had been dug for their protection against the rifle fire, the women and children died like rats when the flames swept over them. One pit uncovered this afternoon disclosed the bodies of ten children and two women." [3]

More than two thirds of those killed by Major Hamrock's men were women and children. American workers were white hot with indignation, while the miners went berserk and set out on a four-day war to burn and kill.

The bitterness of the American workers toward the militia was such that railroad crews refused to take trains filled with reinforcements and munitions to the imperiled militia.

Events such as the Ludlow Massacre reverberated throughout the mine fields of America and made men look to the union as their sole defense against the operator.

The names of those who carried the torch for unionization are, with few exceptions, buried as unknown soldiers in old history books. With few exceptions, too, the leaders were broken by their own miners.

There was John Bates, in 1849, who, after organizing most of the Pennsylvania anthracite miners, led them into a disastrous strike. The miners were disillusioned with unionism, and Bates was discredited.

Twelve years later, the miners of Illinois won a strike and in 1861 organized into a Miners Association under Daniel Weaver. In Pennsylvania there was John Siney, who not only organized a large number of the anthracite coal miners but led them through and won the bitter strike of 1869. He made history by establishing for the first time joint collective bargaining between the union and representatives of the Anthracite Board of Trade.

Siney then joined forces with the Miners Association and formed one union called the Miners National Association. He was elected president, but before this new national union could even begin to test its strength, it disintegrated under the impact of the depression of 1873. Working and living conditions went from bad to worse, and the miners, bitter, suffering, and resentful, crucified Siney. He was cursed and driven out of office in 1876, only two and a half short years after being idolized and cheered by his miners. Again the miners were disillusioned with unionism, and again they turned on and destroyed their own leader.

[3] *The New York Times*, April 21, 1914.

Beaten and disorganized, many bitterly struck back. In Pennsylvania the Molly Maguires sprang up, burning breakers, sniping at particularly hated foremen and superintendents, derailing mine cars, and beating up strike-breakers. Terror soon ruled the tipples of Pennsylvania.

The coal operators brought in Pinkerton's National Detective Agency, which set out to crush this secret society in its own way. Knowing that most of the Molly Maguires were Irish Roman Catholics, Pinkerton assigned young, laughing, Irish Roman Catholic, James McParland, to do the job. McParland was accepted by the leaders of the Molly Maguires, given shelter, food, and affection. In return, McParland urged them to even bloodier violence, then ended by informing and testifying against them in court. Fourteen Molly Maguires were hanged, and the name of James McParland replaced the name of Judas Iscariot for decades afterward.

Concurrently with the explosive, short-lived life of the Molly Maguires came another secret society known as the Knights of Labor. Although the Knights were suspect because of their secrecy, they were in actuality the exact opposite of the Mollys. They emphasized temperance, popular education, and remedial legislation. They were even allergic to strikes, yet a panicky press identified them with the Maguires. Many coal miners affiliated with the Knights of Labor, while others, led by John McBride, met in 1883 to organize the Amalgamated Association of Miners of the United States. The Hocking Valley strike smashed the Amalgamated Association and badly battered the Knights of Labor.

Tenaciously the miners came back in 1884 and organized the National Federation of Miners and Mine Laborers. Yet they were still divided, for many of the miners were still with the Knights of Labor.

Then it happened on January 25, 1890, in Columbus, Ohio. Here both groups merged into a new organization, the United Mine Workers of America, which received a charter from the also newly formed American Federation of Labor, which had been created in 1886. Leaders of both factions wept with joy as, at last, disunity was ended. Recognizing that a basic weakness of the past organizations had been the lack of control over the strike weapon, the new union forbade any local strike without the approval of the national president and at least one board member. Now the union could try to utilize its strike weapon as a cannon, rather than having it dissipate itself in grapeshot strikes.

From that time until the days of John L. Lewis, there were eight presidents of the United Mine Workers Union, of whom two were outstanding. One was Michael Ratchford, who at thirty-seven became president. He led the miners into a twelve-week strike on July 4, 1897, and won. Victory had a strange, sweet taste in the mouths of these miners who had never known anything but the bitter dregs of defeat. From a claimed paper membership of 11,000 the union jumped, in one year, to 33,000 active dues-paying members. The foundation was set.

Then came the man still revered in the coal pits as the patron saint of the union, John Mitchell. His career was meteoric. Becoming acting president of the union at the age of twenty-eight, Mitchell soon held the position by right of election. It was under Mitchell that the anthracite coal miners were organized. On May 15, 1903, Mitchell led them into a strike that was to last almost twenty-four weeks and end in the defeat of the anthracite operators. It was during this conflict that the famous "divine right" letter was written by George F. Baer, president of the Philadelphia and Reading Company, to W. F. Clark of Wilkes-Barre, Pennsylvania. In this letter, Baer pointed out: "The right and interests of the laboring man will be protected and cared for—not by the labor agitators, but by the Christian men to whom God in His infinite wisdom has given the control of the property interests of the country, and upon the successful management of which so much depends."

Mitchell went on leading the miners to successive gains and building the union to the giant of today. In the field of legislation the union had promoted and seen enacted mine-safety laws and child-labor laws. The union seemed to prosper on every front, except financially, and then dissension began to develop. There was a growing impatience and scorn for Mitchell's temperate moderation and the Christian charity that was ingrained in him. Many aggressive local union leaders turned against him. Mitchell became the target for fantastic charges and in the end was practically crucified by his miners. Once he protested, shouting, "You are not going to do with me as your

fathers did with John Siney." But they did. Mitchell retired
from office at the 1908 convention. Here even his most vindictive foes joined in praising and in actually burying the career
of the man so beloved by the miners, "Johnnie da Mitch."

The next year his successor, still fearful of the rank-and-file
feeling for Mitchell, tried to have the union's constitution
amended to bar Mitchell permanently from ever again holding
office in the union. It was unanimously rejected, but the very
next year the miners' convention forced a tired and sick Mitchell to resign from a $6,000-a-year post with the National Civic
Association on penalty of expulsion from the union! *Sic transit
gloria.*

The companies' degradation of the miners in forcing them
into slavelike dependency; the rotting decay of the company
shacks infecting the spirit as well as the body of their inhabitants; and the miners having witnessed the butchering in
torture of their fellow coal diggers—all filled the miners with a
hatred so deep and turbulent that it spilled over among themselves. Out of their dark despair, seemingly tormented in a
death agony, they struck down their own leaders again and
again with the blind fury of their own bitterness.

These miners seemed akin to powerful, unbroken, man-killing, wild horses. Mitchell's gentle ways had quieted them for
nearly eight years, but in the end they had unseated and
trampled him.

The mine workers union would only be united by some
man who would know not only the economics of coal but the
miners and their self-destructive hatred. It would have to be a
man far tougher and much more ruthless than all of them put
together. It would have to be, as the miners said, "something
of a man."

Chapter 2

John Llewellyn Lewis

ONE of the shames of Western industrial civilization was and is the misery and stark poverty of the coal miners of Wales. Here generations of men have burrowed in the coal pits under extremely hazardous conditions, reaping a reward of lifetime poverty, broken backs, and broken hearts.

During the last century they, as did the poor of all Europe, turned their faces toward the warm glow of the promised land across the sea. It was said that in America the streets were paved with gold and every man was a prince. This might not be true, but what they did know was that in America, while a man might not be a prince, he could be a man.

The hardier ones leaped at every chance for escape to the New World. Welsh miners packed their large families and few belongings and sailed to the land of opportunity. Driven by the need for an immediate job, they at once sought the only work they knew: the mining of coal. They clustered in different parts of America, and one of the parts was the tiny mining town of Lucas, Iowa. Hither in the late 1870's flowed a steady stream of them, among whom was the Watkins family, including their daughter Louisa, and a burly, brooding miner named Thomas Lewis.

Thomas Lewis worked all day in the coal pits and spent half his nights helping to organize his fellow workers in the big union of the Knights of Labor. In the 1880's Iowa was the catalytic agent precipitating the waves of unrest which were the growing pains of a young democracy. From this state came General James B. Weaver, who as the leader of the Populist party gave Wall Street one of its blackest nightmares of terror. Iowa was in a ferment of ideas and all of these on the radical side.

This was the climate which spurred on Thomas Lewis in his desire to organize the miners into a union.

Shortly after his arrival in Lucas he met Louisa Watkins, and in 1878 they were married. John L. Lewis told the writer that in looking over his family background he felt:

"My background was one of contrast. On my father's side, my family were fighters. They roved a great deal. They were very much interested in the world about them. They were tough people. My mother's side of the family was the quiet kind. They were scholars, teachers, sort of retiring and shy."

Two years later, on February 12, 1880, their first child was born. They named him John Llewellyn Lewis. When young John Lewis was two years old, his father helped to lead his fellow miners in a bitter strike against their employers, the White Breast Fuel Company. He fought the company so bitterly that it became apparent that regardless of the outcome he would never again be employed by them. The strike was won; and Thomas Lewis stood alone, watching his friends and fellow miners return to work while he, who had fought so unreservedly for them, was forgotten. But the White Breast Fuel Company did not forget, and Thomas Lewis was placed on a blacklist as a radical and unionist.

From that time on Thomas Lewis was condemned to a wandering exile, seeking here and there for work to support his family. Now there was another child, Thomas Jr., and the Lewises moved to Colfax, Iowa, where for a time Tom Lewis worked as a night watchman, then again as a miner in an adjacent mining town until the blacklist reached his employers. Then the Lewis family moved to the state capital, Des Moines. Thomas Lewis again began to work as a night watchman and later was appointed custodian of the city jail. Danny Lewis was born in 1889. Three years later came Howard Lewis and, in 1894, Hattie Lewis. Eventually two more sons and one more daughter were born to Louisa and Thomas Lewis, so that the Lewis family consisted of six sons and two daughters.

Young John was an aggressive, pugnacious youngster. John first attended the Grant Park School, which was close to the Iowa state fairgrounds. From there he went to the Lincoln School in East Des Moines, then the old Washington School, and finally attended briefly a junior high school close to the state capital. He rebelled against the formal curriculum of school and quit before he finished the eighth grade. Lewis told the writer: "I never went to high school. I got along all right in school, but I was just more interested in outside things than I was in classroom work." As a boy he thirsted for action and was eager to settle arguments with the fist. Seeing his father in physical fights made it seem natural to the son. Early in life he subscribed to and frequently tested the slogan that "the bigger they come the harder they fall." And yet, for all his fighting, the boy possessed a natural talent for public speaking which even at that age awakened the admiration of his teachers.

As a boy of twelve he sold newspapers, and other newsboys quickly learned not to poach on his territory. Sports attracted young Lewis, particularly baseball. Here, as in everything else in Lewis's life, he played it seriously and for keeps. However, young John did not play baseball very long, as, by the age of fifteen, he was in the mines augmenting the family budget by working every day digging coal. Every night he listened to his father expounding upon the virtues of trade unionism, the infamy of the coal operators, and the general subject of human nature, both of the miners and of the operators. John listened and became imbued with an implacable, life-long hatred for the coal operators and a distrust for the myth of nobility as applying to the great mass of common people. He heard over and over again how his father had fought their cause in the 1882 strike and how the miners had not fought for him when the company not only refused to rehire him but blacklisted him.

In 1897 the blacklists were destroyed, and Thomas Lewis was free to return to the coal fields. At once the Lewis family left Des Moines for their home town of Lucas, Iowa, where John Lewis, now seventeen years old, his brother Thomas, and his father all began to work in the Big Hill Coal and Mining Company. Ventilation of the mines was unheard of in those days. They sweated it out, working ten to eleven hours a day, working in the suffocation of power fumes. Robert Wilkinson, an old neighbor of the Lewis family who worked in the same mine, recalled, "Lewis drove mules—pulled coal for me at the Big Hill. He was a hard worker. He was a good man—and his folks were nice." However, Wilkinson had some bitter memories about the mines: "The air was generally pretty thin. We came home more than one day because there wasn't any air in the mines." [1]

But still the Lewis family was much happier than they had been in Des Moines. Here they were at home among their own folk, Welsh miners who were hardy, rugged people. They were a unique breed, dramatic both in speech and gesture, a strange paradox of sentimental romanticism and hardened realism. They could be tender and yet ruthless. They sang their old Welsh folk songs and quoted Shakespeare in their daily conversations. To understand them was to understand much of what went into the make-up of John L. Lewis.

His energy was boundless. After the day's work was done, John organized and managed both a debating team and a baseball team. He was a human sponge soaking up both information and knowledge from his avid reading. Lewis loved to read and devoured book after book, practically all of them of the sensational stripe. His interests, like his reading habits, were very disorganized until he went to a party and became attracted to young Myrta Edith Bell. It has always been assumed that Lewis met Myrta Bell at this party. However, Lewis told the writer, "I had already known Mrs. Lewis [Myrta Bell] for fifteen years before I married her."

Myrta Bell was the eldest daughter of an Ohio doctor who had moved to Lucas when she was ten years old. The Bell family tree had its roots in the American colonies before the American revolution. It was peopled primarily by scholars, educators, and physicians. It possessed stability and security, and these were reflected in Myrta Bell. She was a calm girl, possessed of an inner security that bloomed into serenity as the years passed. Few ever realized her incredible inner strength. She was in a profound sense stronger than John Lewis. Underneath the tender gentility was a will of inflexible steel.

Myrta Bell organized Lewis's reading habits and introduced him to Dickens and to Homer and other classics. She encouraged his interests, guided him, and loved him. Myrta Bell was to become the most important single force in the life of John L. Lewis.

He restlessly tried his hand at varied occupations from run-

[1] *Des Moines Register and Tribune,* December 1, 1941.

ning a mill to carpentering to managing the local opera house, where he sponsored traveling shows ranging from Shakespearean actors to trained dogs. While the various shows differed greatly they were as one in their rank mediocrity. Some observers have attributed Lewis's dramatic flourishes to his association with these traveling shows. Also, on the side, he became a justice of the peace, although he was not elected to the post.

At twenty-one a deep restlessness possessed John Lewis, and he left home to begin a trek that was to last for five years before his return. He told the writer: "I was too impatient to sit still and go to school. I got my main education during five years when I knocked about the country, in different kinds of work. I saw the suffering that went on, the way people were pushed around, and the misery among large parts of our population. I would say that those five years of my life did more to shape my feelings and my understanding of how people behave and why they behave than anything else in my experience. Those five years were probably one of the most important parts of my life. I suppose if we talk about formal education, I would count that five years as my education. It was a very important part of my life."

His travels were to become a pilgrimage. During those five long years Lewis wandered all over the West. He lived from hand to mouth and traveled by anything he could ride, whether it was stagecoach, a passenger train, or the rods beneath a freight car. Lewis's rise to national prominence has brought forth many tales of his experiences on this sojourn that are strongly reminiscent of the exploits of the fabulous Paul Bunyan. The real significance of these stories is not in their validity but in their expression of the bellicose, driving vigor and almost superhuman courage and strength that are popularly attributed to Lewis.

There is the story about Spanish Pete, a man-killing mule, which cornered Lewis with his back against the wall of a mine corridor and tried to kill him. Lewis is reported to have smashed the animal off its feet with a right-hand punch and with a quickly grabbed piece of timber met the mule's return charge and drove the club with pile-driving force through its brains. Realizing that the killing of the mule might cost him his job, he covered the gaping head wound with clay and reported the death of Spanish Pete as the result of heart failure.

Another often-told tale is how John Lewis stunned two veteran stagecoach drivers by swimming across the racing, turbulent waters of the Big Horn River in Wyoming during a high flood period. This exploit is supposed to have nearly cost him his life.

As Lewis went from place to place, he looked and listened with a profound intentness. He felt driven by the desire for knowledge of people and the conditions under which they worked and lived. At night he asked questions and listened to their hopes, their frustrations, and their suffering. They were inured to their lot, but even stoicism had its limits.

Lewis's wanderings carried him deep into the bowels of the earth as he mined copper in Montana, silver in Utah, coal in Colorado, and gold in Arizona. His journeyings also carried him deep into the bowels of human anguish and horror as a cursing, shocked Lewis helped carry out the torn bodies of two hundred and thirty-six coal miners killed in the great Union Pacific Mine disaster of 1905 in Hannah, Wyoming. The descent into the mine that had become a charnel house was for Lewis a descent into hell, but what ripped his emotions to shreds was the sight of the numb, mute faces of the wives now suddenly widows of the men they loved. It was at Hannah, Wyoming, that John Lewis was baptized in his own tears. It was a grim man matured by tragedy who returned to Lucas, in 1906.

Back home, Lewis went into the mines. His fellow miners quickly realized that young John had reached manhood. His comments and decisions were seasoned with experience. When he talked of the need for safety in the mines, his listeners knew that he had seen the awful carnage that he was trying to prevent. And yet with the gloom of his words there was a bold, militant self-assurance that attracted his companions. Even at that age the dynamic drive of Lewis's personality awed his audiences. He knew their worries and fears; for the shadows that hung over the lives of the coal miners of Lucas, Iowa, were the same as those that hovered over the gold miners of Arizona, the silver miners of Utah, the copper miners of Montana, and the men everywhere who worked and died under the earth. The shadows might vary slightly in form or intensity; but they were the same shadows of fear, frustration, and insecurity. John L. Lewis was not only their kind but he could articulate what was in their hearts. He spoke so that his listeners not only understood the problems of the miners but felt them. It was not surprising, therefore, that within a few months the coal miners of Lucas should elect him as their delegate to the national convention of the United Mine Workers of America.

Lewis went to this convention as he had gone west, keeping his eyes and ears open and his mouth closed except for questions. No one at that convention thought of the shaggy-haired youngster in the hall who looked like a tintype of a professional prize fighter or barroom bouncer eventually becoming their leader. But Lewis did. The opening thump of the gavel called not only the convention but also Lewis's life to order.

More important than all this was his marriage on June 5, 1907, to Myrta Edith Bell. Shortly after his marriage Lewis was bitten by the political bug and ran for the job of mayor of Lucas. A strange family drama developed when his father-in-law, Dr. Bell, bitterly opposed Lewis's ambition and campaigned so effectively against his son-in-law that it resulted in Lewis's defeat. Dr. Bell saw in his young son-in-law the potential characteristics of a future greatness. He was deeply concerned over the fact that if Lewis was successful in becoming mayor of Lucas he would be taking a road leading to a future of being a petty county politician. It was not long before Lewis appreciated that his father-in-law's action was a magnificent gesture of friendship.

Lewis was deeply concerned about the best starting point for the launching of his career. He knew that his ladder must be anchored in a major coal-producing area. This was essential if he were to have a base of support that would be meaningful in his career. Furthermore, he would be able to gain an understanding of the coal miners as an enormous group of varied nationalities rather than the small Welsh group of Lucas.

Lewis looked around; there were the great anthracite coal areas of Pennsylvania and vast bituminous coal fields of West Virginia, Ohio, Indiana, and Illinois. Lewis selected the latter as his vantage point. There were a number of probable reasons for this choice. First the proximity. Not only Lewis and his wife were to make the move but also Lewis's five brothers. The fact that Lewis had made friends in that section of the country was another argument for that selection. It has also been suggested that a subconscious reason operated in reaching that decision, and that was Lewis's strong feeling of identification with Abraham Lincoln because of a common birthday. One thing was certain: Lewis from Illinois would mean more to the miners than Lewis from Lucas, Iowa.

In 1909 John and Myrta Lewis permanently pulled up stakes in Lucas and moved to Panama, Illinois. The Lewis family followed them very shortly. Here in the heart of the Montgomery coal fields, Lewis began passionately to orate on the injustices besetting the miners. The five Lewis brothers formed a loyal claque and vigorously led the applause. Lewis's machine of his five brothers soon captured control of the union local, and John was elected president within a year.

With his wife's invaluable aid, Lewis began to write and practice the art of speechmaking that would both arouse his listeners and establish his dominance as a leader. Many of his gestures, mannerisms, vocal inflections, and phrases were practiced in the privacy of his home and on an audience of one, Myrta Lewis. His wife would patiently correct, modify, change, and polish his delivery. Then as all intelligent wives have done and always will do, she applauded her husband for *his* finished delivery.

Lewis was not only the president of his local but also a one-man grievance committee. This was his first introduction to the whole field of grievances and collective bargaining. Now John Lewis began to attract the attention of the district officers of the union.

Before another year had passed, he was elected by the union's district convention to the post of state legislative agent. His job was that of lobbying in the state legislature for safety measures in the mines.

Then came the Cherry disaster, a mine explosion and fire that killed one hundred and sixty miners. Lewis stood before the state legislature like a mad bull. He raged and banged his fists on the rostrum. He did everything but personally promise physically to demolish each legislator. Intimidated, they passed

bill after bill, including a workmen's compensation law. News
of this victory traveled far; and even Samuel Gompers, founder
and president of the AF of L, asked about this young man in
Illinois.

Nineteen eleven found Lewis in Indianapolis attending the
convention of the United Mine Workers. This was a fateful
convention for Lewis, as the main issue before the delegates
was approximately the same one that Lewis was to face twenty-
four years later when he broke with the AF of L and started
the CIO.

The metal miners of the West had a militant union known
as "The Western Federation of Miners." Both the Western
Federation and the United Mine Workers had been promised
an industrial charter from the American Federation of Labor.
The hostility of the craft unions generally, and particularly the
machinists union, toward the whole idea of industrial unions
blocked the granting of the charter. This negative position of
the AF of L was softened by the explaining golden words of
Gompers.

At this convention the miners were informed that for the
tenth year the promise of an industrial charter to them or the
Western Federation had not been kept. Many of the miners
then had radical backgrounds, and the announcement was as
a flame to a powder keg, and the convention exploded with fury.
A wire was sent to Gompers not asking him but ordering him
to grant the charter at once or else both the coal miners and
metal miners unions would secede and form a separate labor
movement. Lewis was profoundly impressed to see the effect
of a straight brute threat upon Gompers and his craft-union
associates. It came the next morning with the sudden granting
of the charter. Lewis never forgot the cringing capitulation of
these craft-union leaders as well as that of the brilliant Gompers before a show of naked strength.

The clash between the mine workers and Gompers fertilized
a great opportunity for Lewis. Gompers, apprehensive over the
hostile upsurge within the mine workers' ranks, began to cast
about for ways and means to prevent a recurrence of such rebellions. This man Lewis was a comer in the union.

Lewis was the answer to Gomper's need for a tough, forceful
ally in the insurgent ranks of the mine workers. The storm of

indignation against Gompers had scared him into beating a hasty retreat. He remembered and was reassured by Lewis's silence through the tirade at the convention, and so Lewis was personally appointed by Gompers to become a field representative and legislative agent for the American Federation of Labor.

A curious relationship bloomed between Gompers and Lewis. The cold, crafty, cautious, compromising old master was attracted to the bellicose, fiery, fighting bull from the Middle West. They became intimate friends. Gompers trusted Lewis implicitly, and it is reliably reported that whenever Gompers would go on a carouse he would trust Lewis to stand guard against any unfavorable repercussions. They were a curious pair, this slight Dutch-English Jew and this burly Welshman.

Lewis found in Gompers the greatest labor tactician of the era; and he listened to Gompers, questioned him and learned. The greatest basic education in labor that Lewis received was absorbed at the feet of the old master. To this day, even when criticizing Gompers, Lewis refers to him with deference, admiration, and a touch of as much reverence as can come from Lewis.

Samuel Gompers was the great apostle of trade unionism; and he rejected and fought the idea of industrial unionism which was implicit in the structure of the miners' union. The craft type of union espoused by Samuel Gompers and the American Federation of Labor was and is based upon specific skills in a particular occupation. The development of modern industry with assembly lines and systems of mass production serviced in the main by unskilled labor drastically curtailed the percentage of skilled craftsmen in industry. If organized labor was to bargain with industry, it would have to recruit this vast mass of unskilled workers into its ranks. This all-inclusive union that would embrace all members of an industry regardless of skills or lack of skills is known as an industrial union.

Gompers was carefully grooming Lewis to be a potent ally of craft unionism in this war of ideas. History delights in ironically shuffling the plans of men. John Lewis, picked by Gompers to forestall this surge of industrial unionism, was later to become the avenging angel and to be more responsible for industrial unionism than any man in the history of American labor.

In his new post, Lewis officially represented the American Federation of Labor at the sessions of many state legislatures and the federal Congress. In 1916 he served as a member of the Interstate Scale Committee. He was receiving invaluable experience and was being recognized as a coming labor leader.

Lewis traveled widely and learned first hand of the problems of the workers in all the mass industries. What he saw and heard he never forgot and later put to use. Lewis tells the story of how "back in 1911 the Congress had recommended in the form of what was known as the 'Flood Amendment' that a referendum of the people of New Mexico be held in order to make the constitution of New Mexico amendable. There were changes that had to be made in terms of electing their national representatives and other things of that sort.

"About that time I was down in New Mexico representing the American Federation of Labor and speaking on behalf of the Blue Ballot amendments of New Mexico which were amendments concerning the welfare of labor unions. One day I came out of my hotel and was sitting around on the veranda and I saw all these coarse-looking politicians getting together and closing all kinds of deals and deciding who was going to be senator and who was going to be congressman and who was going to be anything. It was a case of blatant corruption. Political offices were being bought in the same manner as one would go in and buy a pound of bacon. After listening for a while, I began to believe that a pound of bacon actually cost more than becoming a public official of the state at that time. One of the main officials chosen was Fall. I don't remember for what office, but I think it might have been for the Senate. This was all as a result of a pretty corrupt deal.

"Years later, while we were involved in some negotiations for legislation favorable to the United Mine Workers of America we found Fall, who was then Secretary of Interior, objecting to and opposing as well as torpedoing our program. One afternoon we ended a conference with him and I stalled and stayed behind until the others left. Then I had a little talk with Mr. Fall, and the very next day Mr. Fall switched and supported our program.

"People have often wondered what happened in that little conversation. Well, as a matter of fact nothing happened. I just began to reminisce with Mr. Fall and told him about my presence in New Mexico in 1911 at the time all of these political activities such as the Flood Amendment and the referendum and the selection of national officials for the State of New Mexico. I told Mr. Fall about some of the conversations that I had heard on that veranda in which he had been mentioned and of other meetings and conversations in which he had been present. I reminisced further about my knowledge of how certain political arrangements had been established and then ended up by simply saying that the entire experience had been extremely interesting to me. Then I left. Apparently my interest in New Mexico's politics made Mr. Fall quite a bit more friendly to organized labor than he had been in the past."

Lewis tried to organize the steel workers and failed. He tried to organize the rubber, the lumber, and the glass industry and failed. He tells the story of a mass meeting of the Westinghouse Electrical Company workers in Pittsburgh that took place on a street that was in the process of being repaired. The street adjoined the plant, and mounds of bricks to be used in the repair work were heaped along the curb. The meeting had been called in order to take the strike vote, and Lewis was the main speaker. As Lewis was preparing to take the vote of the workers, a great number of them came off their shift and streamed out of the plant into the meeting spreading the news that the company had just acceded to their demands. This move of the company tore the heart out of the union organizing campaign. The workers refused to vote for a strike and lost interest in the union. Lewis recounted the story of the meeting to his AF of L associates saying that when the strike vote was taken "the 'yeas' shook the houses but the 'noes' leveled the mountain."

These same citadels of industry, steel, rubber, lumber, glass, and electricity, were to yield to him a generation later. Their conquest was not to be attributed simply to the fact that Lewis had through the years developed into an extraordinarily able and ingenious leader, but that Lewis later became independent, having such powers within his union that he could move as he chose, as well as having control of the union funds, which gave him the necessary finances so vital to an organizing drive.

Most important of all, however, was the fact that the workers in all of these industries wanted to be organized, and they were ready to fight for the right to organize.

But while Lewis failed in his attempts to break the open shop of these major industries, he was extremely successful in organizing and building a Lewis machine within the United Mine Workers of America. Lewis's job with the AF of L gave him a golden opportunity to develop the large personal following that later turned into his machine. He could travel wherever and whenever he wished at the expense of the American Federation of Labor and could personally meet and become friends with a host of key mine workers' leaders throughout the nation. Secondly, Lewis also had the advantage of an American Federation of Labor expense account, which enabled him to entertain these various miners. Thirdly, he had the great advantage of not only possessing a miner's background and being a member of the union, but also the prestige derived from his post as organizer and legislative representative for the American Federation of Labor. This latter position gave him entree into many quarters in the United Mine Workers. The position of his office was such that during the mine workers convention of 1916, Lewis temporarily served as president pro tem. It was soon after this that John P. White, president of the mine workers, offered Lewis the post of chief statistician. Lewis accepted this job and resigned as special representative of the AF of L.

The Lewis family moved to Indianapolis, where the national headquarters of the United Mine Workers was located. The family now included three children, Kathryn who was born on April 14, 1911, John L. Junior, November 25, 1918, and Margaret Mary who was born in 1910 and later died at the age of eleven.

Shortly afterward, John P. White resigned his presidency in order to accept a position as a permanent arbitrator. White was succeeded by Frank Hayes, who was a mild, unaggressive, and ineffectual person for the job. Hayes appointed John L. Lewis as vice-president. Shortly after assuming the presidency Hayes began drinking heavily. From that time on until Lewis's election as president of the United Mine Workers Union in

1920 there have been many whispers and stories as to how he gained control.

There is the most commonly told tale that Frank Hayes was kept constantly drunk while Lewis steadily moved in to seize more and more control of the union. A pamphlet put out by the Communist party in 1929 charged that among other things, Lewis assigned one of his trusted aides to keep Hayes perpetually drunk.

These innuendoes and accusations are without evidence and appear to be unwarranted. However, what is probably true is that, while Lewis was not aiding and abetting Frank Hayes's excessive drinking, he certainly did not discourage it.

For many years, while Hayes was in Colorado after resigning as president of the United Mine Workers, he constantly praised Lewis and spoke about him in such terms as to give the complete lie to all of these wild and fantastic tales surrounding this period.

While Lewis was statistician of the United Mine Workers he also had as a duty the preparation of the union's paper. Lewis used this job, just as he later used the job of vice-presidency of the union, first to learn every single thing there was to be learned about the coal-mining industry and the union so that he would become what he is today, the best-informed man in the entire coal industry, which no coal operator will dispute. Second, he used his job as a means of acquiring more power for himself. He corresponded on a vast scale with the coal miners, always bearing in mind that the union elected its officers by correspondence.

Two years after first becoming an official of the union, Lewis found himself presiding as acting president in the place of President Frank Hayes at the 1919 mine workers convention. As a matter of fact, for the past two years, what with a change of presidents and the new president Frank Hayes showing a great deal more interest in alcohol than in the problems of the coal miners, Lewis had been handling most of the union's business. As acting president, Lewis found himself shouldering practically the entire administrative burden. He spent a great deal of time in consultation with the union attorney, Henry Warrum, of Indiana, with particular reference to a million-dollar law suit that had been lodged against the union by the

Coronado Coal Company charging the union with violation of the Sherman Anti-Trust Law. Six years later, in 1925, the union finally won its case before the Supreme Court, but only with the help of Charles Evans Hughes as their counsel and the payment of a large fee to him for his services. For six years this suit cast a shadow over the mine workers union with the ever present threat of a two-million-dollar judgment, which would have wrecked the financial structure of the union.

The new acting president of the United Mine Workers was in many ways a new man. John Lewis was beginning to stand independent of Gompers. He began to make decisions that were at variance with those of the "old fox." During this year a significant episode occurred at the AF of L convention that was to influence materially Lewis's thinking in the future.

Lewis clashed with Gompers at a meeting of the resolutions committee of the convention of the AF of L when Lewis demanded a resolution calling for a vigorous organizing campaign among the unorganized workers. Lewis told the writer, "I believe it was at the resolutions committee at the AF of L convention of 1919 in Buffalo. I felt that here was the perfect opportunity to launch an organization drive and build the ranks of organized labor in this country. I would have organized all of the unorganized coal miners through the South, West, Virginia, and other places at that time; but I was stopped when Gompers came to me and told me about the status quo agreement which he had with Woodrow Wilson which forbade any disturbance or unrest such as a union organizing drive. Gompers insisted that the agreement be respected. When Gompers told me that, I must say to you that it chilled the very marrow of my bones; and I decided right then and there that I would never permit a union or myself to get so involved in and so dependent upon a federal administration that in times of crisis the ties of loyalty and agreement and obligation to that administration would paralyze me from acting in the interests of labor as it did with Gompers in 1919. The favorable opportunities for labor to organize are precious few and they cannot be waived at the whim of a president. Every opportunity must be exploited to the full whenever it arises."

Looking backward, it is now clear that Lewis's convictions arising out of this experience foreshadowed not only his coming break with Gompers, but also the events of twenty years later when he would break with Franklin Delano Roosevelt.

The climate of the nation was definitely hostile to the strike upon which the young new leader of the coal miners union was about to embark. The Russian revolution of 1917 had sent a hysterical fear through the nation. United States Attorney General A. Mitchell Palmer launched a reign of terror in which everyone suspected of militant socialism or any other kind of "ism" was promptly arrested, indicted, and jailed. Socialist legislators of the N.Y. State Assembly were arrested and placed in jail. Riots raged in some of the cities against this specter of "bolshevism." The hysteria reached extremes that were as irresponsible as the conditions prevailing today in this nation. Attorney General Palmer's shameful violation of those civil liberties basic to the democratic process spread to other branches of the Government, and Postmaster General Burleson began censoring and suppressing publications critical of the administration's war activities. The Postmaster's actions were not confined to the war but extended some time after the war period.

Over on the industrial side of the repressive, undemocratic national scene we find William Z. Foster,[2] formerly a left-wing Socialist and Wobbly, but then an AF of L organizer, leading a national strike against the steel industry in September, 1919. The strike was of short duration as the combined force of the steel industry, the state police, hired sluggers, political organizations, the press, and the Department of Justice smashed the strike. The steel workers did not have the kind of an organization that could stand up to the wave of unbridled violence that poured down upon them. Gompers and the AF of L only gave lip service to support the steel strike. The AF of L lost considerable face during this strike.

The year 1919 found the Government, business, and the press hysterical with fear. Organized labor was suspected of being the advance guard of the unbelievable bolshevik red menace that had captured Russia. While on the international scene Russia was to be quarantined, here at home any individual or organization suspected of infection with this red virus was also to be quarantined—in prison. Those who questioned

[2] Now chairman of the Communist party, U.S.A.

the divine right of capitalism were instantly suspect; and therefore repression, hostility, and suspicion were rampant through the year. Into this forbidding climate, John L. Lewis was to lead and general his first strike.

Throughout World War I the miners had worked for a wage of five dollars a day. They had approved an agreement with the Government binding themselves not to seek any changes in their wage structure or working conditions "during the continuance of the war and not to exceed two years from April 1, 1918." It was clear that the agreement was actually only for the war period; and the two-year extension meant that, if the war was still underway on April 1, 1920, the miners could again negotiate. Further to corroborate this clear intention, Section 24 of the wartime Food and Fuel Act stated "that the provisions of this act shall cease to be in effect when the existing state of war between the United States and Germany shall have terminated and the fact and date of such termination shall be ascertained and proclaimed by the president."

At their convention in the fall of that year the miners called for Government ownership or nationalization of the mines. Lewis, too, supported this proposal as a disorganized coal industry seemed on the verge of collapse. One lone dissenter was howled down with charges of being a company stool pigeon. Then an overwhelming majority of the miners demanded a 50-per-cent increase in pay, a five-day week, and a six-hour day. The miners were in a rebellious mood against being tied to a wartime wage-stabilization agreement while an unstable economy was skyrocketing prices. They were convinced to a man that their agreement was only for the duration of the military war, which had ceased almost a full year before. The administration's protest that the war was not yet over, as no official peace treaty had been signed, was correct only in the sense of pure legalism. Lewis was ordered by the convention to fight for their demands and if necessary to strike.

Negotiations with the coal operators quickly reached an impasse, and in late October Lewis issued the order to all miners to strike on November 1. The repercussions of Lewis's order came instantly as recriminations and attacks against Lewis and the miners filled the air. President Woodrow Wilson, who had permitted his attorney general to run amuck on his red inquisition, now stormed that the strike was ". . . not only unjustifiable but it is unlawful. The law will be enforced and means found to protect the national interest in any emergency that may arise." Administration officials added to the abuse of the union by blaming the union and exonerating the coal operators.

Smarting under their attack, Lewis slashed back at the President, charging that "President Wilson's attitude is the climax of a long series of attempted usurpations of executive power."

Here, young thirty-nine-year-old Lewis, with a shaky union organization, stood up and publicly attacked the President of the United States. To Lewis, Wilson was the man who had cajoled and flattered Samuel Gompers into tying labor's hands with a no-organizing campaign pledge. Now this same Wilson was trying to tie labor's hands on wage increases. To Lewis and the miners the name of Wilson evoked only profanity.

The President then demanded that Lewis and the coal operators agree to arbitration. Lewis tartly replied that, when the steel industry had struck two months before, Judge E. H. Gary, chairman of the board of U.S. Steel, had rejected arbitration and that the Government had not applied any pressure on him. Lewis then went on to remind the President that the steel strike was permitted to go on without any Government intervention. Lewis did not publicly state what was common knowledge, that the Department of Justice had vigorously helped to break the strike.

Wilson then assailed Lewis as a dictator, charging that the strike action ". . . has apparently been taken without any vote upon the specific proposition by the individual members of the United Mine Workers of America through the use of an almost unprecedented proceeding . . ."

The nation's press grabbed their cue from this attack by Wilson and began publishing reams of stories to the effect that the miners did not want to strike and were being forced to do so by this "tyrant Lewis." *The New York Times* reported that two thirds of 11,000 miners in an Ohio district felt that they were being coerced into a strike.

Lewis refused to retreat from the strike action, answering Wilson by saying, "I am an American, free born, with all the pride of my heritage. I love my country with its institutions and traditions. With Abraham Lincoln I thank God that we have a country where men may strike. May the power of my Government never be used to throttle or crush the efforts of the toilers to improve their material welfare and elevate the standard of their citizenship."

Congress was working itself into a rage at this upstart who was defying everyone from the President down. Senators angrily told newsmen that this time this fellow Lewis had gone too far. The Congress could not envisage that this uproar would become a routine issue in their agenda for the next thirty years or more. Newspapers which were to run the headlines: "U.S. Acts to Stop Lewis" might well have saved the type composition, for it was to be a regular banner headline for the next thirty years. Lewis was being initiated with a vengeance into the ordeal of public and Government attack that was to become as routine to him for the next three decades as buying a new suit of clothes.

Colorado's Senator Thomas introduced and had passed in record time a resolution calling for the use of federal troops for the purposes which were in actuality just plain strike-breaking. The President then nodded toward his attorney general's office and Mr. Palmer promptly mounted his red horse and charged off to the courts to use legal power against Lewis.

The Attorney General brought suit in Indianapolis, Indiana, the then site of the national headquarters of the miners union. Federal Judge A. B. Anderson issued an injunction forbidding the Union officials to call a strike. Judge Anderson's court order is still remembered as a classic in its attack upon the rights of labor. The AF of L executive board referred to Judge Anderson's injunction as being "so autocratic as to stagger the human mind" and voted to support the strike and Lewis's defiance of the order.

For John Lewis was defying the court injunction. November 1 arrived, and every coal miner left his job. The strike was on, court order or no court order! The Government gasped in its helplessness and goaded public opinion to new heights of fury. The coal operators charged the whole strike was a bolshevik revolution. Thomas T. Brewster, chairman of the Scale Committee of the coal operators and also spokesman for them, charged it was all financed by "Moscow gold" and that the whole strike was engineered by Lenin and Trotsky. The charges were so wild, fantastic, and irresponsible that the history of those days could well bear the dateline of 1949. Lewis denied Brewster's charge, telling him to put up his evidence or shut up. T. T. Brewster shut up.

The strike was creating a public emergency; and the Government, confronted by a man who refused to yield to the President, the Congress, or the courts, was beginning to temper its attitude. Sheer force was not going to prevail against this young man with heavy eyebrows and a heavier determination to refuse to budge or bow before the public storm. The eleventh day of the strike was Armistice Day, and Lewis threw out a feeler suggesting that he would consider ending the strike if the operators would bargain in good faith.

Lewis was getting concerned and apprehensive about the violence of the attack against the union and himself. The extent of the public emergency, at least as reported in the press, made him uneasy. This was a young, inexperienced Lewis who was getting his feet wet in leading his first national strike by being tossed under Niagara Falls. The Lewis apparently devoid of nerves that America was to know too well had not evolved as yet. Furthermore, the miners union was riddled with dissension and was conspicuous for its lack of discipline and finances. Lewis, still only acting president, was worried about the internal structure of the union. He wanted to get out of the situation in which he now found himself. He greeted the announcement of AF of L support of the strike and defiance of the injunction with the perfunctory remark, "Very interesting. I have no other comment." Actually the AF of L militancy was going to make the course of retreat more difficult.

Negotiations were resumed with the coal operators but to little avail. The administration, now realizing that Lewis had to have a face-saving agreement in order to end the strike, began for the first time to say some kind words for him and to put pressure on the operators.

On December 3, Judge Anderson, after observing the miners flouting his court order for more than a month, ordered eighty-four union officials cited for contempt. Lewis and all the union's national officers were arrested and released on bonds fixed at $10,000 each.

The press and major business organizations continued to

convey the impression that America was now in the throes of a major national disaster. The President of the National Association of Manufacturers, S. C. Mason, scolded Eastern cities for not rationing coal and for following a normal routine of work.

Late in the afternoon of December 6, Lewis and William Green, Secretary-Treasurer of the miners union, arrived in Washington and went to the White House, where they were closeted with President Wilson until late that night.

On December 7, John L. Lewis called off the strike with the public statement, "I will not fight my Government, the greatest government on earth." Twenty-two years later this same John L. Lewis was to fight his "Government, the greatest government on earth" tooth and nail in the famous captive-mine strike of 1941. He was to beat that Government in that battle and emerge victorious on the very same day of December 7. Also on that very same day of December 7 his "Government, the greatest government on earth," was to be attacked by Japan.

The Government was so cocksure of Lewis's capitulation that Attorney General Palmer in Indianapolis on the morning of December 10 wired the President, saying, "The miners will meet promptly at two o'clock and will promptly acquiesce in President's plan."

The press featured Palmer's telegram, which was a classic of arrogant contempt for the miners who were meeting later that afternoon to decide as to whether or not they would accept the President's plan. The miners were so resentful of Palmer's telegram, which openly implied they had no independence and would simply rubber-stamp Lewis's decision, that Lewis had to spend time pacifying the miners and Palmer was forced to announce he had been misquoted.

On the afternoon of December 10, Lewis was back in Indianapolis facing a hostile miners convention. He uncorked all of his dramatic talents from thunders to whispers, from baleful looks to compassionate gestures, while down on the convention floor Lewis's lieutenants worked feverishly with oral and physical arguments to rally support behind their boss. Lewis beat his breast bellowing his "Americanism." He charged that anyone who was against the agreement was against the Government, and waved the stars and stripes for an hour. He tried to paint the defeat as a victory and finally the agreement was passed with the heavy rumble of the steam roller drowning out criticism and dissension.

The terms called for an immediate raise of 14 per cent and the appointment of a commission of three to study the wage situation and report their findings within sixty days. The commission's final judgment resulted in a 34-per-cent increase for tonnage men and wage increases of 20 per cent for day men. More than a third of the day men resented this disparity of wage increases and responded with a flurry of wildcat strikes that eventually got them, through local district arrangements, an increase of $1.50 a day.

The new acting president of the miners had entered the strike as a novice but emerged a seasoned veteran. In his first strike he had fought everybody. He had battled the nation, the President, the Congress, the Department of Justice, the courts, and the press! There was little that could be done to scare Lewis in the future.

It had been quite a first experience. He had learned that he could win over any power if the miners were united and stood together as one. That was the important job ahead and so Lewis turned to the battle within the union.

Chapter 3

The Bloody Twenties

IN 1920 Lewis was officially elected president of the United Mine Workers of America.[1] His election was due as much to the factional fights and divisions within the ranks of the United Mine Workers as to the organization he had built up within the union.

Lewis was now nominally king; but, as he surveyed his domain, he was confronted with a vista of destitution, disorganization, rebellion, and conflict. There was little that was encouraging in the bleak picture of the coal fields. The rank-and-file membership of the union was tough, individualistic, defensive, and cynical. The suspicion they held concerning the outside, hostile world was accompanied by a skepticism of the motives of their own union leaders. They had seen too many of their officials depart from office only to enter the ranks of the coal operators. Many of them were convinced that the office of the presidency of their union was simply an avenue to the financial security on the coal operator's side of the fence. Even their great patron saint, John Mitchell, had gone to work for the Civic Federation, an employer-dominated organization, detested by much of labor.

Lewis, in turn, also reflected a certain cautious suspicion with reference to the rank and file of the miners. He remembered the number of UMWA presidents who had given their very life's blood for the union only to be kicked out of office by an ungrateful rank-and-file membership. He felt that was

[1] When Lewis was acting president of the union his salary was $3,000. Immediately after taking office, he raised it to $5,000 a year. One year later it was raised to $8,000. Subsequently, it mounted to $12,500, then $25,000, and now is an annual salary of $50,000.

one reason some of the union officials joined the operators. He also remembered back to his early childhood when his father, Tom Lewis, had fought so selflessly for his fellow miners in the Lucas, Iowa, coal strike of 1892. He would never forget those strikers returning to work and leaving Tom Lewis in a blacklist exile. Lewis's concept of human nature was not one of optimism.

The new miners' president realized that the union was a union in name, but in fact was a group of large, individual, autonomous domains loosely tied together in a national organization. Each mining district and its local chiefs zealously guarded their own independence from invasion and domination by the national office. The miners summed up their conception of their rights in the term "autonomy." This included the right to elect their regional officials. While these local practices of autonomy were in keeping with the basic traditions of democracy they were resulting in severe disunity within the union. "Autonomy" was developing into a fatal weakness. Each district would try to get the best deal it could, regardless of what happened to the miners in other parts of the country. This was exemplified particularly in Illinois, where the district officers would try to make their own contracts with the Illinois operators regardless of what happened to the rest of the miners.

This practice was encouraged by the operators as it tended to set off one district union against the other and to breed discord and disunity within the union. The local officers seemed unaware of the disastrous effect of separate agreements, which undermined the whole idea of national collective bargaining. For one district to get higher pay than an adjoining district simply meant that the lower wage rate prevailing outside would, in the last analysis, become the standard and shortly destroy the higher wage rate. The only hope for the miners was in a closely integrated national union which could deal with the coal industry on a nationwide basis.

In the union were individual leaders who nominally acknowledged the authority of the national union officers but in practice carried on the affairs of their own districts as though they were not responsible to any other union authority. There was a rank-and-file feeling of revolt against the current leadership, but this feeling was no different than it had always been in the mine workers' ranks. The union had always been a boiling kettle of unrest and change. Many of the factions were more concerned with getting the upper hand over the rival groups than in getting it over the coal operators.

Confronted with this situation, Lewis coldly decided to unite the union into a single, disciplined force. The only way to do it was to develop a machine that would ensure control over the entire union. Of course, there were also Lewis's personal ambitions to rule with complete security. Where his personal desire for power began and where his desire for unity left off is impossible to determine. The two became as opposite sides of the same shield. He knew that in the past every campaign for unity had ended in compromises with the individual power blocs. Past experience was replete with proof that the union could not be mobilized into a single force on the basis of a working coalition of different, independently powerful districts. This passive compromise policy had failed in the past, and Lewis was determined that he was not going to repeat the error. He was convinced from everything he knew and had seen in the union that the only way that this loosely tied organization could be welded into a single, powerful force was to root out completely local autonomy and division of authority. It would mean taking over control of the union, lock, stock, and barrel. He knew that for the building of this machine he would have to be ruthless and uncompromising, for the miners did not fight by Marquis of Queensberry rules. It would be a perilous course to start out on, because in the last analysis it might well mean the destruction of the union. In actual essence it was going to mean either rule or ruin.

But this would have to wait, for in May, 1920, shortly after Lewis's election, a crisis developed in West Virginia.

In the southern part of the state lay the rich Williamson coal fields. There the miners were unorganized and suffering from low wages, long hours, and hazardous working conditions. They were completely at the mercy of the coal operators, who had substituted the gold standard for the golden rule. In turn, the miners union was suffering from the effects of the huge West Virginia coal tonnage (which was 79 million tons in 1919) produced and sold at lower rates than that in the unionized coal fields. It was unfair competition to the organized coal mines whose wages and, therefore, costs of production were higher. The operators of the organized coal mines would always point this out to the union as a defense against wage increases. Furthermore, the organized mines charged they were being cut-rated out of existence. The standards for which the miners union was fighting were in jeopardy.

Lewis ordered the southern West Virginia coal fields organized. The coal operators regarded the union as a burning plague and were determined to fight fire with fire. The appearance of the mine workers officials in the area set off months of violence. The operators not only fired any miner suspected of union sympathies but evicted him and his family from the company-owned houses. These lockouts, coupled with many strikes, resulted in thousands of homeless miners and their families wandering over the countryside. The union provided tents, and cities of tents mushroomed in the fields as miners with their wives and children huddled sick and starving in their rudimentary shelter.

The American Red Cross was appealed to for aid but refused to be "At Their Side" since their suffering was not "An Act of God." The Red Cross's definition of "An Act of God" would be extraordinarily interesting. The Red Cross then pointed out that the bickering miners could get all the necessities of life if they would only go back to work on the coal operators' conditions. Apparently the Red Cross was at the side of the coal operators as was the Young Men's Christian Association, which would not get involved in "controversial" issues. It is no wonder that the coal miners felt that everyone's hand was raised against them. They had sought faith, hope, and charity and gotten fake, hoax, and chicanery.

The coal operators owned most of the law-enforcement officers, body and soul. Reinforced by private detectives, these minions went out of their way to be cruel and terrorize the miners. In return the miners and their few friends vengefully struck back.

The violence burned at white heat in the southwestern coal fields of West Virginia, which bordered on Kentucky. Here in Mingo and Logan counties along the Tug River the main battle was joined between the mine workers union and the coal operators.

Life had always been cheap in this part of the country and the whir of a passing rifle bullet did not cause undue excitement. This was a battle ground over which had raged a forty years' war with no holds barred, a war which was to become a part of the immortal American legends and to be known as the Hatfield-McCoy Feud.

There were still Hatfields and McCoys around, and they still did not run from trouble. One of them, Sid Hatfield, was known as the "Terror of the Tug" and a dead shot with a gun. He was the chief of police in the small mining town of Matewan which was situated in the heart of the union-operator battleground and was the headquarters of the Stone Mountain Coal Company.

At Matewan all the miners were being evicted. The operators had hired the Baldwin Felts detective agency as a supplement to their mine-police force. The Baldwin-Felts agents were in charge of the evictions and were passionately hated by the miners. The hatred was mutual; and there were many reports of the cold callousness of these agents.

On May 19, a group of these detectives headed by their chief, Albert C. Felts, and his brother Lee Felts, came into Matewan from Bluefield, West Virginia. They went from house to house routing out the miners and their families. Mothers and children wandered in confusion through the streets of the town not knowing where they were going to sleep that night.

Police chief Sid Hatfield lost his temper at the spectacle of misery. Hatfield got C. C. Testerman, the town's mayor, and they walked up to Felts to protest. They exchanged some heated words while Felts and his men nervously gripped their guns as they tensely watched Hatfield.

The meeting ended when Mayor Testerman walked away, with Hatfield audibly urging the Mayor to sign warrants for the arrest of Felts and his detectives. Testerman balked at issuing the warrants, and Hatfield's temper began to run out. He is reported to have remarked to a neighbor, "We'll kill those sons of bitches before they get out of Matewan."

Later in the day he saw Albert Felts and warned him that he was going to arrest him and all his detectives before they left town. Felts and his men went back to the hotel to pack and get the next train returning to Bluefield. At the hotel, Felts is reported to have threatened to "get" Hatfield.

This was the background for the death orgy that was to come that afternoon. As Albert Felts and his men, all armed, were walking to the railroad station they passed Hatfield. Felts approached Hatfield and tried to arrest him with a false warrant. In a moment the street was full of gunfire. In five minutes there were eleven dead bodies on Matewan's Main Street. There were Albert Felts and his brother, Lee Felts. Albert Felts had been given a *coup de grace* with a gun held next to his head as he lay wounded and writhing with pain. Five other detectives were dead, as were Mayor Testerman and a boy bystander and two miners. A moment later the train from Bluefield pulled across the main street. There are stories that those who got off the train blanched with horror at the carnage strewn up and down the main street. There is another tale that the engineers took one look down the street and hastily began to back the train out of the town that had suddenly become a morgue.

Guerrilla warfare broke out throughout the territory, and many a man suddenly went down before an unseen gun. The daily casualties looked like a war report. Finally on August 24 the climax came in the form of a revolution when a "citizens' army" of 6,000 armed and disciplined miners, accompanied by nurses adorned with UMWA instead of the Red Cross, opened battle at Madison, West Virginia, with 2,000 very well-armed strike-breakers, detectives, and imported thugs. It bloomed into a full-fledged war that was covered by the press with their ace war correspondents.

Three days later the U.S. Army moved in, and the miners promptly stopped and surrendered their guns. It meant a surrender, too, of their hopes for a union. Fifty thousand union-minded miners had been thrown out of their homes and wandered about helplessly with no food or medicine. Finally most of them capitulated and went back to the open-shop mines. For the next thirteen years the idea of the United Mine Workers of America in southern West Virginia was dead. Lewis no longer had a problem in West Virginia. He had nothing.

The union was yielding to pressures everywhere except in Illinois. In Pennsylvania, the mine owners were emulating their fellow operators of West Virginia and the union was receiving a horrible beating.

The outlook during the year 1921 was bleak and forbidding. That year Lewis took another defeat. The American Federation of Labor convened that June in Denver, Colorado. Here at its fortieth convention Lewis entered into a campaign to dethrone Gompers and become the president of the AF of L. Gompers had been president since Lewis was a two-year-old infant.

Why Lewis decided to fight for the presidency against Gompers will never be known. Some attributed it to an overweening ambition plus the fact that he had come so far in so short a time that he began to feel infallible. Lewis remembered, too, that Gompers had been defeated only once in his career and that by a mine worker president, John McBride, in 1895. Others suggest that the barren prospects facing Lewis in the coal miners union made him anxious to climb out of the grim morass in which he seemed to be mired. Lewis electioneered for a program of health and unemployment insurance, old-age benefits, Government ownership, and all in all, a radical program for those days.

Lewis told the writer, "I ran against Gompers for the presidency of the AF of L in 1921 because a number of unions were sickened by Gompers's depending upon the federal administration. They could not stomach the reverent awe which he had in his heart for presidents. I want to tell you that at that convention I did not campaign for a single vote. I never asked for a vote. I never asked for a vote in my life for anything. When the count was completed, I got one third of the votes of the federation body against Gompers."

At any rate, Lewis ran and was beaten two to one. Some of his own coal-miner delegates voted against him, which was an index of the disorganization and hostilities in the union. Lewis wanted to start the purge within the union, but again he had to wait, for the union wage demands were rebuffed by the operators. If the operators would not yield it meant that 1922 would be another year of strike.

On April 1, 1922, Lewis ordered a nationwide coal strike. Out of this, a small southern Illinois town named Herrin became forever identified with terror and carnage.

Herrin is located in the heart of the great coal field running under Williamson County. The deposits include some thirty square miles of coal, most of it lying close to the surface.

The mine workers in southern Illinois had fought for and won union recognition as far back as 1898 so that union conditions prevailed and were accepted when the huge coal beds were discovered in the early 1900's. Under these circumstances, the coal operators were unable to set up company towns or to force miners to live on company property as they did in West Virginia, Kentucky, and elsewhere. Herrin had a strong, solid union that was part of the community's way of life.

Herrin's way of life also included a tradition of violence. As early as 1899 a mine operator tried to break a strike by importing nonunion miners. Many of these strike-breakers were killed and the community not only sanctioned but approved this violence and loss of life. Later on, another operator tried the same tactics and this time permitted his guards to display Gatling guns. The striking miners interpreted this armed exhibition as a challenge that they accepted, and with much gunfire and community approval.

Violence was not confined to the miners and operators as civil war raged in Williamson County between the Ku Klux Klan and its opponents. Guns blazed in broad daylight on the main street of Herrin, and many a family went into mourning.

There was also gang war and gang rule in Williamson County and killing was the order of the day. Life was cheap in southern Illinois or, as it was known, "Little Egypt." It is small wonder that Williamson County became known throughout the country as "Bloody Williamson County" even before the event that was to horrify the nation.

The spring of 1922 found Illinois's 60,000 union miners joined with other union miners in the nation on strike. The profit of the coal operators had dwindled to approximately 3 per cent on their investment, and they refused to agree to Lewis's demand of a wage scale of $7.50 for day men.

In the midst of this strike, William J. Lester, an absentee owner of a strip mine near Herrin, Illinois, decided to pull a fast march on his competitors. He made arrangements with the mine workers local in Herrin to permit members of the Steam Shovel Men's Union to work off only the top coverings of his coal beds. This meant that the moment the strike was settled the coal could be quickly mined and shipped to market well in advance of the other mines. At this strip, known as the Southern Illinois Coal, was a gigantic steam shovel which had originally been used to help dig the Panama Canal. Over it all was a tough, strike-breaking mine superintendent from Kansas named C. K. McDowell. Back in Kansas McDowell had tangled with the short-tempered Alex Howat, and had busted Howat's strikes as fast as they arose. The strikers, in turn, had broken his leg and he walked with a limp. He came from Kansas filled with contempt for the miners union.

Both McDowell and his boss, William J. Lester, were utterly oblivious of the character of the people who lived in Williamson County. Only this ignorance can explain their next move, which in Williamson County could only result in the bloody consequences that followed.

McDowell converted the mine into a bristling arsenal and announced that he was going to mine and ship coal. This was not just a violation of the agreement with the union but open strike-breaking. For strike-breakers, in addition to using members of the Steam Shovel Men's Union, McDowell turned to Chicago's Madison Street. Skid Row's hoboes were rounded up and brought down to the mine. En route they were warned by the authorities that they were going into a dangerous venture. But high pay for no work and plenty of liquor was an inducement beyond any warnings. Their job was to be that of being physically present at the mines so that striking miners would become apprehensive of their jobs, demoralized, and then try to return to work.

Anyone acquainted with "Bloody Williamson County" could have told McDowell that he was inviting certain death for himself and his associates in this scheme. It is also certain that McDowell, supremely self-confident, would have sneered at all warnings.

His action antagonized the entire community. The Sheriff, Melvin Thaxton, was a former miner and the State Senator, William J. Sneed, was an official of the United Mine Workers Union. McDowell and his cohorts would have been safer in a cage of wild lions, but McDowell blindly plunged ahead. His manner was arrogant and belligerent. He seemed to go out of his way to try to intimidate the strikers. The passing of each day brought a new blunder and an increasing hatred by the community. His armed guards careened around the country side blazing away at everything in sight, from cattle to windows. The farmers, now in a rage, arrayed themselves on the side of the miners. The area was seething with vindictive passion, and Williamson County had become a powder keg eagerly awaiting a spark.

State Senator Sneed desperately tried to argue McDowell out of what was now utter madness. McDowell, by this time slightly sobered by the intense hatred that he could almost feel, and getting a bit bewildered by a situation he had never before encountered, told Senator Sneed that he was not strike-breaking, since in his strip mine, coal was mined by a steam shovel and the steam shovel operators were union men.

Since Illinois District president Frank Farrington was unavailable, Sneed wired Lewis on June 18, wanting to know how union steam-shovel operators could participate in breaking the coal strike. The next day came Lewis's reply:

> Your wire of 18. Steam Shovel Men's Union was suspended from affiliation with the American Federation of Labor some years ago. It was also ordered suspended from the mining department of the American Federation of Labor at the Atlantic City Convention. We now find that this outlaw organization is permitting its members to act as strikebreakers at numerous strip pits in Ohio. This organization is furnishing steam shovel engineers to work under armed guards with strike breakers. It is not true that any form of agreement exists by and between this organization and the mining department or any other branch of the AF of L permitting them to work under such circumstances. We have, through representatives, officially taken up this question with the officers of the Steam Shovel Men's Union and have failed to secure any satisfaction. Representatives of our organization are justified in treating this crowd as an outlaw organization and in viewing its members in the same light as they do any other common strike-breakers.

It came on June 21. How it started no one will ever know. Coleman in his *Men and Coal* states that on the afternoon of that fatal day, a young striker visiting with a group of his friends a half mile from the strip mine was killed by a bullet fired from a high-powered rifle at the mine.

The *Chicago Daily News* charged that Lewis's telegram branding the steam-shovel operators as "common strike-breakers" was responsible for the holocaust. The *News* added that the striking miners had opened fire on a truck carrying ten men to work in the mine.

The *Tribune* and other papers echoed this charge. The accounts all varied with one exception. Everyone from New York to California knew that on June 21 southern Illinois erupted, and in Williamson County all hell broke loose.

From all over southern Illinois came men carrying guns. There were miners, farmers, shopkeepers, legionnaires, and members of recreational and fraternal societies. Young and old they came, and their women urged them on. They had taken all they would and to them that strip mine was their Bunker Hill. Hundreds and hundreds merged to become a mob thinking and feeling only as a mob can. Individual consciences and humanity were buried by the mob mind. It was a human pack hungry for the kill. They came and they killed. They came in battle lines. They hired an airplane to bomb the mine with dynamite. They advanced in waves. It was war in its rawest and most primitive form, for here there were to be no quarter and no prisoners.

The night was an inferno as intense gunfire went on without even a moment's interruption. More than a thousand guns in the hands of the striking miners were firing steadily on the mine. From the mine came the staccato hammering of machine guns sweeping the fields. Finally the miners blew up the pumping station that supplied water to the mine. A moment later a freight car loaded with food for McDowell's men was blown sky high by dynamite. Now there was no food and no water.

Shortly after dawn a white flag was waved from the mine. With rebel yells and war whoops the hundreds of striking miners now stormed over the embankments surrounding the mine. The miners dynamited the steam shovel and other parts of the mine. It was reported that they guaranteed safe conduct to all in Herrin. What happened afterward is a matter of history. It was what it has always been called—a massacre.

". . . Then the enemy, yelling like Indians, swarmed over the top and down on us. We were helpless. . . . Many of them were reeling drunk. First they struck us with their fists and then, as they tasted blood they started in to hammer some with the butts of revolvers." [2]

The miners demanded the identification of those who had operated the machine guns against them. One was pointed out and instantly killed. They draped his body over the machine gun.

Superintendent McDowell was taken for a walk, shot and killed and his dead body riddled with bullets. Under a scorching sun thousands of men and women and children lined the road from the mine to Herrin, screaming and attacking the prisoners as they were stoned, clubbed, shot, knifed, and tortured. The captives ran a never ending gauntlet of kicks and punches.

"They tied five men with me, took us out on the road and told us to run. We ran and hundreds of bullets followed us. We staggered on. . . . Some fell, pulling others tied with them, down. Several bullets were in me already.

"I laid there while men came up and fired more shots into us from three or four feet. Then everything went black. I woke up later and begged for water but there was not any. I remember being dragged along the road but I don't know by what. They carried me then to the hospital. . . ." [3]

When the miners tired of exhibiting and abusing six of their prisoners before the cheering audience, they took them to an adjacent cemetery and made them dig a hole. The six were roped together as cattle and for some minutes the crazed miners fired and fired into their bodies.

With others they staged a foxhunt, only the victims were men. They were given a head start and then the mad chase began. They were hunted down, beaten, tied, and dragged in the roads, knifed, shot, kicked, and spat upon. Three were hanged. The air of all Williamson County reeked with the sweet sickening stench of blood and death and was filled with the shriek of men in agony praying for death.

One of the men, wounded, lay on the road with one shoulder

[2] *Chicago Tribune*, June 23, 1922.
[3] *Ibid.*

shot away and his face all bloody, moaned, "Please boys, give me a drink."

A laugh from the spectators was the only reply. A news correspondent rushed to give him water but was forced quickly to withdraw by drawn pistols and told to keep away.

When the man begged again for water pleading, "For God's sake," a young woman with a baby in her arms placed her foot on the mangled body and said, "I'll see you in hell before you get any water."

The union miners denied they killed any strike breakers. A correspondent accosted a striking miner and asked, "How many were killed?"

"No one killed at all."

"Why, the dead are all over," the correspondent countered.

"We didn't kill them, they just dropped dead from fright when we surrounded their camp." [4]

The mob trooped into Herrin carrying about seventeen dead bodies, which were propped up in profane poses. Hundreds of mothers took their children to see the sights. Each corpse brought fresh jeers and laughter from the crowds.

As news of the Herrin massacre began to leak out, a stunned nation demanded to know what had happened to law and order. The answer was almost as grim as the horror of the day. The Sheriff admitted to the press that "he and his deputies stayed away on warning that they would be bumped off" and that he had been advised to do so by Delos Duty, the states attorney for Williamson County.

If that was the unbelievable condition of law and order in Williamson County, the public wanted to know why the Governor had not intervened. That answer, too, came quickly, for Governor Small was in northern Illinois in a Waukegan courtroom being tried on a charge of embezzling $1,500,000 of interest on public funds. Since the National Guard could only come into Williamson County on request of the local authorities or the order of the Governor it was now obvious why the Guard had not been summoned.

A Gilbert and Sullivan episode then developed as Governor Small in righteous indignation blamed Attorney General Brundage for the massacre because the latter's prosecution of

[4] *Chicago Daily News*, June 22, 1922.

the Governor kept him penned in court up in Waukegan. Brundage cryptically replied, "Governor Small is mistaken where the blame belongs. If he and his friends had not taken $1,500,000 interest on public funds, he would not be at Waukegan now."

By the next day the Associated Press reported that they had seen 26 dead bodies over a fifteen-mile area and estimated that the total dead would be between 30 and 40.

Now that it was done, the next question was one of responsibility. Williamson County States Attorney Duty blamed the coal operators for the bloodshed. Some of the strike-breakers who escaped with their lives added to the denunciation of the coal operators, fixing the blame there, saying the ones responsible were "those who sent us here under false promises that there would be no trouble" and that "the miners would not object."

Joseph O'Rourke, of Chicago, described, as he tossed in pain from six bullet holes in his body:

> I was sent here by the Bertrand Commissary on West Madison Street in Chicago. I had no idea what I was running into. I don't blame the miners much for attacking us for we unknowingly were being used as dupes to keep them from their jobs. We were given arms when we arrived and a machine gun was set up in one corner of the mine. Guards were with us all the time and most of the guards were tough fellows sent by a Chicago detective agency. I understand the miners sent us warnings to leave town or we would be run out. We never got them. . . . When we saw the miners approaching yesterday afternoon we did not know what to do. The guards prepared to fight, most of us workers wanted to surrender.[5]

Then came a stream of statements of righteous indignation and shock from various public officials and labor leaders including Samuel Gompers.

Later, John L. Lewis charged that the entire massacre had been instigated by Communists and implied that Farrington could not guard the union against the Communists. Lewis's statement was pure poppycock and knowing southern Illinois as he did, Lewis personally was aware of the nonsensical character of his attacks. During this period, Lewis was at the height

[5] *Chicago Tribune*, June 23, 1922.

of his irresponsible and violent red baiting. His constant attacks upon and blaming of the reds for everything that went wrong was partly the result of his having been labeled a red during the 1919 strike. Lewis resented the charge, and one way of clearing himself before the public was vehemently and unceasingly to attack Communists. Second, the Communists provided an ever present catch basin for all blame such as the Herrin massacre. Third, communism provided Lewis with a smear weapon against his opponents within the union. The moment a critic or foe of Lewis reared his head, Lewis would shout that the man was a Communist.

State-wide indignation on June 24, when Governor Small was acquitted of charges of embezzlement, caused the Williamson County coroner's jury decision to pass comparatively unnoticed. The jury held that "the deaths were due to acts direct and indirect of officials of the Southern Illinois Coal Company and found that C. K. McDowell, slain superintendent of Lester Mines, had killed a union miner."

No one was convicted for taking part in the butchery of June 22.

Blood also flowed in Pennsylvania, but this time it was that of the miners. The Pennsylvania coal fields resembled a huge concentration camp closely guarded by the mine operators' private police. These private police were well supplied with machine guns. Andrew B. Mellon's brother, Richard, before a Senate committee was queried about these machine guns and his police. He replied, "It is necessary. You cannot run the mines without them."

The mine owners' police questioned and searched cars passing through the district. Miners were persecuted and brutally attacked. There were horrible atrocities, such as the Pittsburgh Company police officers, killing miner John Barkoski by beating him with a red-hot poker and twisting his ears until they bled. Barkoski was killed because the two sadistic private police wanted to "warm up" and keep in practice.

A U.S. Senate investigating committee took about 3500 pages of evidence, which constituted a mammoth Black Paper damning the operators. Idaho's Senator Frank Gooding indignantly charged, ". . . The strike-torn regions of the Pittsburgh district are a blotch upon American civilization. It is incon-

ceivable that such squalor, suffering, misery, and distress should
be tolerated in the heart of one of the richest industrial centers
in the world. The committee found men, women and children
living in hovels which are more insanitary than a modern
swinepen. . . ."

Shortly after this, Lewis began the purge. He moved decisively and ruthlessly.

In Nova Scotia, the union officers of the district had their
own political and social philosophy. Lewis branded them as
Communists working for their ". . . revolutionary masters in
Moscow" and revoked their charter and their autonomy. Lewis
then placed the district under the control of his personal appointees. The internal weakness of the district enabled Lewis
to do it here and get away with it, so now Nova Scotia was se-
curely in his camp.

He could get away with it, too, in a West Virginia weakened
and battered from its recent war with the operators. The district's autonomy was suspended and a Lewis lieutenant was
placed in charge. Now he had West Virginia, which in future
years became one of the most powerful districts of the union.

In Kansas, there was a hotheaded, impetuous, extremely militant and courageous Alexander Howat who would, whenever
possible, call a strike. Howat was impatient and resentful of
what he interpreted as Lewis's cautious conservatism. He opposed Lewis and kept the Kansas mines in a constant uproar.
Miners did far more picketing than mining. Lewis moved
against Howat and his followers by expelling them from the
union. For years afterward, it was a common sight at the mine
workers convention to see Howat, refused recognition by the
chairman, charge down the aisle and leap on the platform into
the waiting arms of Lewis's men who then heaved Howat back
onto the convention floor. But Howat was done for, and Kansas was now in the Lewis camp.

Lewis then turned to Illinois. Here was the strongest part of
his union, and here was his strongest menace. Frank Farrington
had many of Lewis's characteristics and mannerisms. He was
physically a huge man and could bull his way through the
opposition or be soft and persistent. He was conservative, cal-
culating, and an unusually capable negotiator with the operators. He hated Lewis as intensely as Lewis hated him.

In Illinois, Farrington had his own machine and was acceptable to the Peabody Coal Company which dominated the coal industry in the state, and to a significant extent the union. Lewis began tentatively probing for vulnerable spots in the Illinois regime. Farrington, in turn, began allying himself with Lewis's enemies in Kansas and Pennsylvania. Farrington would harry Lewis and the union by always threatening to sign a separate contract with the Illinois operators.

Finally in 1929 Lewis proved that Farrington, while still president of the Illinois Miners District, had signed a contract with the biggest coal company in the state, the Peabody Coal Company, to be their "labor representative" for $25,000 a year. How Lewis uncovered the contract has never been disclosed and his only answer to that question was, "It is enough I have it." There is a strong suggestion that the Peabody Coal Company, realizing that Lewis was ultimately going to win over Farrington, permitted it to get into his hands.

Lewis promptly stripped the Illinois District of its autonomy and then moved in by sending his personal appointees to administer the district. This formula, which had worked in the other districts, now backfired. Farrington had been disposed of, but the Farrington machine led by Harry Fishwick was still in the saddle.

Lewis's men were greeted in Illinois by locked doors and loaded revolvers. Fishwick went on to get a court injunction against Lewis and the national union, restraining them from interference in Illinois.

In Fishwick, however, Lewis did not have an opponent who had the intelligence or abilities of Frank Farrington. Lewis bided his time and soon cracks of corruption opened in the Illinois machine, and Fishwick surrendered.

But before Fishwick surrendered, he spearheaded a last attempt at setting up another national miners union. On March 10, 1930, all of Lewis's opponents, John Brophy, Powers Hapgood, Alex Howat, Frank Farrington, and others,[6] met in a separate convention in Springfield and set up a rank-and-file

---

[6] Those interested in the details of these intraunion fights are referred to: McAlister Coleman, *Men and Coal* (New York: Farrar and Rinehart, Inc., 1946); Oscar Ameringer, *If You Don't Weaken* (New York: Henry Holt, 1939); Tom Tippett, "Miners Fight Their Leaders," *American Mercury*, June, 1934.

movement. They elected officers and prepared to do battle with the Lewis forces. For a year the civil war went on, with father against son and brother against brother. Before the year had passed, the insurgent movement had become meaningless splinters. However, Lewis was to have more trouble with Illinois before the state became a docile part of his machine.

The bitterness against Lewis resulted in a number of miners breaking away from the mine workers union and setting up their own organization, which they called the Progressive Mine Workers of America. This union has survived every attack made upon it by Lewis, and today it still numbers approximately 10,000 members. Its unifying force is hatred for Lewis. The bitterness of its members is so deep that they instinctively oppose any position that Lewis adopts. When he supported Roosevelt, they bitterly attacked the President. When he supported the Guffey Coal Act and the Wagner Labor Act, the progressive miners condemned both of these laws. Today the ranks of the progressive miners are thinning out to extinction.

As late as 1932, in the heart of the depression, the Illinois coal miners rebelled against a contract which reduced their wages a dollar a day. They voted it down 25,239 to 10,084. With the country at a low economic ebb, this was the best agreement that could be secured. Lewis campaigned through the state, speaking before hostile miners, urging their acceptance of this contract. The story is told that while in Williamson County he spoke in a high-school auditorium to a mass meeting of angry miners, some of whom were known to be armed. As Lewis finished speaking, he stepped away from the rostrum and sat down. One of his associates admiringly asked him, "Mr. Lewis, weren't you nervous? You knew that there were guns out in that audience." Lewis slowly replied:

"I wasn't concerned about the men in front of me; I could see them, but it was the man with the gun in back of me," and Lewis gestured toward the billowing curtains just behind them. "I've been worrying about that man." Shocked, his associate ran behind the curtain in time to see a man holding a revolver scurry away.

Lewis and his henchmen went on arguing and fighting to have the men vote to accept the contract. Then the miners voted, and it was current gossip that the results were similar to the first vote and the contract had been rejected. Lewis suddenly announced that the ballots had been stolen, creating an "emergency," and just as suddenly signed the contract. With crushing dictatorial tactics of this sort, Lewis brought the Illinois District to its knees.

With Illinois coming under Lewis's control, he now ruled the mine workers union. Lewis had successfully built his machine and now Lewis was king.

Through the years of intraunion struggle the mine workers conventions were scenes of riotous battles. The stories of Lewis's conduct at these conventions are legion. There is the oft-told tale of how Lewis, during the height of his fight with Howat and his Kansas supporters, continuously referred to the "imbroglio" which confused the entire convention. While the delegates did not understand what he was saying, they admired his use of a word which left them so baffled.

A delegate who had once owned a saloon asked a critical question. Lewis pounced on him as a "damned publican." The delegate subsided in shocked silence. During a recess in the meeting he approached Lewis whining, "Why, John, I always thought you were a Republican yourself."

At a meeting of the resolutions committee in the morning of the day the convention opened there was a group led by a delegate named Pat Ansbury who violently opposed Lewis. Lewis sat quietly, never opening his mouth, while everyone was arguing. After some hours of discussion, Lewis summed up all of the arguments and made his decision. Pat Ansbury took violent exception to Lewis's decision and attacked it with vitriolic language. After Ansbury finished, Lewis began discussing every member, every coal miner, delegate and official who was seated in the room. When he came to Ansbury, he looked at him and said, "All I can say is that I mined coal in Illinois when delegate Ansbury was herding sheep in Bulgaria."

That afternoon, on the floor of the convention, Pat Ansbury leaped to his feet shouting, "President Lewis, I demand the floor on a point of order." Lewis turned his head very slowly and stared at Ansbury. Then leaning forward, said:

"And why does the delegate ask for the floor?" Purple with anger Ansbury shouted:

"I demand the floor on a point of order because I insist upon an apology from the President. President Lewis referred to me as one who herded sheep in Bulgaria and by inference called me a Bulgarian. Everyone here knows that I'm Irish. I demand the apology."

Lewis stood there in silent meditation while the entire convention kept looking first at Ansbury and then at Lewis. After what seemed ages Lewis finally raised his head and sweeping his eyes from one corner of the convention to the other he said, very slowly:

"Delegate Ansbury asks for an apology from the President of the United Mine Workers. The President of the United Mine Workers of America does owe an apology, but the apology is not to Pat Ansbury, but to the committee of twelve Bulgarians who came to me at noon and protested this insinuation against their group. I herewith apologize to the twelve Bulgarians for having even suggested that such a person as Pat Ansbury could be associated with them."

One of Lewis's major opponents had been socially prominent Harvard graduate Powers Hapgood, who, because of burning ideals, had turned his back on a life of ease and security to join the miners in their fight.

Hapgood told the writer: "You know, as much as I used to hate Lewis and fight him I just couldn't help being just plain dumbfounded and filled with awe at the mastery with which he would handle situations. Of course, to anyone in the labor movement, Lewis's sudden bursts of rhetoric, or the way he would handle a situation just by the turn of an eyebrow, was something out of this world. Then there was the 1924 convention in Indianapolis. As usual, of course, the fight was on for autonomy and a resolution was on the floor demanding that officers in various districts be elected instead of being appointed by Lewis and his cohorts.

"At this time, Phil Murray was acting as chairman. Van Bittner, chairman of the constitutional committee, presented a resolution that strengthened Lewis's policy of appointing officers for districts and opposed the right of the miners to elect their own district officers, in other words he opposed local autonomy. Murray and Bittner tried to get the resolution through and the entire house of delegates, I swear there must have been five hundred miners from Illinois and from Nova Scotia, just got up and booed and hissed until Murray just couldn't hear himself. For more than an hour Murray continued to bang with the gavel but its sound was drowned in the din. The booing and hissing cries of 'Get off that platform! Let's have autonomy!' were wildly cheered. The stomping and screaming went on and on through the afternoon. Finally Murray moved away from the rostrum and Bittner came forward and tried to speak. If anything, the booing increased. You couldn't even hear yourself think. It sounded like a riot, like a bunch of madmen. We were sick and tired of being pushed around on the autonomy issue. This time we had the floor and we were just going to keep Lewis's henchmen from being heard.

"All this time, Lewis sat off in a corner on the stage with his head down, occasionally looking up at all of us, staring us in the eye. The man had the faculty of sitting there, looking at the convention and every delegate on the floor seemed to feel that Lewis was looking directly at him. He would then take a puff of his cigar and slowly blow the smoke, seemingly right into our collective face. We wouldn't scare, and our booing increased. This kept up for an hour and a half. Finally, what happened at this point no one will ever be able to explain, but if you talk to anyone who was at that convention they'll gasp when they try to explain it to you. Lewis's chair was about twenty-two feet away from the rostrum and it seemed to everyone that Lewis suddenly got up and with one spring, one jump, covered the twenty-two feet and landed right behind the rostrum. Of course, that's impossible and everyone knows it, but we don't know how he did it. Mabye he did it in two leaps, but if so he was on the ground for such a short time in between that no one noticed it. It looked as if he had flown across the stage and that unbelievable feat brought complete silence in the convention hall. Everyone just stared at Lewis. In that sudden silence, Lewis grabbed the gavel and banged it down and then looking at the convention, roared out, 'This beating of breasts like the savages of Africa playing on their tom-toms must cease. You understand? Mr. Van Bittner is chairman of this constitutional committee. He has the floor.' Bittner got up and you could hear a pin drop. Again, we lost autonomy."

At one of the conventions, Alex Howat made his customary Pickett's charge down the center aisle and up onto the platform.

Then came the usual aftermath as Howat was seized and sent sailing through the air back into the audience and Lewis's followers on the platform panted from the exertion necessary from this feat. Howat's demands for recognition by Chairman Lewis were denied and the convention began to shout and hiss and boo its disapproval. Lewis calmly regarded the bedlam for some moments and then boomed, "May the Chair state that you may shout until you meet each other in hell and he will not change his ruling."

At another convention, a resolution was approved and passed in spite of Lewis's opposition. Lewis, then, as chairman, prepared to call the next order of business, but before doing so, addressed the convention saying: "It is deplorable that so much of the valuable time of this convention has been devoted to the discussion and passage of this resolution. All of your energies and all of your passions have been a tragic waste for I tell you that this resolution is going where all resolutions go!"

Another time the issue of antonomy was being debated. The proponents of autonomy seemed to be carrying the day against Lewis. Just before the vote was taken, Lewis addressed the convention with an impassioned and threatening speech, in which he vehemently opposed the issue of local autonomy and ended saying, "And now that I have given you *your* thinking and *your* decision we will proceed with the vote." Obviously Lewis meant *my* thinking and *my* decision but the slip of the tongue was revealing of basic attitudes.

At another hectic convention, Lewis was bulling down the opposition. It was reported that he pounded his gavel as frequently on the heads of his enemies as he did on the rostrum. At one point a critical delegate arose, demanding the floor. Lewis thundered, "For what purpose does the delegate arise?"

The delegate shouted, "I want to go on record as—"

Lewis broke in with a crash of the gavel and snapped, "If you wish to go on record, write it on a piece of paper and hand it to the secretary. Next order of business!"

At another convention, with the Illinois delegation bitterly attacking and threatening Lewis, one of the delegates, well known for his constant carrying of a gun, tore up to the platform. Lewis met him halfway up the stairs and growled, "Take that gun out of your pocket or I'll shove it down your throat." The delegate blanched and backed away.

In the midst of his battle against his union opposition, the "Communist menace" about which Lewis had been railing for years, came to the fore. William Z. Foster had organized a Trade Union Education League popularly known as the T.U.E.L., which was designed to bore from within in a number of unions including the coal miners. Foster was the spearhead of the movement in Pennsylvania which tried to set up a new organization known as the National Miners Union which would then secede from the parent organization and try to recruit the membership of the latter. They also attempted to make an alliance with two of Lewis's chief opponents, John Brophy and Powers Hapgood. In this they failed, despite Brophy's and Hapgood's bitter opposition to Lewis. Hapgood told the writer, "It was around 1928 when the Communist party tried to get John Brophy and myself to sign a petition or a call for a conference to be held in Pittsburgh. The rallying cry was 'Save our Union.' Neither one of us would do it because we firmly opposed the idea of dual unionism. This movement would have resulted in the withdrawal from the UMW of its best elements and left Lewis completely unopposed, in his own organization.

"I was very confused by this action of the Communist party since they, too, have always felt as I do, that dual unionism was a curse to the furthering of the labor movement. I went to see William Z. Foster. Bill Foster and I had been good friends for a long time. I said to him, 'Now look here, Bill, you wrote a book about the bankruptcy of the American labor movement. I think that book is a hell of a good book. In that same book you denounced dual unionism and I agreed with you one hundred per cent. I still feel the same way. Now I am told that you and the Communist party have come out for dual unionism, and frankly, Bill, I just don't understand it.' Foster looked off in the distance for a moment or two and then, turning back to me said quietly, 'Powers, the Communist party decided that policy. As a good Communist I just have to go along.'" [7]

The T.U.E.L. failed; and, of course, in later years with the

---

[7] A letter containing this excerpt was sent to William Z. Foster, chairman of the Communist party of America, on August 23, 1949, requesting his comment for publication. It was unacknowledged.

coming of the CIO, the Communists not only dropped all of their opposition to Lewis, but gave him their unreserved support.

During some of these conventions, William Z. Foster and his associates would be present in the galleries. Lewis would acknowledge them by pointing his finger venomously at Foster and thundering, "Lurking in that gallery is that arch prince of communism who is here between his annual pilgrimages to his Moscow masters." With that, a melee would break out in the gallery and suddenly end with the precipitous retreat of the Communists.

While Lewis was putting his opposition out of business, economic circumstances were practically putting the Northern coal-mine operators out of business. Lewis could force the operators, as he did in 1922, to pay a daily wage of $7.50, but he could not force them to give regular daily work to his miners. The unionized part of the coal industry was finding it almost impossible to compete with the low prices of coal produced by nonunion low-wage mines. Three dollars a day was a common nonunion wage. Almost two thirds of the coal being mined and marketed was now coming from nonunion mines. Cutthroat competition and a shrinking market were tragically reflected in the reduction of the total number of operating mines which skidded precipitously from 9,333 in 1923 down to 6,057 in 1929 and to 5,891 by the following year. The coal industry was a shambles and as it began to go down, it dragged the union down with it.

The union's miners soon became a vast union of unemployed. The only factor that permitted the Northern union's organized coal mines to survive was that the cost of freighting coal from the Southern nonunion mines was almost, but not quite, enough to offset the wage differential.

The explanation for the chaos in the coal industry was "too many miners and too many mines." Even Lewis echoed this refrain. Various plans and panaceas were suggested, tried, and failed.

Lewis's personal thinking zigzagged with the times. From advocating government regulation of the mines he reversed himself in 1925 in his book, *The Miners Fight for American Standards*, where he argued for the free and unrestricted play of economic force. With this laissez-faire situation strangling the union, Lewis sought Government aid. He and the union's attorney, Henry Warrum, and the union's economic adviser, W. Jett Lauck, drafted legislation which included the right of labor to organize and bargain. This section of the legislation was later to be known and passed as Section 7A of NRA. It was to be the birth certificate of the CIO. Lewis, as always, learned from his mistakes. He knew now that the ultimate welfare of the miners depended upon the welfare of all the workers. An unorganized steel industry or rubber or auto, in the last analysis, was as much of a menace to the miners as the unorganized coal mines. He was sick of the coal operators' constant refrain to his wage demands when they would say, "The miners are making more money than the steel workers."

Lewis learned, above all, that it was impossible to have a stable union in a violently disorganized industry. He knew that a solid miners union could only be built upon the foundation of an orderly, stable, integrated industry. He realized that his primary task in building up and organizing the United Mine Workers of America was to organize and stabilize the coal operators themselves and the industry.

Lewis began to encourage mechanization of organized Northern mines as a method to undercut the low-cost coal from the low-wage nonunion Southern mines. While mechanization would reduce the number of miners employed, at least this smaller number would be working. Better a few working regularly than all being idle.

Lewis's battle cry throughout these terrible twenties was "No Backward Step." As wage cut followed wage cut, the slogan became a mockery. Yet the cry of "No Backward Step" revealed the desperate condition of the miners who had forsaken any hope for new benefits or forward progress.

In 1924 Lewis got the operators of Illinois, Indiana, Ohio, and western Pennsylvania to agree to a three-year wage contract. This contract, known as the Jacksonville agreement, was hailed as a great victory as it would protect the wages of the miners for the next three-year period. Shortly afterward, the agreement became another scrap of paper as the operators violated it again and again, all except one coal operator who sided with and tried to help the union. This operator, a woman named

Josephine Roche,[8] was president of the Rocky Mountain Fuel Company. Acting on the basis of ideals, she signed and honored a two-year contract with the union. In later years, when the company ran into financial difficulties the union reciprocated by setting up a private corporation called Lew-Mur-Ken (being the first three letters of the names of the three leading union officers, *Lew*is, *Mur*ray, and Secretary Treasurer *Ken*nedy), and siphoned large sums of money into Miss Roche's mines to try to keep her properties afloat. There was more than sheer altruism involved, as Lewis well knew that the union miners' jobs were dependent upon the continuance of operations by the company.

Through those years Lewis fought an unceasing defensive rear-guard action against the operators, and simultaneously carried on an unrelenting offensive against his internal union foes. The decade of the 1920's was a battle of the union for just survival. Lewis was scarred and graying, but his once great union was not only scarred but practically decimated. The best reports show that the dues-paying members of the union had shriveled from well over 400,000 in 1920 to less than 150,000, and some reliable reports cited 60,000 by 1930.

It had been a heart-breaking decade of trial by fire and starvation. Lewis had carried through with his rule or ruin policy. He had fought for an empire and ended with a wasteland. Lewis rallied his bobtailed remnants and prepared to lead them into the future. The future would be good. The turn of the tide would come with the turn of the decade, but before 1930 came October 24, 1929.

[8] Now director of the United Mine Workers of America Welfare and Retirement Fund.

Chapter 4

The Beginning of the Big Parade

ON "Black Thursday," October 24, 1929, America's economy came apart at the seams. American business leaders, economists, journalists, and the President of the United States all closed their eyes and refused to see or acknowledge the great depression that had arrived and was all around them. America tried hard to avoid facing the facts of life. There were musical sedatives such as "Happy Days Are Here Again." The movie houses featured "happy" pictures. On the best-seller lists were escapist and self-uplift volumes like *Life Begins at Forty* and *You Must Relax*, which a hard-boiled critic described as "the onanistic school of American literature." All those were just samples of the many forms of make-believe which a desperate people indulged in because of fear.

But America couldn't keep its eyes closed forever and when they opened, there were long breadlines in New York City, a municipal soup kitchen in Milwaukee, and parades of protest by growing armies of unemployed everywhere. The skies over Gary and Pittsburgh no longer had their dull red glow as furnaces went out. In Detroit the automobile industry was grinding to a stop. A new business sprang up on every corner with a sign, "Unemployed. Buy apples, 5¢ each." Destitute people began to live in Hoovervilles or in tarpaper shacks, many of them built around garbage dumps. Americans laughed with bitterness as Will Rogers cracked, "We hold the distinction of being the only nation in the history of the world that went to the poor house in an automobile." Women were working for a maximum of 25¢ an hour and many for 10¢ an hour. Taxi drivers in New York were averaging fifteen dollars a week for a six-day week. The salaries and wages of 1925 were more than halved by 1931. The national income dove from eighty-one billion dollars in 1929 to forty-one billion in 1932. By that time there were approximately fifteen million Americans unemployed. The new world aged through those years. A plague was in the land as hundreds of thousands of people hungry, heartsick, and driven by fear took to the road seeking not security but just bread and shelter.

The wave of unemployment engulfed the labor movement, and many of the 15,000,000 unemployed were union men and women. By 1931 the AF of L was losing more than 7,000 dues-paying members each week, and the situation was steadily getting worse. The impact of the depression smashed those standards the AF of L had so patiently and painfully achieved. Working conditions and wage-and-hour standards were gone with the tornado of the depression. The very life of organized labor was at stake. Millions of unemployed desperately walked the streets searching for any kind of a job at any kind of pay.

Yet under Hoover's last-ditch and futile administration came legislation that was to set the foundation for the labor laws of the coming New Deal. The Supreme Court decision of 1930 in the Texas and New Orleans Railway case sustained the ban of the 1926 Railway Labor Act against the employer practice of forcing company unions upon workers. Then came a triumph for the labor movement with the passage in March, 1932, of the Norris-LaGuardia Act, which drastically curtailed the issuance of injunctions by federal courts as a strike-breaking device and forbade the employers from asking their employees to sign a contract pledging not to join a union. This kind of contract was commonly known as a "Yellow Dog" contract. Implicit in the Norris-LaGuardia Act was the thesis that workers had the legal right to protect themselves through "association, self-organization, and designation of representatives of their own choosing to negotiate the terms and conditions of their employment."

The labor movement, buffeted and beaten on every front and praying for survival, was desperately trying to dig in. But as labor leaders huddled together in their common misery and made plans for further retreat, John Lewis was preparing to attack. The depression was no new experience to Lewis and his miners. For them the depression had begun back in 1920.

For a decade, the miners and Lewis, with his slogan of "Never a Backward Step," had fought a bloody retreat. For them it had not been a series of strikes and picketings. It had been a war with all the cruelty and loss of life that make war. The dead marked the bloody trail of "retreat" from West Virginia to Pennsylvania to Illinois.

Lewis had an idea that this was to be the time to unionize all America. This was to be the time to build a union in the steel industry. No longer then would the coal operators be able to point to the low wage of the unorganized steel workers, automobile workers, and others as a defense against the wage demands of the miners. If America's basic industries were organized, labor would be the equal of capital. It was a dream, but its potentialities transfigured it into a vision.

Lewis told the writer, "I had learned the bitter lesson that as long as the great mass of workers was unorganized, so long would it be impossible for organized labor to achieve its legitimate goals. When unions neglect to organize the unorganized they pay the penalty of their own neglect. I was never permitted to forget that lesson because every year as we sat down to negotiate with the coal operators, they would begin by denying my people a raise in wages and attempt to justify their unreasonable position by citing the lower wage of the unorganized steel workers. The coal operators would then declare that since the mine workers were earning more money than the steel workers, we should be satisfied. The low pay of the steel workers was a drag on the wage scale of the United Mine Workers. It became increasingly clear that the mine workers could never really win a just wage until the steel workers were organized and their miserable wages raised to a human, decent standard. This seemed to be a simple elementary, economic fact and it applied not only to the miners, but also to other organized union groups."

As Lewis pondered, his idea became a volcanic obsession that then congealed into a cold plan for action. The blueprint no longer was limited to the nation's basic industry, but to all unorganized workers. Even at that time, he secretly struck off the slogan for the future organizational drive—a slogan that

America was to hear again and again and again, "Organize the Unorganized." In a discussion on this point Lewis commented: "Nothing on the grand scale of CIO ever happens all at once. Things that were the life blood of the CIO, such as NRA and Section 7A, were the product of careful fruition, dreams, and strategy. Social security and old-age pensions stemmed not only from their base of repeated support by the American Federation of Labor, but also from detailed planning. From time to time, fate will create a set of circumstances which will result in an unexpected development. But careful planning on a general, inclusive basis leaves little room for the unexpected, very little of fate playing the part which can completely upset one's plan. The plans for the CIO were so broad and so flexible that they allowed for the quirks of fate and even the sit-down strikes found their place in the general framework. A plan that is strong and elastic is your major tool in your work."

But first Lewis would have to organize his own shattered union. Lewis remarked to the writer, "Of course, also in 1930, the labor movement was having its difficulties; and conditions within the United Mine Workers were not, shall I say, too favorable. However, it was obvious to me that the internal strength of our own organization or any other labor union could not be built up to its maximum point unless the unorganized were also organized."

Lewis stated to the writer, "By 1932 my thinking had reached the point where the general pattern of NRA, and specifically Section 7A, began to appear as the most important single move essential to opening the way for a nationwide organizational campaign of industrial unionism. In the fall of 1932 the Finance Committee of the U.S. Senate made a study of the state of the coal mines of the nation, and in that study I was invited to testify before the Senate Committee. Jett Lauck [1] had prepared a careful economic study which ended up with a general outline of the NRA and a flat specific statement which was later incorporated in NRA and called Section 7A. I remember when I was testifying before this Finance Committee in the fall of 1932 that Senator Smoot of Utah, who was chairman of the Finance Committee, walked out while I was reading the lobby report. This report never received much attention but it was

[1] Economist for the United Mine Workers of America.

the birth certificate of Section 7A, popularly known as Labor's Magna Charta." [2]

Finally 1933 rolled around, and there was a new President in the White House. Franklin Delano Roosevelt had pledged a "New Deal" and professed a deep sympathy for labor. Lewis met him and appeared deeply impressed with Roosevelt's personality and statements, for it was Roosevelt who struck new hope in the nation with his unbelievable self-assurance and confidence. He had said, "The only thing we have to fear is fear itself," and the country had heard and raised its head. The times were desperate, and here was a President who was willing to gamble or as he called it "experiment."

With Roosevelt's New Deal came Raymond Moley, first of what was to be a long line of what Americans called "Brain Trusters." He asked Lewis for suggestions for the administration.

Lewis gave what was to be his stock answer for the next year; he urged Government legislation to protect labor's right to organize and bargain collectively. Moley listened and reported to his chief in the White House.

Roosevelt's advisers began to think along the general lines of an NRA. Foremost among those actively interested in this kind of a program were Bernard Baruch and General Hugh Johnson.[3] They, in common with various top leaders in industry, not only laid down the outline of the National Recovery Act, but also filled in the details.

Lewis reminisced to the writer about the formulation of NRA: "In the spring of 1933 I learned of a conference that was to be held at the home of Bernard Baruch in New York City. This meeting would involve a number of top industrialists of the nation, such as the Chairman of the Board of Standard Oil at that time. (I don't remember his name and he has since died.) Also, Bernard Baruch, General Hugh Johnson, and Ed McGrady were to be there. Baruch had sold Roosevelt on the

[2] Lewis's testimony before the Senate Committee was an effort to promote federal legislation giving the workers "the right to organize and bargain collectively through representatives of their own choosing." It would brand any open-shop employer who would interfere with labor organization as a lawbreaker. It would put the law on the side of organized labor. It was the Norris-LaGuardia Act with big teeth.

[3] Later to be appointed head of the NRA.

idea of having this meeting held in his home for the purpose of serving as a general clearing house for all ideas with reference to a proposed Government action. When I heard of this meeting, I insisted upon attending, and through General Hugh Johnson and Ed McGrady I found myself present.

"It was a peculiar situation because it was at this meeting in the home of Bernard Baruch that NRA was conceived and born. I was the only representative of organized labor present. I insisted on the inclusion of what later came to be known as Section 7A into this piece of legislation. I fought for it and got it."

Lewis soon found himself fighting a two-front war. On the one side was the Congress of the United States, fearful and balky about this thing called Section 7A. On the other side were Lewis's own associates and alleged allies, the leaders of the American Federation of Labor.

Lewis recounted in detail to the writer his struggles with the AF of L hierarchy: "About two days after the meeting at Bernard Baruch's apartment, I met Bill Green at the Lincoln Hotel in New York. I propositioned him again about organizing the unorganized. I told him about NRA. I told him what it would mean if organized labor got that kind of a mandate, that it was a franchise to nationwide organizing campaigns. I told him that this franchise was absolutely meaningless unless certain powers implicit in Section 7A of NRA were broadly interpreted by the leaders of labor and boldly and audaciously used as the weapon for a great organizational attack, and that if this were done, Section 7A might very well be the Magna Charta of the working men and women of this nation. But Bill Green was terribly flustered; as a matter of fact, he was just plain scared.

"Around March or April of that year we met again. Bill Green and I were involved in some controversial issues at that time, and Bill was concerned about being seen publicly with me. Furthermore, I was then involved in engineering some political moves. No one knew just what they were about, but there was talk. Bill felt that being seen with me would involve him in the whisperings and speculations as to what I was up to and cause some reactions in the old-line AF of L unions.

"He met me at 11 o'clock that night outside the St. Regis

Hotel in New York. [Here Lewis grinned.] I can still see him walking up and down outside the hotel with his coat collar pulled up and his hat pulled down. We started to walk down 55th Street toward Park Avenue; but Bill mumbled something about the bright street lights, as well as there being frequent passers-by. So we went up 55th Street, past Madison Avenue, until we came to an areaway which was in a dark shadow. There I talked to Bill for two hours. I told him all about NRA, how it had been engineered, and what Section 7A meant. I explained the full potentialities of it to organized labor. Then I asked him to throw the AF of L into a tremendous organizing drive and organize steel, autos, shipbuilding, rubber—everything. Bill argued against it. He said it would cost money, plenty of it. I said, 'Sure, but it would be worth it.' It wasn't a case of really being 'worth it'; it was a case of it had to, it must be done. I said that I would start the ball rolling with a half million dollars. Bill kept hesitating. He talked a bit about how thirty AF of L craft unions hadn't been able to organize in the basic mass-production industries. I told him that such an experience was simply an argument for industrial unionism as against trade unionism. I emphasized as hard as I could that we must launch industrial organizations into these mass industries. Green hesitated and kept saying, 'Now John, let's take it easy.'

"It was that night in that dark alley that I knew, and knew it irrevocably, that industrial unionization of steel, autos, and the basic industries would never come out of the AF of L. Section 7A or a thousand sections would never inspire the AF of L or Bill Green to this inevitable task. It was then and there that I knew it was up to me. The die of the CIO was cast in those early morning hours in that dark areaway on 55th Street. I went to bed, and the next day I began to plan the CIO."

Lewis continued, "The idea of industrial organization and, specifically, the organization of the vast masses of unskilled workers in this country had been very strong in my mind from as far back as I would say the late 1920's. Around 1930 I had not only sounded out various AF of L leaders, but had also discussed generally the proposition of the AF of L's launching an organization drive amongst the unskilled workers. I ran up against a complete blank wall of fear and ignorance. Most exasperating were the limited mentalities of so many of our so-called leaders of labor, who could not begin to grasp the scope of the nationwide organization drive nor understand its implications. They could not recognize the simple premise that the very welfare of their own unions was completely dependent upon and contingent upon the welfare of the other workers in this country. Over all this lay the shadow of the curse of the labor movement, cowardice, avarice, and those private petty fears and insecurities of individual trade-union leaders who were zealously guarding and jealously fearful of their own little stakes in the empire of labor. They wanted then, as now, to repose in comfort and peace. Unfortunately, too, many leaders of many union groups are more interested in their own personal wages and peace, comfort, and order than in the constant struggle to increase the living standards and wages of their own people. One hears the use of the word appeasement; but for real, unadulterated, criminal appeasement it is difficult to surpass the point of view and the position of some of our so-called labor leaders.

"Repeatedly during this period, we were not only trying to educate the Congress and to get this legislation through, but I found myself in the peculiar situation of having to educate our trade-union leaders and to point out to them the enormous significance of the passage of Section 7A. At that time the leaders of labor were in a panic. The thirty craft unions of the American Federation of Labor were gasping for breath to stay alive. The International Ladies Garment Workers Union was on its knees, both in terms of membership and in terms of finances. We gave them a lot of money. By we, I mean Sidney Hillman, who agreed with me on Section 7A and pledged to me his support. Hillman and I called on David Dubinsky and showed him what the NRA would do for his union. We examined all of his union problems and not only advised him on how to meet issues but gave him financial aid. Dave was in a state of real panic. As a matter of fact he and the union were in a blue funk. I remember once after a meeting with him that Sidney Hillman commented to me that Dave was scared stiff. But it should be remembered to Dave's credit that then he did not have too much experience in running his union. We guided him through many a devious channel. Yes, we did a lot for David Dubinsky. However, we were able to make him see the meaning of NRA, and now we had another potential ally.

"As part of the procedure to insure Sidney's support and alliance with us as well as to use his weight in the American Federation of Labor, I also forced the AF of L to admit Hillman into the Federation at that time. Hillman made more concessions to the AF of L than I wanted him to; but, at any rate, Sidney got in and assumed a good solid position on the issue of industrial unionism; and now I felt I had Charlie Howard, Sidney Hillman, and David Dubinsky ready to support CIO."

Section 7A became Lewis's Holy Grail, and he was determined that his quest would be successful. He fought to rally the support of organized labor behind the Section, while simultaneously waging war on his second front, the Congress and the President of the United States. NRA and Section 7A did not find a receptive administration. The Congress, hostile to the bill, repeatedly tried to destroy the Act through time-consuming revisions. Congressional enemies of NRA also assumed that this process would wear down the patience of its protagonists, particularly John L. Lewis. But they did not know Lewis. It was estimated that there were approximately forty revisions, in many of them Section 7A being either eliminated or emasculated. Each time, Lewis fought back. His patience and determination were endless, for on this he had staked everything.

The storm that accompanied the drawn-out battle for the passage of Section 7A is evident in Lewis's statement to the writer: "I can't tell you how hard I fought for the enactment of Section 7A. I watched the progress almost minute by minute on this one point, but it was an all-important point, one which was to fertilize the egg of the CIO. Senator Bob Wagner was appointed by President Roosevelt to shepherd this piece of legislation through the Congress. Roosevelt was not too friendly to Section 7A; and, if there was any time when I began to question and wonder and have reservations about the President, it was at that time. You see, I never trusted Roosevelt fully. Never. Not even through '33, '34, '35, or the second term, or any time. In my mind there never was a real break with Roosevelt because there never had been a real alliance. An alliance involves a certain mutual confidence and trust, and I had my suspicions about that man. This great friend of organized labor repeatedly fought in a most underhanded way against the inclusion of Section 7A in

NRA and forced us to utilize all kinds of tactics, many of which I have a great deal of distaste for. Flattery was used on the President to an unprecedented degree, trying to assuage his feelings of hostility toward this one section. He was told that he was the great friend of the working man, that American laborers were looking up to him as their Messiah, that while everyone knew it would take great courage, compassion, and humanitarianism to stand by this one section, Section 7A, they also knew Franklin D. Roosevelt was the epitome of courage, compassion, and humanitarianism. That kind of stuff was used not just daily, but hourly. Some of his subordinates, who were completely sympathetic with our views, would repeatedly say to him, 'Now Mr. President, of course we stand on this position because we know that that is where you stand, because that is where justice lies; and we, of course, know your feelings on that subject.' "

'There are many dark stories told of the means that had to be employed on behalf of Section 7A. The tactics went so far as having letters Roosevelt never saw but bearing his signature sent to congressmen. These letters were formulated by White House attachés who were in sympathy with Lewis and were working for his purposes. A number of labor supporters used these letters for lobbying in favor of Section 7A.

By dint of open clamoring, pressure politics, lobbying, both subtle and blatantly threatening, plus devious secret intrigues, the NRA containing Lewis's secret weapon of Section 7A finally became law on June 16, 1933.

Lewis now demonstrated what he meant by a "broad interpretation" of the law. He hired union organizers by the dozens and threw the entire treasury of the United Mine Workers Union into a desperate organizing campaign. Into every coal field swarmed these organizers shouting, "The President wants you to join the union." In every part of the country the miners responded, and thousands upon thousands streamed back into the union they had previously abandoned with disgust. In two years the membership of the United Mine Workers rose from a low ebb of a little over one hundred thousand to a tidal wave of more than four hundred thousand.

On September 21, 1933, Lewis scored a major triumph when he and the coal operators signed the first Appalachian agree-

ment. To the union it was a charter for a new life. Both the
Northern and Southern coal operators signed the contract with
the rejuvenated mine workers union. It meant that even the
die-hard Southern operators recognized and bargained with the
union. The agreement and the NRA code were both long steps
toward the stabilization of the industry so necessary for the
well-being of the union.

Lewis now had his own army and a treasury that was mush-
rooming from the dues of his skyrocketing membership. He
had a solid base from which he could operate with impunity.
Those four hundred thousand and more miners belonging to
the union belonged to his union, for he had exterminated
every vestige or shred of opposition in the previous decade.
Now he was prepared to do battle for his great plan to organize
the unorganized.

Lewis watched the unrest and flareups of violence through
the summer of 1934. He saw the Dunne Brothers in Minneapolis lead a general strike of truck drivers into a virtual civil
war. Blood ran in Minneapolis.

In San Francisco a general strike spearheaded by Harry
Bridges' Longshoremen's Union paralyzed the great Western
city for four days.

Before that year was out, seven hundred thousand workers
had struck. Lewis could read the revolutionary handwriting on
the walls of American industry. He knew that the workers were
seething and aching to be organized so they could strike back.
Everyone wanted to hit out, employer against worker and
worker against employer and anyone else whom they felt was
not in their class. America was becoming more class conscious
than at any time in its history. These were times of hate and
anger.

Lewis watched the inept actions of the AF of L. As multitudes
of workers spontaneously were organized in the mass industries,
they turned for aid to the AF of L. The AF of L's answer came
in the form of vacillation, equivocation, and the strangling of
many of these unions with red tape. He saw the cold water of
craft unionism douse all the burning fires that had flamed up
inside of hundreds of thousands of angry workers.

The bitter experience of Akron Ohio's rubber workers was
typical of the incredible blunderings of the AF of L. In Akron

nearly five thousand rubber workers had organized themselves into one industrial union. Nearly all of them were unskilled and working in various divisions of one big rubber plant.

In response to their request for affiliation and a charter, the AF of L dispatched an old-time craft-union organizer by the name of Coleman Claherty. He was in many respects the type of organizer commonly described as a business agent. Claherty divided and subdivided this Rubber Workers Union into nineteen different local unions ranging from plumbers to blacksmiths and from sign painters to pipe fitters. Actually Claherty divided and divided until there was no Rubber Workers Union left. He left Akron fervently hated by the rubber workers.

Lewis knew that the time to attack was close at hand. That fall, at the AF of L convention, he stormed into the resolutions committee meeting demanding that Akron rubber workers be granted their industrial-union charter. He asked for the same in behalf of the workers in autos, radios, electrical appliances, and others. Lewis could not budge the AF of L. Various gestures were made toward industrial unionism by the Federation, but that was all.

The stage was now set for the climactic convention of the AF of L in 1935.

Fifty-five-year-old John Lewis was ready to fight to the death, if necessary, the fifty-five-year-old AF of L. Almost with the pounding of the opening gavel, the convention was forced to face the issue squarely and choose between industrial unionism as the weapon for a vast organizational drive or a craft-union "status quo." Charles P. Howard, head of the Typographical Union, presented a minority resolution reading:

> . . . In the great mass production industries and those in which the workers are composite mechanics, specialized and engaged upon classes of work which do not fully qualify them for craft union membership, industrial organization is the only solution. Continuous employment, economic security and the ability to protect the individual worker depends upon organization upon industrial lines.
>
> In those industries where the work performed by a majority of the workers is of such nature that it might fall within the jurisdictional claim of more than one craft union, it is declared

that industrial organization is the only form that will be acceptable to the workers or adequately meet their needs. . . .

Matthew Woll, one of the arch-conservative, trade-union officials at the AF of L, bitterly attacked the minority resolution. He assailed Lewis as the master mind behind the resolution and charged him with reneging on his conciliatory position at the convention of the year before. Lewis hotly replied:

". . . At San Francisco they seduced me with fair words. Now, of course, having learned that I was seduced, I am enraged and I am ready to rend my seducers limb from limb . . ."

Then Lewis launched into a detailed, impassioned plea for industrial unionism:

". . . We laid claim to a membership of approximately three and a half million, out of an organizable number of approximately thirty-nine million. There is the answer. . . .

". . . On that basis I submit it to be a reasonable statement that it will be a long time before the American Federation of Labor organizes those 25,000,000 workers that we are all so anxious to organize. There are others among us who believe that the record indicates a need for a change in policy. This convention floor is teeming with delegates from those industries where those local unions have been established and where they are now dying like the grass withering before the autumn sun, who are ready to tell this convention of the need for that change in policy. . . .

". . . There has been a change in industry, a constant daily change in its processes, a constant change in its employment conditions, a great concentration of opposition to the extension and the logical expansion of the trade-union movement. Great combinations of capital have assembled great industrial plants, and they are strung across the borders of our several states from the north to the south and from the west in such a manner that they have assembled to themselves tremendous power and influence, and they are almost 100 per cent effective in opposing organization of the workers under the policies of the American Federation of Labor. . . .

". . . If you go in there with your craft union they will mow you down like the Italian machine guns will mow down the Ethiopians in the war now going on in that country; they will mow you down and laugh while they are doing it and ridicule your lack of business acumen, ridicule your lack of ordinary business sagacity in running your own affairs, because of the caviling in your own councils and the feebleness of your methods. . . ."

Lewis then closed his denunciation of craft unionism with a burst of oratory including statements which today are still remembered and repeated:

". . . The labor movement is organized upon a principle that the strong shall help the weak. That principle of the organizations of America is American, that the strong shall help the weak. . . .

". . . Isn't it right that we should contribute something of our own strength, our own virtues, our own knowledge, our own influence toward those less fortunately situated, in the knowledge that if we help them and they grow strong, in turn that we will be the beneficiary of their changed status and their strength? The strength of a strong man is a prideful thing, but the unfortunate thing in life is that strong men do not remain strong. And that is just as true of unions and labor organizations as it is true of men and individuals.

"And, whereas today the craft unions of this country may be able to stand upon their own feet and like mighty oaks stand before the gale, defy the lightning, yet the day may come when this changed scheme of things—and things are changing rapidly now—the day may come when those organizations will not be able to withstand the lightning and the gale. Now, prepare yourselves by making a contribution to your less fortunate brethren, heed this cry from Macedonia that comes from the hearts of men. Organize the unorganized. . . ."

Lewis finished, and the convention voted on the minority resolution. Hutcheson, Woll, Frey, and other leaders of craft unionism gloated as the delegates turned down industrial unionism 18,024 to 10,993.

The blow came on Saturday morning, October 19. Delegate Thompson of the then tiny union of rubber workers was pleading for an industrial charter as the only basis on which the rubber workers could be successfully organized. Suddenly William Hutcheson, huge, red-nosed boss of the Carpenters Union, reared up, bellowing "Point of order!" Thompson hesitated, confused and uncertain as Hutcheson demanded that all discussion of industrial unionism be declared out of order. Lewis leaped to the floor in Thompson's defense, and the attention of the convention was instantly riveted on both Lewis and Hutcheson. As in all previous conventions, the carpenters' delegates were seated adjacent to the miners' delegates. Both unions were among the largest in the Federation; and repeatedly in years past, whenever a controversy developed, Lewis would either walk across the aisle to confer with Hutcheson or vice versa. The convention would usually watch these "conferences" in silence, knowing that a deal was being made to settle the issue. Now again, the spotlight was on them. Lewis glared at Hutcheson as he ended his remarks with, "This thing of raising points of order all the time on minor delegates is rather small potatoes."

Hutcheson hoisted his nearly three hundred pounds and stretched himself to his full height roaring, "I was raised on small potatoes. That is why I am so small."

Lewis walked up the aisle and approached Hutcheson. As usual, the convention became quiet. Lewis in a low voice said something to Hutcheson that caused the leader of the Carpenters Union to reply profanely. First the word "bastard" was heard, then the crack of Lewis's fist on Hutcheson's face. A few more blows were exchanged and Hutcheson and Lewis grappled and went down amidst collapsing chairs and tables.

For a moment bedlam broke loose in the convention, with the news reporters frantically wiring what everyone knew would be the top news story of that day. The strained peace within the AF of L had collapsed with the crash of the chairs and table under Hutcheson and Lewis as they went down.[4]

There is evidence that more than suggests that Lewis's physical attack on Hutcheson was premeditated and deliberate. First, there is the fact that any study of Lewis's own personality and behavior shows that he has with rare exception taken any action except in accordance with a carefully preconceived and thought-out plan. Second, he knew that Hutcheson symbolized to

[4] A vivid example of the treachery of source material for historical research is to be found in the Official Proceedings of this 1935 AF of L convention which carries no mention or suggestion of this fight which every paper in the country featured.

millions of frustrated workers that craft-unionism policy that had defeated their spontaneous organizations of the early 1930's. All of the passion and wild hopes of these mass-industry workers had been dissipated by those craft-union labor leaders of whom Hutcheson was an outstanding representative. They had expected hostility and attack from their employers but not from their alleged friends, these so-called labor leaders. They had tasted what they felt was treason, and they were bitter. They hated Hutcheson and his group more intensely than they hated their employers. They ached to strike back at Hutcheson and everything he stood for.

Lewis knew that with one punch at Hutcheson he would be doing what thousands of workers wanted to do. By attacking Hutcheson, he was attacking the trade unionism these workers so bitterly hated. He knew that with one blow on Hutcheson's face he would rupture the uneasy peace within the Federation, creating the revolt necessary for secession.

Lewis reviewed the 1935 convention with the writer, saying, "Things were beginning to move, slowly but smoothly. Each move tied into the next one. In the 1933 AF of L convention I had the full support of Charlie Howard of the Typographical Union on a proposition involving organization of the mass industries. I had Howard and others trying to get affirmative action on organizing the unorganized. We fought for it, but again it was running into a stone wall. There did not seem to be a glimmer of understanding, enthusiasm, and really any kind of hope, of great hope for the working people in this country. None of this was present, nothing but a glum, smug apathy.

"By 1935 the workers were in a state of ferment. They had arisen, after the passage of NRA and particularly Section 7A. To them, this was a proclamation of freedom; and, as the workers responded and demanded organization by the AF of L, the AF of L, squirming with fear, shrank from the responsibilities which the workers of the nation were literally thrusting into its hands. Instead of leadership, the AF of L gave them a number of chicken-livered business agents who knew nothing except collecting dues, issuing some charters, and keeping peace and harmony. Their business agents feared any kind of an upsurge as being something 'radical,' or, of course, dangerous. The character and convictions of these business agents were such that they could check out of their union offices on Saturday and begin working for the National Association of Manufacturers on the following Monday.

"The workers were seduced; they were sold down the river; they were betrayed; and only a burning passion on the part of vast masses of the unorganized kept them from being completely filled with disgust and cynicism and running up the white flag and turning their backs on the organized-labor movement. Some of them did give up; some of them were so embittered by their experience with the AF of L business agents that they swore they never wanted to see another union man again. There are parts of the steel industry which never accepted the CIO and it will take at least a new generation to wipe out the foul taste of treason which the AF of L left among steel workers in 1933.

"By 1935 the workers, embittered, frustrated, and filled with a certain degree of hopelessness, began to hate the conservative, short-sighted, ignorant labor leadership of the American Federation of Labor almost as much as they hated their own employers who were exploiting them. They were caught between two interests, both selfish and short-sighted and both grinding their hopes and their dreams into dirty dust. Bill Hutcheson represented symbolically the kind of leadership in the American Federation of Labor that the workers of this country detested. It was Bill Hutcheson's supporters and associates in the AF of L who successfully blocked every single move that was made in the direction of industrial unionism. All I will say is that I never walked across an aisle so slowly and grimly as I did that day in the 1935 convention. An act of some kind, an act dramatic to the degree that it would inspire and enthuse the workers of this country was necessary. Did I say necessary? It was essential. With this in mind, I laid my plans. The 1935 convention of the American Federation of Labor was to be the scene and Bill Hutcheson, unknowingly, was to be one of the main actors of the cast. The reason for this selection and this plan was to be found in the background of Hutcheson and myself in the previous AF of L conventions."

There is a great deal of evidence that Lewis had already decided to bolt the AF of L and was operating according to plan.

An example is to be found in the statement made to the writer by Powers Hapgood: "I remember how I buried the hatchet and went to work for John L. Lewis. It was during the 1935 AF of L convention in Atlantic City. I had been reading what Lewis had been talking about at the convention. I watched him, and then I knew that I was his man. With Lewis as our leader I knew we were on our way. I was in the gallery, and I sent down word to him that I wanted to see him. Later, one of his lieutenants came back and said to me, 'Mr. Lewis will see you later this afternoon.' I remember this was one day or possibly two before he slugged Hutcheson. I then went downstairs and got an aisle seat in the rear of the auditorium. Later that afternoon Lewis came up the aisle; and, as he passed me said, 'Out in the lobby.' I walked out into the lobby of the building. He motioned me to a chair and said, 'Well, Powers, what's on your mind?' I said, 'Well, Mr. Lewis, there are two things on my mind. I think I'll take up the least important one first. You know I've been doing a lot of lecturing around the country on unionization and other issues; and, while I was down in Knoxville, the Knoxville paper came out with a very scurrilous and libelous attack on me. One of the things that they cited was the fact that the Mine Workers District Director down there had said that I had either planned or had flown around in an airplane over the West Virginia coal fields dropping bombs. I brought suit against the paper for libel. I understand they are going to try to get your District Director to appear in court and testify in this suit against me.' Lewis said, 'Well, just a moment.' He called his secretary over and said, 'Take a note to District Director Turnblazer. He is not to testify in court against Powers Hapgood. He is to stay out of that case completely.' The secretary then left, and Lewis turned to me and said, 'Now, Powers, what is the second thing on your mind?' I said, 'I want to come to work for you. I want to help you do what you're talking about. I want to get back in the United Mine Workers. How do I go about it?' Lewis looked at me and said, 'Well, I'll tell you, Powers, there are two ways you can get back into the United Mine Workers Union. One is to get back into the coal pits and start digging coal. Now, I think you have a couple of children, more responsibilities, and you're older. I don't think that would be such a good way. The second course would be to accept a position working for the United Mine Workers of America, and I want you to come with us. We're about to go off into a campaign that I do not feel at liberty to discuss here, but let me just tell you, Powers, that it will be everything you've dreamed about and everything you've talked about. We're going out to fight for those things, and we're going to get them. You see, Powers, I've never really opposed those things. I just never felt that the time was ripe and that trying to do those things back in the days when we had our violent arguments would have been suicide for organized labor and would have resulted in complete failure. But now, the time is ripe; and now the time to do those things is here. Let us do them.' Lewis stopped talking and I can't tell you how I felt. It was just as though everything I had dreamed of had finally come to pass. In the next couple of weeks I got my first assignment. That's how I got back working for John Lewis."

Lewis's attack on Hutcheson served its purpose. From a Kansas City union carpenter came a telegram to Lewis, "Congratulations. Sock him again," which echoed the sentiments of the workers in autos, steel, rubber, glass, and all the basic industries of America. Within a day it was clear that the crack of Lewis's fist on Hutcheson's jaw had reverberated through the unorganized factories of America, just as the first shot at Lexington had through the colonies. The revolution was on!

At 11 o'clock Saturday night, October 19, the annual convention of the American Federation of Labor was adjourned. At approximately 11 o'clock the next morning John L. Lewis sat at the head of the table in a dining room of the President Hotel buried deep in discussion with eight companions. They were out to adjourn the American Federation of Labor, permanently, if possible.

It was a late Sunday breakfast; and seated around the table were Lewis's two henchmen, Philip Murray and Thomas Kennedy; Lewis's old-time enemy in the United Mine Workers, John Brophy, who was now back at his side, just as Powers Hapgood had come back to the Lewis camp; Charles P. Howard, head of the Typographical Union; David Dubinsky, president of the International Ladies Garment Workers Union; Max Zaritsky, chief of the Hat, Cap and Millinery Workers; Thomas McMahon, the leading official of the Textile Workers;

and Sidney Hillman, president of the Amalgamated Clothing Workers of America.

Lewis did most of the talking. His voice was low, and he spoke with passion. He outlined the conditions in all of the major industries of the country. He emphasized that thousands upon thousands of workers were waiting with outstretched arms for unionization to come to them. Lewis then said, "And it can only come from you and you and you," as he dramatically punctuated his statement by stabbing his finger at each man seated around the table. He painted the breathtaking potentialities of a great labor movement embracing almost every working man in the country. He finished with vivid words suggesting this as the fulfillment of dreams that all labor leaders had but dared not admit to themselves.

As Lewis spoke, most of the food on the table went untouched and grew cold; but the men around that table were on fire. They too had caught the vision, and it became their gospel.

Lewis was ready to lead them into the future—the unknown. It meant breaking with the past—the known past. Even with all its faults, the past contained the security of familiarity. They, at least, knew what it was. The future was uncertain, and the future that Lewis painted was one that was lit by lightning and torn with upheaval. It was a future in the skies. If ever anyone had his eyes lifted to the stars, it was Lewis in his discussion of that morning. His words dissolved the fears, doubts, and rationalization of his companions. They were ready for the crusade. Less than three weeks later, on November 9, 1935, the same group met in Washington. Now they were joined by Harvey Fremming of the Oil Field, Gas Well and Refinery Workers of America Union; as well as Thomas Brown, chief of the Mine, Mill and Smelter Workers Union. At this meeting they set up a formal structure, calling it the Committee for Industrial Organization, or CIO. They announced that this Committee would function within the AF of L as a special self-appointed committee with the purpose "to encourage and promote organization of the workers in the mass production and unorganized industries." The Committee also announced that it would be primarily "educational and advisory." John L. Lewis was elected chairman of the Committee with Charles P. Howard as secretary and John Brophy as executive director.

Almost immediately, President Green of the American Federation of Labor notified each member of the Committee of his "deep fears" that there was a possibility that this was going to result in a dual union that would end by opposing the American Federation of Labor. He pointed out that the majority rule at the convention of the AF of L settled the issue of industrial unionism and that he expected those who were subscribing to the Committee for Industrial Organization to accept the majority decision. Howard, as the Committee's secretary, politely replied to President Green claiming that there should be no objection to a minority group's attempt to educate and work among the rank and file of the workers in order to "convert those whose interests are most effective."

These polite paper skirmishes ended on November 23, when Lewis resigned his post as vice-president of the American Federation of Labor. In January, 1936, the members of the AF of L's executive council meeting in Miami were stunned to find this issue of industrial unionism that they believed had been settled and buried at the convention just three months before was now being waved in their faces by this Committee called CIO. It was asking for the immediate granting of industrial-union charters to a number of unions such as the rubber workers and the auto workers. Furthermore, this CIO insisted that an organizing campaign be started at once in the steel industry.

The AF of L indignantly rejected these proposals. Lewis met this rejection by announcing that the United Mine Workers would now withhold their per-capita tax of $48,000. William Green ordered all of the unions of the American Federation of Labor to have nothing to do with the CIO. This heretical CIO was to be excommunicated. On August 4, 1936, the CIO unions were ejected from the AF of L by its executive council for refusing to obey the order of the council that they "cease and desist" in their industrial-union activities. They were convicted for the crime of starting a dual union. The CIO headquarters, too engrossed and involved in the gigantic organizing drive, did not give more than passing attention to the AF of L action. They were too busy even to attend the Fifty-sixth Annual Convention of the American Federation of Labor, which took place that November in Tampa, Florida.

The CIO was busy in Toledo, Ohio, in guiding the flat-glass

workers in the development of an all-inclusive union on an industrial basis. They were busy in Philadelphia organizing the radio workers into an industrial union. They had started to develop their foundation for an organizational drive in steel. Working quickly, and before the AF of L even knew what was up, the CIO had absorbed the Amalgamated Association of Steel, Iron and Tin Workers into their camp. Arrangements were made whereby the CIO would retire this whole alleged organization that did not even pack the weight of its own letterhead.

The CIO was ready to roll into an organizing drive in the steel industry. The UMWA was ready to throw half a million dollars into the drive. Philip Murray, trusted aide of Lewis, was made chairman of the CIO steel workers organizing committee. Organizing committees of different industries began to sprout, and Lewis watered them with UMWA funds.

All this time Lewis was issuing cutting comments that the press was featuring with great delight. With reference to the meeting of the executive board of the AF of L in Florida in January, Lewis stated, "I have neither the time nor the inclination to follow the peregrinations of the council from the Jersey beaches in the summer to the golden sands of Florida in the winter." As President Green threatened the CIO with excommunication, Lewis responded, "Alas, poor Green, I knew him well. He wishes me to join him in fluttering procrastination, the while intoning, *O tempora, O mores!*" Or again he said of Green, "I fear his threats as much as I believe his promises."

In 1936 AF of L President William Green entered the lion's den of the biennial convention of his own union, the United Mine Workers of America. Lewis coolly greeted him and then coldly presented him to the 2,000 delegates. For an hour and a half, Green entreated the mining delegates to return to the AF of L and forget this madness of "industrial unionism" and "organizing the unorganized." Green then changed his tactics and tried to cajole the convention. He spoke as a "brother miner," as one who was for organizing the unorganized, but through the AF of L, when it was "ready" to do so.

Throughout Green's speech Lewis sat rigidly in his chair with his face a blank mask. Finally Green, perspiring and flushed with his efforts, ended his plea and turned from the rostrum. Lewis arose, looked over his two thousand delegates, and then asked those who agreed with Green to stand up. One lone delegate arose as 1,999 of his fellows filled the hall with howls of derision. Lewis, his face still impassive, turned, looked at Green, saying, "There is your answer, Mr. Green." Green hurriedly left the convention.

With the UMWA ousted from the AF of L, the miners suspended Green from their union, temporarily creating the embarrassing situation of a nonunion person holding the highest office in the AF of L. Little James Caesar Petrillo of the Musicians Union rode to Green's rescue by giving him a membership card made of solid gold leaf. So Green was and still is a member of the Musicians Union, although there is no evidence that he can play more than a kazoo.

Lewis, who was now taunting Green to distraction, promptly announced, "That is appropriate. Like Nero, Green fiddles, while Rome burns."

It was not long before Green became a major object of ridicule. Between Lewis's well-turned, caustic comments and the reaction of the press, Green was in misery. Many cartoons depicted him as a cherubic, innocent child, confused and horrified by the storm about him.

Lewis found himself engaged in a three-pronged campaign. First, he was building a corps of organizers for his forces of the CIO. Second, he was fighting a holding action on the American Federation of Labor front to prevent their obstruction of his plans. Third, it was a presidential election year, and Franklin Delano Roosevelt figured heavily in Lewis's plans for the future. Lewis gave a half million dollars in cash to Roosevelt's campaign and contributed more in other ways. He campaigned with the President through Pennsylvania. With Roosevelt's victory, Lewis, feeling assured of White House support, turned his undivided attention to the task ahead. Lewis marshaled his legions for battle. They were a motley group of idealists, hardboiled career labor organizers, liberals, fanatics, Communists, and all those who wanted a chance to hit back. They had been tossed and uprooted by the times, and now they were bent on mastering the times.

Lewis looked about him at a nationwide industrial scene exploding with unrest and discontent. Strikes were breaking out in autos, glass, rubber, and, it seemed, almost everywhere.

America was convulsed with the struggle between labor and capital. In the mass industries, the workers had taken the CIO as their economic religion and John Llewellyn Lewis as its prophet. The time was now; and with his organizers giving rebel yells of "Organize the Unorganized" John Lewis gave the order, "Attack!"

Chapter 5

1937, the Year of Attack

OUT of 1936 screaming and sit-downing into 1937 came the CIO. It was the year of attack. This was it. Hundreds of thousands of men mad with anger and frustration leaped to the battle. They would stop at nothing, and nothing would stop them. The fire of their leaders was the passion of youth and their weapon a shining cause. In General Motors, Bob Travis and Walter Reuther were twenty-nine. In the electrical plants James Carey was twenty-five, and elderly thirty-year-old Lee Pressman was in Washington. Everywhere were youth and ideals. Among the milling sweating struggling thousands upon thousands of workers rode these youthful leaders carrying their crusade "Organize! Organize! Organize!" Over it all fell the brooding shadow of its dark angel, John L. Lewis.

Facing this human tempest stood the vast modern industrial empire employing millions of men and women. Times had changed from the days when fifty to a hundred men working under one roof comprised a "factory" or "industrial center." Now with the factory whistle thousands of workers streamed in and out of the massive gates of giant industry. The basic challenge to the men with the new union gospel was how to reach the ears of these thousands of workers milling through and around the many entrances to the vast plants. Even the strongest bellowing voice stepped up with passion and fervor would be as an indistinguishable whisper in the buzz of these swarms of workers.

The answer came from the same science that had built the modern industrial realm. It came blasting forth from a mechanical contraption now known as a sound truck. Through the

86

amplifier the voice of the speaker thundered and screeched for more than a city block. Speeches alternated with martial union music, and the workers could hear. They not only heard but listened. Their answer came in the surging strikes that smashed the open-shop bulwarks of America. The part played by the sound trucks in the great CIO drive has not been publicly realized. Employers were driven to a frenzy by the constant rolling bombardment on their workers emanating from these loud-speakers on wheels. During the sit-down strikes and mass picketing the sound trucks acted as mobile top sergeants in keeping discipline on the one hand and as roving GHQ's on the other. The voice of the loud-speaker would shift from comforting reassurance to a tough tongue lashing to bolster the morale of the workers. Industry struck back pressuring city administrations to pass ordinances "banning" and "forbidding" the sound truck, but it came too late. The workers had heard, and the big parade was on.

Nineteen thirty-seven was the year in which the sit-down strike reached its high-water mark. This revolutionary seizure of the industrial plants by the workers was the CIO's atom bomb against America's vast open-shop, mass-production industrial empire. Yet it was not a carefully planned and conceived weapon. Actually the sit-down strike sprang spontaneously from an angered mass of workers. All American labor leaders would have been shocked, scared, and instinctively opposed to the initiation or approval of this disorderly revolutionary upheaval. In the American trade-union tradition, particularly the AF of L brand, strikes were approved through regular authorized channels and carefully controlled by the proper duly constituted authorities. This described reaction of American labor leaders would include John L. Lewis and his CIO associates. While Lewis would not initiate the undisciplined sit-down, he had the vision and courage not to be scared and not only to ride with it but clearly to express the inarticulate hopes and drives of the strikers and exploit the sit-down strikes' possibilities to victory. Hundreds of thousands of workers were involved in this revolutionary upsurge.

The sit-down strike was the extremely simple tactic whereby workers suddenly, without warning, laid down their tools and refused to work or to leave their jobs in the plant; they sat down on the job. Ruth McKenney gives a stirring description of how a sit-down strike started on January 29, 1936, at the Firestone Tire Plant No. 1 in Akron, Ohio:

The foreman paced slowly past his workmen, his eyes darting in and out of the machines, eager for any betraying gesture. He heard no word, and saw no gesture. The hands flashed, the backs bent, the arms reached out in monotonous perfection. The foreman went back to his little desk and sat squirming on the smooth-seated swivel chair. He felt profoundly disturbed. Something, he knew, was coming off. But what? For God's sake, what?

It was 1:57 A.M. January 29, 1936.

The tirebuilders worked in smooth frenzy, sweat around their necks, under their arms. The belt clattered, the insufferable racket and din and monotonous clash and uproar went on in steady rhythm. The clock on the south wall, a big plain clock, hesitated, its minute hand jumped to two. A tirebuilder at the end of the line looked up, saw the hand jump. The foreman was sitting quietly staring at the lines of men working under the vast pools of light. Outside, in the winter night, the streets were empty, and the whir of the factory sounded faintly on the snow-swept yard.

The tirebuilder at the end of the line gulped. His hands stopped their quick weaving motions. Every man on the line stiffened. All over the vast room, hands hesitated. The foreman saw the falter, felt it instantly. He jumped up, but he stood beside his desk, his eyes darting quickly from one line to another.

This was it, then. But what was happening? Where was it starting? He stood perfectly still, his heart beating furiously, his throat feeling dry, watching the hesitating hands, watching the broken rhythm.

Then the tirebuilder at the end of the line walked three steps to the master safety switch and, drawing a deep breath, he pulled up the heavy wooden handle. With this signal, in perfect synchronization, with the rhythm they had learned in a great mass-production industry, the tirebuilders stepped back from their machines.

Instantly, the noise stopped. The whole room lay in perfect silence. The tirebuilders stood in long lines, touching each other, perfectly motionless, deafened by the silence. A moment ago there had been the weaving hands, the revolving wheels, the clanking belt, the moving hooks, the flashing tire tools. Now there was absolute stillness, no motion, no sound.

Out of the terrifying quiet came the wondering voice of a big tirebuilder near the windows: "Jesus Christ, it's like the end of the world."

He broke the spell, the magic moment of stillness. For now his awed words said the same thing to every man, "We done it! We stopped the belt! By God, we done it!" And men began to cheer hysterically, to shout and howl in the fresh silence. Men wrapped long sinewy arms around their neighbors' shoulders, screaming, "We done it! We done it!" [1]

It is significant that ten days prior to this, the first major sit-down strike in America, the rubber workers were addressed by John L. Lewis. Prior to Lewis's arrival in Akron, the rubber workers were hopelessly disillusioned with organized labor as represented by the AF of L. They had repudiated William Green and his official representatives. They were angry and bitter and felt they had been "sold out." Despite a blizzard on January 19, thousands of rubber workers massed to hear Lewis.

Lewis faced the mountaineer workers of Akron calmly. He had taken the trouble to prepare himself with exact information about the rubber industry and The Goodyear Tire and Rubber Company. He made no vague, general speech, the kind the rubber workers were used to hearing from Green. Lewis named names and quoted figures. His audience was startled and pleased when he called Cliff Slusser by name, described him and finally denounced him. The A. F. of L. leaders who used to come into Akron in the old days were generally doing well if they remembered who Paul Litchfield was.

The Lewis speech was a battle cry, a challenge. . . .

. . . "What," he said in his deep passionate voice, "have Good-year workers gotten out of the growth of the company?" His audience squirmed in its seats, listening with almost painful fervor.

"Partnership!" he sneered. "Well, labor and capital may be partners in theory, but they are enemies in fact. . . ."

. . . Here was a man who said things that made real sense to a guy who worked on a tire machine at Goodyear.

"Organize!" Lewis shouted and his voice echoed from the beams of the armory. "Organize!" he said pounding the speaking pulpit unit it jumped. "Organize! Go to Goodyear and tell

[1] Ruth McKenney, *Industrial Valley* (New York: Harcourt, Brace and Company, 1939), pp. 261-262.

them you want some of those stock dividends. Say, 'So we're supposed to be partners, are we? Well, we're not. We're enemies.' "

He said these words to an increasingly excited audience. He evoked a dream in the minds of men, a dream of security, and a dream of freedom. . . .

. . . But it was not John L. Lewis' gift for oratory that won him overnight top place among Akron rubber workers. His speech and his appearance was remembered in the valleys because he said what the people already knew.[2]

By the physical occupation of the industrial plant in the sit-down strike the workers nullified all accepted strike-breaking procedures. It was impossible for the employers to continue producing by the use of strike-breakers since their machines and plants were in the possession of the strikers.

All the rigors and hazards of the picket line were eliminated as the men were secure from the weather, skirmishes with the police, company-hired sluggers, from scabs breaking through picket lines, and additionally secure in the feeling of numbers; they were prepared to sit it out indefinitely.

The actual capture of the plant and all of its machinery filled the company with fear regarding the welfare of their property. Hasty and forceful action by management might well result in enormous destruction of their machinery and other property. The strikers' sit-down became a gun at the head of the company.

The living and fighting together under a state of seizure heightened a feeling of friendship and almost kinship among the strikers. They were knit into a solid body by their common ordeal. There was also the stimulus of a kind of war psychology or, as a former General Motors sit-down striker told the writer, "It was like we was soldiers holding the fort. It was like war. The guys with me became my buddies. I remember as a kid in school readin' about Davey Crockett and the last stand at the Alamo. You know, mister, that's just how I felt. Yes sir, Chevy No. 4 was my Alamo."

The origin of the sit-down technique and pattern is, like all origins of human behavior and tradition, uncertain. Actual sit-down strikes are known to have occurred in the United States as far back as 1892, when the steel workers seized the Home-

[2] *Ibid.*, pp. 249-251.

stead plants. In 1896 a large number of New York laundresses sat down and refused to work to show their support of the garment workers' strike. In Telluride, Colorado, the workers seized and occupied the mines. Sit-down strikes were common with the rebellious fighting Wobblies. In Schenectady, New York, the General Electric Company underwent a sit-down experience in 1901. Work stoppages, which were brief periods when workers suddenly stood idly at their posts, began to come with greater frequency. These stoppages were in reality quick and short sit-down strikes and became known as "quickies."

In 1933 the meat packinghouse workers employed in the Jay Hormel plants at Austin, Minnesota, sat down in strike. Two years later the Goodyear Rubber workers of Akron, Ohio, followed suit. But it was in the waning days of 1936 and into 1937 that the sit-down made every American and all of the nation's industry stand up and take notice. It was the sit-down assault and triumph over the vast, powerful General Motors Corporation which caused the nation's newspaper-headline writers practically to leave the words "sit-down" in day after day as part of the banner headline.

John L. Lewis was questioned by the writer on the origin of the sit-down strike. He answered: "No one knows when the sit-down strike began. I have inquired into the subject and the earliest recorded sit-down strike that I know about occurred in the time of King Cheops, who was famous as the builder of the largest of the pyramids in Egypt around 3700 B.C. He did this by the forced labor of the people, who at one point rebelled and sat down refusing to continue building until they got rest." It was a long jump from 3700 B.C. to America's great sit-down spree of late 1936 and the first half of 1937.

December, 1936, and January, 1937, were months of rebellion, violent unrest, and reprisals by workers in many occupations. Everywhere everyone was quitting in protest. Even Edward VIII, King of England, quit his throne during this critical month. Let us take a quick glance over the events of what was to be industry's dark December.

In New York City, WPA artists battled the police, who forcibly smashed a "stay-in strike"; striking AF of L glazers hurled stove bolts through plate-glass windows in every borough. Most of the city's three hundred fifty hotels were either struck or threatened with strike action. The subway workers of the B.M.T. seized the power plant, WPA workers in Central Park and maids in Long Island went on strike, and two thousand shirt makers in Manhattan stopped making shirts. The seamen's union went on strike; and in adjoining Jersey City, the police met them with tear gas, machine guns, and sections of rubber hose.

An hour and twenty minutes away on the Pennsylvania Railroad, Philadelphia, City of Brotherly Love, was having its own acute indigestion. Electric-storage-battery workers, hosiery workers, dressmakers, all sat down. In nearby Chester, Pennsylvania, more than a hundred persons were seriously injured in violence flaring up out of the strike-bound Sun Shipbuilding Yards. Even the Philadelphia prisons were not immune, as convicts staged a sit-down strike in the penitentiary work shop, while miles south the Alabama prison guards organized into a union and prepared to strike.

In Chicago, a sudden sit-down strike of the electrical workers caught city officials with their britches down and the city with its bridges up. The bridges stayed up; and all street lights, including traffic lights, were off during the strike's duration. The Fansteel Company, in a once quiet Chicago suburb, was the scene of a sit-down strike about which the United States Supreme Court would one day comment.

People did more walking as the bus drivers of Flint, Michigan, and the taxi drivers of Baltimore, Maryland, walked off their jobs.

In Akron, Ohio, Goodyear rubber workers, stenographers, bookkeepers, and typists, and Firestone tire workers sat down. The Kelly Springfield Tire Plant in Cumberland, Maryland, copied Akron's new look as did the rubber workers in Eau Claire, Wisconsin.

Paper, shoe, and textile strikes swept the state of Maine. The ticker tape of strikes began to sound like a nightmarish stock-market quotation of everything being "down"; "down," "sit-down," "down," everything from the Detroit plant of the Aluminum Company of America to Pittsburgh Plate Glass, to Illinois Glass, to the entire automobile industry. Steel was being struck in the opening skirmishes of what was predicted to be a titanic struggle.

The cities and villages of America were carbon copies of all this. While Carson City, Nevada, silver miners beat off a back-to-work movement with their heavy boots, the silversmiths of Greenfield, Massachusetts, went on a sit-down strike.

A national coal strike cast its shadow over all this and added to the ferment and hysteria. Everyone began to strike. Eighty-eight women on a sewing project in Pleasantville, New Jersey, seized the City Hall. In this same state Democratic state senators voted a "stay-away strike" from the meeting of the legislature so as to block their Republican opponents. Now that it had reached this level high-school students went on sit-down strikes or just plain strikes. In a New York private high school the strike was for postponement of a German examination; in Cleveland students struck to protest class rings which they said turned out to be a "lot of junk"; in lower Penn's Neck Township, New Jersey, students struck in protest over the dismissal of a police officer.

Newspapers were being struck by printers or reporters from Beaumont, Texas, to Flushing, New York.

College students picketed and protested the high cost of food from Chicago's Central YMCA College to Florida campuses.

The strike fever not only boiled over the top of the nation's thermometer, but it got so hot that it burned through asbestos. The asbestos workers of the Johns Manville factory struck and chased the plant superintendent out of town.

The press and the courts denounced the sit-down strikers for illegal seizure, confiscation of private property, and general insurrection. In their own defense the sit-down strikers advanced the theory that they possessed "a property interest" in their jobs. They pointed out that in the early days the craftsmen and artisans owned their own tools but that now the assembly line and other features of the machine age had eliminated the tool-owning craftsman and that the workers' right of ownership had passed from their tools to the machines they now operated.

John L. Lewis cut through the cumbersome and somewhat tenuous logic of this defense by thundering, *"Americans have a right to work and a right to a job."* Lewis's clear expression and articulation of the sentiments and needs of the workers was one of the striking qualities of his leadership.

The year was the most turbulent of the terrible thirties. The unprecedented wave of 1,860,000 men on sit-down strikes virtually inundated American industry. Through 1936 and 1937 approximately seven thousand strikes brought chaos into the national economy. The following chart on strike profiles from 1927 to 1944 depicts the relationship of 1937 to those other years.

The nation's basic industries broke before the impact of the CIO. Bouncing off rubber, the CIO crashed through glass, tore through textiles, slugged it out with autos, and then cracked steel. In addition to setting up permanent labor unions in hitherto rugged open-shop territory, the CIO scored heavy economic gains for its workers. Spielmans points out that one half of the workers secured substantial gains, one third of them partial gains, and the small remaining fraction little or no gains. But the biggest stake the American workers fought for was won. Far above the pressing demand for higher wages, shorter hours, and better working conditions was the profound urge of human beings to rise out of the abyss of anonymity where they were a cog on an assembly line or a number on a time card. It was the fundamental need of being recognized as a person, as an individual with the dignity and meaning inherent in that term. To hundreds of thousands of these men the "recognition of the union" meant *recognition of themselves, as people. Fortune* magazine in a nationwide survey of the labor scene reported in its February, 1940, issue, "In 1937, when the number of strikes reached its peak, less than a quarter of the workers involved were striking over wages and hours; nearly 60 percent were striking for union recognition. This issue was paramount in the strikes of 1934 and 1936."

By mid-1937 the CIO had gathered 3,083,000 members in its 23 affiliates and was still highballing down the track.

In the wake of the attack lay the victims. Hundreds upon hundreds of strikers gassed, shot, and maimed. They died in San Francisco, Detroit, Youngstown, Chicago, and all over the United States.

The CIO attack rolled on gathering momentum and strength until it broke with full fury upon that great cornerstone of American industry, the General Motors Corporation. Here both industry and the CIO unleashed everything they had. This was certain to be the Armageddon for both. It was here in the

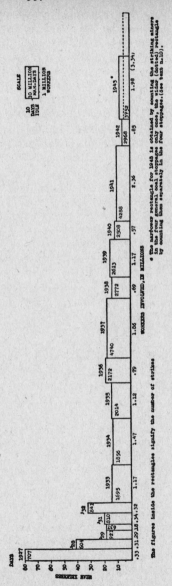

TOTAL STRIKE PROFILES, UNITED STATES, 1927-43 [3]

The figures inside the rectangles signify the number of strikes

[3] John V. Spielmans, *The Journal of Political Economy* (Chicago: The University of Chicago Press, 1944), December, 1944, p. 323.

titanic struggle between General Motors and the CIO that labor stormed the highest bastion of industry. It was in this strike that John L. Lewis became heralded as the unchallenged leader and champion of the workingmen. It was in this strike that Lewis broke the back of the open shop in the mass-production industries. It was also in this strike that Lewis began to break with Roosevelt.

The climax of 1937 came early in the year in the grim, no-quarter struggle of the automobile workers led by John L. Lewis against the General Motors Corporation. In the sit-down strike of General Motors all the forces in the American scene came into play.

Chapter 6

They Sit to Conquer

THE Goliath of American business enterprise, the automobile industry, was alert and waiting. Its vast corporations and multitudes of dependent industries flexed their muscles to brush off the puny, impudent CIO. They would flick off the CIO as they would an annoying insect, for this was the mammoth juggernaut that had always knocked out even the thought of attempting to organize the men who made autos.

But the CIO did not fight as it was expected to; it did not lead with its chin or its cheek. The CIO turned around and attacked with its buttocks! It sat down; and under it sprawled in impotent, choleric rage the fabulous financial and hitherto invincible motor empire.

The saga of the CIO's victory over the automotive industry is a tale of the irony of fate. It is a satire worthy of the gods that thousands of wearied men, angry and bitter with standing for hours beside an inhuman, constantly speeded-up assembly line, should achieve their triumph by the simple act of sitting down.

This is the story of D Day for the CIO. This is the tale of how that giant of General Motors was felled so that it became inevitable that the CIO banners would soon be flying over the automotive empire of America.

The automobile had become the symbol of American genius and the world's highest standard of living. The proud American creed no longer boasted only of a chicken in every pot, but also of a car in every garage. America was on wheels, and this revolution in transportation resulted in a transformation of every aspect of the American way of life.

To satisfy the public's hunger for cars, enormous factories

were constructed around one of the greatest industrial inventions of the era—the assembly line. In the course of the movement of the assembly line more than fifteen thousand separate parts were brought together to assemble the modern automobile. The Ford Motor Company was producing sixty assembled autos an hour. In 1936 the automotive industry produced 3,543,857 cars, and in 1937, despite shutdowns, slowdowns, and sit-down strikes, this number was topped with a production of 3,903,531. Americans demanded cars, and by now the auto was no longer a luxury; it was an essential.

Into the maws of this gargantuan industry went more than three and a half million tons of steel, a million and a quarter tons of copper, and the same amount of zinc. With this went thousands of tons of aluminum, chromium, nickel, and tin. This was just a part of the raw materials involved to keep Americans riding. The list does not include the vast quantities of textiles, rubber, glass, plastic, paint, and innumerable other products that are combined to produce the automobile.

What of the men needed to assemble (and in some cases fashion the items to be assembled) this stupendous mass of materials into automobiles? Well, exclusive of the hundreds of thousands of men and women working in steel mills, textile mills, tire, glass, and paint factories, exclusive of the hundreds of thousands of coal miners producing coal for the power needs of all of these, the copper miners, the men operating the boats and trains to transport these materials, the thousands working in oil fields and refineries, the hundreds of thousands employed indirectly but definitely in the production, sales, and maintenance of the automobile, exclusive of all these, four hundred thousand men were employed directly in the building of this high-speed, streamlined American dream.

The colossal automobile industry centered its major production plants in and around Detroit. Detroit became a synonym for the automobile, for the assembly line, for power. No matter where one went in this world, Moscow or Tokyo, Cairo or Prague, Paris, Capetown, or Melbourne, the name Detroit conjured up the greatest genii of industrial power known to mankind.

Our story concerns the human element in this vast, incredibly complicated mechanical network. It is the story of the four hundred thousand men and women flanking the assembly lines, turning, wrenching, pulling, hammering, screwing, pushing, going through all the motions that went into the work of assembling the finished automobile.

Many of these four hundred thousand were Middle Western farmers who tired of reaping debts as their main crop. The collapse of portions of the coal and lumber industries set up large pools of unemployed that flowed into the automobile centers. Both skilled technicians and unskilled workers were attracted by the high wages offered by the automobile industry. The higher wages of the automobile industry over those prevailing in other major fields of production were exaggerated until they exerted a tremendous attraction upon the nation's labor supply. The economic depression drove even more people to the assembly lines of Detroit. "In desperation, I hit upon the scheme of going to Detroit to crash the gates of the automobile factories. In that city, according to the stories I had heard from workers who had worked in the auto plants, fabulous wages were paid in the shops that turned out millions of cars every year." [1]

It took no longer than a year for these people rudely to discover that the "high wages" of the automobile industry, which had originally attracted them, were a delusion. The regular seasonal layoffs for retooling for the new year's models, and layoffs for other reasons, shriveled the auto workers' annual income to the point of bare subsistence. In 1934, the annual earnings of half the auto workers amounted to less than a thousand dollars. Even by 1936 their average annual income was $1,294, less than $25 a week.

This low income of the auto workers reflected itself in their housing and way of life. In Flint, Michigan, General Motors' stronghold, "The city's housing condition was frightful, with substandard ramshackle dwellings of the 1910 period renting at exorbitant rates. According to a survey, half or more of the homes in a number of working class districts had no private indoor toilet, bath or running water." [2]

The misery of the auto workers outside the auto plants was surpassed inside the plant. The workers silently railed and

[1] Clayton W. Fountain, *Union Guy* (New York: Viking Press, 1949), pp. 16-17.
[2] Henry Kraus, *The Many and the Few* (Los Angeles: Plantin Press, 1947), p. 6.

cursed at the man-killing speed-up system. Sheer physical fatigue from the incessant, uninterrupted repetition of the same motions was accompanied by a mental exhaustion that bordered on neurosis. The noted comedian, Charlie Chaplin, in "Modern Times," a pantomime of the effect of assembly-line speed-up, depicts a scene during a five-minute rest period where for the first four minutes his hands continue the specific motions of his hands on the assembly line, gradually slowing down until he is finally able to grasp a glass of water. This satire was not amusing when witnessed by auto workers. They winced at its realism. The human havoc resulting from the speed-up bordered on the incredible. "During July, a torrid heat wave sent the thermometer boiling over 100 degrees for a week straight. But the assembly lines pounded away mercilessly while many workers fell at their stations. Deaths in the state's auto centers ran into the hundreds within three or four days, and the clang of the hospital ambulances was heard incessantly as they dashed to and from the factories in Detroit, Pontiac, and Flint." [3]

The speed-up was not alone in driving workers to distraction. Piecework contributed its share.

> Our major gripe was the piecework system. I don't recall exactly what our piece rate per cushion was at the time, but we made something like about $6.50 or $7.00 a day. According to the theory of incentive pay, the harder and faster you worked, and the more cushions you turned out, the more pay you received. The employer, however, reserved the right to change the rules. We would start out with a new rate, arbitrarily set by the company time-study man, and work like hell for a couple of weeks, boosting our pay a little each day. Then, bingo, the timekeeper would come along one morning and tell us that we had another new rate, a penny or two per cushion less than it had been the day before. [4]

To add insult to injury, the automobile workers early discovered that the automobile empire was possessed of its own "law and order." Workers were spied upon, insulted, searched, intimidated, and at times physically beaten up. The Ford Motor Company under its former personnel chief, Harry Bennett, was the extreme example of this medieval policy.

[3] *Ibid.*, p. 23.
[4] Fountain, *op. cit.*, p. 28.

For years after Bennett came to power, it was the proud, un-disguised aim of the Service Department to blot out every mani-festation of personality or manliness inside a Ford plant. Striving for such an end, Bennett's mercenaries finally mastered every tactic from the swagger of the Prussian drill sergeant to out-right sadism and physical assault. On the night shift they would jolt an incoming worker out of his wits and take the starch out of his system by flashing a light in his face and shouting at him, "Where did you get that badge?" or, "Who's your boss?" An-other intimidating practice that came into being under Ben-nett's rule was the act of "shaking 'em up in the aisles." In this case a workman summoned to the employment office for any reason at all, even one that was totally unrelated to his work, would be shoved and pushed along the aisle by a pair of officious Servicemen, like a felon in the custody of the police. . . . But the disciplinary whip which caused greater dread than periodic bullying or an occasional show of force at Dearborn was the fa-cility of Ford Service in exploiting fear of the job. This practice at Ford's was the talk of the trade. In an industry which was characterized by chronic job insecurity even in the 20's, the op-eratives of Ford Service made matters worse by invoking the right to fire without appeal.[5]

At Ford's the workers' lunch boxes were searched and one man was fired for "smiling." Workers were so cowed and fear-ful that they wouldn't speak to each other during their lunch period, for who knew but that their companion might be a com-pany spy. Men were watched from the timecard to the toilet and back again. Even *Fortune* magazine stated, "Ford's organization does show extreme evidence of being ruled primarily by fear of the job." [6]

This rule of terror became a fixture in the mentality of the motor magnates. The violent union-busting of the notorious Black Legion that flourished in Detroit and its environs was viewed with sympathy by some of the top officials of motordom. General Motors in 1936, in conjunction with Standard Oil, U.S. Steel, Du Pont, and others, formed a "Special Conference Com-mittee" to crush the challenging CIO. "In May, 1936, the in-vestigation disclosed, William B. Foster, advisory director of

[5] Keith Sward, *The Legend of Henry Ford* (New York: Rinehart and Com-pany, 1948), pp. 306-308.

[6] Reprinted from *Fortune*, December, 1933, by special permission of the editors. Copyright, Time, Inc.

the service department of E. I. du Pont de Nemours and Co., requested E. S. Cowdrick, director of the 'Special Conference Committee,' to obtain for him information concerning 'The Sentinels of the Republic,' the notorious pro-Facist organization. Cowdrick canvassed his constituents. Among those replying was Harry W. Anderson, G.M. vice-president in charge of personnel. A copy of Anderson's letter was published in the files of the La Follette Committee:

" 'Dear Mr. Cowdrick: With reference to your letter of June 1, regarding the Sentinels of the Republic, I have never heard of the organization. Maybe you could use a little Black Legion down in your country. It might help.' " [7]

The mechanical character of the industry tended to make its leaders think in mechanical terms of everything including their employees. It became devoid of human feelings and regarded its people as automatons—necessary adjuncts to the assembly lines. With this kind of attitude it was understandable why rule by actual terror developed as it did and why human life came to be regarded in such a cheap denomination in the automotive production formulae.

Yet only this kind of callous cruelty could have swept such vast numbers of workers, few with any union background, into the arms of the CIO. In the last analysis, the greatest organizers of the coming automobile workers' unions were the executives and owners of the industry.

The general economic collapse of the 1930's added terrifying pressure to an already ugly situation. The squeeze of unemployment and competition for fewer jobs added to the other destructive forces in the automotive industry and started the pot boiling. Wages were driven down; unemployment threatened every auto worker. The threat soon became the fact, and thousands upon thousands of them found themselves out of work. The workers, enraged, bitter, resentful, filled with hate and fear, struck back.

In mid-1930 a Communist-led union struck the huge General Motors Fisher Body Number One plant in Flint, Michigan. It was beaten. By 1932 it was estimated that from a third to one half of all of the workers in the automobile capital, Detroit, were unemployed. The federal relief programs had not yet

[7] Kraus, op. cit., p. 37.

been organized to deal with this problem, and municipal and private agencies, completely swamped, found their resources were totally inadequate to meet this crisis.

It was in March of that year that the famous Ford Hunger March took place. That Communists were active in the formation of this mass demonstration is undeniable; but what is more important is that the thousands of workers, seething in their own helplessness, were more than willing to join in to make the only gesture by which it was possible to express themselves—a public demonstration. Several hundred of these workers, consisting primarily of former Ford employees, unemployed auto workers, and others, as well as a few Communists, set forth to march in a public orderly demonstration to the Ford Motor plants, at Dearborn. The obvious intent was then to send in a delegation to Harry Bennett with various requests for employment as well as a statement of their grievances against the company. What happened is now a matter of odious record. They were met with tear gas, gun fire, and fire hoses; and, when it was over, four were dead and about sixty were wounded. Practically every newspaper in the country bitterly condemned Harry Bennett and the Ford Motor Company for this murderous attack. Few pictures exist, since the Fort Dearborn police confiscated all film in the cameras of the news cameramen. The camera in the hands of the photographer of *The New York Times* was shot out of his hand. If the press had been aware of the arrogant attitude of the automobile industry toward their employees, they would not have been as shocked as they were by this outrageous attack.

In 1933 the Skilled Tool and Die Makers struck. Minor stoppages and disorganized protests flared up throughout the industry but were quickly quelled. Nineteen thirty-three was the year of NRA, with labor's magna charta, Section 7A. In early 1935 the American Federation of Labor armed with Section 7A approached the 400,000 angry men and women in the automobile industry who were aching to be organized so that they could strike back and stand up on their feet as men and women. With the protection of their numbers they believed they could start correcting the conditions that were goading them to the point of explosion.

The American Federation of Labor, based as it was primarily

on craft unions and on a craft-union philosophy, approached the problem of organizing the automobile workers with a certain diffidence and reservation. It was clear to everyone, even including the American Federation of Labor, that the automobile workers would have to be organized on a mass, industrial basis. Here was an industry which could only be effectively approached with the industrial-union philosophy. Everyone who worked in an automobile plant would belong to a single labor organization. To introduce the multitudinous, various craft-union locals and jurisdictions into an automobile plant would have hamstrung the workers to the point of paralysis. It would have created a condition whereby a thousand or more people working on one assembly line would belong to thirty or forty different unions. This condition would naturally have made it impossible for the workers in the automobile industry ever to bargain collectively with any effectiveness. To remedy this situation the AF of L set up what is called the federal local, in other words, locals which are affiliated directly to the national headquarters and not assigned to the jurisdiction of any of the craft unions making up the Federation. Into these federal locals by early 1935 thousands of automobile workers streamed.

Now organized, the auto workers prepared to lash back at their tormenters. The people who had worked and suffered in the auto industry knew that these vast corporations would listen only to the voice of power. Now they were ready. But the AF of L was not. The Federation's leaders and their organizers were totally incompetent to enter the arena in which they now found themselves. There is considerable evidence that the AF of L, which had become fat, soft, and afraid, was actually more fearful of the explosive power inherent in the thousands upon thousands of organized, angry, resentful, bitter automobile workers than they were of the opposition of the automobile industry.

It did not take very long for the labor leadership to discover that the automobile industry not only would not bargain collectively, but was impatient at the very idea of wasting any time conferring with union representatives. In desperation the AF of L turned to the Government. The personal intervention of General Hugh S. Johnson, head of NRA, was greeted by the automotive industry with bored indifference. The corporation

heads of the automobile industry likewise ignored the request
and gesture of President Roosevelt. Finally, upon Roosevelt's
personal plea, one last meeting was held between the motor executives and the AF of L officials. In this meeting, the officials
of the AF of L retreated on one point after another, finally ac-
ceding and capitulating to the adamant position of the companies. They even went so far as to accept the companies'
position of no recognition of the union. In short, the workers
were left high and dry.

The reaction of the automobile workers to the AF of L was
one of disgust and nausea. They made bonfires of their union
books and cards. Thousands of them quit the union, vowing
they would never have any further truck with what they considered the rottenest sellout in their experience. If this was what
a labor union was like they didn't want any part of it. The
AF of L for its own part, anxious to get rid of the troubled
complications and mass headache the automobile workers represented to them, in May, 1936, handed over independence and
complete control of the Automobile Workers Union to the automobile workers themselves. At this point it became question-
able whether the automobile workers hated the tycoons of their
industry as much as they did the leadership of the American
Federation of Labor.

The Automobile Workers union lost no time in joining up
with the newly formed CIO. This resulted in its suspension
from the American Federation of Labor.

The condition of the union was grave. It was estimated that
in Detroit one worker out of every 275 belonged to the union,
and in Flint, Michigan, which was to become the Bunker Hill
of the automobile workers, only one out of every 400 employed
in the automobile industry belonged to the Automobile Workers Union.

General Motors from January, 1934, to July, 1936, spent
$839,764 for spies, or as they were termed, agents. During the
year of 1935 the Chrysler Corporation spent $72,611.89 for the
same purpose. The business of labor espionage mushroomed to
monstrous proportions. The Senate La Follette Committee reported that industry expended a minimum of $80,000,000 a
year in the pursuit of industrial happiness. These undercover
organizations riddled the labor unions and became industry's

fifth column. Spies held many key positions in the unions and used their posts for purposes of betrayal. Bribery and blackmail were common daily tools used by these labor-spy companies in achieving their aims.

In Flint the effective operations of these spies so disorganized the automobile workers that this espionage was a major force in practically decimating union organization among the workers. In one year from 1935 to 1936 the enrolled membership of the Auto Workers Union was reported by Huberman to have dropped from 26,000 to 122!

The curtain was about to go up on one of the greatest upheavals in the history of labor in America. The cast starred the General Motors Corporation, the CIO, the sit-down strikers, John L. Lewis, Governor Murphy of the state of Michigan, the President of the United States, and the Secretary of Labor. The supporting cast included the National Guard, the courts, the police, the politicians, an alarmed press, and hundreds of thousands of extras.

The giant of the automotive world was and is the General Motors Corporation. In 1937, the latter employed 261,977 of the approximately 400,000 employees in the entire industry. The corporation's net capital was $1,040,665,000. Its total annual pay roll for that year (including executive salaries) was $460,-452,000, which was roughly 42 per cent of the total sales of the industry. It produced and sold 2,116,897 cars and trucks. Its plants were located in 57 different communities in the United States from New Jersey to California, and from Canada to Georgia.

In its colossal size and intricate network lay both its strength and its weakness. Each plant made essential parts which were then shipped to a central point such as Detroit, where they were assembled on the lines. The absence of one vital unit such as motors, springs, wheels, batteries, and similar items would bring the entire corporate production process to a halt. The various parts circulated through the General Motors system always returning to its heart in Detroit. A stoppage at any vital point reacts as a clot in the bloodstream which eventually deprives the heart of its life blood and brings death to the whole system.

Flint, Michigan, a city of more than 150,000 population is the basic stronghold of General Motors. Flint is the birthplace of the Buick Company, and it grew with the speedy development of the automobile and General Motors. The five huge corporation plants included the two largest units of the entire General Motors empire, Buick and the fantastically huge Chevrolet No. 4. It was in Chevrolet No. 4 that all the motors were built for the Chevrolet cars, the biggest-selling, biggest-money-making product of the corporation. If ever Chevrolet No. 4 fell, General Motors would quickly follow. But that was an impossible conjecture, for Chevrolet No. 4 was a mighty, impregnable fortress. Its enormous power plant and nine tremendous shops encompassing eighty acres was built, guarded, and policed in the finest General Motors tradition.

As for the town of Flint, General Motors owned it body and soul. The newspaper and local radio station carried out General Motors' bidding, not only editorially and by biased news reporting but even by refusing to carry ads of the new CIO union. The police, the politicians, and the judges were not the only ones genuflecting to the great god General Motors. So with few exceptions did the ministers, the priests, and the school officials. General Motors owned everything in Flint, except the people; all they owned of them was their implacable hatred.

It began in the autumn of 1936, by which time the accumulated frustrations and resentments of the auto workers had fused into deadly hatred against the industry. A prison expert who toured the assembly line in November reported that the tensions and expressions on the faces of the men were similar to those observed in a prison yard just prior to a mad riot. On November 18, there was a flare-up when a General Motors Fisher Body plant in Atlanta, Georgia, was struck. In the light of the coming struggle, this was tantamount to a brief feeling-out skirmish. Finally, in December, as one General Motors executive commented, "All hell broke loose."

Violent upheavals in the industry began to spread. On December 13 the employees of the Kelsey Hayes plant, which made brakes for the Ford Company, struck. On December 15, men in the General Motors Kansas City Fisher Body plant sat down.

The feeling-out period was drawing to a close. Soon the main forces would be joined in the struggle to a decision.

Homer Martin, the president of the United Automobile Workers Union, was a product of the depression period. Only out of the mad disorganization which characterized the terrible thirties could a Homer Martin be propelled upward to the official leadership of this union. A former minister, who lost his church because of his liberal sermons and then went to work in an automobile plant, Martin was a college graduate and a former national track and field champion of the hop, skip, jump. His critics held that he was also champion of the mental hop, skip, and jump. Certain it was that he possessed a most chaotic and incoherent picture of the auto industry and its workers. His lack of knowledge of industrial problems and the power politics of collective bargaining was appalling. No questions were ever raised at that time with reference to his personal integrity or idealism, but with the coming battle of corporate finance power against corporate manpower, Martin was to be in all actuality a minor and pathetic figure. True, he made many public statements, but it is also true that he was eliminated from the scene at every important showdown. He was vaguely aware of his inability to master-mind the situation and willing to follow Lewis and to respond to his cues, when he understood them.

On December 17, Homer Martin met and conferred with John L. Lewis on the volatile situation in autos. The next day Lewis issued a public statement, "It is the hope of the United Automobile Workers that General Motors will agree to meet peaceably and work out these questions without any disturbance of production. Collective bargaining is the law of the land and we think General Motors should now do a little collective bargaining." Lewis added the "hope" that a strike could be averted, but at the same time emphasized that the auto workers' organizing drive would be stepped up.

This statement was a significant sign of the forthcoming facility of Lewis's strategy. The sit-downs were coming in force, and some had already occurred. Lewis, well aware of the illegal aspects of the sit-down strike and the possible repercussions of public opinion, opened with a demand on General Motors that *they obey the law,* inferring that General Motors was the law-breaker and not the sit-down strikers.

On December 19, the United States Senate's La Follette Civil Liberties Committee announced that it would investigate General Motors. Throughout the course of the events that followed, the Senate Civil Liberties Committee constantly pursued General Motors and repeatedly uncovered information damaging and acutely embarrassing to the corporation, actually performing yeoman service for the CIO offensive against G.M.

Now began what was to become the saga of the forty days of General Motors. Forty days of battle, climaxed by the ultimate capitulation of the corporation to the young, squalling, kicking, sit-downing union. On the twenty-first Homer Martin, following his conference with John L. Lewis, telegraphed William Knudsen, executive vice-president of G.M., demanding that General Motors meet with the UAW for purposes of negotiations on "flagrant discharge of and discrimination against union men." Martin also attacked the absence of seniority rights among the auto workers as well as the speed-up. The point of seniority rights was of great importance to the automobile workers, as it is to workers in all industries; for their absence meant that a man who worked for years in the industry had no more security in his job than one who had worked for only a short time.

General Motors' answer was a conference the next day between Knudsen and some of his associates, and Martin and George Addes representing the union. Knudsen announced that this was not a meeting of G.M. and the union but a "personal interview." General Motors' strategy obviously was first to get out of the spot where it had been placed by Lewis's statement accusing it of being an arrogant corporation that regarded itself above the law and would not meet with its workers. At the same time, General Motors was determined that the meeting should not be construed as an unofficial recognition of the union. Further to remove any ideas of informal recognition of the union, Knudsen told Martin "to take up matters with the plant managers." This was the same answer General Motors would give to any complaining worker.

If General Motors could force the union to deal on an individual basis with each plant, it would never complete its organization. Since all local plant policies were determined on a national scale by the top-level executives of the company, it could fight the union in its many plants, plant by plant. In each plant a relatively small number of workers would be forced to face the entire strength of G.M. The industry could decide strategically where it would permit a strike in order to crush the union in a particular plant. Suppose, for example, there are four plants assembling one make of car and negotiations begin in one. General Motors could be very tough and uncompromising with the union in one plant and force it to strike. In the meantime the company could go along with the unions in the other three plants, and grant union demands. Production could be boosted in those three plants to offset the closing down of the strike-bound plant. With that kind of situation, General Motors could operate with little loss and less jeopardy. With the company prepared to keep the strike-bound plant closed indefinitely the inevitable result would be the end of the strike and the return of the workers economically smashed and with crushed spirits. The union would disappear in this plant for a long time. Having achieved this, G.M. could then repeat this strike strategy in the other plants, one at a time.

Furthermore, plant-by-plant bargaining would result in many varied contracts, which would arouse resentments of workers within and against the union. The workers in a Detroit General Motors plant might get a contract whereby those doing job "X" would get ninety cents an hour. In Milwaukee the workers in a General Motors plant might get a contract whereby the workers doing the same job "X" might get eighty-two cents an hour. Disparity in wages for the same work breeds discontent and bitterness among the workers, much of it directed toward their own union. Furthermore, local plant managers possessed no powers for real collective bargaining and settling of grievances. In the last analysis, General Motor's plant-by-plant strategy was the ancient one of "divide and rule."

Homer Martin, blissfully unaware of what it was all about and pleased with meeting with such important General Motors executives, announced on the next day, December 23, that the meeting with Knudsen and his colleagues was "completely amicable."

In Washington, Lewis cursed as Martin's statement was reported to him. Lewis well knew that to the auto workers the situation was the antithesis of being "completely amicable," and that Martin's statement could have a disastrous effect upon the fighting morale of the auto workers. Completely disregarding Martin's dignity or office, Lewis thundered from Washington, "That's not collective bargaining. That's just evasion of the responsibilities on the part of G.M. It will be unsatisfactory to the union." He then went on to warn that the UAW "will press their claim" and charged General Motors with full responsibility "for the continuing confusion which will logically result" from their adamant defiance of the Wagner Act and refusal to bargain. Homer Martin, now contradicted and publicly spanked, hurriedly fell back in line. He sent a hasty letter to Knudsen requesting a national conference. General Motors didn't even bother to acknowledge it.

But below Martin there were thousands upon thousands of General Motors auto workers led by tough, militant leaders like Bob Travis; Wyndham Mortimer; the three Reuther brothers, Roy, Walter and Victor; Dick Frankensteen; George Addes; and local leaders of the stripe of Bud Simon. These men were young, many of them in their late twenties; and they were passionately devoted to their "cause." These leaders and the auto workers knew their General Motors; and they knew that there was only one way to get General Motors to "acknowledge" Martin's letter, to speak the language General Motors would understand—force.

Three days after Christmas, the offensive began. The General Motors Fisher Body plant in Cleveland sat down. Tensions had reached the point where the workers' nerves were sensitive to the point of rawness. This entire plant went down because a conference between the union and management set for the morning had been postponed until 2:30 that afternoon. At 2:30 the plant was shut down and in the initial throes of a sit-down strike. Any ideas entertained by General Motors of moving their machinery to another town died a-borning when the railroad switch crews refused to cross the automobile workers' picket line. It was a common tactic among major industries that when plagued with strikes they would remove all their machinery to another locale and hire a new labor corps that had not been, from their point of view, "infected with labor-union germs." This meant that the strikers would permanently lose their jobs as the plant they had struck had become defunct. Therefore, striking workers fought against any removal of machinery as it meant removal of their jobs.

Wyndham Mortimer, vice-president of the UAW, then issued a statement in Cleveland that this sit-down strike would and could only be settled as part of a *national* agreement and there would be no talks with local management. Mortimer and other officers of the UAW knew what they were doing and were prepared to follow the line laid down by Lewis. To confirm officially this policy the UAW called a planning conference for January 3 to lay down an approved and agreed-upon program in dealing with General Motors.

December 30 was D Day for the auto workers. The General Motors empire was rocked with four major sit-down strikes. It was now clear that the sit-down was to be the chief weapon in the attack against the company. To date all New Deal figures, including labor leaders, were loathe to indicate even indirectly the most remote approval of this revolutionary and seemingly illegal tactic. Even the sit-down strikers themselves were uneasy concerning both the legality and validity of this weapon. Sensing this, but believing General Motors could be beaten only by the sit-down, Lewis boldly blessed the sit-downers and told the nation, and what was more important, many of the sit-downers, what the purpose of the strike was. *"The CIO stands squarely behind these sit-downs.*[8] Local conferences, such as Knudsen proposes, would only be confusing. It is up to General Motors to make the next move."[9]

The New Year opened with a bang. While Michigan's new governor, Frank Murphy, was being inducted into office the crescendo of battle was rising rapidly throughout the state and the nation. The first issue of *The New York Times* for 1937 carried a four-column headline:

35,000 MEN ARE MADE IDLE
SIT DOWN STRIKE CLOSES
7 GENERAL MOTORS PLANTS

General Motors' reaction to the sit-down came speedily.

[8] Italics the writer's.
[9] *Cleveland Plain Dealer,* January 1, 1937.

Knudsen officially informed Homer Martin that first, collective bargaining would only be considered after the sit-down strikers evacuated General Motors' plants and second, that national recognition or bargaining was unthinkable; the union would have to bargain with individual plant managers.

Out of this exchange of views emerged the clear issue of the conflict. The UAW and Lewis demanded national recognition of the union as the bargaining agent for the workers of General Motors. To this, General Motors was adamantly opposed. All other issues were secondary in importance.

The area of conflict began to expand beyond the principals involved. Rev. Charles E. Coughlin, of Detroit, delivered a radio broadcast on January 1 with a so-called New Year plan for peace in the industrial world. The reaction in many quarters to Coughlin's remarks was the same as to his previous broadcasts, "more than a bit on the crackpot side." Before many days were to pass, Coughlin was to come out in a bitter attack against Lewis and the CIO.

A more formidable attack against the sit-down strikers came from Coughlin's superior, the Catholic Bishop of Detroit's Catholic Archdiocese, Bishop Michael J. Gallagher. On January 11, "addressing a cathedral congregation he said he did not doubt that the automobile company's employees should get higher wages, but he called the sit-down strikes 'illegal and Communistic. We're fearful that it's Soviet planning behind it,' the Bishop asserted. Many pastors told him of complaints of low pay and high-speed production methods. He added, 'But these sit-down strikes are illegal. They are borrowed from the Communists of France. You will remember there were many of them in France when Blum came into office. The Communists advocated these strikes—often followed by riots—as a smoke screen for revolutions and civil war.' " [10]

On January 2, General Motors secured an injunction from Judge Edward Black, ordering the sit-down strikers out of the plants. The sheriff who tried to serve the court order was laughed out of the plant. Homer Martin, visibly wilted by the threat of the law, announced that the court order would be obeyed and the union would not fight the law. He then went on to say that if Knudsen would only start to discuss "broad

[10] *The New York Times*, January 12, 1937, p. 12, col. 3.

principles covering seniority, speed-up, hours, non-discrimination for union activity," the UAW would be willing to have other matters dealt with in the local plants. Here Martin was actually throwing away the major objective of the sit-down strikes and of the union—national recognition and national bargaining.

In Washington, John L. Lewis, now beginning to doubt Martin's ability, softly remarked to his lieutenants that a couple of husky automobile workers sitting down on Homer Martin's mouth would be almost as important as sitting down in a G.M. plant.

The next day two hundred UAW delegates meeting in Flint created a board of strategy and gave it authority to call a general strike. They also reiterated Lewis's demand for national recognition. Thus in one day the union repudiated Martin's statement and actually stripped him of real authority for the struggle with General Motors.

General Motors continued to refuse to meet with the union, and strikes spread further. The January 4 battle map showed Atlanta, Georgia; Cleveland, Ohio; Flint, Michigan; Kansas City; Norwood, Ohio; and Anderson, Indiana, in the union's camp. That day President Sloan of General Motors lashed back at the union with charges of labor dictatorship, saying, "the real issue in the controversy is will a labor organization run the plants of the General Motors Corporation or will the management continue to do so?" With this blast, G.M. went to work plastering announcements of ". . . Will you pay to a private group of labor dictators for the privilege of working? . . ." over all the bulletin boards in their plants.

Homer Martin, scared by both General Motors' thunder, and Lewis's and the UAW officials' ominous reaction to his previous irresponsible utterances, maintained a discreet silence for one day and then issued a carefully worded denial of General Motors' charges.

Now the national administration began to be concerned with the rapidly expanded battlefront of the General Motors–CIO war. President Roosevelt and his Secretary of Labor, Frances Perkins, conferred twice on January 5 on this critical labor-capital conflict. Roosevelt was noncommittal after these conferences, while Secretary of Labor Perkins made some veteran reporters grin sarcastically by stating that F.D.R. and she had discussed the strike "only superficially."

That day the General Motors strongholds in Toledo, Ohio, and Janesville, Wisconsin, toppled. Now that all forces were rapidly being joined for the final decision, conflict began to revolve around these questions.

1. The issue was national recognition of the union as the exclusive national bargaining agent for the factory employees of General Motors.

2. The union's basic weapon was the sit-down strike. If the sit-down strike was defeated either by the courts, public opinion, or the state or national governments, the cause of the union would be lost.

3. Although the strike was spreading all through the General Motors network, the major and decisive assault was converging upon the General Motors plants in Flint, Michigan, and specifically on the gigantic Chevrolet No. 4 plant. If that went, then the fatal bloodclot would be formed in the General Motors system. The battle of Flint was fully recognized by both adversaries as the locale of the ultimate showdown.

4. In the last analysis, it would be a struggle on the part of General Motors to use the courts, citizen groups, police, and governmental authorities to break the union's stranglehold on General Motors in Flint. On the other side, victory or defeat was to be determined by the ability of the workers and Lewis to maintain the sit-down strike unbroken by the opposition forces.

With this compass before us, we can now intelligently chart the maneuvers and drives of these two titans. G.M. had resorted to the courts and secured eviction writs. The strikers and their leaders in the Flint plants were apprehensive and uncertain in the face of the legal weapons pointed at them by G.M. The injunction of Judge Black could not be long ignored. If enforced it might well mean the collapse of the union. At this point, a brilliant maneuver saved the day for the union. Clever Lee Pressman, general counsel of the CIO, had been sent to Detroit by Lewis. The thought crossed Pressman's mind that it might be interesting to find out if Judge Black, who had issued the injunction for General Motors against the union, might be a General Motors stockholder.

According to Pressman, what happened was this: "I phoned a friend of mine in New York City and asked him to go over to the General Motors offices and ask to look at the list of stock-holders. He did this and called me back in about six hours. While I would not have been too surprised to have discovered that the Judge was a stockholder, I can tell you I was practically bowled over with joy when I was informed that this particular Judge Black was not only a stockholder, but he possessed 3,365 shares of General Motors stock currently valued at $219,000. Well, as you know, we went to town on the issue and by the next morning, Judge Black was as far out of the fight as though he lived on another planet. The Michigan state law barred any judge from presiding over a case in which he was an interested party. Well $219,000 is more than a slight interest. As for the injunction, it wasn't worth the paper it was written on. If G.M. was calling us 'red' it was nothing compared to the red face General Motors had after we broke this. It was a real break for us." [11]

Although Pressman calls it "a real break for us," the fact is that through his own alertness, imagination, and in this case, brilliant idea, he made the "break." The same ingenious ma-neuvering and sensitivity to all possibilities in the situation by Lewis and his associates made nearly all the "breaks." In Flint, it was Bob Travis and the Reuther boys; in Detroit, Wyndham Mortimer, Maurice Sugar, a skillful labor attorney, and Lewis's lieutenants, Pressman, Brophy, and Powers Hap-good; and over it the old Napoleonic master of power and strategy: cold, ruthless, ingenious John L. Lewis.

The devastating effect of the disclosures of Judge Black's holdings in General Motors stock blasted him and his injunc-tion permanently out of the picture. In fact, the UAW peti-tioned the State House of Representatives to impeach Judge Black for sitting on the case while being a stockholder of Gen-eral Motors. Here is another sample of the play to the public, probably by both Pressman and Maurice Sugar. General Motors issued embarrassed denials of any knowledge of the Judge's financial investments and hurriedly prepared to go to

[11] Interview with Lee Pressman, New York City, December 6, 1948.

another court for a new injunction to evict the sit-down strikers. With the union now having temporarily extricated itself from the legal hot box of the injunction concerning the sit-down strike, it began to issue statements to the general public to the effect that sit-down strikes were just and legal on the basis that a man's right to a job transcends the right to private property. G.M. met this propaganda attack by their own publicity, which was along the line that people have a right to work and the vast majority of workers in General Motors were being denied that right by a sit-down strike in which only a handful of radicals were engaged.

On Friday, January 8, for the first time both sides were becoming apprehensive. G.M. was definitely restless now that operations in Flint were at a standstill. The corporation began hinting that it might be willing to negotiate nationally if the plants were evacuated. This was accompanied by another G.M. statement that they would be willing to promise not to move out their machinery if this evacuation were to take place.

On the other side, the UAW informed Governor Frank Murphy of Michigan that it was willing to waive its demands for recognition, if G.M. would start negotiating. Friday, January 8, was a day of jitters for both sides. G.M. for the first time was fearful, UAW uncertain as to how long it could continue to maintain the sit-down strike.

The nervous tension gripping both the union and General Motors was reflected in Flint, where fights and demonstrations broke out. Father Coughlin in *Social Justice* of that week attacked Lewis. Coughlin stated that he did not and would not ever support any organization of union labor to sovietize industry. This statement was almost an exact paraphrase of what General Motors had been charging, and the same statement was paraphrased later in the official statement of the New York Merchants Association in their attack on the CIO.

The unrest of Friday the eighth resulted in G.M.'s sending a brief and unacceptable offer to UAW through Governor Murphy. In Washington that day Lewis, aware of the nervous tension of both the auto workers union and G.M., decided upon a dramatic act to restore confidence to the union and also increase G.M. apprehensions. Lewis had tried to get F.D.R. to make a public statement insuring unimpaired federal relief to the strikers, which would have been a terrific morale factor. The President would not budge. Roosevelt, as President of the United States, could not possibly indicate any approval or even moral support for an action as patently lawless as the sit-down strike. The auto workers worshiped him and always assumed that he was completely on their side. Lewis then decided to do what he had done before and did so many times afterward— maneuver to make it appear the President was actively behind him even if he was not.

He decided to exploit the general public opinion that he had F.D.R.'s positive support. Lewis prepared a situation that would be publicly interpreted as his possessing confidential information that the President would shortly throw his weight on the side of the union. This, plus a personal air of unruffled confidence, would be certain to tighten even more the already taut nerves of General Motors.

Edward McGrady was Roosevelt's right-hand labor conciliator and very much in the public limelight. Lewis asked McGrady on Friday night to make an appointment for the following morning to see the President on the subject of the automobile strike and then to meet Lewis later that afternoon at the Willard Hotel. McGrady innocently agreed to this. The Roosevelt calendar of appointments was public property, and anyone who saw Roosevelt that day was not only known, but it was actually printed in the paper. Lewis then tipped off the press that he had a very important appointment with Ed McGrady late that afternoon. The press put two and two together. McGrady was seeing Roosevelt in the early afternoon and was going to see Lewis in the late afternoon, and something big must be brewing. Roosevelt was finally acting in this situation and obviously was going to act on the side of Lewis. McGrady showed up for his appointment with Lewis and was dumbfounded to find a room full of newspaper reporters all buttonholing him and saying, "Mr. McGrady, you've seen the President this morning and, now of course, you're carrying a very important message from him to Mr. Lewis. Can you tell us what happened?" While McGrady was still in a state of shock, Lewis came out and said, "Come on into my room, Ed," and pulled McGrady into his room and shut the door. McGrady then looked at Lewis and said, "Why all the newspaper re porters?" Lewis said, "Oh, well, they just heard you were coming. Forget them." Lewis then engaged McGrady in conversation for an hour, and as McGrady left, said, "When you leave, ignore the reporters with a 'no comment.' That's all, and I'll appreciate your doing this for me."

McGrady stayed for an hour and then left, elbowing through the reporters saying, "No comment." All the while Lewis looked very mysterious and bore a look of triumph as though something terrifically important had taken place. The press then began pounding that Roosevelt was beginning to step into automobiles. Lewis was about to square off with General Motors with President Roosevelt's full support behind him. The fact that F.D.R. was furious over this maneuver leaked out; but at the same time repudiation of Lewis and organized labor was unthinkable, so F.D.R. could do nothing but sit there and hold the bag, for the time. . . .[12]

At this point the forces engaged in the battle appeared to spread, including other seemingly spontaneous movements that unfurled the banners of General Motors and rushed onto the warpath against the union. In Flint a new organization, the Flint Alliance, suddenly mushroomed, headed by George E. Boysen, a former paymaster of the Buick Motor Company. There seemed to be ample funds supporting this movement, judging from their headquarters and organizational tactics. Company foremen, executives, doctors, politicians, and others worked enrolling members.

Frequent charges that General Motors was the hothouse for this new flower of the Flint Alliance have never been legally proven though it was of interest to note that after the strike Boysen sued G.M. for money he claimed to have spent developing the organization.

The Flint Alliance announced that it represented thousands of workers and that, if there was going to be any collective bargaining between General Motors and its workers, the Alliance had as good a right if not a better one to represent the workers than did the union. The Flint Alliance's daily announcement of its growth in "membership" defied the tales of Paul Bunyan.

Public opinion was not entirely with General Motors. The social-action department of the National Catholic Welfare Con-

[12] Interview with Lee Pressman, New York City, December 6, 1948.

ference, the Industrial Division of the Federal Council of the Churches of Christ in America, and the Social Justice Commission of the Central Conference of American Rabbis sent a joint telegram to Knudsen urging collective bargaining. They also went a step further and offered their services to resolve this conflict. It was becoming clearer by the hour that the fight was one that would be determined strictly by the strength of the opponents and that both sides in the last analysis had the attitude, "the public be damned," unless the public would be on their side. This was a straight power struggle, which suited John L. Lewis.

The reaction of General Motors to the telegram of the three major religious groups was in accord with this. They announced they "would stand pat," and then having rejected these requests from these major organizations announced any action they would take would depend upon "public opinion." On that day Governor Murphy announced that he had ordered the State Welfare Department to provide relief on the basis of need. This meant that the strikers were eligible for relief and were removed from the shadow of starvation. It was now clear that G.M. was not going to be able to starve the union into submission. This action was one of the most important administrative decisions in behalf of the automobile workers that took place throughout the strike. Murphy was not only leaning over backward as far as the union was concerned but actually siding with them. He demonstrated this in many other ways. Committees of so-called "loyal" workers and other alleged citizen committees favorable to General Motors attempted to see the Governor and demand the eviction of the sit-down strikers. With few exceptions Governor Murphy either side-stepped these groups, ignored, or reprimanded them.

The spurt of strikes continued, however, and Oldsmobile and the Fisher Body plants in Lansing, Michigan, went down. General Motors was being pushed more and more to their last line of defense.

January 12 was a day of blood. Twenty-four strikers were injured, some seriously, in a riot that broke loose in Flint. There seems to be little doubt that a good part of this riot was the result of the inflammatory action of the Flint Alliance. Certainly, statements like Boysen's would not hasten peace. The union offensive continued, and five more plants were shut down. General Motors was no longer producing Chevrolet cars, Cadillacs, or LaSalles. Pontiac and Oldsmobile production was seriously curtailed. The mammoth G.M. organization was grinding to an almost complete standstill. The job of paralyzing the G.M. structure was practically done. The question now was, would the workers be able to continue the sit-down and hold down the brakes on the General Motors juggernaut? General Motors was feeling the pressure and beginning to spar for time to find a way out of this tempest. They announced that they would not use strike-breakers, which was somewhat ludicrous, since one of the main features of the sit-down strike was that physical occupation of the plant made it impossible to bring in strike-breakers.

Tension was mounting through the country. Newspaper editorials appeared, demanding that Roosevelt intervene. The *Detroit News* came out with a front-page editorial headed, "Let Roosevelt do it." Rumor was chasing rumor that G.M. was willing to discuss a number of points of controversy on a national basis. Added to the pressure on General Motors was the knife-in-the-back "co-operation" of the rest of the automobile industry with the union. If the other automobile companies, Ford, Chrysler, Studebaker, Nash, and Packard, had been willing to support General Motors in its fight, probably the union could have been defeated. That is, if Studebaker, Ford, and Chrysler had said to General Motors, "Look here, we recognize that you are carrying on our fight. We fully share the policies that you have and the employment practices which you try to maintain, including your opposition to having your workers organized into a union. Your defeat by the union now means our defeat later. If you continue your fight against the union, we will stop producing cars so that you need not fear loss of your market." But they did not. The profit motive transcended everything else. Pressure began to build up on General Motors from its dealers throughout the country and particularly from Chevrolet dealers, who now could no longer guarantee delivery on automobiles. At the same time other automobile companies cut in on the General Motors market, to an unprecedented degree. The squeeze was on, not only from the union, but also from the other automobile companies, G.M.'s competitors.

Through all this, Lewis continued to exude an air of supreme confidence. By word and gesture he would intimate that the President of the United States and the Government of the United States was behind him. He announced that the Government's La Follette Committee was going to be asked to investigate General Motors and that this investigation should encompass the entire financial structure of General Motors, excessive salaries of executives, possible dictation of policy by foreign stockholders and also their "arsenal" and "armies." While Lewis's words encouraged the sit-down strikers, they had just the opposite effect upon Knudsen, who, it is reported, was so disturbed he sat up all night. The boys in the plants, the army of labor, the people without whom no general and no one individual could have forced General Motors to its knees, continued their advance. The Fleetwood Body plant in Detroit and the Pontiac plant fell; and General Motors production lines now were as silent as the tomb. Threats by the Flint Alliance of open physical warfare resulted in a stream of reinforcements for ___ ___ion. The union leader in Toledo, Ohio, announced that a thousand workers in his town were coming into Flint to help the union. Rubber workers from Akron, coal miners from Ohio, men from different industries in the Middle West were filing into Flint, and a revolutionary spirit surged through the town.

At this point, Murphy invited Knudsen and Homer Martin to come to Lansing, Michigan state capital, for a conference. Following the meeting, Governor Murphy announced that the deadlock had been broken with a truce, whereby the union had agreed to evacuate the sit-down strikers out of five of the major plants that week end and that in return General Motors had agreed to start negotiations with the union, at 11:00 A.M. the following Monday. On the next day the sit-down strikers began to evacuate the plants. They were marched out of the Cadillac and Fleetwood plants in Detroit, with flying banners and brass bands. Preparations were being made for similar evacuations in the other plants, when suddenly the truce blew up with a roar. The sit-down strikers who were halfway out of the plants turned and ran back in to assume their positions. Other plants in the midst of their marching-out preparations locked the doors and prepared for an indefinite siege. The union had discovered that General Motors had agreed also to meet and negotiate with the Flint Alliance. Organizer Bob Travis had secured this information before it was released to the press. Thus the union could countermand its evacuation orders in time.

John L. Lewis issued a statement saying, "The representatives of the workers in these conferences will insist upon formal recognition of the union as the *exclusive* bargaining agent before the industry. When General Motors accepts this formula, it is reasonable that the other items in the controversy will quickly respond to negotiation." This was obviously the major issue. General Motors' agreement with the Flint Alliance was defined by the union as a betrayal of the agreement. With the rupture of the truce, G.M. began to use the law.

Governor Murphy tried to save the truce from complete destruction by phoning Knudsen and trying to persuade him to drop his scheduled conference with the Flint Alliance. Knudsen refused. At this point, Lewis issued a public statement. "G.M. was caught in a barefaced violation of the armistice and so the evacuation of the plants was stopped. The men are not going to leave them. It was an amazing action for the motor manufacturers to take but the union will protect itself."

With the battle now hopelessly deadlocked between General Motors and the union, Frank Murphy left for Washington to confer with Roosevelt and Perkins. He also planned to see John L. Lewis. Murphy now realized the impossibility of dealing with subordinates in this situation and announced that if he could see Lewis he would then go to see Alfred P. Sloan, chairman of the board of directors of General Motors. Here were the very top powers in both camps, Sloan for General Motors and John L. Lewis for the CIO.

On January 20 while Roosevelt was giving his now famous inaugural speech, ". . . I see one third of a nation ill housed, ill clad and ill nourished . . ." Governor Murphy was closeted with Secretary of Labor Perkins and the G.M. chieftains, Sloan, Knudsen, Brown, and John Thomas Smith in a "peace" conference that ended in a dismal failure.

The next day Lewis charged that ". . . a united front of financial groups interested in steel, automobiles and rubber and glass and coal is intent on ending what they consider the menace of the CIO." This statement carried within it the revolutionary implication of class warfare which began to permeate the CIO during these months.

The same day, the CIO began calling off strikes in the aluminum and plate-glass industry to insure a free flow of materials to Ford, Chrysler, Packard, Nash, and Studebaker so that they could not only maintain but boost production to invade the market formerly dominated by General Motors. The CIO was employing a hard, shrewd policy of using even the rivals of the auto industry as unwitting allies.

On Thursday, January 21, Lewis, before a press conference equal in attendance to the White House conferences, publicly asked for the support of President Roosevelt: "The administration asked labor for help to repel this attack and labor gave its help. The same economic royalists now have their fangs in labor. The workers of this country expect the administration to help the workers in every legal way and to support the workers in General Motors plants."

It is interesting to note that Lewis deliberately used the term popularized by the President of "economic royalists." Here was his open bid for a dividend on the more than $500,000 contributed to Roosevelt's 1936 campaign by the United Mine Workers of America.

Sloan, after seeing the newspaper stories about Lewis's demand for the President's support, packed his bags and left for New York City. Before leaving he announced that General Motors would not bargain with any group "until negotiations with the United Automobile Workers Union were concluded successfully or otherwise." This was a slight retreat from General Motors' fixed position.

On Friday, Roosevelt, smarting under Lewis's pressure to get him involved in the strike, tartly commented, "Of course I think in the interests of peace that there come moments when statements, conversations, and headlines are not in order."

The New York Times headlines were "Roosevelt Rebukes Lewis." Lewis, undaunted, then began to turn the screws on the President by replying, "I cannot undertake to interpret the President's words. He alone can define his statement and of course, I do not believe that the President intended to rebuke the working people in America or his friends." By this statement Lewis broke through the generality of Roosevelt's phraseology and challenged him openly to say that he would not help the automobile workers. This, of course, Roosevelt would not do, by virtue of both his personal attitudes and his personal politics. Then Lewis, having fended off Roosevelt's intended rebuke, returned to the attack: "We have ample evidence here that in the end the President will do what he thinks necessary. We think that the President thinks about as we do on these things. . . . Labor is on the march. . . . That is what Sloan asked for and he'll take that and more."

In the meantime General Motors continued to denounce the union and the sit-down strikers as representing a minority of its employees. Also the corporation charged that the strike was engineered by "radicals" or "left-wingers." There was considerable truth to these statements; for, while the union represented the frustrations and hopes of most of the automobile workers, comparatively few of them officially belonged to the union. As for the charges of "radicalism" and "left-wingers" there was no question that the political thinking of the two prime leaders of the General Motors strike, Robert Travis and Wyndham Mortimer, was to the left.

Lewis continued indifferent to all attacks from General Motors. The UAW told the administration and the country that they would do what Lewis told them to do when they stated, "Homer Martin was directing strike activities under the *leadership of* John L. Lewis." [13]

January 24 Frances Perkins stepped into the picture to announce she was calling a conference of the union and the company two days from that time.

Lewis viewed the conference with General Motors and Secretary of the Labor Perkins with wariness and caution, if not suspicion. He felt that Frances Perkins was accustomed to far different behavior and standards than the dirty, slugging power battle which was raging between General Motors and the union. Lewis also felt that because of this she would be unable to understand that this was a battle where anything went and that the decision would come as a result of sheer power.

[13] Italics the writer's.

Sloan's rejection of Madame Perkins's invitation to the meeting opened the door for Roosevelt to counteract his first statement against Lewis with a second one against Sloan. On January 27 he stated at his press conference, "I told them [meaning General Motors] that I was not only disappointed in the refusal of Mr. Sloan to come down here, but that I regarded it as a very unfortunate decision on his part." But it was obvious to the nation that President Roosevelt's personal "disappointment" was not going to influence the policy of General Motors.

The same situation was repeated on the thirtieth. Frances Perkins had Sloan in her office. After a couple of hours of conversation she assumed that he was prepared to sit down with Lewis and Governor Murphy and commence negotiations. Instead of that, Sloan after leaving her office, took a train for New York City, and slammed the door on a settlement under Madame Perkins's auspices. Perkins's reaction to Sloan's departure was typical of what Lewis felt with reference to her ethics and standards. Perkins, emotionally very upset, protested, "Really, it is not what one should expect from a man in his position." The sit-down strike that had paralyzed General Motors should have been some clue to Frances Perkins as to "what one should expect from a man in his position." However Sloan's action was popularly interpreted as G.M.'s placing itself above the Government and swung considerable public opinion toward the union.

Lewis also balked at conferences with Perkins and the General Motors officials because he felt that Perkins might suggest that the sit-down strikes stop and the strikers leave the plants as a condition for bargaining. Of course the evacuation of the plants would have meant the end of the strike for the union and victory for the company. Perkins could not see it that way.

On Sunday, January 31, Lewis's fears were confirmed when Perkins told the press that one of her proposals to Sloan on the day before had been that the strikers were to evacuate the plants "as an expression by the union of good faith in General Motors."

The Washington negotiations or rather lack of negotiations began to resemble a Mack Sennett comedy. On Monday, Roosevelt would spank the union, on Friday he would spank General Motors, and all other days he would turn somersaults to stay out of the whole situation. A few blocks away, Frances Perkins was continuously wringing her hands and deploring the ungentlemanly conduct of Alfred Sloan. Alfred Sloan seemed to spend most of his time jumping off and on trains, going to Washington and returning to New York, while Madame Perkins's blood pressure rose and fell accordingly. A few blocks away, John L. Lewis glowered and persistently tried to force the President to throw the weight of the White House behind the union. But trying to catch and hold on to the elusive Franklin Delano Roosevelt appeared to be impossible.

Governor Murphy, now in a state of despair, realized that this issue would not be settled in Washington, that Frances Perkins was unable to do anything about it, and that the President would not be coaxed, taunted, or threatened into it. It would be decided right on the battleground of Detroit between the leaders of General Motors and the leaders of the CIO.

The crisis came on Tuesday, February 2. What the sit-down strikers and their leaders had long feared now came to pass. Judge Paul V. Gadola issued an injunction ordering the sit-down strikers out by 3 P.M. the following day. This time the writ was not signed by a G.M. stockholder. The injunction and the proceedings were legal.

General Motors waited silently. The courts had acted. The law of the State of Michigan was now openly invoked in behalf of the corporation. These sit-down rebels must now get out or be forced out. The red nightmare of property seizure was now to have its back broken. Chaos was to go, and order was to come. General Motors' silence was the sudden stillness auguring the oncoming storm.

General Motors' tense quiet, of stop, look, and listen, was not the case with the sit-down strikers. Bellows of defiance, mad rage, and frenzied curses could be heard coming from the occupied plants. "Damn the injunction, damn the courts, damn the army, and double damn General Motors." They would be damned if they would budge! Out of this inferno came the now famous blood-bath telegram to Governor Murphy:

> Unarmed as we are, the introduction of the militia, sheriffs or police with murderous weapons will mean a blood-bath of unarmed workers. . . . We feel it proper to recall to you the assur-

ances that you have given many times publicly that you would not permit force or violence to be used in ousting us from the plant. . . . The Police of the City of Flint belong to General Motors. The Sheriff of Genesee County belongs to General Motors. The judges of Genesee County belong to General Motors. . . . It remains to be seen whether the Governor of the State also belongs to General Motors. Governor, we have decided to stay in the plant. We have no illusions about the sacrifices which this decision will entail. We fully expect that if a violent effort is made to oust us many of us will be killed and we take this means of making it known to our wives, to our children, to the people of the State of Michigan and the country, that if this result follows from the attempt to eject us, you are the one who must be held responsible for our deaths!

General Motors, shaken by this incredible reaction to the injunction, tried to pacify the sit-down strikers with a public statement that the union's observance of the injunction would demonstrate "union responsibility." The sit-down strikers and the union, now in a frenzy of defiance, didn't even give a thought to General Motors' "gentlemanly request."

The hours went on for the sit-downers with the outlook becoming steadily darker. Finally in desperation, Lee Pressman and Bob Travis phoned Lewis in Washington at 3 A.M. Pressman pleaded with Lewis to come out to Detroit at once. Lewis inquired, "What will you have for me when I get there?" Pressman replied, "Nothing, except that we will have you out here and you can do what has to be done. If you don't come it will mean injunction enforcement, defeat, and blood filling the streets of Flint." Lewis spoke three words, "I am coming," and hung up.

Before leaving for the train Lewis faced a press conference equal in size to one that met with the President that day. *The New York Times* reporting this conference notes that Lewis was asked point blank, "Have you talked to the White House or Secretary Perkins during the afternoon?" Lewis answered, "I am noncommittal on that." At Roosevelt's press conference, the President parried similar questions as being "iffy."

Before leaving for the railroad station, Lewis conferred privately with Roosevelt's right-hand labor adviser, Ed McGrady. Then he literally led a parade of news reporters to the railroad station. There, surrounded by the press, labor leaders, and hundreds of interested citizens, he dramatically announced, "Let there be no moaning at the bar, when I put out to sea," and then boarded the train.

Reporters scampered aboard, staying on until Baltimore, machinegunning questions, "What would he do?" "Would the sit-down strikers defy the injunction?" "Would they march out?" "Was the President going to intervene?" "Did Mr. Lewis have anything to say about anything?"

Lewis was in a jovial mood, answered questions with questions, laughed frequently, and exuded complete self-confidence. He appeared unruffled and assured of victory. Reports of his apparent lack of concern came as a trumpet call of courage to the tension-ridden strikers.

That day *The New York Times* headlines ran:

COURT ORDERS STRIKERS OUSTED TODAY
MEN WIRE MURPHY THEY WON'T SUBMIT.
LEWIS GOES TO DETROIT TO FACE CRISIS.

The next morning, February 3, Lewis arrived in Detroit. His prime concern prior to meeting and negotiating with General Motors was to find out exactly where Governor Murphy stood in terms of enforcing the injunction. Would the sit-down strikers be permitted to sit or would they be forcibly evicted?

Frank Murphy was sincerely devoted to the liberalism of the New Deal. His heart was with the union in this no-quarter war with General Motors. Yet as governor of the state of Michigan he would have to carry out the laws of the state and support the courts and their action—and one of their actions was the Judge Gadola injunction against the sit-down strikers in General Motors. Frank Murphy was also ambitious. He was an excellent possibility for the Democratic party's presidential nomination in 1940 to succeed F.D.R., and he stood an excellent chance of winning in spite of being of the Roman Catholic faith. The climate of the nation had changed drastically since the ill-fated campaign of Alfred E. Smith in 1928. Frank Murphy knew that organized labor and particularly the CIO ranked at the top of the New Deal family. To antagonize the CIO might well annihilate his future career.

It is reliably reported that on the first day Lewis was in

Detroit he was informed by Governor Murphy that President Roosevelt wanted the sit-down strikes ended. Lewis was dumbfounded. He told Murphy: "I was given to understand by the President before I left Washington that the sit-down strikers could continue to sit as far as he was concerned. He said, 'Let them sit, John!'" [14] Murphy then replied: "Look, the President has told me one thing and now you tell me that he told you just the opposite. I do not intend being caught in the middle. I will call the President and you can listen in on an extension." The call was made and when Governor Murphy quoted Lewis's report of what the President had told him, Roosevelt's reply was, "Disregard whatever Mr. Lewis tells you." This answer started the deadly feud between Lewis and Roosevelt.

Lewis, in reviewing his relationship with Roosevelt, stated to the writer: "It was during the winter of 1937 when we were gripped in fatal conflict with the corporation of General Motors that I discovered the depths of deceit, the rank dishonesty and the doublecrossing character of Franklin Delano Roosevelt."

Murphy gambled with time. He decided to ignore the injunction for the moment and stake everything on a quick settlement of the strike between Lewis and General Motors.

On the first day of negotiations, Lewis took a short walk with Knudsen. Upon his return he announced that Knudsen and he had agreed upon national recognition of the Automobile Workers Union by General Motors and also a closed shop. When they heard this, the General Motors associates of Knudsen almost went berserk. They pulled Knudsen off into another room for a twenty-minute, behind-closed-doors huddle. Later they emerged and in the presence of a flaming-faced Knudsen informed Governor Murphy that they would sever negotiations if Lewis again talked privately with Knudsen. Knudsen stood there, the picture of mortification, but silent. Lewis's success with Knudsen was partially the result of careful research. It should be noted that Lewis usually is well armed with data whenever entering a controversy. As Lewis tells the story:

"I had Mr. Knudsen investigated during the early days of the strike and I was repeatedly impressed with the assembly-line character of his mind. There was no question that he was a production genius, however, and his mind operated with the methodical inflexibility of a mechanical assembly line. His mind must logically proceed from step to step with a rigidity that did not permit too much imagination. For example, years ago, while he was an executive with Ford Motor Company, some mechanical condition developed which caused a great number of complaints from many Ford owners. It became sort of a standing joke that you were never certain whether the Ford you drove out would be able to bring you back.

"Knudsen decided to find out what was wrong and then go about fixing it. My information was that he spent about seven months traveling around the country, going from one Ford agency to another and inquiring at each service place what the major complaints were with reference to the Ford car. After this seven months' investigation he discovered the trouble was something that had to do with a spark coil. Knudsen then corrected this condition so it did not recur.

"Now the main lesson of this experience of Knudsen's to me is that I found it difficult to understand why he simply did not send out telegrams to every Ford agency in the country saying, 'Please inform me by return wire what is the major complaint you have on the mechanical operation of the Ford.' He would have secured all this information in a couple of days. But not Knudsen. He, as I tried to emphasize, with this assembly-line type of mind, had to see things for himself, he had to talk directly with the people he dealt with, the people servicing the cars, and in many cases, see the cars themselves. Now with that kind of a mind, once you can get it to accept an initial step it will automatically accept all the implications that follow.

"With that in mind I got Knudsen first to agree that if the workers did not look out for their own welfare, no one else would and that, therefore, they had a right to organize into a union. Once he agreed to this, the next logical step was the closed shop—which he also agreed to. (Here Lewis roared with laughter.) I will never, never forget the looks on the faces of his associates—his fellow officers of General Motors—when Bill Knudsen nodded his head after I announced we had agreed upon national recognition of the union and the closed shop." [15]

Meanwhile the strikers were at bay before the onslaught of

[15] Interview with Lewis, 1940.

the courts. On one side there was an injunction carrying a penalty of fifteen million dollars on the union and all its officers in the event the injunction was not immediately obeyed. In the meantime a military force of 1300 troops had already been concentrated in Flint by Governor Murphy and was suddenly doubled in size as 1200 troops, including light artillery and cavalry, moved in. A blockade was thrown around the strike-bound area, pickets were driven off at the point of bayonets, crews of union sound trucks were arrested, and then the military made their first direct move against the sit-down strikers by barring shipments of food into the plants, which meant forcing the strikers to submit by starvation. This tactic was quickly stopped by an order from Governor Murphy and food shipments into the plants were resumed.

A curious and overlooked detail of that day was that suddenly the 26th Infantry, which had been occupying the Fisher Body plant sector No. 2 area in Flint, was relieved by the 125th Infantry. The 125th was made up mainly of boys coming from Detroit, many of them auto workers and many of them knowing the strikers or known by them or related to them. *The New York Times* reported considerable fraternizing between strikers and national guardsmen. However, at many points in the sit-down area sullen suspicion prevailed. The smell of possible carnage was in the air. Union men were walking around armed with clubs; and a horde of automobile workers from Detroit, Lansing, Pontiac, Saginaw, Bay City, and Toledo descended upon Flint. Here was to be the Waterloo of General Motors or the union. The union was further reinforced by rubber workers from Akron, steel workers from Pittsburgh, and coal miners from Pennsylvania, Ohio, and Indiana. Street fights broke out with coal miners and steel workers right in the middle of them.

The city of Flint had by this time recruited a special police force of five hundred and tolerated armed vigilantes inspired by such groups as the Flint Alliance. The tension was somewhat eased when the National Guard got an agreement from the union that its followers would stop walking around with clubs in their hands and assembling in large groups well stocked with clubs. The authorities of Flint agreed to demobilize their five hundred special policemen and to keep armed vigilantes off the streets. Here we find the municipal administration of Flint, for the first time, recognizing the growing political power of labor.

Friday, February 5, found both General Motors and Lewis refusing to budge. *The New York Times* headline read:

AUTO DEADLOCK UNBROKEN
BUT MURPHY REPORTS GAIN
ROOSEVELT INSISTS ON PEACE

John L. Lewis, flanked by Wyndham Mortimer and Lee Pressman, stood pat for recognition of the UAW–CIO for a beginning period of at least six months. Lewis assumed that within that six-month period the union, with possession of the exclusive right of collective bargaining, would so increase its strength that there would be no question of the indefinite continuance of this arrangement.

General Motors treated this demand as too preposterous to merit discussion. They were willing to say, "We'll recognize you but not for any fixed time period." General Motors felt invincibly armed with the injunction and was convinced that Governor Murphy could not stall longer than another week before being compelled to enforce it and smash the strike.

In Flint that day the strikers held "victory parades," shook wooden clubs out of car windows, and established mass picket lines around the struck plants. The tension began to affect Homer Martin, and he sought help from the AF of L. The answer was a sarcastic rejection.

Between Detroit and Washington the telephone wires were humming. Governor Murphy and Madame Perkins had lengthy conversations, which Perkins then reported to Roosevelt. That evening Murphy recessed the negotiations for an hour and asked Lewis to step into the next room. Murphy closed the door behind Lewis and pointed to a telephone with its receiver off the hook. "The President wants to talk to you, John."

Lewis strode to the phone and picking up the receiver said, "Yes, Mr. President," and the voice that came back was that of Franklin D. Roosevelt.

"Hello, John, how are you? John, we're having sort of a party up here at the White House, but I'm talking to you from my bedroom upstairs and things are very quiet here. As a matter of fact, Sidney Hillman is here, and I've asked him to come upstairs. He's sitting right along side of me. I've had a long talk with Sidney about this situation out in Detroit, and we came to an agreement. John, I think I can get an agreement for you for General Motors to give you recognition for one month. What do you say, John?"

Lewis replied, "Mr. President, my people tell me it's got to be six months. One month is not satisfactory."

There was some hesitation, and then the President continued. "Now, now, John, let's be reasonable about this. How about two months? I'm not sure I can get two months, but I think I can. As a matter of fact, I think I can. Now what about two months, John?"

Again came the answer. "Mr. President, my people tell me it's got to be six months. Nothing less than six months will be satisfactory."

Roosevelt then became irked: "Now look here, John, this is no time to be arrogant about this whole thing. This is a pretty dangerous and critical situation that you're in. How about three months? I don't know whether I can get it, but how about three months?"

Lewis again repeated, "Mr. President, my people tell me it's got to be six months. No less than that."

A few more words were exchanged and then Lewis turned the phone over to Murphy, "Governor Murphy, the President would like to speak to you." With that Lewis left the room.

The next day Roosevelt sent his famous message to Congress requesting that the Supreme Court be reformed. It cannot be questioned that Roosevelt's sole interest in this message was to change the Supreme Court. However, his attack on the judiciary reverberated through the General Motors war areas to the advantage of the strikers. Roosevelt's onslaught on the Court tore the gown of infallibility surrounding all the courts and lessened the popular sanctity of the law. For the moment it rendered the flouting of the injunction less reprehensible; and moments were desperately needed by the union.

In Detroit that night, Murphy, Knudsen, and Lewis met as a subcommittee to discuss and prepare reports for the conference to be held the next day. At this meeting, Lewis dropped his demands that the union be the sole bargaining agency for everyone in G.M.'s sixty-nine plants and limited it to the twenty strike-bound plants. As these were the key plants of the

General Motors structure, Lewis's concession was not as much as it might seem. Actually the organization that bargained for the workers of those strategic plants really controlled the total personnel policy of General Motors. G.M. was rumored to be willing to grant six months' recognition to the union in six plants. If this was true, General Motors was on the road to defeat; for it would mean they had abandoned their "no-six-months" recognition position and the door was open for the union to build up the figure of six plants to twenty.

General Motors through this period continued to participate in negotiation although possessing writs for the arrest of all union leaders because of the defiance of the Gadola injunction. Murphy's ignoring of the injunction placed General Motors in a tight spot. If they forced Murphy's hand so that he would use force against the sit-down strikers, General Motors' public reputation might be boiled in blood. From their point of view Murphy must, as governor, enforce the injunction on his own initiative so that the blood would be directly on his hands and not on law-abiding General Motors.

That day, February 6, Judge Gadola issued a writ of body attachment against all the sit-down strikers, pickets, and union officers. The Sheriff's office, obviously unable to carry out the order of the court alone, requested the use of the National Guard. Sheriff Wolcott wired Governor Murphy:

> Please advise me by wire whether you will place the National Guard now on duty here at my disposal to carry out the orders of the Court or will it be necessary to deputize a sufficiently large group of deputies to uphold the court decree. Your immediate reply is respectfully requested.
>
> Thomas Wolcott

It was squarely up to Murphy, and he could not evade the issue much longer. The issue was whether or not Frank Murphy as governor of the State of Michigan was going to enforce the law of that state. If he did, he would go down in labor history as the Benedict Arnold of labor. If he did not he would have failed to live up to his oath of office as governor. It was a bad Saturday night for Murphy.

General Motors gave Murphy and themselves a forty-eight-hour reprieve by announcing they would refrain until Monday from demanding the enforcement of the law. General Motors was fearful of the possibilities inherent in the immediate enforcement of the order. *They were fully cognizant of the fact that the battle to evict the strikers might well result in the destruction of General Motors' plants and a pyrrhic victory. The General Motors strike bordered on revolution.*

The press reported that day that Governor Murphy was about to declare martial law, which would render civil court decisions ineffective during the period that military rule prevailed. This course of action appeared as too crude an evasion of the issue. There were also press stories that Murphy was going to be impeached, that Murphy was going to evict the strikers, that he was not going to evict the strikers. In essence it was becoming clear that no one knew what Governor Murphy was going to do including Governor Murphy.

The next day Murphy announced that nearly all points of differences had been ironed out and the chief obstacle remaining was sole recognition. Of course, this was the basic issue from the beginning, but Murphy's statement cast the shadow of a possible union victory over all its foes. Into this shadow promptly fled all officials dependent upon the electorate for their badges and bellies. Sheriff Wolcott suddenly wheeled on both the anti-union vigilante groups and the Flint Alliance, warning them that if they attempted to take the law into their own hands, they "will be the first ones arrested." In Flint, the hitherto bitterly anti-union City Commission called a special meeting to try to disband the "special police force." A newspaper reporter cynically commented that Flint was changing its clocks from General Motors time to the United Automobile Workers Union time!

February 7 was a bad day for General Motors. The G.M. directors met and cut their dividends in half. G.M.'s biggest stockholder, Pierre S. du Pont, owning ten million shares, was estimated to have lost a minimum of $2,500,000 on this day. Other auto makers were having a Roman holiday at the expense of General Motors. Nash reported their sales had doubled. Studebaker jumped their production from 6,000 units a month to 7,700. But General Motors was at a standstill, sweating it out.

The tension was terrific on both sides. Homer Martin was discovered walking down a street in Detroit's main business section weeping hysterically. Lewis then dispatched Martin on a nationwide speech-making tour in order to get him out of the picture.

The next day, General Motors, with its back to the wall, stiffened and lunged to the offensive demanding the enforcement of the injunction. Murphy began to wilt. Suddenly the entire strike-bound Chevrolet area was surrounded by bayonets and machine guns. The picket lines that had fraternized with the sit-downers were dissolved. Sit-down strikers were barred from leaving the plants to visit the union office or their homes and then returning to the plants. The morale of the strikers was visibly waning. Murphy was on the spot, and his morale was keeping pace with that of the strikers. General Motors, now having tasted blood, struck again. The weather was icy cold, and they were prepared to turn off the heat in the struck plants and freeze the workers out of the plants. The sit-down strikers countered by opening all the windows. This meant that the fire-fighting equipment would freeze and all the General Motors insurance policies would be voided. Some of the UAW leaders, probably Robert Travis, had carefully read over the insurance policies of the corporation and spotted this one loophole whereby the insurance companies could be freed of any responsibilities for destruction by fire of the General Motors plants. For some hours the key plants of General Motors were completely unprotected by insurance until General Motors capitulated.

General Motors, now in a frenzy from the results of their turning off the heat on the workers, really turned the heat on the Governor. Murphy on his last legs blew up under the additional pressure and stormed into Lewis and Pressman. His voice shaking with anger, he said, "The sit-down strikers over at Chevrolet No. 4 have opened up all the windows. This means that everything inside that plant is going to freeze, including the fire equipment, and all of the policies that General Motors has will lapse; and you've got to do something about this, Mr. Lewis. I demand that you do something."

Lewis looked stonily at Governor Murphy for a moment and then said quietly, "I did not ask these men to sit-down. I did not ask General Motors to turn off the heat. I did not have any part of either the sit-down strike or the attempt to freeze the men. Let General Motors talk to them."

Through Monday, February 8, General Motors pushed its last-ditch legal offensive and stalled on negotiations. The conferences continued only because of the firm insistence of Governor Murphy, who now was stalling for time with the fervent hope that something might occur that would stave off his evicting the sit-down strikers and also evicting himself out of public life. Unquestionably Murphy was emotionally on the side of the union. The sincerity of his liberalism was later borne out by his many opinions as a member of the United States Supreme Court. But the calm, deliberative atmosphere of a judicial chamber did not surround Murphy in 1937. This was an ordeal that he was never to forget.

General Motors again insisted on a secret ballot to be supervised by Governor Murphy to determine how many of their employees actually belonged to the union. This was a shrewd maneuver by the company as first, they felt that the union only represented a minority of their workers. Second, it would result in the suspension of negotiations until the vote had been taken and during this interval Murphy would have to evict the strikers. Third, by stipulating that Murphy was to supervise the election, they prevented the union from raising any question of the honesty of the election, and they also put Murphy in a spot where the corporation was willing to trust him. For these reasons General Motors put forth this proposition, but the union rejected it. The union well knew the validity of G.M.'s charge that the union's membership consisted of a minor part of G.M.'s working force. Lewis publicly announced that the UAW must first be recognized as the sole collective-bargaining agency for the twenty plants closed by the strike and that afterward all other points at issue were to be settled by continuous collective bargaining.

Into this stalemate stepped the American Federation of Labor. William Green, president of the AF of L, phoned Governor Murphy and wired William Knudsen demanding that the "rights" of the AF of L be protected and therefore he and the AF of L were opposed to General Motors' granting exclusive recognition and bargaining to the CIO. Actually Green here was supporting the position of General Motors.

At the afternoon meeting Knudsen suddenly produced his telegram from William Green stating that the AF of L opposed any recognition of the CIO Automobile Workers Union or John L. Lewis. After Knudsen had read this telegram, he looked up at Lewis awaiting his comments. Lewis calmly rose, turned his back on all of the representatives of General Motors and Frank Murphy, then crossed the room to the closet. Slowly and silently he put on his coat. Pressman, startled, followed suit. Frequently not knowing what was in Lewis's mind CIO representatives just imitated his actions. One could hear a pin drop. Lewis then slowly walked to the door. The silence was unbroken until he put his hand on the door knob. Murphy then cleared his throat and called out, "Oh, Mr. Lewis, where are you going?" Lewis slowly turned and stared coldly at Mr. Knudsen for a moment and then turned his gaze on Governor Murphy. After a moment he said slowly: "Why, now that Mr. Green and the American Federation of Labor have entered into this picture, I suggest that you gentlemen also invite Haile Selassie, because he certainly has as much of a following and as much representation among your workers and as much right to be present as Mr. William Green!"

Knudsen and Murphy burst out laughing. Murphy then called, "Oh, forget it, John. Come back here and sit down. Come back here." Lewis took off his coat and strode back to his seat. Never again was William Green or the American Federation of Labor mentioned in the conferences.

Later that evening General Motors continued to maintain an aloofness from any actual discussions. They made it clear that they were present by sufferance because of Governor Murphy's insistence that the negotiations go on. Time was running out, and Lewis was harassing and maneuvering in every possible way to break through the icy disinterest of the General Motors representatives. The leader and strategist of the G.M. position was John Thomas Smith, general counsel of General Motors. Smith was the toughest and most hostile to the union of G.M.'s negotiating triumvirate, which included William Knudsen and Donaldson Brown, who was a son-in-law of the Du Ponts. Lewis focused his attention on Smith, who was sitting next to him.

Lewis has described the scene: "John Thomas Smith was one of the most ruthless individuals I have ever encountered. He was as impersonal and as void of feeling for the workers as though he were a soul-less corporation in human form. He was truly a worthy representative of General Motors. He was the major obstacle to any spirit of negotiations. Finally I turned on Smith, glared, then looked down at the space separating our chairs and cleared my throat noisily with a sound of complete disgust. Then I looked away. A moment later I turned again on Mr. Smith, glaring at him and then with as disgusted an expression as I could possibly muster, I stared down at the space separating our chairs again, noisily clearing my throat. This time Mr. Smith seemed to become aware of my actions and began to shift uneasily in his chair. Again I turned, glaring at him; and as he caught my eye, I turned my head downward staring at the space between our chairs clearing my throat once more as noisily as I could. This time, Mr. Smith, too, looked searchingly and apprehensively at the space between our chairs. I repeated this performance a moment later and this time Mr. Smith, practically in a panic, turned to me and said, 'Why, Mr. Lewis, is anything wrong?'

"This time I brought up my best frown and turning to him I said very slowly, 'Wrong, Mr. Smith? Yes, there is something wrong.'

"Mr. Smith said, 'Well, what is it, Mr. Lewis?'

"I replied, 'Mr. Smith, would you mind moving your chair a bit closer to mine?'

"Smith looked down at the space between our chairs and ejaculated, 'Move it closer to you? Why, we're practically sitting in each other's laps right now, Mr. Lewis. My chair is only about six inches away from your chair. Why should you want me to move closer to you?'

"I then stared at him and with a wistful tone I said, 'You see, Mr. Smith, for the past hour I have been thinking about how someday in the future I would be able to tell my grandchildren about how at one time I sat just six inches away from one and a half billion dollars, but I would so like to tell them that I sat only three inches away! Please, do you mind moving your chair a little bit closer?'

"Smith, purple with rage, leaped out of his chair. He started off with, 'I'll have you know, Mr. Lewis, that I worked my way up, that I was a . . .'

"I interrupted. 'Newsboy, when you were a child . . .'

"Smith said, 'That's right and later on I worked my way through school . . .'

"I interrupted again. 'I'm sure you took some correspondence courses too!' At this point Smith's success story became ridiculous even to him and amidst giggles even from his associates he subsided. The icy reserve of General Motors was now broken." [16]

An experience along the same line occurred later that night. At one point, late in the evening, conversation ceased. General Motors representatives, realizing Lewis was baiting and irritating them to start conversations that might conceivably lead into negotiations, decided to shut up. Finally in a body they got up from the table, put on their coats, and prepared to leave. Governor Murphy remaining at the table, said, "Gentlemen, the conference is not adjourned as yet." The three General Motors representatives then stood in the room with their hats and coats on and their mouths grimly silent. Murphy's invitation to be seated was politely declined.

Lewis coolly surveyed the three representatives of General Motors and then turning to Murphy he inquired, "Governor, is there an Army and Navy store open at this hour?"

The Governor, taken aback, replied, "Why do you ask this, Mr. Lewis? Is there anything you need? I don't think there is a store of that type open at this hour, but I suppose arrangements can be made. What is it you want, Mr. Lewis?"

Lewis again turned and carefully looked over the standing G.M. executives and said: "Well, Governor, I would like to purchase three long suits of red flannel underwear and present them to these gentlemen with my personal compliments. I think they would be much more comfortable standing in this warm room in red flannel underwear than as they are in hats, coats, suits, and what have you."

Murphy tried, unsuccessfully, to refrain from laughter but roared. The spectacle conjured up by Lewis of these three great leaders of the General Motors Corporation decked out in red flannel underwear was too much for the Governor, and he continued to shake with laughter. Lewis joined in the merriment. The G.M. officials looked sheepishly at each other and then

[16] Interview with Lewis, 1940.

without a word took off their hats and coats and sat down again. at the negotiations table.

However, the meeting finally broke up with General Motors still refusing to bargain.

The next day, Murphy displayed an outward confidence to the press which was actually ninety-nine per cent bravado and one per cent wild hope. If a settlement was not forthcoming by the next morning, he would have to order the National Guard to enforce the court's injunction against the strikers and the union. Murphy's back was to the wall. He knew it and General Motors knew it. *The New York Times* reported Murphy's position as of that day:

> Talk that a state of insurrection might be declared by Governor Murphy if present peace conferences fail and that under such a proclamation the National Guard would assist Sheriff Thomas Wolcott in evicting the sit-down strikers . . . It was said that Governor Murphy felt he had done everything possible to prevent bloodshed through his repeated conferences with General Motors and union officials. It was pointed out that he had never issued any statement justifying the sit-downers in seizing possession of other people's property or in defying the courts. He has limited himself to discouraging and delaying any drastic action until the last hope of peace has been dissipated. Reluctant as he still is to do anything that might cause the killing or shooting of anyone, it is understood that the Governor feels that the strikers are in a state of insurrection against the local authorities, especially in their action in defying an injunction issued by Judge Paul V. Gadola, ordering them to evacuate the seized factories by 3:00 o'clock last Wednesday afternoon.[17]

Murphy tried one last desperate compromise. He suggested that General Motors sign a contract recognizing the union not as the sole bargaining agent, but that in practice they would do so. All this time the General Motors proposal for a secret ballot was receiving more and more public support. The union's position was grim.

At this crucial point Lewis refused to retreat. He decided to try to bull his way through. He issued the following succinct public statement:

[17] *The New York Times*, February 10, 1937.

Our position is substantially this: These plants are shut down and operations are suspended throughout General Motors. General Motors and the Governor in these negotiations are recognizing the United Automobile Workers as the bargaining agency to start this industry going again. We are the only agency in this conference. There is no other qualified to negotiate. If we are the bargaining agency to start these plants in operation we must be the bargaining agency after an agreement is reached. That is very simple, very concise and perfectly understandable.

With Lewis now hanging onto the union's demands with bulldog tenacity and General Motors demanding the enforcement of the court order, Governor Murphy was at the end of the road. No one could have done more than he did to help the union. He had stood by now for almost a week turning his back while thousands of strikers defied the law. Now he must give the fatal order.

Around Flint that night of February 9, 1937, the National Guard sprang into action. All units were alerted. Preparations were made to seal off all highways, railroads, and every entrance into Flint so as to prevent CIO members and sympathizers from reinforcing the strikers. The civilian police were mobilized and used for the first time.

In Chevrolet No. 4 and the Fisher Body plants that night, the men were depressed and angry. Was this the end? They nervously clutched sections of door hinges, bars, cushions for shields, and anything else they could hold in their hands. Some wanted to fight to the death, some wanted to run, and all were scared. There was that tightness in the air and inside their chests; the feeling that men have just before they do battle.

In Detroit, that night, the General Motors chieftains were on edge. With nerves at the breaking point they waited for Murphy's order. Maybe they had erred in forcing the Governor's hand. What if there was a horrible massacre? What if their plants were destroyed in the reign of terror that seemed certain to erupt with the Governor's decision? How long would it take them to rebuild their plants and how much more of their shrinking market would their competition raid? General Motors' customers were buying Ford, Chrysler, Studebaker, and Nash products. Was it too late to retract and sign a contract? The nerves of General Motors were snapping. If Murphy now did not put through the order they would recognize the union and avoid the nightmare that now enveloped them.

In Detroit, that night, John L. Lewis went to bed.

In Detroit, that night, Governor Murphy, torn up inside, prepared the order that was to convert Flint into a battlefield and sound the death knell of the union.

In Detroit, later that night, Lewis told the writer, he was awakened by a knock on the door. He opened it to find Governor Murphy standing there tense and pale. The Governor entered and turned to Lewis. "Mr. Lewis, I have here in my hand an official order as governor of the State of Michigan, declaring a state of insurrection and ordering the National Guard to enforce the injunction of the court of the State of Michigan to evict the sit-down strikers from those plants of General Motors which they are occupying by illegal seizure." Lewis, equally pale, glowered silently at the Governor. Governor Murphy continued, "I want to give you an advance copy of this order so that we can avoid violence."

Lewis took the order and read it carefully. It was a brief announcement by Frank Murphy that as the governor of the state he was sworn to uphold the laws of the state; that an injunction of a court of the State of Michigan was now being flouted and that he was sworn to uphold the law and therefore compelled to enforce this injunction. It went on to order officially that on that morning the sit-down strikers were to be asked voluntarily to evacuate the plants. If they refused there would be no alternative except forcible ousting.

Lewis wheeled on the Governor, thundering, "Governor, do you know what this means?"

Murphy, shaken, replied, "Yes, I do, but there is nothing else I can do."

Lewis then turned his back on the Governor, walked across the room and stared broodingly out of the window.

For some minutes the silence in the room alone was audible and then Murphy said, "Well, Mr. Lewis, what are you going to do about it?"

Lewis turned on Murphy. "I repeat, Governor Murphy, why are you doing this?"

Murphy's voice trembled. "You know why I'm doing it. As governor of the State of Michigan, I have no recourse. I'm do-

ing it because I am sworn as governor of this state to uphold
the laws of this state, and I have to uphold the law. Now do you
understand?"

Lewis fixed a stony stare upon the Governor and then began
in a very low voice, "Uphold the law? You are doing this to
uphold the law? You, Frank Murphy, are ordering the National
Guard to evict by point of bayonet or rifle bullet, the sit-down
strikers? You, Frank Murphy, by doing this are giving complete
victory to General Motors and defeating all of the hopes and
dreams of these men. And you are doing all of this because you
say, 'to uphold the law!'" Lewis continued with his voice rising
with each sentence. "Governor Murphy, when you gave ardent
support to the Irish revolutionary movement against the British
Empire you were not doing that because of your high regard
for law and order. You did not say then 'uphold the law!' When
your father,[18] Governor Murphy, was imprisoned by the British
authorities for his activity as an Irish revolutionary, you did
not sing forth with hosannas and say, 'The law cannot be wrong.
The law must be supported. It is right and just that my father
be put in prison! Praise be the law!' And when the British government took your grandfather [19] as an Irish revolutionary and
hanged him by the neck until dead, you did not get down on
your knees and burst forth in praise for the sanctity and the
glory and the purity of the law, the law that must be upheld at
all costs!

"But here, Governor Murphy, you do. You want my answer,
sir? I give it to you. Tomorrow morning, I shall personally
enter General Motors plant Chevrolet No. 4. I shall order the
men to disregard your order, to stand fast. I shall then walk up
to the largest window in the plant, open it, divest myself of my
outer raiment, remove my shirt, and bare my bosom. Then
when you order your troops to fire, mine will be the first breast
that those bullets will strike."

Then Lewis lowered his voice. "And as my body falls from
that window to the ground, you listen to the voice of your
grandfather as he whispers in your ear, 'Frank, are you sure you
are doing the right thing?'"

---

[18] Governor Murphy's father, John Murphy, was jailed at the age of sixteen
in Canada for taking part in a Fenian disturbance.
[19] Governor Murphy's grandfather was hanged in Ireland by the British.

Governor Murphy, white and shaking, seized the order from Lewis's hand and tore out of the room.[20]

The order was not issued, and the next day General Motors collapsed and capitulated at 2:45 A.M. Thursday, February 11. Lewis was confined to his bed with a severe cold, and the Governor and the General Motors' executives shuttled from their conference room to Lewis's bedside. When the agreement was reached, General Motors' John Thomas Smith stood alongside Lewis's bed and said, "Well, Mr. Lewis, you beat us, but I'm not going to forget it. I just want to tell you that one of these days we'll come back and give you the kind of a whipping that you and your people will never forget."

The nation's press bannered the settlement in headlines. The National Guard began to evacuate Flint. The agreement signed at noon on February 11 provided that General Motors agreed to recognize the UAW as the bargaining agent for its members, not to bargain on the matter of general corporate policy with any other group from the twenty struck plants without Governor Murphy's sanction, no discrimination to be shown against the union members, to drop court proceedings, rehire all workers and resume operations as soon as possible. The United Automobile Workers agreed to call off the strike and evacuate the plants, not to have any intimidation or coercion in its membership drive, not to recruit members on company property, to exhaust negotiations before striking again, and not to have a strike when negotiations were about to begin. Both agreed to begin bargaining Tuesday on wages, hours, production "speed-up" and other working conditions.

After the signing of the agreement, which Governor Murphy signed first, the Governor suggested to Lewis that he sign his name above all the signatures on the pact. Lewis replied, "If it's all the same to you, Governor, I will put it last." He signed as "Counselor for UAW and representative of the CIO."

Lewis then issued a statement: "Automobile workers can rejoice in their achievement. The efficiency and precision of their

[20] The order was never seen until about two years afterward, when Frank Murphy was nominated for the post of U.S. Attorney General. Violent criticism was leveled at his past handling of the General Motors sit-down strikes during his gubernatorial administration in Michigan. Among the materials publicly presented in defense of Frank Murphy's "legal responsibility" was this unissued order.

strike has been magnificent. Their devotion and self-sacrifice has been rewarded. They can now perfect their union and go forward. Governor Murphy has contributed greatly to the settlement. The nation is the beneficiary of his statesmanship."

Knudsen told the newsreel cameras, "Let us have peace and make cars."

The union told its members, "Let us get back to work to build cars and build our union."

The UAW was on its way now. The CIO shifted into high gear and raced on to new battlefields.

Flushed with triumph, astride both General Motors and the CIO, stood John L. Lewis. He had generaled an undisciplined but fighting small army against the fabulous entrenched power of the General Motors Corporation and won. He had not flinched from the storm of the sit-downs, but instead had assumed leadership of them. He had captured not only General Motors, but the hearts and imaginations of America's workers. Out of this victory over General Motors was born the legend of Lewis's invincibility. A later, unbroken series of conquests permanently fixed Lewis in the minds of the workers as a man who always won. Labor's tomcat had become a lion. But he was a lion not without wounds. He was hurt and angry with Roosevelt. Lewis felt betrayed. He was convinced that if this President, who had benefited just ninety days before by almost a million dollars contributed in support of his re-election did not stand fast then, he never would. Here were planted the seeds of what was to grow into one of the most bitter feuds and hatreds of the generation—that of Lewis and Roosevelt.

Chapter 7

The Rout

W ITH the defeat of General Motors, the CIO turned the flank of American industry. Now the CIO began to roll up the line of industry, and the war turned into a rout. The giants of commerce were successively and speedily toppled. The roll call of the CIO conquests was the listing of the New York Stock Exchange: Armstrong Cork Company, Caterpillar Tractor, Chrysler Corporation, Firestone Tire and Rubber, General Electric, B. F. Goodrich Rubber Company, Goodyear Tire and Rubber Company, Hudson Motors, Jones and Laughlin Steel, Libby-Owens Ford Glass, Pittsburgh Plate Glass, Studebaker Motors, Timken Roller Bearing, United States Steel, and a host of others.

Some of these made a hopeless last-ditch fight while others capitulated. But all America gasped as United States Steel surrendered without a struggle. There were various explanations offered for this drastically sudden capitulation by the giant of American industry. Among the stories of how this came about is one about an episode at the Mayflower Hotel, Washington, D.C. In December, 1936, this story goes, Myron Taylor, chairman of the board of U.S. Steel, was dining with his wife. Mrs. Taylor noticed Lewis at another table and turned to her husband, saying, "Myron, I want to meet that man. Bring him over here." Taylor did, and a friendship was established that served as the foundation for the agreement between U.S. Steel and the CIO.

This may have contributed to the settlement, but it would be naïve to assume that U.S. Steel's action was based on this personal factor alone. It is known that Great Britain, in anticipation of possible war in Europe, was placing enormous orders with

U.S. Steel, and interruption of steel production would have constituted a menace of the first magnitude to the empire. Because of this, it is reported, Britain subjected U.S. Steel to considerable pressure to take steps necessary to avert any unrest or stoppage. There were also the economic facts of the costs of labor spies, police, and above all the staggering profit losses that could result from sit-down strikes such as were suffered by General Motors.

There were, however, other factors that contributed to the surrender of U.S. Steel. First, Lewis personally engineered the entire move, working with Tom Moses. Moses, a prominent official in U.S. Steel, was a former associate of Lewis in the United Mine Workers of America. Through a series of private meetings between Moses and Lewis, and Lewis and Myron C. Taylor, the arrangements were worked out.

But it is uncontradictable that Lewis singlehandedly won collective bargaining from U.S. Steel without a strike and thereby built the Steel Workers Union. Without this accomplishment the outlook for a steel worker's union was grim. Lee Pressman, then general counsel of the CIO's Steel Workers organizing committee, admitted to the writer, "I don't know what we would have done without Lewis's brilliant move. There is no question that we [the steel workers] could not have filed a petition through the National Labor Relations Board or any other kind of machinery asking for an election. We could not have won an election for collective bargaining on the basis of our own membership or the results of the organizing campaign to date. This certainly applied not only to Little Steel but also to Big Steel."

Following the denouncement of the U.S. Steel–CIO agreement of March 2, 1937, the steel workers streamed into the union by the tens of thousands. The first steel agreement obtained by Lewis was the decisive force in organizing the workers in that industry into a union.

But others, like the Chrysler Corporation, made a last stand. The Chrysler strike was far different from the General Motors one. The bitter hatred of General Motors workers against the heads of their corporation was not felt by the Chrysler employees. Walter P. Chrysler was regarded with admiration and affection by his workers. Lewis told the writer, "Walter Chrysler was a just, decent man, and I always respected him."

Almost immediately after the victory over General Motors, the Chrysler Corporation was gripped by the sit-down strike. Even at the height of the conflict, the slogan on the signs carried by the strikers read, "Mr. Chrysler, we still think you're fair. Prove it!" or, "Will Chrysler lead again with human rights?"

Again Lewis rode into Detroit, and again Murphy left the Governor's Mansion in Lansing. This time, when they met, it was not with General Motors' Knudsen or Smith under the icy shadow of Sloan. This time, it was with the humane, warm-hearted Walter Chrysler and his hard-boiled, anti-union production boss, K. T. Keller. Where in the General Motors situation Knudsen as production chief was the warm, human person and Sloan hostile and unapproachable, the roles were reversed in the Chrysler setting.

Again, Governor Murphy wearily sat at the head of the table. On one side was Lewis flanked by Lee Pressman and UAW's organizer Richard T. Frankensteen; on the other side sat Walter Chrysler with his high command, K. T. Keller and Nicholas Kelley, general counsel. Chrysler appeared helpless against the threats of Keller and Kelley to resign along with other key officials if any concession was granted the CIO. It was also known that Keller and Kelley had the full support of the Chairman of the Chrysler Corporation's Finance Committee, who was also chairman of the Republican party's Finance Committee. Chrysler was reported to have been in misery as his hands were tied by these threats.

Throughout these negotiations Chrysler's Keller sat sneering across the table, disdainfully looking beyond Lewis and his cohorts with cold arrogance. His insulting stares infuriated the CIO leaders. Finally Lewis decided to break down Keller.

The meeting on the day following this decision began as its predecessors had with a lame, strained conversation between Governor Murphy, Pressman, Frankensteen, and Kelley. Occasionally Walter Chrysler would join in with a friendly, humorous story. Everyone was acutely uncomfortable and conscious of the frozen aloofness of Keller. His grimaces were beginning to tell on the nerves of Pressman and Frankensteen as they kept stealing glances at their impassive chief. The hours went by, with Lewis sitting in complete silence. Across from him sat Keller with his manifest scorn becoming more obnoxious to the CIO spokesmen with each passing minute. To Lewis and his associates, Keller's face began to symbolize the attitudes and position of a giant corporation toward its employees.

The tension heightened, and suddenly Keller broke his silence. Turning to Lewis, with a sneer in his voice, he said, "Mr. Lewis, you haven't said a word about this situation. Do you happen to have any comment or contribution?"

Lewis very slowly rose to his feet and with a murderous stare at Keller softly replied, "Yes, Mr. Keller, yes, I have. I am ninety-nine per cent of a mind to come around this table right now and with one fell swoop wipe that damn sneer off your face!"

There was a dead silence in the room. Governor Murphy hastily cleared his throat and announced a brief recess. The Governor got up quietly, nervously looking at Lewis and Keller. Keller seemed to be in a state of shock. Suddenly he shook his head and came around the table toward Lewis. Lewis deliberately turned his back on him and began to walk over to the other side of the room. Keller followed him, then put his arm around Lewis's shoulder. Everyone heard Keller in a pleading voice say, "I'm really not as bad as you make me out to be, Mr. Lewis, really I'm not as bad as that. Believe me, I'm not as bad as that."

Lewis turned to Keller and still with complete dignity said, "Well, Mr. Keller, in the heat of controversy, one is bound to be indiscreet." Keller's resistance cracked after this episode.

Lee Pressman, when questioned by the writer about this incident, remarked, "It is impossible to put into words just what everyone felt at that moment. Lewis, the man, was not threatening Keller, the man. Lewis's voice in that moment was in every sense the voice of the millions of unorganized workers who were exploited by gigantic corporations. He was expressing at that instant their resentment, hostility, and their passionate desire to strike back. There just was no question that Lewis's threat was not against Mr. Keller as a person, but against the Chrysler Corporation and every other giant, soul-less corporation in this country. It was a moment of real greatness, because Lewis transcended his own person and was speaking out the deep yearning of millions to force a great, sneering, arrogant corporation to bend its knee to organized labor. I cannot remember when I have been so moved in my life. I had never before experienced anything so completely devoid of individual personality, for those two voices of Lewis and Keller were really the spokesmen of two opposing fundamental forces."

The next day Lewis cleared the decks as he demolished Nicholas Kelley. Although not possessed of Keller's icy arrogance, Kelley had constantly insulted Pressman and Frankensteen and gone out of his way to bait and goad them. Suddenly Lewis turned on him and began a bitter excoriation. He reminded Kelley of the different position on social issues which his mother had represented as over against Kelley's anti-union stand.

Lewis went on and on and on developing his denunciation in low, cold, withering words. Lewis continued driving and driving into him until everyone thought that Kelley was about to have a fit of apoplexy.

Finally Kelley leaped to his feet and screamed, "STOP IT, STOP IT, MR. LEWIS!" After a good deal more in this vein he finally ended up by shouting, *"Mr. Lewis, I want you to know, Mr. Lewis, that I—I—I am not afraid of your eyebrows."*

Lewis's laughter rolled Kelley out of the fight, and Chrysler gave up. Just after the signing of the contract, Walter Chrysler turned to Lewis and voiced the deep fear of many American industries, saying, "Mr. Lewis, I do not worry about dealing with you, but it is the Communists in these unions that worry me a great deal."

If Lewis could then have talked to Chrysler, he would have told him about the Communists. He would have told him that he had no choice but to accept the support of the Communists. Even after the debacle of 1933 and 1934, when the American Federation of Labor smashed the spirit of unionism, it was the left-wingers who zealously worked day and night picking up the pieces of that spirit and putting them together. We have already seen how a fearfully rigid, unwilling, unbelievably inept, bureaucratic AF of L nearly wrecked the surging uprise of the hundreds of thousands of industrial workers. When the auto workers, filled with disgust, built bonfires with their AF of L membership cards, it was the left-wingers mainly who kept fighting against the disillusionment and cynicism that swept the workers. It was they who kept organizing and organizing and organizing.

When Lewis turned to help the auto workers, he saw that they were being organized and led by the leftists. The leaders and organizers of the UAW group in General Motors were the left-wingers, Wyndham Mortimer and Robert Travis. These two built the union inside the great General Motors empire. If Lewis wanted to take the auto workers into the CIO, he had to take in their left-wing leadership. The UAW officers were split into two camps; President Homer Martin was guided by Jay Lovestone, a former top Communist. Opposed was a co-alition of Communists, Socialists, and other militant union leaders. In the coalition were such outstanding leaders of the auto workers as First Vice-President Wyndham Mortimer; Second Vice-President Robert Travis; Edward Hall; the Reuther brothers, Walter, Victor, and Roy; George Addes; Richard Frankensteen; and R. J. Thomas.

Every place where new industrial unions were being formed, young and middle-aged Communists were working tirelessly. It was the decade of the great depression. The Communist party was then operating in a climate of mass disillusion and bitterness. A generation was growing up that did not know the reality of a job in private industry. The frustration and common misery of the people created a sympathetic interest for all those bearing a gospel of and guidebook to the promised land of security.

In these receptive circumstances, the Communist party was welcomed into many quarters. Their issues and actions appealed to countless Americans. The then Communist program of the United Front enabled them to work with all groups. Then, as is now commonly known, the Communists worked indefatigably, with no job being too menial or unimportant. They literally poured themselves completely into their assignments. The Communist party gave its complete support to the CIO.

The CIO was waging economic war, and as do all organizations and nations in time of war, it welcomed allies wherever they could be found. The fact is that the Communist party made a major contribution in the organization of the unorganized for the CIO.

Throughout this period from 1935 to June 22, 1941, John L. Lewis was idolized by them as well as by the liberals and vast masses of the workers. After Russia was invaded by Hitler, the Communists attacked Lewis in every conceivable way and would have welcomed his being court-martialed and shot during the 1943 war strikes. Lewis was well aware of the degree and proportions of the Communist power within the CIO. To charges of harboring Communist organizers, he would answer, "I do not turn my organizers or CIO members upside down and shake them to see what kind of literature falls out of their pockets." Or again, speaking of Communists, "If they are good enough for industry to hire, they're good enough for us to organize."

When the CIO was being daily attacked as Communistic, Lewis angrily took up the cudgels against red baiting. Yet when a CIO official once began a conversation with Lewis saying, "You know that I am a member of the Communist party," Lewis cut in crisply with, "I did not know. You are dismissed. I will not have a Communist employed by us!"

Lewis always believed that he could control the Communists. Possibly one reason for this error of judgment was a record of more than six years in which the Communists slavishly followed Lewis's line from the beginning of the CIO—to the fatal June day of the invasion of the Soviet Union.

Lee Pressman, former general counsel of CIO and popularly described as a leading left-winger of the CIO, was questioned by the writer on the common charge that the CIO was engineered by the Communist party. His reply to the question is, "Was the CIO engineered by the Communist party? I can answer that question and answer it very clearly without any reservations. The answer is definitely, 'No.'

"John L. Lewis had carefully prepared the groundwork for the formation of the CIO. The timing and initiation of the steel-organizing campaign—the initial activity of the CIO—stemmed primarily from Lewis. The basic objectives of the CIO were formulated by Lewis.

"The leadership of the movement in every sense of the word revolved around John L. Lewis. A common denominator was offered to all who might care to participate in the crusade—

organize the unorganized—to achieve economic and political democracy for the common people.

"Support for the movement came from many sources, including the Communist party. But it was not the Communists or the left which engineered the CIO."

But Lewis could not then discuss the Communists with Chrysler and had to hurry to other battlefields. Not even the drama of the CIO drive could interfere with his first love, the UMWA. Lewis took time out to beat down the coal operators again for another wage increase for his miners. Mindful that the coal industry must be stabilized if his miners were to keep working, he engineered and had passed the Guffey-Vinson Coal Bill, which fixed the price of coal, setting minimum prices for all coal marketed through interstate commerce. At last Lewis smashed the cutthroat price war that was suffocating the industry.

The CIO attack was on in full force, and there was yet much of the steel industry opposed to unionization. The surrender of Big Steel accelerated the organization of the workers in the independent steel companies known as Little Steel. Such companies as Youngstown Sheet and Tube, Bethlehem Steel, Inland Steel, Weirton Steel Company, and Republic Steel made up the array of Little Steel.

In Republic Steel was ruthless Tom Girdler, who prided himself on being as hard as his steel. Girdler was chosen by these companies to lead the fight against CIO.

Little Steel seized upon a question of legal semantics for the issue of conflict. They claimed that while under the law they were compelled to engage in collective bargaining, they would make verbal but not written agreements. There was nothing in the letter of the Wagner Act that specifically stated that agreements must be written and signed.

Girdler seemed to glory in his toughness. His statements were embellished with that touch of profanity and table pounding popularly associated with toughness. His adamant refusal to yield resulted in the long and bloody Little Steel strikes.

There was violence everywhere, and then came the now infamous Memorial Day Massacre of 1937. At 3:00 P.M. Sunday afternoon, May 30, a large group of striking workers, friends, and sympathizers, estimated at between one thousand and twenty-five hundred, assembled in a union meeting at a hall known as "Sam's Place." Many of them had their wives with them and some their children. The meeting was the usual kind of strike mass meeting, or as a *Chicago Daily News* reporter testified in describing the scene, ". . . the typical crowd that I have seen since in various strike mass meetings . . ."

There was a general holiday atmosphere in the crowd. After listening to speeches, the assembly adopted resolutions criticizing the police and their behavior toward the strikers. The meeting was adjourned with a motion that all present parade about a mile to the gate of the Republic Steel Mill and there establish a picket line. Two young strikers then picked up the American flags on the sides of the speakers' platform, and the crowd fell in behind these flag-bearers. As they approached the gate the parade came to a stop before 264 policemen. Then, according to the investigation, with no provocation whatsoever, the police suddenly attacked the crowd with tear gas and then opened fire upon the fleeing men, women, and children. Thirty were shot down, sixty sadistically beaten, and ten died. *Every man shot by the Chicago police was shot in the back.* Following this mass murder, the police seemed to go berserk, beating and gouging the wounded on the field, and their behavior was actually pathological. The nation was horrified, and as each story corroborated the worst, the Chicago police department was denounced from every responsible quarter.

Investigations were immediately launched into this homicidal orgy of the Chicago police. New killings kept pace with each investigation, and twenty days later blood was spilled in Youngstown, Ohio. Here, the deputy sheriffs, tiring of shooting tear gas, switched to bullets and shot down men and women almost as indiscriminately as the Chicago police did on Memorial Day. In Youngstown, however, the men were not shot in the back.

In Ohio, the National Guard came in to maintain the *status quo* of the strike but ended their martial law by strike-breaking. When they arrived they had been warmly greeted by the workers, but they left with their hatred and curses.

Tom Girdler held fast to his refusal to sign a union agreement, and the triumphant sweep of the steel workers organizing campaign was abated. Until Girdler, there was no stopping the

CIO, but Girdler was willing and eager to fight it out. Unlike most other employers, Girdler did not back away from bloodshed. There are those who felt that he almost welcomed it. To some he was a hero—to many others a man so obsessed with what to him were the virtues of hard toughness that he momentarily delayed the trend of the times. The legal technicalities upon which Girdler rested his refusal to sign a written labor contract were upset by the Supreme Court of the United States[1] long after the first Little Steel company had negotiated and signed a CIO contract.

The U.S. Senate Committee on Education and Labor investigated the Memorial Day Massacre. One phase of the inquiry was a Senate hearing that took place three weeks afterward on July 22. The transcript of the testimony is fantastic and indubitably established a large number of Chicago police officers as being either moronic liars or lying morons.

A Chicago police sergeant testified that the strikers advanced "with military precision" plus a flanking maneuver "on the double." The testimony verged on the comic when the police sergeant attempted to square his military terminology with photographs of the crowd. Conceding that the line of march was obviously irregular and apparently unorganized, he said the marchers resembled an army—the Mexican Army. He also identified three of the men at the head of the strikers as the leaders of the army, "because these three men in front seem to have a determined look on their faces, and if they were not leaders they would not be at the head of the column."[2] A police captain testified in support of his sergeant's unique version, after which another police captain's report, filed May 31, which the city police commissioner introduced, described the union marchers as "a very disorganized mob."

As one police officer contradicted the next, the testimony became a classic of pathetic, clumsy lying, as the police tried to extricate themselves from a pure and simple case of deliberate murder. A patrolman seriously testified under oath "that a good many of them [the strikers] were under the influence of marijuana," and "a good many of them seemed to be under

[1] H. J. Heinz Company v. NLRB, 311 U.S., 514 (1941).
[2] Report of the U.S. Senate Committee on Education and Labor, Report No. 46, Part 2, July 22, 1937, p. 13.

the influence of liquor. . . . *Some of them had a monotonous chant, 'CIO, CIO!' "*

Where the Chicago police officers did not personally contradict their own "testimony," their fellow officers promptly did. No police disclaimers could refute a Paramount newsreel depicting the unreasoned callousness of the killing. The newsreel was backed up by the obviously impartial testimony of Ralph Beck of the *Chicago Daily News*. The transparent lies of Chicago custodians of law and order were so nauseating that some of the news reporters at the hearings held their noses. The one fact that stood out clearly was that the Chicago police, on May 30, set a new record for shooting people in the back.

But unknown, even today, to anyone except Lewis and Murray, is the fact that there were other consequences of the Memorial Day Massacre. The blast of police gunfire reverberated to the very top of the CIO and opened the first cracks of what was later to become a violent civil war. Lewis, in reviewing the story of the CIO and steel to the writer, stated, "This began as a result of my conversations with Myron Taylor, which started in October, 1936, and went on until February, 1937. These talks were finally consummated with an agreement whereby the CIO was recognized as a collective-bargaining agency for union members of U.S. Steel, which I believe, at that time, comprised approximately 60 per cent of the steel industry. This victory in steel, coupled with the magnitude of our successes in General Motors and Chrysler, apparently set a stage for Phil Murray's inner feelings and insecurity whereby he decided he was going out and win a battle all by himself. He also felt the general air of success which permeated the nation at that time, the feeling that the CIO was unstoppable, and was convinced that the unbroken string of victories, the very momentum of the organizing drive and the psychology of the times would carry him to victory. With that in mind, Phil Murray then called the strike against Tom Girdler's Little Steel. This was the first time in Murray's life that he acted without requesting my advice. I told him what I thought, and he has never forgotten that." [3]

[3] Two letters from the author to Philip Murray, requesting an interview in which his point of view could be recorded, were unacknowledged. One of those letters was sent registered, June 8, 1949, with receipt requested, registration number 872811. It was received.

However, there was much to transpire before Lewis and Murray were to square off against each other. Topping the list of unfinished business was steel, and beyond that was Franklin Delano Roosevelt, for with the CIO and Little Steel now at each others' throats, Lewis looked to Roosevelt for help. It came on June 30, 1937, with Roosevelt's hostile reaction to the CIO and steel with his quote from Shakespeare, "A plague on both your houses." Lewis, who had been crouching, licking his wounds from what he later referred to as "Rooseveltian catlike scratches," glowered at a vast assemblage of news reporters, "Which house, Hearst or Du Pont?" Although Lewis here again attempted to parry Roosevelt's thrust, he was consumed with anger. Friends of Lewis reported that his face resembled a black thundercloud when informed of Roosevelt's remark. This public rebuff coming fresh on the heels of Lewis's experience with Roosevelt in the General Motors strike was too much for Lewis. The President, apprehensive at the resentment to his remark, tried to relieve the tension by sending out word that he meant not the steel industry and the CIO, but those segments of business that refused to engage in collective bargaining and those labor groups that were engaging in violence. The President's attempted apology was a weak gesture that was increasingly irritating to the CIO.

Thirty days later, Lewis lashed back in words that are now remembered as one of the high points of that year. On Labor Day, September 3, 1937, speaking over a coast-to-coast network of the Columbia Broadcasting System, Lewis publicly attacked the Roosevelt administration:

"Shortly after Kelly's police force in Chicago had indulged in their bloody orgy, Kelly came to Washington looking for political patronage. That patronage was forthcoming, and Kelly must believe that the killing of the strikers is no liability in partisan politics. . . . Labor next year cannot avoid the necessity of a political assay of the work and deeds of its so-called friends and its political beneficiaries. It must determine who are its friends in the arena of politics and elsewhere. It feels that its cause is just and that its friends should not view its struggle with neutral detachment or intone constant criticism of its activities.

"Those who chant their praises of democracy but who lost

no chance to drive their knives into labor's defenseless back must feel the weight of labor's woe even as its open adversaries must ever feel the thrust of labor's power."

Lewis then personally assailed Roosevelt, thundering, "Labor, like Israel, has many sorrows. Its women weep for their fallen, and they lament for the future of the children of the race. It ill behooves one who has supped at labor's table and who has been sheltered in labor's house to curse with equal fervor and fine impartiality both labor and its adversaries when they become locked in deadly embrace."

The friendship between Lewis and Roosevelt was now darkened with suspicion and hostility. As fighters who had exchanged the first blow, they now warily waited for the next move. The storm signals were flying as the revolutionary year of 1937 exploded into the past.

Chapter 8

The Lewis-Roosevelt Break

THE dawn of 1940 found Lewis champing at the bit to break away from what he was now convinced was "an unholy alliance" of the CIO and Roosevelt. The cold war between them was now capped with a frigid personal hatred.

Even before 1937 there had never been the intense tie between these two leaders that the public so devoutly believed. Roosevelt and Lewis had been bound together by the times and their need for each other. Events between them had been piling up since 1937, and by 1940 they began to press upon each other until they broke into a stampede.

Lewis had dedicated himself to a campaign to organize all American workers and set up a mass base that would be the decisive instrument in the creation of what he referred to as an "economic democracy." He found himself swept up in the great crusade for industrial organization. The fire of the CIO had kindled within Lewis a flaming zeal and burning impatience for a new world for workers, their families, and their children. He was now obsessed with impatience. There had been long years, years of bitter defeats for labor, not only for other unions but for his as well. It had been a hopeless year-in and year-out struggle at AF of L conventions trying to start a drive toward organizing the mass industries. Then came the break with the AF of L. Now, with a number of major unions following him, the hour was at hand.

There was a back-drop feeling in Lewis's mind that this Roosevelt, dawdling while precious hours passed into eternity, was an aristocrat with an intellectual sympathy for labor but incapable, by virtue of his background, of grasping the real needs, feelings, and the solidarity of labor, born of common travail. On this point we find Roosevelt's Secretary of Labor and close friend throughout his reign, Madame Perkins, in agreement.

> There are many things about trade unions that Roosevelt never fully understood. I doubt that he understood what solidarity really means in the trade union movement. He tended to think of trade unions as voluntary associations of citizens to promote their own interests in the field of wages, hours, and working conditions. He did not altogether grasp that sense of their being a solid bloc of people united to one another by unbreakable bonds which gave them power and status to deal with their employers' terms.[1]

It had been a long, rough, and dirty road for both Roosevelt and Lewis. The terrific pace of the times made it seem ages back when Lewis made the first draft of Section 7A of NRA.

Lewis had been confused by Roosevelt's uncertainty and lack of enthusiasm for Section 7A. He had begun to believe that the New Deal was to be a profound social program that would include a new deal for organized labor. This President, who talked boldly and decisively, had acted with hesitation and procrastination. It was during his battle for the Section that Lewis developed a campaign strategy against Roosevelt that, with few variations, became his standard tactic against the President. It was the method of using the President's publicly stated position as a weapon against him. For example, the President was for organized labor, therefore he was on Lewis's side. Lewis would announce that he had the President's support, placing the President in a spot whereby if he were to deny the validity of Lewis's announcement it meant repudiation of his labor policy, which at that time would have been a major political mistake.

In the fight for Section 7A Lewis even entered into White House intrigue with a labor-minded White House assistant to the President. Lewis would write to the President, and in the latter's reply to the letter this assistant to the President would insert a brief statement or change a word that would favor the

[1] Frances Perkins, *The Roosevelt I Knew* (New York: Viking Press, 1946), p. 325.

passage of Section 7A, and which would pass unnoticed. Upon receipt of this letter Lewis would promptly get word to many congressmen and senators, saying the President wanted Section 7A passed. Then Lewis would quote the statement in the letter.

Section 7A passed, and with it, through Lewis's mind passed doubts and questionings on the depth and sincerity of this artisan of the New Deal. From that moment there was a cautious skepticism on the part of Lewis, a dislike for the Rooseveltian approach, bordering on the contempt held by a slugger for a boxer.

Nineteen thirty-six was a presidential year. Nineteen thirty-six was also the year that Lewis was to unleash the nationwide organization campaign that was to culminate in the CIO. Mindful that an unfriendly President in the White House might spell the doom of his dream of organizing the unorganized, Lewis chose to give unreserved support to Roosevelt's re-election. To this end Lewis's union made cash contributions and loans to the Democratic party of $486,288.55. Of this total, a large portion of which had been designated as loans, approximately $50,000 was repaid. Added to all this was a sum nearly equal to the cash contributions spent for maintenance and operation of Lewis's political organization, "Labor's Non-Partisan League," salaries of labor organizers assigned to political activity on Roosevelt's behalf, printed material, advertisement billboards, radio time, and the countless elements of a political campaign.

On the heels of Roosevelt's victory came the memorable General Motors sit-down strike. Lewis, hard pressed and desperate for help, publicly called upon the President demanding payment.

Lewis's open call to the President to pay off a political debt resulted in Roosevelt's losing his temper at what he felt was the "unfairness" of Lewis's tactics.

In this constant clashing of personalities the jockeying of Roosevelt by Lewis repeatedly incensed the President. Roosevelt found himself maneuvered into positions not of his own choosing. Lewis's statements were so toned and phrased that for the President to issue a denial would have meant placing himself in an undesired and politically untenable position. For example, in the very beginning of the New Deal, with the passage of Section 7A, Lewis flooded the coal fields with union organizers shouting the slogan, "The President wants you to join the union." This slogan put Roosevelt on the spot where if he were to disavow Lewis's statement he would really be in the position of saying that he did not want the coal miners to join the union, which, of course, was not Roosevelt's position. The President, therefore, remained silent, although recognizing that his silence would be popularly interpreted to the effect that Lewis was correctly quoting the President. Although the power of the presidency is such that it becomes practically impossible for any individual successfully to wage battle against the President, nevertheless, it is also true that the dignity of the office can impair, impede, or actually obstruct retaliation by the President.

Roosevelt's penchant for vagueness and generalities in his statements presented a vulnerable target for Lewis's blunt specific approach. Implicit in Lewis's strategy against the President was the constant challenging threat of insisting that the President be specific and name names. Lewis refused to accept any generalities or nonspecific statements from the President. Since there were many situations in which Roosevelt could not in his right political senses speak concretely and specifically, the end result would be that Lewis would have the final say on the subject.

It was during the General Motors strike, as we have seen, that the first fundamental break came between Lewis and Roosevelt. Lewis, prior to departing for Detroit, was given assurance by the President that the sit-down strikers could continue sitting, and upon arrival in Detroit discovered not only that the President had instructed Governor Murphy to the contrary but had added the postscript, "Disregard whatever Mr. Lewis tells you."

To Lewis this was the rankest perfidy. In 1933 he had felt the President was indecisive, procrastinating, and lacking a deep sympathy for labor, but nevertheless honest. Now Lewis lost faith in Roosevelt's integrity. He distrusted him and realized that he would have to proceed with caution. He felt that the President had fleeced his union out of about three quarters of a million dollars, that if Roosevelt did not express his appreciation at a time as fresh in his memory as only two months after his re-election, the prospects of real support for the future were dim. Lewis, in reviewing his relationship with Roosevelt, stated to the writer: "It was during the winter of 1937, when we were gripped in fatal conflict with the Corporation of General Motors, that I discovered the depths of deceit, the rank dishonesty, and the doublecrossing character of Franklin Delano Roosevelt."

However, Lewis had staked everything on the CIO, and the power of the President would be a telling factor not only in the pace of the organizing drive, but also in its actual success. Lewis then decided that if he and the CIO did not in actuality have the warm support and blessings of the White House, he must proceed as though he had.

For this purpose there was some effective stage scenery available for heightening the illusion to the point where, to the country and particularly to industry, the fiction would appear to be the fact. First, there was Roosevelt's reputation as a friend of organized labor. Second, Lewis's enormous financial contribution to the 1936 campaign, which, at the current diplomatic rate of exchange, was sufficient to purchase fifty ambassadorships to the Court of St. James's and was assumed to be given on a quid-pro-quo basis. The average American assumed that Lewis would be in enormous favor with the administration and on a pragmatic basis would be repaid by strong presidential support in his activities. With this as background, Lewis then proceeded to try to manipulate events to the advantage of the CIO.

The ever increasing hostilities between Lewis and Roosevelt were not monopolized by Lewis. A clue to Roosevelt's feelings on Lewis are to be found in a story told by Max Lerner, New York educator and journalist, who, after an interview with President Roosevelt during this period, reported that the President at one point said, "You know, Max, this is really a great country. The framework of democracy is so strong and so elastic that it can get along and absorb both a Huey Long and a John L. Lewis." [2] When this statement was repeated to Lewis, he snapped, "The statement is incomplete. It should also include 'and a Franklin Delano Roosevelt.'" [3]

It is significant that, despite Roosevelt's expressed private

[2] Personal interview with Max Lerner, December 7, 1948.
[3] Personal interview with John L. Lewis, fall, 1948.

attitude toward Lewis, he, too, publicly simulated strong friendship for Lewis. Roosevelt as the champion of the common man could not afford the shock of a break with the idolized leader of the most militant and active section of the labor movement. Thus both men played their role of mutual affection and unshakable alliance in the public spotlight, but behind the scenes the masks were pulled off and the stilettos pulled out. It is important here to pause and scan Roosevelt's behavior during the General Motors strike.

It must be remembered in this connection, as well as in others, that, with few recorded exceptions, because of the death of the President we cannot learn the facts as Roosevelt saw them. The President cannot answer in his defense. Every picture of Roosevelt conveyed by Lewis is the Roosevelt that Lewis knew. Each person has his own particular conception of another person. The character of the relationship between two people largely determines the picture that each person has of the other. Where a man is an "unethical politician" to his foes, he is a "realistic statesman" to his friends. One of the wisest expressions in Frances Perkins's book is the title, *The Roosevelt I Knew*. One thing we do know is that Franklin Delano Roosevelt was an extraordinarily complex personality possessed of many facets. In these quotations of Lewis we see the Roosevelt that Lewis knew.

We find Lewis charging the President first with a dishonorable action in violating his given word to him. If the Lewis charge was true, then it is a possible conjecture that overnight Roosevelt changed his mind, and fearing a public scene with Lewis, did not inform him of his reversal of thought. With reference to Lewis's second charge that the President did not extend the expected support to the CIO in its hour of trial, one might raise the question what or how much support would comprise the "expected" support. When one remembers that the sit-down strikes were illegal and revolutionary and that, with the exception of Lewis, no recognized labor leader dared to sanction or approve them, it might well have been "expecting" too much to have Roosevelt openly support strikers engaged in a tactic so unprecedented. It could be argued that passive condoning of the strikes or nonintervention was a great deal of support. Secretary Perkins, in describing President Roosevelt's reactions to the sit-down strikers, quoted him as thinking they were doing "something quite wrong and hazardous," but on the other hand reports Roosevelt as saying, "Well, it is illegal, but what law are they breaking? The law of trespass, and that is about the only law that could be invoked. And what do you do when a man trespasses on your property? Sure, you order him off. You get the sheriff to order him off if he tries to pitch a tent in your field without your permission. If he comes on your place to steal, why, you have him for theft, of course. But shooting it out and killing a lot of people because they have violated the law of trespass somehow offends me. I just don't see that as the answer. The punishment doesn't fit the crime. There must be another way. . . ." [4]

Here, then, are these two great leaders of humanitarianism and social justice trotting together, harnessed by public opinion, and yet distrusting each other and bearing a resentment for each other approaching hatred.

To Lewis, Roosevelt's doublecross on the General Motors sit-down strike on top of what he felt was a faithless vacillation by the President during the grim crisis of the CIO was unforgivable. This doublecross became the main factor in a newly outlined picture that Lewis conceived of the President. Events and incidents that followed from that point on served primarily to color and fill in the background and accentuate this mental image of Roosevelt now fixed in Lewis's mind.

Lewis was deeply angered, at times almost desperate, with what he felt to be one of the greatest hoaxes ever perpetrated on the organized labor movement. To the public President Roosevelt presented a figure of forthright courage, of the highest principles, of a man of decisive action, imbued with the deepest humanitarianism and strong convictions, and a devoted ally of the working man and his labor union. Lewis now was convinced that the reverse was true, that he, as the head of the CIO, was actually dealing with an individual, with a President who in reality was convictionless, unprincipled, weak, and vacillating. From Lewis's point of view, Roosevelt was enjoying the New Deal, not because of the deep feelings of positive benefits that were being secured for the workers, nor because of the satisfaction of using power to bring security, health, and other

[4] Perkins, *op. cit.*, pp. 321-322.

benefits to the working class of this country, but rather because Roosevelt enjoyed the use of power purely because of the pleasure of using power—that the organized labor movement was a fascinating toy to him and one with which he could indulge his capriciousness.

Once the field of what was to develop into a life-long struggle of bitter hatred between these two men was plowed, the first seeds were irritatedly planted by Roosevelt when steel and the CIO in 1937 prepared to lock horns in a titanic battle that promised unlimited bloodshed. The pressure of this impending struggle intensified, and in midyear the CIO looked to the Great White Father of labor for a clue, for a sign of his support.

On June 30, 1937, came the fiery exchange with the Presidents' flip comment of "a plague on both your houses," and Lewis's slugging retaliation sixty days later with: "It ill behooves one who has supped at labor's table and who has been sheltered in labor's house to curse with equal fervor and fine impartiality both labor and its adversaries when they become locked in deadly embrace."

The growing tensions and hostility between Lewis and Roosevelt eased off in 1938. Roosevelt was encountering severe resistance in the Senate. A group of Southern senators combined with the Republicans to harass and torpedo successive Roosevelt-sponsored legislation. The President, unaccustomed to Congressional resistance, and not having learned from his disastrous attack upon the Supreme Court, was angered, and again took the offensive. He determined to "purge," among others, the spearhead of his opposition, Senators Millard E. Tydings of Maryland, Walter F. George of Georgia, and "Cotton Ed" Smith of South Carolina.

Roosevelt personally sponsored the opponents to each of these senators in their state Democratic primaries. As we shall see later, the President could not get financial co-operation from the national Democratic party, including the National Chairman of the party, James E. Farley. In fact his "purge" plans were frowned upon by the Democratic party political chiefs.

In desperate need of funds, Roosevelt turned to Lewis and received huge contributions to subsidize this retaliation. A major beneficiary of the money of the United Mine Workers was the Roosevelt-Democratic faction in Maryland that opposed Senator Millard Tydings. One of the leaders of this Roosevelt group was Congressman Allen E. Goldsborough of Maryland, who was later rewarded by the President for his personal loyalty with a federal appointment as a jurist. This is the same Congressman Goldsborough, now Judge Goldsborough, who nine years later fined John L. Lewis and his union three and a half million dollars. This is one of the many instances where Lewis has extended help with the open hand only to be rewarded ultimately with a closed fist.

While Roosevelt was busily trying to purge his enemies, he found his friend and devoted supporter, Senator (now Vice-President) Alben Barkley of Kentucky, facing defeat at the hands of the electorate. This was the campaign where Barkley's defeat seemed probable, the campaign where Roosevelt gave him his official blessings in his widely publicized "My dear Alben" letter, which was the President's personal endorsement. Lewis contributed a large sum of money to Barkley's campaign at the behest of Franklin D. Roosevelt. As a matter of fact, he refused to make the contribution unless the President personally requested it. Roosevelt was away from Washington on a train, and when notified of Lewis's refusal to deal with his representatives, the President then phoned him personally from Albuquerque, New Mexico, requesting the money.

In the light of Lewis's opinion of Roosevelt, one might examine the motives for Lewis's coming to the President's aid. From a cursory point of view it might seem like throwing good money after bad. But the practical considerations in relation to the Barkley contribution were obvious to Lewis. With one contribution, made at Roosevelt's personal request, Lewis expected to achieve two objectives: gratitude from the President and political "co-operation" from Senator Barkley.

It should be remembered that Senator Barkley was the Democratic whip in the Senate. After his November re-election he was re-elected Democratic majority leader, and as such Barkley could reciprocate for the generous aid extended by Lewis by aiding legislation in which Lewis was vitally interested, such as the renewal of the Guffey Act. Senator Barkley responded to Lewis's contribution with a glowing letter of appreciation. To Barkley, assistance was a concrete matter to be concretely reciprocated. He was and always has been loyal and grateful to his friends and those who have extended a helping hand at a time of need.

Second, on a power basis, Lewis was preparing the stage for requesting presidential approval of organization of the WPA by the CIO, by placing Roosevelt under further obligations to Lewis for his aid in securing support for the President. In spite of Lewis's strong feelings against the President he still hadn't abandoned hope that Roosevelt might yet deliver the kind of help that Lewis "expected" of him.

The purge failed and was forgotten; as far as Lewis was concerned, so were he and his contribution. Lewis felt, and with cause, that since he had made a substantial contribution at the direct, personal request of the President, the latter was under obligation to him.

By 1939, Lewis's political thinking had gone far to the left of Roosevelt. Lewis was becoming increasingly interested in the establishment of a third political party. He now fully recognized the sterility of the kind of thinking that would segregate trade unions from direct political participation. By that time Lewis had already spoken out publicly for a third party and had begun to move in that direction. The building of Labor's Non-Partisan League was his first step toward this objective. That year Lewis proposed to the President that the CIO be permitted to organize the hundreds of thousands of workers enrolled on the WPA projects. Lewis recognized, as did everyone else, that the WPA represented a large mass of citizenry that had been particularly effective politically for the Democratic party during its election campaign. WPA had become a significant part of the Democratic party. To Lewis, the organization of the WPA would mean the addition of an enormous number of citizens, who, added to the CIO and Labor's Non-Partisan League, would provide a base for a third party, by which its machinery might ultimately be captured, or else serve as a Trojan horse within the Democratic party. At that time, Lewis assumed, as did everyone else, that when Roosevelt's second term in office expired, he would enter the shadows of the quasi-public life of all ex-Presidents. When this event came to pass, Lewis believed that the Democratic party would then revert to its predepression, pre-Roosevelt character, and there would then be no substantial difference between the Democratic party and the Republican party. Organized labor, and particularly the CIO, would then be at the mercy of the Democratic party, whose resemblance to the character of the Republican party would not be just a matter of coincidence.

Harry Hopkins vehemently opposed Lewis's proposition that the CIO be permitted to organize the WPA, and on the basis of Hopkins's position plus other factors, Roosevelt rejected it. Lewis was reported to be livid with anger when he heard of Roosevelt's decision. He now knew he could not look to the President for any kind of political support or aid in developing the organized labor movement as a potent political weapon. One of his major reasons for making the large 1938 contribution to Roosevelt's attempted Southern purge was to set the scene for the securing of a favorable decision to move in on the WPA. Now Lewis was convinced that he had again been betrayed and was determined that he was completely finished dealing with or supporting Franklin Delano Roosevelt.

Where the first public move toward the break would be made, or who would make it, were matters of conjecture. Both Lewis and Roosevelt laid claim to the loyalty of the CIO membership, their families, their friends, and the hundreds of thousands of progressive liberals—having an estimated voting strength of from eight million to twelve million. This bloc of our population, while insufficient to elect an administration, did hold the balance of power and could defeat an administration. Both Roosevelt and Lewis were the great champions of this crucial segment of our population. The militancy and open political participation of the CIO caused considerable concern in Roosevelt quarters as to what might be the political consequences of such a split.

Furthermore, the public identification of these two as part and parcel of the same philosophy and objectives made it psychologically extraordinarily difficult to make an open break. Both Lewis and Roosevelt found themselves penned together in a prison of joint popularity by their common followers. While everyone was dimly aware of friction and tension between Lewis and Roosevelt, yet the common agreement and feeling was that although Roosevelt and Lewis were engaged in a tug of war, they were both clinging to the rope of the New Deal and neither would ever let go of his particular end. Lewis might pull Roosevelt this way for a bit, then Roosevelt would pull Lewis his way; but in the last analysis they were both pulling forward for those objectives held in common by both the New Deal and the CIO. The fact that the New Deal dream had become a nightmare between these two did not even begin to pierce the popular imagination. Just as a minute part of an iceberg is visible above the surface and almost ninety-eight per cent of it concealed below water, so was the Roosevelt-Lewis struggle obscured to the public view.

It is dubious whether Roosevelt or Lewis ever really believed that a public break would come, in spite of their mutual hatred and fear of each other. They felt caught in the embrace of the popular conception of their role of unity by the working people who supported both of them. This popular interpretation was so strong that to both Roosevelt and Lewis it seemed to be beyond the control of either of them to change or break this relationship. To the coal miner in the pit, the steel worker in the mill, the packinghouse worker in the slaughter houses, the lumber worker of the sunny Northwest, or the man who worked in New York's dark subway, Franklin Delano Roosevelt was not only the greatest President they had ever known but the greatest friend they had ever had, and John L. Lewis was their great knight in shining armor who was leading them out of the economic jungle to the promised land. Both of these men were working together in a common cause, and to both flowed love, admiration, and almost worship from the working men and women of this country. The working class's and liberal's religion had set up its holy trinity. Lewis was their economic god, Franklin D. Roosevelt was the God Almighty. In a significant sense, Franklin D. Roosevelt was the Father, Lewis was the Son, and the New Deal was the Holy Ghost. In that sense, these two men were almost indivisible. They had worked together and built a philosophy and a movement that made it seem inconceivable for one to break off from the other.

Both Roosevelt and Lewis were fearful of the test. This fear, plus practical power politics, forced a public concealment by both Roosevelt and Lewis of the deteriorated relationships between them. One of the phenomena of the age was the curtain of silence that so successfully cloaked the depths of bitterness and hostile maneuverings between them that when the break eventually came it was a bombshell. For weeks afterward, liberals and union leaders were shaking their heads in dazed, incredulous disbelief.

The year was just about three weeks old when Lewis lashed out. On January 24, 1940, at the Golden Anniversary Convention of the United Mine Workers of America at Columbus, Ohio, John L. Lewis delivered the first directly aimed personal attack on Franklin D. Roosevelt and the Democratic party. His words were featured on the front pages of every paper in this country. ". . . Labor today has no point of contact with the Democratic administration in power, except for casual and occasional interviews which are granted its individual leaders. In the Congress, the unrestrained baiting and defaming of labor by the Democratic majority has become a pastime, never subject to rebuke by the titular or actual leaders of the party.

"As the current year opens, the Democratic party is in default to the American people. After seven years of power, it finds itself without solution for the major questions of unemployment, low national income, mounting internal debt, increasing direct and consumer taxation, and restricted foreign markets. There still exists the same national unhappiness that it faced seven years ago.

"Labor and the people are losing confidence. They fear for the future and rightfully so. It is estimated that approximately twenty-five million men are under arms in Europe and Asia. Nearly seventy million other men are engaged in servicing these contending armies. When these men are returned to the pursuits of peace as eventually they must be, the effect upon our nation's remaining foreign trade will be devastating.

"The present Congress is without a program, except to enact necessary appropriations in ample time to engage in the national quadrennial political marathon.

"I am one who believes that President Roosevelt will not be a candidate for re-election. Conceding that the Democratic National Convention could be coerced or dragooned into renominating him, I am convinced that, with the conditions now confronting the nation and the dissatisfaction now permeating the minds of the people, his candidacy would result in ignominious defeat. . . ."

But Lewis was wrong. Roosevelt was nominated for a third term. Opposed to him was Wendell Willkie as Republican standard bearer, and between the two stood Lewis, trying desperately to plot his political course. The CIO was sailing before the stiff wind of the Roosevelt New Deal, and to slam down the tiller now and change drastically in the Republican direction might well capsize the CIO. If he decided upon this change, would the CIO follow his leadership? That was a moot question. Lewis, victorious and determined, constantly praised and eulogized by the unions of the CIO, was confident that his people would follow.

There was the course of not endorsing either candidate and repaying Roosevelt by repeating his "plague on both your houses" on both Roosevelt and Willkie. This Lewis was sorely tempted to do, but he recognized the untenability of this position for three reasons, all of them purely pragmatic. He could not find it possible at that time to abstain from direct participation in either camp—there was too much at stake. He felt that if he were to follow a hands-off policy, nearly all CIO members would vote for Roosevelt. He was keenly aware of the role of the left wing within the CIO. The Communist party at that time was following a line of condemning the war in Europe as an "imperialistic war" and attacking Roosevelt as a war monger. On the other side, they attacked Wendell Willkie as a barefoot Wall Street boy. If Lewis came out with a condemnation of both the Republican and Democratic parties, he would be supporting the left wing's position on the election, thereby greatly enhancing their prestige and consolidating the position of all the left-wing leaders in the CIO. They would then turn to their people and say, "Look, even our great John L. Lewis agrees with us." On any one of these three counts abstaining was made impossible. The remaining avenue was to support Roosevelt for the third term. By late summer of 1940 Lewis was fighting circumstances that he felt were trapping him into the support of the President.

Everyone knew that to millions of working men and women, John L. Lewis was the labor messiah who had come to deliver them from evil working conditions and low wages, and to give them security in their jobs. These were the same men and women who loved and followed Roosevelt. The consequences of such a reversal of the political relationship between Roosevelt and Lewis were too enormous to contemplate at that time.

During this period, the growing hostility between them was stimulated and given considerable impetus by most of the gossip columnists and the general climate prevailing in Washington. Trivial events became magnified out of all proportions; and, when events did not occur, they were invented. Regardless of all this, however, there was a universal opinion that Roosevelt would have a reluctant Lewis in his camp by November. The idea that Lewis might politically oppose Roosevelt was still completely incomprehensible to anyone.

By early fall all avenues of communication between Lewis and Roosevelt were closed. Dan Tobin, ardent New Dealer and president of the AF of L's Teamsters Union was Roosevelt's personal labor representative and the man who made contact with most labor leaders in trying to secure their support for the President. Tobin's visits to Lewis's office in the United Mine Workers Building gradually ceased. This was one index of the strained relationship between the President and Lewis. It is doubtful whether Tobin's presence at this point would have made any difference, since Lewis was convinced that Tobin was so completely committed to Roosevelt that in any liaison activity between Roosevelt and Lewis Tobin's sole concern would be Roosevelt's interests. Sidney Hillman was constantly with Roosevelt and in him there was a potential line of communication. The use of Hillman as an intermediary, however, was impossible for two reasons. First, Lewis no longer trusted his own lieutenants, including Sidney Hillman. He felt that they were unduly influenced by the President's personality and his office. Second, it would be an impossible situation for the chief of the CIO to have to deal through one of his own union subordinates with the President of the United States. Furthermore, any agreement between Lewis and Roosevelt would have to be of such scope and character that it could only come from a direct meeting between the two. The great and only contribution that could be made to this effect by an intermediary would be simply to facilitate this meeting and arrange it in such a manner that it would "save face" on the part of both parties, so that neither one would feel that he was in the position of having asked for the meeting.

Time was running out and there were only about sixty days remaining before the election. The political weather around Lewis and the Roosevelt New Deal was sultry and ominously silent. If nothing was done now, the break would be inevitable. At this point, a last attempt was made to bridge the rapidly increasing gap between Lewis and Roosevelt. The final negotiators were the author and the Roman Catholic Bishop Bernard J. Sheil of Chicago. An arrangement was devised whereby Lewis, expressing complete confidence in the integrity of the author and the Bishop, was willing to enter negotiations with the President. Bishop Sheil got in touch with the President and was informed that the President was fully prepared and eager to try to close the breach and that he definitely wanted Mr. Lewis's support in the campaign.

The long, close friendship between Bishop Sheil and the writer enabled the negotiation of arrangements to be carried out with dispatch. Bishop Sheil not only supervised the arrangements at the White House, but was present when a number of Lewis's statements were made. The objective of a Roosevelt-Lewis rapprochement, which Bishop Sheil and the writer were striving for, was a cause that all liberals and such CIO leaders as Philip Murray and Sidney Hillman were anxious to see realized. The only group in the CIO which at that time would have disapproved the negotiations were the Communist-led unions, which were then unalterably opposed to Roosevelt.

Negotiations began first with a series of personal conferences between John L. Lewis and the writer. In the beginning, Lewis expressed an intense anxiety about the situation and a desire to bridge the gap between Roosevelt and himself. Lewis, despite personal dillusionment and anger with Roosevelt, was willing to make one more attempt on a *different basis* to work along with the Roosevelt administration. Previously, Lewis had always given the President support, financial and otherwise, without any prior commitments except the simple belief that the President would reciprocate in concrete terms. This reciprocation had not materialized. Now Lewis intended to reach an agreement with the President whereby Roosevelt would commit himself in advance of Lewis's delivery of support. Lewis hoped to carry on the New Deal to a point where a solid progressive labor-farmer base would be developed. This labor-farmer organization would serve as the foundation for a progressive pressure bloc within the Democratic party that might eventually capture the party or else serve as the base for a third party. Lewis favored the latter to the point of almost declaring and starting a third party. He was angry and disillusioned almost to nausea with labor's being forced to depend upon the actions or pledges or "whims" of one individual, Roosevelt, or one party, the Democratic party. Lewis expressed his distrust of Roosevelt's integrity, particularly with reference to Roosevelt's friendship toward the labor movement or the CIO. A presentation of the verbatim statements made by Lewis in these meetings with the writer will be more revealing of the issues and the intensity of feeling than any description.

At the first meeting the writer queried Lewis: "You say, Mr. Lewis, that you want assurances, guaranteed assurances, from Mr. Roosevelt of his friendship to organized labor? It seems to be a sort of commonly accepted idea that Mr. Roosevelt is one of the greatest friends of organized labor in the history of this nation. Certainly under his administration more pro-labor legislation has been passed than any other national administration can claim. How do you reconcile that fact with your present feelings about Roosevelt?"

An angry look came over Lewis's face. He looked squarely at the writer and snorted: "I have sat quietly and patiently, Saul, while the press and various other groups have drawn their own conclusions of my relationship with the President. You see, Mr. Roosevelt is a peculiar person. Everybody says I want my pound of flesh, that I gave Mr. Roosevelt $500,000 for his 1936 campaign, and I want quid pro quo. The United Mine Workers and the CIO have paid cash on the barrel for every piece of legislation that we have gotten. We have the Wagner Act. The Wagner Act cost us many dollars in contributions which the United Mine Workers have made to the Roosevelt administration with the explicit understanding of a quid pro quo for labor. These contributions far exceed the notions held by the general public or the press. Is anyone fool enough to believe for one instant that we gave this money to Roosevelt because we were spellbound by his voice? It is common knowledge that we spent approximately three quarters of a million dollars in the 1936 campaign. And you might be interested to know that the $500,000 direct contribution wasn't my price, but was the figure named by the White House, and I was given approximately forty-eight hours to get that money. Certainly there was a quid pro quo—the right for labor to organize. But there was more than that. The sums we spent in 1936 were not only cash contributions that were made to the Democratic party, but also were money expended in terms of salaries for organizers and other personnel who worked full time organizing and electioneering for Roosevelt. Radio time purchased, billboards, hand bills, literature, and all the other paraphernalia that are part and parcel of the process of being elected President of the United States did not come gratis.

"But there is much that the public does not know. In 1938 when Franklin D. Roosevelt decided that the time had come for him to execute the 'Southern purge,' he not only selected the opponents to these men for the election but threw what personal weight he could in terms of his own prestige and what strength he could muster out of the Democratic party behind them. He did everything he could to purge these dissenters with his program. I believe that it was here that the first great real break between Franklin Delano Roosevelt and many of the financial interests and the power interests of the Democratic party took place. Where was Jim Farley at this time? Where did the money come from that Franklin D. Roosevelt siphoned into these Southern states to try to bolster up the fight against the anti-New Deal senators. Where did the money come from? I'll tell you where it came from. Right here, from the coffers of the United Mine Workers of America. It came by request of the President of the United States through one of his trusted aides. You tell this to the President, and if he questions it, and I'm certain that he will not, you may inform the President that I am perfectly willing to name names and sums, chapter and verse, to satisfy any slight amnesia that there might be on this particular issue. You ask me for gratitude in terms of an administration that we have literally poured our life's blood into supporting! You wonder that I do not express the feeling that one should have for a great champion of labor. I say that labor's champion has to a large extent here been a bought and paid-for proposition. There is nothing we should be grateful for when we paid cash on the barrelhead at the price demanded for it.

"I have never spoken of that before, but I am telling you this just so that you will know whatever President Roosevelt asked me for, at no time and in no way did I ever fail. Of course, you will at least give me the benefit of the doubt to recognize that if my feelings are strong on the subject, there are reasons and plenty of reasons. After all, I am a sane man, and I didn't suddenly wake up one morning on the wrong side of the bed and say, 'From this day on I do not like President Roosevelt.' Now there have been a great many things that have happened, a great many actions which have convinced me that with reference to organized labor the man has played an ingenious role of holding out with his right hand and offering all the benefits of the world and then quickly taking away these benefits with his left hand. Let me give you an example of what I mean.

"You know that Representative Howard Smith of Virginia is a labor-baiting, crackpot fool, a menace to the nation. When that—shall we call him a gentleman?—appeared in the House of Representatives he was the butt of ridicule of all decent-minded, good-thinking representatives of the people; and even those who were reactionaries, and there were plenty of those— even they regarded Howard Smith as a buffoon. But the CIO took no chances, and every time Howard Smith introduced a union-busting bill we fought it with all of our strength. We supported the interpretation of the representatives that this man was a bigoted fool. It wasn't long before Howard Smith had no influence at all in the House of Representatives excepting the fact that whenever he opened his mouth, he would force those others who happened to be in the hall to yawn—and then like a bolt out of the blue it happened. Howard Smith was invited to lunch with the President! He returned from that luncheon adorned with the prestige of a White House luncheon, a person recognized by the President. He quickly gathered about him a new following, and just as quickly was he transformed from a harmless clown into a tremendously dangerous person of authority.

"I went in to see the President that afternoon and asked why he had done that. The President turned to me. 'Why, John, you seem to be upset about it.' I said, 'Well, I am angry, definitely so.' The President said, 'Why, John? I just can't understand it. I called him in here to tell him that I disapproved of his anti-labor actions. I thought I was doing you a favor.'

"I told the President that he should have known better, that he should have known that his luncheon would enhance the prestige and influence of Howard Smith, and it would certainly aid and abet his labor-baiting progress. The President shook his head, 'Why, John, I just don't understand it. Here I try to help you fellows out, and you come in feeling that way.' " Lewis grimaced at the writer, shrugged his shoulders and continued, "He expected me to believe that! Would he expect anyone to believe that? Even a precinct captain would have sufficient political savvy to recognize the consequence of that kind of an action, and with Franklin D. Roosevelt's political sagacity, to give that kind of an answer to me was not audacity, it was a bare-faced lie that only a damn fool would believe. I would challenge anyone in this country, even Roosevelt's most devoted admirer, to accept that kind of a statement as being the truth. He has done the same thing with Martin Dies that he did with Howard Smith."

A meeting was arranged between Roosevelt and Lewis. The President phoned Lewis inviting him to come to the White House the next afternoon. Lewis accepted the invitation. Shortly after Lewis's return from the meeting he gave the writer the following report: "The President and I spent about twenty-five minutes together. When I came in he was cordial and began to discuss a report or a plan which he had before him which involved the setting up of a co-ordinated production schedule for this nation in the state of the present world emergency. He asked me for my reaction and I gave him some of my opinions. We chatted generally and then I left, with the understanding that we would probably have another meeting in the near future. That's all."

From other comments made by Lewis and his daughter Kathryn Lewis[5] to the writer on this meeting with the President, it was evident that while the President was discussing his

[5] It will come as a shock to many Lewis critics who have attributed Kathryn Lewis's feelings toward and advice to her father as a factor in the break with Roosevelt to know that this attempt to reunite Lewis and Roosevelt had her ardent support. Kathryn Lewis was determined to avoid the break and fought to maintain negotiations until the end.

plans for a general over-all commission to accelerate efficient production for the defense program, Lewis pulled out a memorandum from his pocket and said to the President that he too had been thinking over ideas for improving the defense program and that here was what he had in mind. Lewis then told the President of his proposed plans. From a White House source it is learned that at that time the President's reaction was: "After I told John something of the general outline of my plan, he pulled out a plan from his pocket and practically told me in so many words, 'Well, your plan is pretty good. Now it just happens that I have given some thought to the matter and here is a real good plan and one which takes in a lot of matters which you haven't thought about.'" Either way, whether it be by Mr. Lewis's report or by the White House report, it is quite certain that this conference was unsatisfactory.

The writer asked Mr. Lewis whether anything was discussed about labor in terms of Roosevelt's actions toward the CIO or about any of the grievances Mr. Lewis had, and the answer was, "No. The situation was not conducive to that kind of a discussion, and the President did not bring up anything. I just discussed what happened to be in the President's mind."

The next day another meeting was held with Lewis, at which the writer asked Lewis for solid and specific terms necessary for reaching an agreement with Roosevelt, that it was essential to know exactly what was to be the quid pro quo so that these terms could be laid before the President. The writer expressed his hope that a reconciliation could be effected very quickly and that his deep concern was that time was operating against the possibilities of a reconciliation. Lewis's jaw jutted forward, and he paced the floor for some minutes, chewing solemnly on his cigar; he then turned to the writer and spoke very slowly, "Specific terms? I am not prepared to bargain the fate of the CIO and the hopes of the working men of this country for a few paltry, specific terms. Sir, I want and insist upon a general understanding, a general trust, and above all integrity. I want to know what Mr. Roosevelt's intentions are with reference to the labor movement; and, if his intentions are those of a friend, then he has my support. Along the line of that general understanding, there are certain specific gestures that he could make, questions that he could answer if he would. Yes, he could reappoint J. Warren Madden as chairman of the National Labor Relations Board. At the present time he seems to be hesitating a good deal on this point. He could accord organized labor the recognition of real consultations on our defense policies and not courtesy political consultations. Why has he failed to appoint a commission from labor, industry, and the Government to plan a real program to meet the national problem of unemployment? Does he think he and his fawning lackeys know all the answers? If he is a friend of labor why does he turn his back and permit the emasculation of the Wages and Hours Law? I repeat, sir, why? Why, if he is such a great staunch friend of labor does he condone his administration's policy of awarding defense contracts to violators of the National Labor Relations Act, the Wages and Hours Law, and the Walsh-Healy Act? Why, if he is a friend of labor?" Here Lewis paused, then continued in a grim voice, "If he is a friend of labor, why are there no answers to these questions? Evasions, yes; answers, no! Apparently the real answer to all these questions is that Franklin Delano Roosevelt is not labor's friend. He is listening to the voices of reaction and not to the voices of labor. If Mr. Roosevelt is sincere in his friendship for labor, *then I insist he desist from raiding the ranks of the CIO.*"

The writer was startled and asked, "What do you mean, raiding the CIO?"

Lewis wheeled, thundering, "What do I mean? Why isn't he content to be the President of the United States? Why does he also insist upon trying to be the president of the CIO?"

The writer sat quietly, as Lewis continued, "He has been raiding the CIO for the past three years. He has been carefully selecting my key lieutenants and appointing them to honorary posts in various of his multitudinous, grandiose commissions. He has his lackeys fawning upon and wining and dining many of my people. At proper intervals he has unveiled to them the glory of admission to the White House and permitted them to bask in his presence. He has been engaged in a deliberate conspiracy to wean away the primary loyalty of many of my lieutenants from the CIO to himself. This has been apparent and has been going on, I would not say consciously and deliberately, from 1937 to 1939, but during the past months it has been deliberate, conscious, and of extremely vicious and evil intent.

"It is difficult enough for me to maintain the organizational structure and discipline necessary to carry forth the ideals and the aspirations of the CIO so as to be able to meet and surmount successfully the titanic obstacles in opposition which confront the workers of this country. Now Roosevelt has rendered it increasingly and unbearably difficult with his contemptible boring from within. This has resulted in the dilution of the drive and singular loyalty which is necessary for my lieutenants to have to complete successfully the task which we have set for ourselves—the organizing of all of the unorganized in this nation. I can give you, and I'm perfectly willing to give you and the President of the United States, chapter and verse to support this statement which I now make to you.

"Take the appointment of Sidney Hillman to the Advisory Commission to the National Defense Council. Why, the first I knew of that appointment was when I read about it in the morning papers at breakfast. Franklin D. Roosevelt knows better than anyone else the importance of clearing through proper channels and the proper form and the proper respect due to organizations. If any outside group went into his organization and deliberately took one of his lieutenants without consulting him, Roosevelt or the leader of any organization so involved would regard this as an act of war and proceed accordingly. I do not. I regard it for what it is, another example of the deliberate raiding policy engaged in by Franklin Delano Roosevelt against myself and the CIO. Roosevelt could just as easily have called me on the phone and said to me, and I can see him doing it, 'John, I want Sidney Hillman on my Labor Advisory Commission to the National Defense Council. Now John, what do you think of that?' My answer would have been, 'Mr. President, I believe that your choice is a wise, prudent one, and I shall not only call in Sidney Hillman tomorrow morning and inform him of your choice, but also tell him that in this new position he would have the full and unreserved support of the CIO and myself in every human way.'

"But instead of that, what did Roosevelt do? He did just what he has been doing for the past year and a half. In a quiet, confidential way he approaches one of my lieutenants, weans his loyalty away, overpowers him with the dazzling glory of the White House, and appoints him to a federal post under such circumstances that his prime loyalty shall be to the President and only a secondary, residual one to the working-class movement from which he came, here, in this case, to the CIO. You mark my words, if Franklin D. Roosevelt ever tells Sidney Hillman to break a strike, Sidney Hillman will issue the order to break a strike. Of course, Sidney's head was so turned by Roosevelt's personal attention that he didn't think it worth while consulting with his associates. Sidney often told me I could never understand what it meant to a person who was an immigrant not only to be welcome in the White House but to have the President call him by his first name. But the seduction of Hillman by Roosevelt is not particularly propitious for a trusting, co-operative relationship."

Lewis leaned back in his chair, tired from the outburst; then he smiled and began reminiscing, chuckling here and there. Finally he got back to Roosevelt and still smiling continued: "Mr. Roosevelt has a sense of humor about some things, but when it involves his own person, you can't very well discuss it. After all, he is President of the United States, but during the old days of 1936 I remember once being notified that a gentleman wanted to see me who had something very important, very confidential to discuss. I saw this gentleman, and he turned out to be some kind of a lunatic, a crackpot who claimed to have discovered some kind of an invention, and when you turn it on and aim it in one direction you can read what the people are thinking. Turn the contraption toward Moscow and turn the lamp on, and according to this man it would start broadcasting all the things which were going on in the minds of the Russian Communist government. Well, I told this lunatic if such an invention were true, it would be a great aid to the United States, and it was too important to be entrusted to any subordinate officers of the Government. I gave him an extraordinarily urgent letter to the President. The President immediately saw him, and I understand that the lunatic took about thirty minutes of his time explaining his invention. Then the President retaliated by sending out orders for the FBI to pick up another crazy crackpot. He gave that man a letter of introduction to me. Of course I saw the man, and it took me almost an hour to get rid of him. I suppose you could call it kid stuff, but he had a sense of humor about this." Lewis's face suddenly hardened.

"There were other times that were humorous in a tragic sense such as the afternoon I went to see the President about a month ago on a certain very important matter concerning the NLRB and some other issues—issues of vast importance. Well, when I came into his study he was bent over a big map of the oceans, the Atlantic Ocean, British Channel, etc., and he had a lot of little boats representing the British fleet and the American fleet and kept moving them up and down saying to me, 'You see, John, if we move this one over here, they will be able to get in over there.' I would listen respectfully and say, 'Mr. President, I would like to bring this matter up.' He would wave it aside. 'On the other hand, if I get these boats over here, we could block it off there.' I got a bit sarcastic and remember muttering something about sending him an electric train for Christmas so he would have more to occupy his time, and walked out.

"Well on top of all that, there is all the intrigue and the gossip and the mental quirks of Washington. You walk through a lobby with a big smile and you set loose a million rumors that something good has happened. You walk through with a frown, and the papers come out with editorials about planning something with the President. And I am sure that the same thing happens at the White House, and I suppose we are a little at fault, and we see windmills where there aren't any." Lewis laughed out loud, and then suddenly frowned. "People think that I am a prima donna, but I say that all of us have our personal quirks and prides and eccentricities, but Franklin Delano Roosevelt shouldn't be the person to bring up that point about me."

The negotiations limped along, and Lewis began suggesting to the author that Wendell Willkie was an honest, capable, socially minded person who could make a good President. As more and more statements along this line were dropped by Lewis, the author became convinced that Lewis was not uttering them simply as a tactical move to force the President into an agreement. It became increasingly clear that unless this situation was resolved within the next ten days Lewis would break with Roosevelt and join in the support of Wendell Willkie for the presidency.

I sent an urgent message to this effect which was carried to the

President. He seemed to grasp the seriousness of the situation and indicated concern. Within the next forty-eight hours word began coming back that Roosevelt's advisers were convinced that this threat of Lewis was unadulterated bluff and that they were so advising him. It was definitely established that Harry Hopkins was adamant in his conviction that Lewis was trying to high-pressure the President.

There is a reliable account of an episode at a Sunday-night White House supper that took place the first week end after the warning. One of the guests at this supper who was then chief of the Farm Security Bureau, Will Alexander, told the author some years later that the President suddenly threw a bombshell into the dinner conversation by saying, "I have a message or call it warning that John L. Lewis may support Wendell Willkie. What do you think?" With that, a New York woman highly publicized for her activities with labor-union officials and in whom the President expressed great confidence by high appointments, leaped to her feet in great excitement. She almost screamed, "Mr. President, how can you say such a thing with any seriousness. It is too fantastic and absurd. Whoever told you that is a liar or a fool!" She then raised her purse high, thumping it, and continued, "Mr. President, I have Mr. Lewis right here—don't give him a second thought. Lewis will support you—he wouldn't dare not to!"

This miscalculation of the President, stemming from his advisers, was one of the misjudgments resulting in the collapse of this last-ditch attempt at reconciliation.

The last meeting between John L. Lewis and the President occurred eight days prior to Mr. Lewis's coming out for Wendell L. Willkie. It was on Thursday morning, October 17. The conference took place in the President's bedroom. Mr. Lewis was ushered in. The President was in bed. This is the account of what took place, told to me that afternoon by John L. Lewis and repeated a few hours later by his daughter, Kathryn Lewis:

"The President seemed to be quite uncomfortable. His face had an unhealthy pallor, and he seemed to be laboring under a great deal of tension. After greeting me, he said, 'John, sit down over here by my side.' I sat down. After a moment's silence, he said, 'John, I want your support.'

"I said, 'You mean, Mr. President, you want the CIO's support. If you want the CIO's support, what assurances can you give to the CIO?'

"The President became irritated and snapped at me, 'Well, what do you mean? Haven't I always been friendly to the CIO?' I didn't answer. He continued, and his voice rose angrily, 'Haven't I always been a friend of labor, John?'

"I said, 'Well, Mr. President, if you are a friend of labor, why is the FBI tapping all my phones, both my home and my office, and why do they have instructions to follow me about?'

"The President said, 'That's not true!'

"I said, 'I say it is true!'

"The President said, 'That's a damn lie.'

"I got up, looked down at him and said, *'Nobody can call John L. Lewis a liar and least of all Franklin Delano Roosevelt!'* Then I started walking out and got my hat and coat. Just as I got to the door, the President called out, 'Come back, John. I want to talk to you.' I walked back and I said, 'My phones are tapped, and they are, and everything I said is true, and whatever I said I know because I can prove it by Frank Murphy, who told me so and who knows about it because he has seen your orders to the FBI to do so.

"The President changed the subject. I stood there with my hat in my hand and my coat on my back. We engaged in small talk about minor and different things for about ten minutes. Finally I stretched out my hand and said, 'Good-by, Mr. President.' The President was quite upset and nervous. I guess I wasn't feeling too game myself. His face became quite hard, and he turned it away from me, and even when we shook hands he was looking the other way. I walked out. Roosevelt and I are done."

The negotiations that had begun with such high hopes burst like a skyrocket across the sky, and now there was nothing left, no way to try to bring these two leaders of the working people together again. Lewis was going for Willkie. Lewis and his family knew it. Franklin Delano Roosevelt knew it. Bishop Bernard J. Sheil and the author knew it, but to all others there was no sign of even a break.

The week end passed quietly, and then on Monday, October 21, it was announced that John L. Lewis would deliver a nationwide political broadcast on the coming Friday night.

Lewis turned aside all queries as to the nature, purpose, or content of the broadcast with the simple statement, "The die is cast."

Friday evening, October 25, found 25,000,000 to 30,000,000 [6] Americans listening to the sonorous tones of an undreamed-of Lewis castigation of the Chief Executive. Over America's three major radio broadcasting chains involving 322 radio stations, Lewis hurled every weapon in his arsenal at Roosevelt. Throughout Lewis's attack upon Roosevelt he constantly hammered upon one theme. Roosevelt means War! War! War!

". . . Those who hear these words, and who have studied the public addresses of the President, from his Chicago 'quarantine speech' to his Charlottesville 'stab in the back' address, and thence to Dayton and Philadelphia, will understand his motivation and his objective. It is war. His every act leads one to this inescapable conclusion. The President has said that he hates war and will work for peace, but his acts do not match his words. I am opposed to any involvement of our country in foreign wars. I believe that every thoughtful and normal citizen is similarly opposed. They are willing, as I am willing, to contribute everything for any necessary defense of our geographical integrity, our families, our possessions, our liberties, and our lives . . .

". . . The present concentration of power in the office of the President of the United States has never before been equaled in the history of our country. His powers and influence in this republic are so far-reaching that they intimately and vitally affect the lives and fortunes of every citizen. In like measure, they may affect the lives and fortunes of other nations and their populations.

"How startling, therefore, is the spectacle of a President who is disinclined to surrender that power, in keeping with the traditions of the republic. The suggestion of a third term under these conditions is less than wholesome or healthy. Personal craving for power, the overweening abnormal and selfish craving for increased power, is a thing to alarm and dismay. . . .

". . . Power for what? Personal and official power to what end? In all history, the unwarranted exercise of continuously vested authority has brought its train of political and social convul-

[6] Estimated by *The New York Times*.

sions for which humanity has paid an appalling price in loss of liberty, in disorder, tragedy, and death.

"America needs no superman. It denies the philosophy that runs to the deification of the state. America wants no royal family. Our forebears paid the price in blood, agony, privation, and sorrow, requisite for the building of this republic. Are we now to cast away that priceless liberty, which is our heritage? Are we to yield to the appetite for power and the vaunting ambitions of a man who plays with the lives of human beings for a pastime?

"I say 'No,' and whether I stand alone, or whether I am sustained, as I think I will be, by the overwhelming number of American citizens, I should retain these convictions. It is time for the manhood and the womanhood of America to assert themselves. Tomorrow may be too late. . . .

". . . President Roosevelt is asking the American people to contribute to him at least four more years out of their individual lives. What will be done with those lives and this nation in the next four years, and how does he propose to do it? He has not said, and he asks from the people a grant of discretionary power that would bind him to no course of action, except the unpredictable policies and adventures which he may later devise.

"After all, Americans are not a nation of guinea pigs, constantly subject to the vicissitudes of the economic and political experiments of an amateur, ill-equipped practitioner in the realm of political science. . . .

". . . If not Roosevelt, whom do I recommend to do the job of making secure our nation and its people? Why, of course, I recommend the election of Wendell L. Willkie as the next President of the United States.

"He is a gallant American. He has opened his heart to the American people. He is not an aristocrat. He has the common touch. He was born to the briar and not to the purple. He has worked with his hands, and has known the pangs of hunger. . . . He has had experience in various fields of American enterprise, and is an administrator and an executive. . . .

". . . He is strong enough to enlist the services of other strong men to do the job of saving our nation, whether from attack by external foes, or disintegration from disunity within. . . .

". . . It is obvious that President Roosevelt will not be re-elected for the third term, unless he has the overwhelming support of the men and women of labor. If he is, therefore, re-elected, it will mean that the members of the Congress of Industrial Organizations have rejected my advice and recommendation. I will accept the result as being the equivalent of a vote of no confidence and will retire as President of the Congress of Industrial Organizations, at its convention in November. This action will save our great movement, composed of millions of men and women, from the embarrassment and handicap of my leadership during the ensuing reign of President Roosevelt.

"To the leaders of the CIO, its executives, staff officers, and field representatives—I know and have worked with each of you. Upon some of you, I have bestowed the honors which you now wear. Through the years of struggle, you have been content that I should be in the forefront of your battles. I am still the same man. Sustain me now, or repudiate me. I will not chide you and will even hope that you will not regret your action.

"To the mine workers of the nation who know me best, and who have always been the shock troops in the forward march of labor, I say it is best for you, and for those you love to help oppose the creation of a political dictatorship in free America.

"To the steel workers, the automobile workers, the shipbuilders, the maritime workers, the lumber workers in the far northwest, the textile workers, the white-collar workers, and the men and women of labor in the miscellaneous industries, I say I have worked for you and have fought for you. Believe me now, when I say that your interest, and the interests of the families you support, lie in the acceptance of the truth of the words I speak tonight."

Next morning *The New York Times* headlined the break:

LEWIS DECLARES FOR WILLKIE
SAYS ROOSEVELT MEANS WAR
AND DICTATORSHIP IN NATION
STAKES CIO RULE
TELLS WIDE AUDIENCE ON
RADIO HE WILL QUIT OFFICE
IF PRESIDENT WINS

Union men and women wept with bitter disappointment at this break between their two idols. Liberals and many adherents of the CIO cursed Lewis for what they felt was a major betrayal. Ten days later Franklin Delano Roosevelt stepped into the spotlight of history as America's first third-term President, and John Llewellyn Lewis stepped into the long twilight.

Chapter 9

Post Mortem

THE spectacular break between Roosevelt and Lewis produced a host of theories and endless speculation. Many reasons and so-called inside stories were advanced to explain both the break and the consequent feud that raged uninterrupted by a world war until the death of the President. It is now possible to examine critically the most popularly told and accepted stories, and to dissect those elements that would be most revealing as to the character of the Roosevelt-Lewis relationship. The part of the story that will probably never be known is locked in the strange, dark, psychological tug of war of affinity and hostility between these two complex, strong-willed personalities.

Leading in common acceptance as the major reason for the violent rupture between Lewis and Roosevelt was Lewis's personal political ambitions for the vice-presidency of the United States. Many varied stories along this line had appeared in the press—in both news and feature columns, in magazines, and in books on politics and labor; and they were spread also by radio commentators. Most of the tales dealt with Lewis's telling Secretary of Labor Perkins that she should inform the President that his sole chance for a third-term victory lay in John L. Lewis being his running mate.

In November, 1946, Frances Perkins published her *The Roosevelt I Knew*, where for the first time she personally recounts the story as follows:

> A strange light on this third term came one evening when I went with Daniel Tobin of the Teamsters Union to see the President. I cannot recall now why we went. We finished our

business shortly. The President, seated in his second-floor study, was in a relaxed mood.

As we prolonged our visit in pleasant conversation, Dan said, "Mr. President, you just have to run for the third term, you know you do. Don't talk to me about your fishing trips next winter—you are going to be right here in the White House."

"No," said the President, "no, Dan. I just can't do it. I tell you, I have been here a long time. I am tired. I really am. You don't know what it's like. And besides, I have to take care of myself. This sinus trouble I've got, the Washington climate makes it dreadful. It's the Washington disease. I never had it until I came here. How can I get over it? The doctors say I have to go into the hospital for a month of steady treatment. But I can't do that, you know. When a President does that, the bottom drops out of the stock market, the Japs take advantage of what they think is a serious illness, the Germans starts propaganda that I am dying and that the United States is in a panic. No, I can't be President again. I have to get over this sinus. I have to rest. I want to go home to Hyde Park. I want to take care of my trees. I have a big planting there, Dan. I want to make the farm pay. I want to finish my little house on the hill. I want to write history. No, I just can't do it, Dan."

Tobin expostulated, giving his emotional arguments. The President laughed. "You know, the people don't like the third term either."

"That's all right," said Tobin. "Labor will stand by you."

The President laughed again at some private joke. "I want to tell you two a very interesting thing," he said. "About two months ago John Lewis came to see one evening. He was in a most amiable mood, and he talked about the third term too, Dan, just the way you have, only much smoother." Roosevelt could not resist teasing a friend. "When I told him what I told you that the people wouldn't like a third term and that it would be very hard going politically, what do you think he said, Dan? He said, 'Mr. President, I have thought of all that and I have a suggestion to make for you to consider. If the vice-presidential candidate on your ticket should happen to be John L. Lewis those objections would disappear. A strong labor man would insure full support not only of all the labor people but of all the liberals who worry about such things as third terms.' "

The President paused. He could see Dan was astonished. "Can you beat it?" he said. "What do you think of it?"

Tobin exploded. "Why, Mr. President, he isn't even a Democrat. How does he think he'll get the nomination?"

We were both curious. Tobin asked the question. "How did you answer him, Mr. President?"

"Why, he didn't press me," said the President, "he didn't press me. He just asked me to think it over and give it consideration."

As I drove home that night I recalled that only a few days earlier I had conferred with Lewis about some labor legislation and had suggested that the support of the labor organizations ought to be forthcoming. He had said that he did not wish to commit himself on this legislation yet. Then he observed, in a very ceremonious way, "I have just made some suggestions to the President and I think that I shouldn't commit myself until he has time to think about them and come to some conclusions." [1]

When the writer questioned Lewis on the Perkins story, he replied: "If this happened as Madame Perkins stated it, and mind I emphasize *if*, then the President used his office to give credence to a fantastic cock-and-bull tale he himself manufactured out of whole cloth. That would be a typical Roosevelt maneuver to stir the antagonism of others against one whom he opposed, or else typical Madame Perkins gossip."

In view of this categorical denial of the Roosevelt story, some observations on the circumstances prevailing at the time might be of aid in attempting to evaluate these two diametrically opposed statements of fact.

First, in support of the veracity of the Roosevelt story, one must remember that John L. Lewis was a daily headline that greeted you at breakfast through 1936 and 1937 and frequently afterward. As a dramatic, dynamic figure in the national life, he was second only to Roosevelt, and during the year 1937 eclipsed the President in the public eye. *In the year of 1937 John L. Lewis and his activities took in* The New York Times *99,816 column inches or 4.2 per cent of the total news coverage for the year, foreign or domestic. This meant that about one-twentieth of* The New York Times *day in and day out was devoted to Lewis and his operations.* His name became a synonym for the power of the workers pitted against the entrenched wealth of the nation. He was labor's avenging angel. He was an invincible win-

[1] Frances Perkins, *The Roosevelt I Knew* (New York: Viking Press, 1946), pp. 126-127.

ner. His voice, his thoughts, his actions, were in perfect pitch and attuned to the conflict and storm of the depression period. John L. Lewis was the nation's most lauded and cursed individual. As with Roosevelt, masses of the population either adored or abhorred him. There was no middle ground of mild opinion concerning Lewis. He was either the greatest demagogue or the foremost protagonist for democracy in modern times. The nation was more class-conscious than at any time in recent generations, and John L. Lewis was the unchallenged leader of the working classes.

With this came a growth of political consciousness of a magnitude and depth labor had never before experienced. The CIO and innumerable other groups in the country, stirred to the core and on fire with the times, began thinking of an independent political organization to be born of a fusion of organized labor and the farmers. This political ferment gravitated into two conceptions for future action, either a third political party, which was personally favored by Lewis, or else a drive for the political capture of the existing Democratic party.

In both the camps of those driving toward a new labor party and those attempting to capture the Democratic party, John L. Lewis was the only potential presidential candidate. This thinking was translated into a tremendous amount of talk about Lewis and the presidency.

During the 1936 campaign, Phil Hanna, business and financial editor of the former *Chicago Sun* and now associated with the *Chicago Daily News,* addressed the Montana Bankers' Association in Yellowstone Park, charging, "Mr. Lewis and the Roosevelt administration made a horse trade in which Lewis agreed to support Roosevelt this year in return for the President's support for the Democratic presidential nomination in 1940."

William Hutcheson, head of the Carpenters' Union, AF of L, still nursing the jaw that Lewis had slugged and a much more wounded ego, supported this statement with the assertion, "A vote for Roosevelt is a vote for Lewis."

Cecil Carnes, writing on Lewis in 1936, quotes Heywood Broun, "Of course, it is anybody's guess. But it seems to me that the political and economic history of America in the next ten years will be largely written in terms of the success or failure of John L. Lewis."

Carnes also cites an interview on Lewis with the late Senator Huey P. Long, "There ain't an ounce of foreignism in him, but he may be forced to become the second George Washington in this land. See what I mean? I mean there is enough Tories here, God damn them, to cause anything. Huey sees that if things get worse why somebody is going to have to tromp on the Mellon and the Morgan, the twin bed mates of disaster. And old John L. could do it. They tell me he fights moving locomotives in the early morning just to warm up. He's the Huey Long of labor. That's what he is, the Huey Long of labor." [2]

Carnes concludes:

> He would like to be President of the United States. He has repeatedly turned down Republican offers of cabinet positions. Just before the last Republican convention he was approached on the possibility of becoming the nominee for the Vice-Presidency. But the Republican Party, as constituted in 1936, does not have the labor principles which he desires.
>
> But what, you say, if 1940 finds conservatives in full command of both parties in opposition to "radicalism," which is the old guard synonym for the demand of a fair return to labor? While it seems unlikely, do not put entirely out of mind the possibility that Mr. Lewis will then use more vehement and practical means to secure his ends. Pragmatist that he is, Mr. Lewis is rather a master of events than a slave to any ephemeral theory. So he can be very dangerous if his hand is forced. If he ever turned into a General Coxey, an improbable supposition, there would be no compromise. Beyond that there is a reasonable doubt that he himself knows exactly what he would do. [3]

During this period many labor leaders honestly felt that Roosevelt would later support Lewis in a presidential bid. The thought of any President serving beyond two terms never occurred to any of them. Even Sidney Hillman, who later broke with Lewis on the political issue of Roosevelt, was at that time thinking and working for Lewis as President.

> Sidney Hillman is a smart man. . . .
> . . . A shrewd, hard-boiled, guttural individual who operates

---

[2] Cecil Carnes, *John L. Lewis, Leader of Labor* (New York: Robert Speller Publishing Corporation, Inc., 1936), pp. 303-304.

[3] *Ibid.*, p. 306.

with finesse and acumen, Sidney Hillman toys with a great ambition. He wants to make John L. Lewis President of the United States. He lies awake nights, thinking about it.[4]

It would be absurd to assume that Lewis was impervious to the wind blowing from these quarters and whipping out the banner of Lewis for President. Lewis became the god of the left wing, and they daily heaped editorials and articles of adulation at his feet. All these stories were flushed with the hope that some day John L. Lewis would be America's greatest President.

> During the last presidential campaign a man close to Lewis said to me meaningfully, "Roosevelt will only serve to hold the fences until . . ." Until when? Until labor becomes competent to protect itself politically while it keeps going ahead economically. Lewis himself refuses to discuss his political plans, but, talking with him, one has no doubt that they include the White House and the country.[5]

Even *Fortune* kept pace with the Communist *New Masses* when it reported in the October, 1936, issue:

> When the Washington labor correspondents filed into the headquarters of Labor's Non-Partisan League on the fifteenth of last July, they were welcomed by Major George L. Berry, Sidney Hillman, and John Llewellyn Lewis. Major Berry, the President, announced the news. The league had decided to perpetuate its existence beyond its current support of Roosevelt. It looked for a realignment of political forces before 1940 and wanted to have a hand therein. Yes, in New York State the league was already backing a pure labor ticket. Whereupon the reporters all looked at John L. Lewis, who rotated his cigar and said nothing. And the reporters, probably to a man, asked themselves whether this vast and glowering Welshman would really wind up in the White House.[6]

It would be equally absurd to believe that Lewis did not possess White House aspirations. This ambition, latent as it may be, is nevertheless common to most citizens in a democracy when even the most minute possibility exists for its realization.

[4] C. L. Sulzberger, *Sit Down with John L. Lewis* (New York: Random House, 1938), p. 134.

[5] *Forum*, March, 1937.

[6] Reprinted from *Fortune*, October, 1936, by special permission of the editors. Copyright, Time, Inc.

When asked in 1937 concerning himself as a presidential possibility Lewis answered direct questions by saying: "I have tried to avoid any public discussion of the idea of the presidency. I am not seeking public office. I have turned down public office. I could have been Secretary of Labor years ago. When the workers are organized, there will be by-products of that organization, but this is not the time to discuss them. What they will be will be up to the workers, after they are organized."

Most individuals are basically fearful of power and its utilization. Lewis, however, always reached for power, enjoyed both its possession and application to the resolution of issues. He was completely committed to a national program that could only be achieved with the leverage of sheer power. His realistic grasp of labor's needs and the essential role of political power in the securing of these objectives had blasted him out of the mental quarantine of sectarian, segmental trade unionism. Through the CIO he was wielding power with both hands to the point where he was popularly regarded, with the exception of the President of the United States, as being the most powerful single individual in America.

It must also be observed here that Lewis was no stranger to American Presidents, their attitudes and their policies. He knew that Roosevelt was giving to organized labor a more sympathetic interest and aid than any President before him, at least in Lewis's lifetime. How else can one explain his tremendous all-out political support of Roosevelt in 1936? If Lewis wanted more pro-labor power in the White House, it could only come from labor itself occupying the White House or John L. Lewis as President or vice-president as per the Perkins story.

On the other hand, it must be remembered that prior to the occurrence of the Perkins story, Lewis had already attacked and denounced Roosevelt. It seemed unlikely that Lewis, feeling as he did, would ask to be placed on a ticket with a man he already opposed. By this time, Lewis had already acquired his deep personal contempt and hatred for Roosevelt that bordered on actual loathing.

Lewis and Roosevelt were both extremely dynamic, strong-willed, possessive individuals. One of their many similarities was their inability to brook competition that might be a personal challenge to their running the whole show. No one knew this better than Lewis, who recognized the human impossibility of such a political alignment.

Lewis had steadfastly rejected political offers made at a time in his life when they must have loomed as large to him then as the presidency did in 1939 or 1940. These political invitations ranged from a senatorship from the State of New Mexico and later from Illinois, to membership in the Cabinet of President Coolidge, to a bid from top Republican powers to be Herbert Hoover's running mate. All of these bids were instantly rejected by Lewis. His public and private record through the years had been one not only of personal disinterest in public office but even of actual aversion. In the light of much of our knowledge of Lewis as a person it would definitely have been a most unusual action for him. The course of the final negotiations between the two, presented in the last chapter, also do not argue for Lewis's driving for the vice-presidency.

These are the facts. Whether the truth lies wholly with Roosevelt or wholly with Lewis or partially with each will never be known. Historians and biographers writing in the future will draw their own judgments with the ink of their prejudices, but they will never have more evidence on this point than has been presented here. These facts and a personal knowledge of Lewis's stubborn and almost abnormal pride make the writer lean toward the Lewis version of this episode.

Another basic disagreement between Roosevelt and Lewis appeared to stem out of America's foreign policy. During these years, civilization stood at the brink of catastrophe as Europe rapidly reverted to the dark ages. Fascism with its super-racism and a bloodletting never before experienced by mankind was sweeping the continent and threatening the world.

Both Roosevelt and Lewis were unalterably opposed to Hitler and everything he represented. To the country as a whole, Roosevelt's position on foreign affairs was defined as interventionist while Lewis's was regarded as isolationist. Instead of yielding to the temptation of labels and dismissing the problem as solved, it is essential here that Lewis's isolationism and Roosevelt's interventionism be scrutinized.

Lewis believed that the best way of defeating fascism was to make America so strong internally that the democratic way of life would be invulnerable. His definition of "internal strength" was to strengthen the labor movement.

The Spanish Civil War of 1936 and 1937 found both Roosevelt and Lewis silent. Here, in the prelude of World War II, with open and armed intervention in Spain by Hitler and Mussolini, both interventionist Roosevelt and isolationist Lewis were passive. Lewis told the writer that he did not take a positive public position against Franco at that time because of Philip Murray's personal plea to him prior to the 1937 CIO executive board meeting. Murray's arguments were based on the pro-Franco position of the Catholic Church. The latter was also responsible for Roosevelt's refusal to raise the arms embargo, thereby barring a duly constituted legal government from purchasing arms to defend itself against an uprising sponsored, financed, armed, and largely manned by Hitler and Mussolini.

On this issue, Lewis appears in a better light than Roosevelt. He, at least, did not render a positive contribution to Franco's ultimate victory as did the administration's arms embargo. On March 15, 1937, Lewis addressed a huge mass meeting in New York City:

". . . Fear is king in Germany. By day and by night each man's hand is against his brother. The days and nights of the Swastika terror have swept one hundred thousand men and women into concentration camps where the torture of defenseless prisoners seems to be the choice pastime of Nazi heroes. The mothers, wives, and children of these prisoners must mourn in secret lest their grief be punished with further bloody reprisals. . . .

". . . Forced labor is extended to the soldiers who have been sent as 'volunteers' to Spain. These soldiers were told that they were to be sent to other parts of Germany for secret maneuvers, and the absolute censorship of the press served again as a useful tool for the imperialistic ambitions of the Nazi dictatorship. . . .

". . . The establishment of a Fascist dictatorship in the United States would undoubtedly assure a retrogression from which civilization might not recover for ages and from which it would certainly not recover for many years. I know of only one means of insuring our safety—the workers of America must find self-expression in economic, in social and in political matters. . . .

". . . The horrors which have been visited upon the Jewish people in Germany and which have been visited upon the representatives of free organization of labor should be proof sufficient to every American citizen of the imperative necessity of maintaining the economic stability of our own domestic household and maintaining our stern national disapproval against that nation which has persecuted a great race and debased the living and cultural standards of its own people."

Approximately seven months later, on October 5, with the Spanish Republican government virtually dead, the President speaking in Chicago made his famous "quarantine the aggressor" speech. From that point on, he embarked upon an interventionist program.

Almost from the same time Lewis became more and more set upon a course of staying out of war. It must be remembered, too, that Lewis had a long record of abhorring war. This attitude was evident again and again during the First World War. Many of Lewis's statements and private reactions to war are similar to those of the Quakers.

It should be noted here that students of labor and politics have commented that the personal bitterness already existing between Lewis and Roosevelt was so intense that Lewis would automatically have developed a position opposed to Roosevelt on any issue, foreign or domestic, that he was by then obsessed with being "agin the administration." This speculation, like all conjectures or theorizing based upon one facet of the Lewis-Roosevelt relationship, was gross oversimplification. Unquestionably Lewis's hostility toward Roosevelt made it much easier and more comfortable to oppose him on this issue. It must also be remembered that by 1940 Lewis passionately believed that Roosevelt was determined to get into war. On the basis of pure power politics, certainly Lewis recognized that Roosevelt would be and was more vulnerable to attack in this area than almost any other. "Peace" is a cause of perennial popularity.

Any discussion of Lewis and foreign policy always brings up the story of Lewis's relationship with an international oil speculator by the name of William Rhodes Davis. With this tale are mysterious hints of Lewis's being involved in commercial transactions with the Nazis, plus his bearing a peace offer from Goering to the White House, which was rejected. There is con-

siderable evidence that Lewis did present an offer from a high
Nazi official to the President looking toward an attempted
peace. Lewis never accepted the fact that peace with the Nazis
was impossible.

The writer put the following question to Lewis,[7] "What was
your relationship with William Rhodes Davis, the international
oil speculator, who was rumored to be finally working in business transactions, at least, with such prominent Nazis as Her-
mann Goering?"

Lewis drew a detailed background of his association with
William Rhodes Davis, which came as a part of the times, particularly the years 1933 to 1939. There were many things on
which Mr. Davis and Lewis saw eye to eye. This was during the
period following the Mexican government's shaking off the
shackles of outside finance and expropriating the British- and
American-held oil properties in Mexico. Lewis felt these properties properly belonged to the Mexican people. The Mexican
government was an extraordinarily progressive government at
the time, and the cause of the Mexican people was close to the
heart of the American workers. The Mexican labor movement
had grown into a powerful instrument. The CIO felt many a
common tie with the powerful industrial-union movement
sweeping through Mexico at that time. Many CIO leaders
shared the Mexican labor leaders' resentment of a British financial blockade, and just as many shared the Mexican government's avowed sympathies for the Spanish Republican
government.

Great Britain at that time was engaged in both attempting an
economic blockade of Mexico and leading the so-called nonintervention policy on Spain, which was really an arms and
economic blockade of loyalist Spain. This action ultimately
defeated the Republican government and delivered it to the
Fascists.

During this period William Rhodes Davis had purchased outright and also leased a significant number of oil tankers and
was trying to sell Mexican oil wherever he could. This meant
opening the foreign market and striving to break the British
blockade of conservative capital against the Mexican government. The Mexican government fully supported Davis's ef-

[7] Interview with Lewis, Carleton Hotel, Washington, December 17, 1948.

forts; and, if it happened that one of the few places where Davis could break through the British stranglehold on the world market was in Germany, then he would sell there. What a strange paradox of oil being sold to Hitler in order to help the progressive anti-Fascist government in Mexico stabilize itself in its struggle against British finance! Actually all American industry was trafficking, whenever it could, with Hitler, Mussolini, and the empire of Japan.

Commenting on this situation Lewis said: "At the time when William Rhodes Davis was trying to make these sales to German interests, I think it only fitting and proper that inquiry be made as to what American business in this country was doing with the Nazis—whether it be Ford Motors or the working relationships between cartels such as the Farben Die Trust. This is all a matter of common knowledge today.

"I believe it also pertinent that one inquire into the fact that if William Rhodes Davis was such a democratic leper, why did Franklin D. Roosevelt regard him as one of his close friends in 1936? Why did Franklin D. Roosevelt give him a personally autographed photograph of himself which included one of the warmest and strongest written personal statements that I have ever seen on a Roosevelt photograph? Also why, and of course, it is significantly related to this warm Roosevelt inscription on this photograph, did President Roosevelt gratefully accept the $400,000 contribution that William Rhodes Davis made, part of it directly from himself and the remainder from others acting as his fronts? However, Franklin Delano Roosevelt knew that every nickel of that $400,000 actually came from William Rhodes Davis.

"I could answer the question also by saying that if William Rhodes Davis was good enough for Roosevelt, he was good enough for me. That, of course, would be a false answer. The fact that a person was good enough for Franklin Delano Roosevelt really was not an exalted criterion."

In this survey of the Roosevelt-Lewis relationship it is imperative that we analyze their political and economic outlooks. The Social views of Roosevelt and Lewis were startlingly similar in that neither was anchored by a central philosophy. Both possessed a generalized desire for a better society. However, this desire was characterized by a diffuse humanitarianism operating on an opportunistic basis with the future fading into a vague panorama not to be concerned about until it became the present.

In 1936 both Roosevelt and Lewis subscribed to the current capitalistic structure. Their political and economic thinking was best reflected in their statement on this issue. The President is reported to have had the following reaction when questioned on his philosophy: "Philosophy? I am a Christian and a Democrat—that's all." [8]

In 1936 John L. Lewis, speaking at the National Press Club, described his political thinking, "I am not a Republican. I am not a Democrat. I am not a Fascist, Communist, nor a Socialist." [9]

Here were their "philosophies," for what they were worth. Both of them were concerned with the issue at hand and not on the horizon. Both relegated "a philosophy" to the category of an unnecessary encumbrance. Roosevelt's New Deal, although geared into the thesis of increasing purchasing power to start again the wheels of industry, was nevertheless a makeshift day-to-day approach strongly resembling a volunteer fire brigade that was willing to throw in everything but the bucket to put out the fire. Roosevelt's constant reiteration of "priming the pump" was much more than a suggestion that he wanted to get the old system working again.

Lewis told CIO delegates that he had no inclination "to indulge in philosophical cogitations or academic meanderings about the philosophy or the academic benefits that might come to posterity through the work that you are doing in this pressing day and year."

By mid-1936 Lewis began to drive left of Roosevelt and continued to go even further to the left. In this left-bound political voyage Lewis became intensely critical of the status quo and began thinking and talking about economic democracy and the development of a more democratic political life.

In the ferment of the New Deal the revolutionary fires burned highest and hottest on the economic front. It was here that the upsurge of labor gave birth to the CIO. Standing in the midst of this flaming violence and the sweeping hopes of the

[8] Perkins, *op. cit.*, p. 330.
[9] *Fortune*, October, 1936.

workers, Lewis glimpsed the soul-stirring vision of the world these workers were battling for with their all, and was profoundly moved. It would not have been humanly possible for anyone, let alone Lewis, not to have been deeply affected. The power, the frustration, the drama of the workers, began to flow through Lewis. He began to articulate for the workers and also for himself. The CIO was a religious crusade and revolution all wrapped together in one movement. Its followers and leaders fought with religious fervor and the fanaticism of new converts. Theirs was a sacred mission, and the road turned ever left. Lewis became the prophet of this new crusade, and all liberals and radicals of every stripe swore eternal fealty to the prophet and the cause.

Lewis began to question whether there was any difference between the Democratic party and the Republican party and whether either one really represented the workers. On Monday, February 1, 1937, John L. Lewis, speaking at a dinner meeting sponsored by the magazine *Common Sense,* came out for a third party based on a popular front of labor and the farmers. The names of other people present who were in accord with a new third-party movement are of particular interest. They were Roger Baldwin, Congressman Amlie, Congressman Maury Maverick, Congressman Vito Marcantonio, Lewis Corey, Sidney Hillman, Alfred Bingham, Selden Rodman, and Ernst Toller.

That same year Lewis publicly proclaimed the revolutionary credo that the right to a job transcends the right of property. He generaled the sit-down strike to the consternation of the vested interests and the acute discomfort of Franklin D. Roosevelt.

By 1939 Lewis was privately charging Roosevelt with "out-Hoovering Hoover." Lewis and the CIO were on the rampage. Lewis knew that if he and his cohorts slowed down and lost their invincible momentum, they would have lost their chance to win what they believed would be an America with full economic and political democracy. He hurled the challenge of labor at the status quo in early 1937 with revolutionary emphasis: "They [the workers] must become conscious of their responsibilities and of their privileges. They must become articulate, and they must be free from industrial oppression, so that they may assume the power which is theirs by right. . . .

The workers must be made economically free, in order to assure them the maximum of opportunity to champion and defend the elemental principles of human liberty. . . . If we can free them from industrial servitude, we can, in the fullest sense, free them from the political shackles which in the past have restrained and limited their strength. There is no reactionary force which can stand against the untrammeled and crystallized voice of the two-thirds of our population represented by labor. . . ." [10] In 1940, in his radio attack on Roosevelt he stated: "War . . . kills off the vigorous males who, if permitted to live, *might question the financial exploitation of the race.*" [11]

Lewis had already gained a vast independent labor movement; now he stood on the threshold of gaining a nation. All that was needed was a Roosevelt leaning left and rendering the necessary political aid. But Roosevelt by 1939 was headed full speed to the right. Roosevelt's followers explain this drastic turn on the basis of the need for appeasing and courting the co-operation and friendship of industry in preparation for national defense and possible war. The administration's domestic policy became the captive of the chaos in the Old World. Thus, by late 1939 Roosevelt and Lewis were straining in opposite directions.

Throughout this change of Roosevelt, Lewis was almost blinded with anger because of his impotent realization that the strength of the CIO could have forced Roosevelt to the left; but this power was dissipated by many of Lewis's associates who supported the President without asking payment. As a result, the President did not have to be politically concerned about jeopardizing his support from the CIO. This left Lewis in a hopeless bargaining position.

It should be noted at this point that the CIO in 1939 and even in 1940, following Roosevelt's re-election, adopted a position on foreign policy that was identical to that of Lewis. Their resolutions echoed Lewis's every word. When Lewis stated his position on the war, he was stating the position of the CIO.

Yet with all these criticisms and attacks on the prevailing economic and political system, Lewis never crystallized it into a creed or working philosophy. Instead, he went as Jeremiah

---

[10] Speech by John L. Lewis, Madison Square Garden, March 15, 1937.
[11] Radio address by John L. Lewis, October 25, 1940. Italics the writer's.

did, crying in the wilderness and calling upon some "power somewhere in this land of ours that will be capable of protecting the worker against the great corporations."

Roosevelt's philosophy was even less substantial than this. It has been suggested that both Roosevelt and Lewis, as outstanding leaders in the field of action and conflict, were overly concerned with the daily improvisations and tactics necessary to meet the issues of each particular day.

Lewis as a onetime disciple of Samuel Gompers had absorbed the Gompers dictum that the labor movement was built by tactics not ideals. Lewis was primarily a tactician and secondarily concerned with ideals. Roosevelt, too, the practical politician, was primarily concerned with daily politicking and maneuvering. Both of them were tacticians with little philosophy.

The pressure of circumstances was not conducive either to creating the inclination or permitting the time to develop an organized pattern of procedure. Both of them were geniuses in pragmatism, but for the hour, not for the future.

Another question that has puzzled those interested in labor and politics was why Lewis announced that he would resign as president of the CIO if Roosevelt was re-elected. It is common political practice for those on the losing side of an election to realign themselves or work out some arrangements with the victor. Lewis's gesture has always appeared as a highly dramatic and senseless act.

In May, 1947, the writer was interviewing Lewis when the conversation turned to the mistakes of the past. Lewis turned to the writer, saying, "What is in your mind when we talk of mistakes—errors or failures?"

The writer replied: "Well, whenever we talk about mistakes my mind goes back to 1940. I believe, as you knew very well at that time, that it was a serious misjudgment on your part to have broken politically with Roosevelt. However, that decision is open to question, but what I believe is not open to question and was in fact, a catastrophic blunder, was for you to have made the public commitment that if Roosevelt was re-elected for a third term you would regard this as a vote of no confidence on the part of organized labor and resign from the presidency of the CIO. That was unnecessary and a wild gamble that was politically pointless."

Lewis puffed for a moment on his eternal cigar and then rose: "You're wrong about that. I carefully examined that election, and there was never a momentary doubt in my mind but that Mr. Roosevelt was going to be re-elected. That was the very reason I deliberately publicly committed myself and my organization to the camp of Wendell Willkie. You see, I wanted to, I had to get out of the presidency of the CIO if I were to be effective in uniting the divided forces of labor. The CIO presidency placed me in an impossible situation, insofar as I could personally strive to unite the CIO and the AF of L. I had to get out, and this was the time and the opportunity. Furthermore, for me to have remained in that office after opposing the President would have been politically embarrassing to the CIO."

In making this statement Lewis had either forgotten or dismissed the fact that the writer was constantly with him during this critical period when the "die was cast." He had forgotten the long political discussions of that time between him and the writer. There were many reasons compelling Lewis to act as he did, but to the best knowledge of the author, the above reason advanced by Lewis this May afternoon of 1947 was nowhere in the vicinity of Lewis's mind on October 25, 1940. There was no question of Lewis's sincerity when narrating his 1947 explanation, but the author would judge it as a rationalization seven years after the fact.

It has been suggested by those who were convinced that Lewis desired the vice-presidential post that once Lewis was denied this opportunity, he attempted to inject himself into the campaign on a par with Roosevelt. He tried to do this by telling the membership of the CIO and many of his followers that if Roosevelt was elected it meant Lewis was defeated and would retire. He was pitting himself politically against the President.

The author rejects both Lewis's explanation and that of his critics. We know now of Lewis's implacable opposition to Roosevelt, his abhorrence of war, and his complete identification of Roosevelt with war. This, plus the author's personal and intimate knowledge of the thinking and actions taking place at that time lead him to the conclusion that Lewis simply did everything in his power to lead the CIO into the Willkie ranks.

Roosevelt never cared for the little man or what was popularly referred to as the common man. He never cared or felt for him because he never had the vaguest conception of what the little man or the common man or the working man was. Franklin Roosevelt never understood or had any idea what the working man was any more than Franklin D. Roosevelt had ever worked himself for a living.

"Whenever Franklin Delano Roosevelt had to deal with men of strong personality, he, Roosevelt, became upset with his basic fear and understanding of his own personal inadequacy. When forced by circumstances to deal with some such men, he would resort to any technique that expediency justified. Such technique when utilized disregarded the ordinarily recognized virtues affecting the relationship between men. He began to connive for no objective except the unholy satisfaction of connivance.

"As for Franklin D. Roosevelt and myself, you can say we—that is, Roosevelt and I—we dipped the well dry, there wasn't any aqua pura left." Here Lewis grimaced saying, "Strike out 'pura.'" [14]

Yet with their differences there were also strong similarities. Both Roosevelt and Lewis were conscious of their historical role. Repeatedly with both of them the factors adding up to a decision would include the question, "How will this look in history?" They both lived and acted with an eye to history.

Many facts on this point argue for the pattern they both followed. Neither Roosevelt nor Lewis would permit the development of a strong lieutenant who might become a rival and challenge his leadership. These facts even suggest that their acute concern with history resulted in their refusal to permit an outstanding successor to follow in their footsteps. To be succeeded by rank mediocrity would elevate their historical stature by stark contrast. The successor becomes an integral part of the background of the canvas of history.

In Roosevelt's case it would have been difficult to have found a more colorless and seemingly mediocre successor than Harry S. Truman. It has been stated and with validity by political sages that Franklin Delano Roosevelt would have carried through to victory with a Hottentot as his running mate. No

[14] Interview with Lewis, Washington, April, 1948.

President in American history had so captured the hearts and the loyalty of the people. Roosevelt knew this better than any of his lieutenants, and explanations advanced that Roosevelt "needed" Truman to win were patently absurd. To be succeeded by mediocrity causes the generation to shake their heads and yearn, "It wasn't like this when F.D.R. was alive—if only he were still in the White House."

Looking at Lewis and the United Mine Workers Union, we find no competent successor in sight, and no one knows that better than Lewis. With conditions as they are, Lewis's death will leave the union leaderless. Incompetent successors plus certain factional fights for power will cripple and set back the strength and the gains of the mine workers. The ensuing decline of the fortunes of the miners will cause them for years to come to shake their heads, saying sadly, "It wasn't like this when the great John L. Lewis was alive."

Looking backward over the Roosevelt-Lewis trail, we see that it probably was tragically inevitable that two such forceful leaders should clash head on as they did. They both felt that they had "a rendezvous with destiny." They were both impressed with their historical importance. They were as different as the sledgehammer is to the stiletto, but they were alike in their intentions in cutting down their opposition.

The break between them ruptured an incipient new American revolution. If Roosevelt had turned left, with Lewis, it would have profoundly changed the course of history. If they had been committed to a philosophy or way of life, they might have found there a common cause that could have transcended their personal drives and ambitions. But lacking that, both began operating against each other on purely personal grounds, which was not in keeping with the broad human sweep of their actions and thoughts. The break between them broke the militant surge of the labor movement and broke much of the New Deal. Historians will describe it as the great American Tragedy of the labor movement.

Chapter 10

The Lewis-Murray Break

T HIRTY million Americans heard Lewis throw down the gauntlet to Roosevelt. "If he is, therefore, re-elected . . . I will accept the result as being the equivalent of a vote of no confidence and will retire as president of the Congress of Industrial Organizations, at its convention in November." [1]

The morning of November 5 found Franklin Delano Roosevelt finishing his second term and re-elected to a third term as President of the United States. Thirteen days later, the morning of November 18 found John L. Lewis finishing his second term as president of the CIO and now prepared to resign as the official leader of the organization he had conceived and nurtured from an idea to a vast giant of approximately four million members.

To most of the delegates assembled at Atlantic City in this third convention of the CIO it was inconceivable that the great John L. Lewis would retire as their champion. His first appearance before the convention resulted in an ovation lasting more than an hour. Some, such as the leaders of the Amalgamated Clothing Workers Union, who were already completely committed to Roosevelt, sat warily, cautiously hopeful that Lewis would step down and future events would shift the distribution of power in the CIO.

Foreshadowings of the future of Lewis and the CIO appeared in the none-too-subtle, indirect attacks at Lewis from the Hillman forces. The first move was an attempted jab at Lewis's battle with Roosevelt through criticism of the policy of the CIO official newspaper. Leaders of Hillman's Amalgamated Clothing

[1] Speech by Lewis, October 25, 1940.

Workers Union charged "that the CIO *News,* especially with reference to the last national campaign, should have had the decency, because even the most reactionary press in America, including the Hearst papers, had the decency, to publish and print the picture of the new President of the United States. . . ." [2] Another Amalgamated delegate accused, "In the issue of November 11th I read every item and in not one single instance did I find the name of President Roosevelt mentioned in the entire eight pages of the CIO *News.* Secondly, I will say this, the two issues prior to that carried a full statement of the President of the CIO when he made a speech for Wendell Willkie, and it was printed in full without one single line missing. I don't know whether the CIO as an organization authorized the president of our organization to speak for Wendell Willkie. . . ." [3]

Lewis bulled down his opposition by assuming full responsibility for the policy of the paper, and challenging the attack to continue, stated, "Any aggrieved unit of this organization or any member of the organization that is dissatisfied or aggrieved has a right to file a complaint either with the editorial staff of the CIO *News,* the executive officers of the CIO, or the executive board of the CIO, which, after all, between conventions is responsible for the policies and the acts of its paper. Mr. De Caux [publicity director of the CIO] is quite correct in saying that CIO did not take a position in the recent campaign. That is right. The President did in his individual capacity. That is right. And if he had the same thing to do over again he would do precisely what he did for the reasons for which he did it. . . . The editor of the CIO *News* published my speech opposing Franklin Delano Roosevelt and supporting Wendell Willkie for President of the United States. He did so because I requested him to do so, and for no other reason. I requested him to do so because some thousands of members of this organization wired and wrote in for copies of the address. They wanted to see what the President of the Organization said; and I requested, merely as a matter of information, the publication of that address, and no blame can accrue to Mr. De Caux; any

---

[2] Daily Proceedings of the Third Constitutional Convention of the Congress of Industrial Organizations, 1940, p. 123.
[3] *Ibid.*

blame, if blame arises, can accrue to me. . . . If there is any gentleman that wants additional information on the CIO *News*, ask me. . . ." There were no further questions.[4]

This was followed by pressure from Hillman's Amalgamated Clothing Workers Union for unity and peace with the AF of L. The basis for this intense desire for peace was that a merger would reduce the Lewis menace. No longer would he be the all-powerful, dominant force. There is considerable evidence that Hillman here was acting for Roosevelt. Roosevelt openly favored this move at that time. Lewis met this head on with one of the most vitriolic and devastating speeches of his career: "Five years ago a little group of men representing some eight organizations in the American Federation of Labor in a hotel on the Boardwalk, a stone's throw away, highly resolved that come high or come low they would go forward . . . some of them did so and they have kept the faith, while others have fallen by the wayside.

"And one of those men was Mr. Dubinsky, representing the International Ladies' Garment Workers' Union, who swore by every God that ever sat on high that he, Dubinsky, would never waver in the cause, and he signed the scroll and by book, bell, and candle vowed to affiliate to this movement. And where is Dubinsky today? . . . He has crept back into the American Federation of Labor. He abandoned his fellows, and he abandoned what he claimed was his principle. And he has gone into that organization on his adversary's terms. He is crying out now, and his voice laments like that of Rachel in the wilderness, against the racketeers and the panderers and the crooks in that organization.

"And Zaritsky, he was the man representing the Millinery and Cap Workers. He said, 'Me too.' And now above all the clamor comes the piercing wail and the laments of the Amalgamated Clothing Workers. And they say, 'Peace, it is wonderful.' And there is no peace.

"There is no peace because you are not yet strong enough to command peace upon honorable terms. And there will be no peace with a mighty adversary until you possess that strength of bone and sinew that will make it possible for you to bargain on equal terms. . . .

[4] *Ibid.*, pp. 123-124.

"Why, the resolution read here this afternoon by one of the speakers said that we should go into a peace conference, or explore the mind, or explore the possibilities. We have explored every proposition. What have we all been doing? I have been an explorer in the American Federation of Labor. Explore the mind of Bill Green? Why, Bill and I had offices next door to each other in the same corridor for ten years. I was a member of the same executive council that he was for years. I have done a lot of exploring in Bill's mind, and I give you my word there is nothing there.

"Explore Matthew Woll's mind? I did. It is the mind of an insurance agent, who used his position as an officer of the American Federation of Labor and a member of the executive council to promote his insurance business. It is so because I told him so, and he agreed with me.

"Explore Tom Rickert's mind, of the United Garment Workers, who was on the negotiating committee? I did, and here is what was in his mind: He said he did not propose to let the Amalgamated Clothing Workers into the American Federation of Labor if he could help it. I said to him that he was getting $20,000 a year graft out of the advertising monopoly in the American Federation of Labor, and I had a paper in my pocket to prove it. He knew it and agreed to that as true. And I thought then I had explored his mind enough.

"Well, after all I think there is a limit to which the membership of my organization should permit me to waste my time and their money. . . .

"Now Mr. Green says that there will never be peace until the shadow of John Lewis grows less. Well, the official shadow of John Lewis is growing less. [Cries of, "No," "No," "No!" from the floor. President Lewis continued.] That shadow is diminishing. And yet, if I read the temper of this convention aright and if I understand what is in the hearts and minds of the millions of members backed by the men and women of this convention, regardless of John Lewis's shadow, you are not going to dishonor yourselves or to sell the right of those people that you represent. I don't care about some of the delegates of this convention who dissent from the tenor of those remarks. It annoys me not at all. I have great concern for those who are possessed of little faith and whose courage is waning. If they find the night too dark, if they find the way too rough, let them sit by the wayside. Let them forgather in the shadow of some friendly tree while those other valiant spirits go on in this great movement. They will carry on! They will carry on! And those who prefer to be a follower of the army rather than in the vanguard of its enterprise, so be it! . . ." [5]

Staring steadily at Hillman, he took the bull by the horns and invited Hillman and his union to get out of the CIO. "Dubinsky took the easy way. Zaritsky [6] took the easy way. If there is anybody else in the CIO who wants to take the easy way, let them go on. . . ." [7]

Hillman's rejoinder was based on the belief that a soft answer turneth away wrath. He flattered Lewis and said the Amalgamated Clothing Workers and its protégé, the Textile Workers Organizing Committee, would remain within the CIO and abide by majority rule. He then attacked a portion of Lewis's supporters by a vigorous denunciation of communism. Still fearful that a draft movement from the delegates would re-elect Lewis immediately after his resignation, Hillman spoke up: "I

[5] *Ibid.*, pp. 159-162.

[6] Lewis's use of Jewish names, such as Dubinsky and Zaritsky, gave rise to the feeling of anti-Semitic overtones to his attack on Hillman. It is probable that his words did stir some anti-Jewish reaction, but it is definite that such an intent or thought was most certainly not present in Lewis's mind. Lewis used the names because they happened to be the names of the individuals who did what he charged, and also because they went together in the same euphonious, dramatic way as Roosevelt's use of the names, Martin, Barton, and Fish. It should also be borne in mind that many of the delegates and supporters of Lewis against Hillman at this convention were Jews.

An incident occurred the evening of the day Lewis made the speech that substantiated the validity of both the reaction that his statement created bitterness against the Jews and also the fact that Lewis had no intention or thought of that possibility in his mind.

Two coal miners were standing in the lobby of the Chelsea Hotel making very derogatory remarks about Jews. This was without question the result of their chief's speech that afternoon. Lewis passed through the lobby and overheard these comments. He walked up to the two miners and in a voice seething with anger, said, "If I ever hear another word like that coming from either of you, I will personally see to it that you are expelled from the United Mine Workers of America." He then wheeled and walked out of the hotel. The two miners were completely overcome with this threat on the part of their sacred hero, and both were very pale. This episode was witnessed by a union official and also the writer. A brief notation is made here because there have been charges of anti-Semitism because of statements made by some of Lewis's associates and in the UMW *Journal.*

[7] *Ibid.*, p. 162.

regret that John L. Lewis will not be the leader of this organization. I know there is nothing else that he can do and will do and will agree to do, but what he believes to be the best for the organized labor movement. I have greater respect for a man who in a crisis stands by his guns . . ." [8]

Hillman also publicly revealed his fear of Lewis: ". . . And I know that when John Lewis speaks he speaks effectively. And when I can be in agreement with him I like his effectiveness. And when I am in disagreement with him I am scared of his effectiveness. . . ." [9]

The convention went on record in support of John L. Lewis's antiwar position, which was the public basis of his radio attack of October 25, 1940, on the President. Resolution R-26, entitled "Preservation of Peace and Democratic Institutions," was unanimously passed.

> *Resolution* R-26 Preservation of Peace and Democratic Institutions
>
> *Whereas,* (1) The people of this nation are more determined than ever to prevent this country from being dragged into the foreign wars now raging throughout the rest of the world; and
>
> (2) John L. Lewis in his masterful Labor Day address in September of 1939 warned the nation of the dangers which would beset the country through the efforts that would be made to drag us into the war; and
>
> (3) Because of the expression on the part of the people of their grave fears regarding these efforts to drag this country into war, the candidates of both major political parties in the recent presidential campaign gave their sacred pledge that this nation would be kept at peace; and
>
> (4) Under the guise and false pretense of furthering national defense the enemies of labor and democracy are attacking the living standards of the common people, the existence of labor unions, and the democratic institutions of the nation in their drive towards war; now, therefore, be it
>
> *Resolved,* that:
>
> (1) This Convention reaffirms its determination that this nation must not enter into any foreign entanglements which may in any way drag us down the path of entering or becoming involved in foreign wars. Eternal vigilance by organized labor

[8] *Ibid.*, p. 192.
[9] *Ibid.*

will be the basic guarantee that a repetition of 1917 will be avoided and that peace and security for our nation will be preserved; and

(2) The Executive Board of the CIO at its meeting in June 1940, unanimously adopted a policy relating to national defense and constituent unions and membership are fully prepared to discharge our responsibilities in the approaching national emergency to the best interests of the United States of America. The Executive Board made it clear and declared in unequivocal terms that we will defend the free institutions of this republic under which the Declaration of Independence and the Constitution give us the greatest democracy on earth—a government of the people, for the people, and by the people. This policy is reaffirmed in clear unmistakable terms.

The Congress of Industrial Organizations and its millions of members and the members of their families are determined to protect and defend this nation not only against foreign enemies who may dare to attack us directly but also against those forces within our nation who place the profits of their financial and industrial enterprises above the well-being of the millions of common people.

(3) Labor believes that national defense means the creation of a nation of strong, healthy, well-fed people employed at work at decent and substantial wages and dedicated to the belief that the democratic way is the best way of living. Labor believes that national defense means the continued growth and expansion of powerful industrial unions which will protect and defend the interests and status of their members to achieve economic security. Labor believes that national defense means the vigilant protection and constant safeguarding of the exercises of all of our cherished civil rights of speech, press, assembly, and worship. Labor believes that ignoring these fundamental principles and limiting our nation's activities to the building of mere armories, of aeroplanes, tanks and guns will not serve but rather defeat the basic interests of national defense.[10]

With this support of Lewis by the convention, Hillman's organization recognized the futility of further open opposition. Finally the time came. Despite tearful pleas, an hour-long demonstration, petitions, telegrams, and demands, the hour for Lewis's resignation struck. In a sense it was anticlimactic; for Lewis had referred to his resignation in one way or another

[10] *Ibid.,* p. 227.

since the opening of the convention. One leader of the Amalgamated Clothing Workers was overheard to say bitterly, "He's been resigning all week." And yet, like a death that is expected in the case of a hopeless malady, when it came it came as a shock.

The silence in the vast auditorium was such that, as one delegate put it, "you could hear yourself breathe." Lewis, visibly moved, redeemed his pledge. All over the convention hall sat tough, hard-bitten, seasoned, scarred veterans of countless picket lines and bitter union struggles, weeping unashamedly like children. At one point in the convention, discussing his resignation, Lewis cried out, "But that is the way of life. Some are able to carry through and some fall. But there is nothing to worry about; we should not dwell on the past. . . . tomorrow is also a day. And I am concerned with tomorrow, and I care not what happened yesterday except insofar as the events of yesterday may bring wisdom to us to guide our steps tomorrow. Some great statesman once said, 'The heights are cold.' I think that is true. The poet said, 'Who ascends to the mountain's top finds the loftiest peaks encased in mist and snow.' I think that is true. It is just as true in the ranks of labor. Maybe it is in other fields of human endeavor. That does not make an awful difference. That is the way of men and life, and we cannot stop to weep and wear sackcloth and ashes because something that happened yesterday did not meet with our approval, or that we did not have a dream come true. Tomorrow is the day that always faces men and women. . . ." [11]

Many observers and delegates at this point felt eerily that they were witnessing an act that is denied to mortal men: a man preaching his own funeral eulogy and yet continuing to go on living. This reaction was felt in common by a great number of observers. Most accounts of Lewis's speech at this convention will and have already touched upon this strange, almost ghostlike phenomenon.

And what of Philip Murray through all of this? He made one talk decrying any desire for the office of president of the CIO. "Now perhaps what I am about to say has no particular relation to the subject already presented to this convention. Each man, I suppose, no matter who he may be, has a heart and soul and

[11] *Ibid.*, pp. 9-10.

mind of his own, exercises the right to express his own convictions upon certain situations. I happen to be that kind of man. For the past week or ten days the news columns of America have been literally flooded with statements to the effect that Phil Murray had some aspirations. I want this convention to know before I take my seat that I do not have any, that I am not a candidate for the presidency of the CIO. That decision has been reached by me, and I imagine, *I think that I have a right to make a decision once in a while in life.*[12] I have a wholesome respect and great admiration, an affection bordering upon actual love, for the President of this Union—let us not have any demonstration. Personally, I disagreed with the President of the National Organization in the recent election. But I did not disagree with him upon some fundamental issues, nor did he disagree with me upon fundamental questions. Those things were matters that really related themselves to the question of individual opinion again. Rumors have been circulated throughout the country about division, division between President Lewis and me, and division between other officers. A division between officers, President Lewis, and myself has never been true, and I trust in God that it never will be. . . ." [13]

Rumors went around the convention that Lewis was having difficulty getting Murray to accept the presidency and that he had to try to persuade him to do it. The idea that Lewis had even to speak twice to Murray, let alone "try to persuade him" came as a shock to the general opinion held by everyone with reference to the relationship between Lewis and Murray. This rumor, coupled with the visible fact of Murray's constant conferring with four outside friends, one a close spiritual adviser, made the convention stir uneasily. Lewis himself found Murray saying, "I'll give you my answer after I talk it over." Never had this happened to Lewis before.

What with Lewis orating his own funeral eulogy and acknowledging the applause for it, what with Communists haranguing and pursuing their hard, ruthless course and then giving vent to their sentimental human attachment to Lewis in very human tears, what with Hillman meekly accepting Lewis's bitter lashes, what with Murray huddling with his spiritual

---

[12] Italics are the writer's.
[13] *Ibid.*, p. 134.

advisers, the convention began to take on the cast of a strange night of *Macbeth*, "prophesying with accents terrible of dire combustion and confused events." It was an omen of the strange, unpredictable occurrences that would be the lot of the CIO henceforth.

On November 22, Murray was nominated for the presidency of the CIO by Lewis, and the nomination was seconded by Hillman. He was unopposed and unanimously elected. In his acceptance speech he struck publicly the chord that he was to sound over and over again. He wanted to be recognized as Philip Murray, President Murray, and not a pawn or puppet created by John L. Lewis. He wanted to breathe more than the air exhaled by John Lewis. He wanted to stand independently of Lewis, and yet he feared Lewis far more than did Hillman. In Lewis's presence he was overpowered with awe. While Lewis treated Murray with the affection of a father for a favorite child, nevertheless he regarded him as a child. With great emotion, Murray struck at the umbilical cord fastening him to Lewis.

"I have no illusions concerning the peculiar twist of fate that thrusts me into this position this morning. I am conscious that under ordinary circumstances this convention would have elected to its presidency the man we all love, John L. Lewis, and I would have supported him. . . . I find that many of the news organs in this country observed and suggested that if this terrible man Lewis were pushed out of the way, this mild man Murray, this moderate, vacillating, weak individual would immediately rush somewhere to perfect an agreement with the American Federation of Labor. Well, I just want you to know, my friends, as I told you the other day, I think I am a man. *I think I have conviction, I think I have a soul and a heart and a mind. And I want to let you in on something; they—with the exception, of course, of my soul—they all belong to me, every one of them. . . .*" [14]

One of Murray's closest and most publicized associates, who later was to join him in the break with Lewis, commented on Murray's "peculiar behavior at the convention. He kept repeating to people every day in some way or other 'Look, I'm not a

[14] *Ibid.*, p. 274. Italics the writer's.

child; I'm a man! A man!'" It was clear that Murray the child was cutting his own umbilical cord.

Whether or not Lewis was aware of the major metamorphosis that Murray was undergoing is a matter of speculation. On the one side is Lewis's dogged devotion and loyalty to Murray (as described later) and his refusal to brook any criticism of Murray by anyone and later to believe what was common knowledge. On the other side is Lewis's statement made to the writer:

"I began to first be concerned about Philip Murray's loyalty in 1939. In the middle of 1939, Mrs. Lewis had a long conversation with me, asking me to withdraw from the presidency of the CIO and use my energy to unite the labor movement. After all, the CIO was now a large, independent organization, strong in its own right, and fully prepared to meet the AF of L on at least equal ground, and the stage was ripe for unity or at least for preliminary moves in that direction. At the same time, a strong uncompromising public position had to be maintained because the climate was such that any offer of unity to the American Federation of Labor would be interpreted as a sign of weakness and would jeopardize the strength of the bargaining position of the CIO. Therefore, while I knew that the time for unity was not ripe or present, nevertheless, I felt as Mrs. Lewis did, very strongly that the time had come when I should withdraw from the presidency and begin to regain my strength and prepare for the campaign for unity. When I say regain my strength I need not remind you that the rigors and the attrition accompanying the organization of the CIO took their toll from all and I was certainly not the least exception.

"That year the CIO was convening in San Francisco, and a few weeks before the convention I had agreed with Mrs. Lewis that I would attempt to withdraw from the CIO. Phil Murray accompanied me on the train ride to San Francisco, and on that trip I told him what my plans and intentions were. I also told him that I wanted him to succeed me in office, and Murray made protests that were somewhat on the feeble side for some hours, and then during the next hours were too strong. I could not help sitting there and thinking to myself while Murray expostulated that he was not the man to succeed me, and over and over again the thought came into my mind, he 'doth protest too much, methinks.'

"To the CIO executive board I announced my intentions; I said I was going to resign. The board absolutely refused to consider anything along that line, and considerable pressure was brought to bear upon me unanimously by every single member of the CIO, all to the effect that my name and my person had become a symbol for the CIO, and this was a critical period, and my withdrawal at this time would tend to jeopardize everything that we had built up together. I also emphasized another reason for my withdrawal, and that is that inevitably during the hectic years of the building of the CIO I had not been able to give my full attention to my duties as president of the United Mine Workers of America. I felt deeply about this because I felt then as I do now, and as I always will, that the coal miners of America have the first call and the first right on whatever John L. Lewis has to contribute. However, I acceded to the pressures of the executive board and reconsidered and announced that I would continue in office. Then came a very definite surprise to me, because knowing my Phil Murray as I have long known him, I could see that he was completely crushed with disappointment. It had never occurred to me before that Phil Murray wanted to be president of the CIO and wanted that position. I did not know that my Phil Murray was so filled with ambition.

"As I have told you before, the first real rift between Murray and myself occurred in the Little Steel Massacre in 1937 on Decoration Day. This was the first time in Phil Murray's life that he had ever acted independently of my advice and judgment; that he had gone ahead without requesting my advice and judgment.

"And, of course, there was the Atlantic City convention, when I resigned, following my public statement that if Franklin D. Roosevelt were re-elected I would resign as head of the CIO, and I would do it, not only for the reasons I have expressed to you, but also to save the CIO from any embarrassment by being led by anyone who was in such disfavor with the President of the United States.

"I saw Murray at the convention in Atlantic City, and I saw him with his advisers. I saw Phil Murray turn to me and say, 'I'll have to think this over and talk it over with my friends.' And I saw Phil Murray adjourn, as did everyone in that convention hall, with the four advisers who constantly accompanied him as he came and as he went. I began to feel, here for the first time, a great power from the outside was being exerted into the organization of the CIO, and that Philip Murray was the subject of its intentions, and that Philip Murray might well be the vulnerable Achilles heel in this great American labor movement. I watched Murray sweating out his decision, because he knew in his speech to the convention that he was breaking off from me. The sweat poured from his face. He knew it and felt it. However, there was nothing else I could do at the time. Phil Murray was the only possible man to succeed me in office, and if you look over the rostrum of CIO leaders there wasn't anyone else who would have been acceptable to the unions that composed the Congress of Industrial Organizations.

"When I left the CIO, it was operating on a balanced budget. At that time, all it really needed was confidence and administration. The days when it required personal leadership and everything involved in the storm and fury of the building of the CIO—those days were past. It was straight administration—that was the only ability required for the post at the time when I stepped aside." [15]

Whether this statement is a later rationalized appraisal or whether Lewis knew it at the time will never be known. Lewis explains his loyalty to Murray's actions through most of 1941 as a desperate attempt and hope to avoid what he realized then might probably happen, and what later did happen—the break with Murray.

A subdued and worried Lewis returned to Washington. He was determined not to permit the development of circumstances that would aggravate Murray's tremendous insecurity. Despite Lewis's reservations about Murray's loyalty, he felt a deep devotion to his successor. He and Murray had been intimate friends for a quarter of a century. He could not bring himself to believe that Murray under any circumstances could ever defy or oppose him.

Lewis appraised the array of forces surrounding Murray at that time. Hillman's Amalgamated Clothing Workers Union

[15] Personal interview with John L. Lewis, United Mine Workers Building, Washington, D.C., December 17, 1948.

and its satellite, Emil Rieve's Textile Workers Organizing Committee, Murray's personal ambitions, a number of top CIO chiefs such as Haywood and Brophy, who Lewis felt were already "seduced by Roosevelt," and probably also Van A. Bittner—all were against Lewis. The question mark on Bittner stemmed from Lewis's personal opinion of Bittner: "Van A. Bittner was nobody's man but Bittner's."

Behind all of this was the driving power of the President of the United States.

On the pro-Lewis side were, first, the long friendship between Lewis and Murray; Murray's recognition of Lewis as his superior over a period of years; the strength of Lewis's own union, the United Mine Workers, which constituted the base of the CIO, both in terms of leadership as well as finances; and the multitude of left-wing-dominated unions that seemingly worshiped Lewis and hated Hillman and Roosevelt. Aside from other considerations, the left-wing or Communist-dominated unions adored Lewis for his antiwar isolationist position on foreign affairs. To the Communists the war between Hitler and France and England was a "phony imperialist war," and America must stay out of it in every possible way. To them Roosevelt and Hillman were warmongers to be fought without quarter.

While events to come were to play havoc with these lineups, Lewis seemed to overlook one enormous psychological factor in Murray and his lieutenants and one in himself.

First, he continued to look upon Murray and Bittner and others as his chief lieutenants in the UMW. For years they had been princes in the empire of the United Mine Workers of America, of which Lewis was the emperor. The relationship had been that of an emperor and his princes, in terms of allegiance and accepted status. Lewis forgot that in the wide arena of the CIO he had carved out new empires like steel and meat packing, and over these empires he placed his princes as emperors. Having become accustomed to the homage, the independence, and the prestige of being emperors they were loathe to return to the lower levels of princehood. Furthermore, their desires and ambitions were being encouraged by a super-emperor far above their former chief—none other than the President of the United States. Lewis did not realize that the enormous change in power of his subordinates would be accompanied by equal personality changes.

Both Murray and Bittner knew that Lewis made ninety-nine per cent of the decisions in the UMW and that to a major extent his lieutenants were the bits of the tail on the kite. They knew that Lewis knew how much less in stature they were compared to him, and it was a human reaction that underneath all of their professed love and loyalty there should be a deep hatred.

There was also inside Lewis a stubborn personal pride that made him feel it was infinitely beneath his dignity to engage in controversy with any of the CIO leaders whom, with the exception of Hillman, he regarded as his creations.[16]

Lewis returned to the second-floor office of the president of the UMW and went into veritable seclusion. CIO leaders after calling on Murray would troop downstairs to pay their respects to, and seek the advice of, the man everyone in the nation, including themselves, still regarded as the real head of the CIO, John L. Lewis.

Lewis would snort when they would try to review their discussions with Murray or request advice. "Philip Murray is your president, not I, sir," became a frequent refrain of Lewis's.

Lewis was very sensitive to Murray's reactions; and he was certain that Murray would and did resent this, despite Murray's holding the official position of top officer of the CIO. With two exceptions, Murray's own union, the Steel Workers, and Hillman's Amalgamated Clothing Workers with its affiliate of the Textile Workers, all the other unions continued to look to Lewis. Lewis felt that Murray was bitter about being overshadowed by Lewis and by being popularly regarded as Lewis's Man Friday, and he took another step to relieve the pressure of the situation. He not only refused to discuss CIO problems with CIO leaders, but strongly discouraged them from even stopping at his office for a social visit. This action was to be a major factor both in accelerating and in ensuring his break with the left-wing unions that was to erupt in a few months.

[16] A typical example of his attitude was manifested on December 18, 1948, when Lewis and the writer were lunching at the Carleton Hotel. Two tables away sat a national officer of the CIO. Lewis frowned at him, then turning to me chuckled, "When I see any of them, I feel like a mastiff dog stalking down the street while a puny Pekingese pup skulks well behind eating of my leavings."

Lewis went out of his way to make Murray feel secure and assured of his full support as president of CIO in fact as well as in name. An example of his concern is to be found in the following statement from Lewis. "Some weeks after Philip Murray's election to the presidency of the CIO, a number of organizers of the United Mine Workers who were closely identified with Philip Murray came to me and said that District 5, which is the Pittsburgh District, where Murray came from, was going to give a big banquet in honor of Murray's being elected to the presidency of the CIO. They wanted me to come as their guest to the banquet. I said, 'No, I would rather not.' They seemed somewhat surprised about this and continued to press me. I said, 'Look, this is a banquet for Phil Murray, and I don't think it would be proper for me to be there.' All that I was thinking of at the time was that it would be difficult for Phil Murray to be the center of attention, as it is only fitting for guests of honor at a banquet, when his chief was sitting at the same table, and that most of the attention would probably be directed toward me and result in deep resentment on the part of Murray. I did not want any more of his resentment. I wanted to avoid any kind of conflict situation or controversy. With this in mind, I continued to refuse to attend this dinner. However, the pressure began to develop, and I soon saw that if I continued to persist in refusing to be present at this dinner it would be interpreted as an insult to Phil Murray, and under these circumstances I then announced that I would be present.

"The dinner was held in the vaulted room of the William Penn Hotel in Pittsburgh, and it was a tremendous banquet. Phil Murray spoke, and I said a few words.

"Next morning I went into breakfast in the coffee shop of the hotel, and there at the central table at breakfast was the Murray retinue, all of them sitting around the table looking extremely depressed and all looking down at the front pages of newspapers on their table. I walked by, saying good morning, and received a very melancholy good morning in return. I was seated at the table and opened up the front page of the paper to see what had happened that had plunged Murray's followers into such a black depression. All I could see was a story on the front page announcing that 'John L. Lewis last night stated . . .' and went on giving in full detail what I had to say and ending with a very short paragraph to the effect that this speech was made at a dinner in the William Penn Hotel that had been given in honor of Philip Murray.

"To get a picture of their chagrin and disappointment was to get an index of one of the things characteristic of Murray and his followers and the issues which they developed in their campaign against me, and that is the utter and complete pettiness of the man and his associates." [17]

Despite the tensions and undercurrents of hostility, no overt hostilities were manifested until some months after the convention. The first indication that Murray was beginning to strike out alone came in a situation involving the Packinghouse Workers Organizing Committee. Following Lewis's break with Roosevelt, certain officials of that union rallied behind Lewis and went all out in support of Willkie prior to the CIO convention. Van A. Bittner, who was chairman of the Packinghouse Workers Organizing Committee, summarily transferred these top union officials to distant parts of the country. Following Murray's election to the presidency, they appealed to Lewis's office and were told to request a meeting with President Murray. Lewis expressed every confidence that Murray would not support Van A. Bittner. The situation stalled for weeks while a civil war raged inside the Packinghouse Workers Union. Finally Murray agreed to see the Lewis supporters. He met them with general phrases of fraternal sympathy but gave no decision. The Lewis supporters, blindly assuming that Murray would side with Lewis, were stunned.

They turned to Lewis and discovered to their horror there suddenly was no Lewis. Lewis had been struck down by a coronary attack. For days Lewis's condition was critical. During this period was first observed the first development of a Murray machine. News of Lewis's grave condition leaked out. Using the battle cry of "King Lewis is dead, long live King Murray," the Murray followers began maneuvering, forcing unions into the Murray camp. An example was found in the case of a minor CIO official in Chicago who went around saying, "Lewis is dying of a heart attack. If you know what's good for you, you'd better line up behind Murray."

[17] Interview with John L. Lewis in his office in the United Mine Workers of America Building, Washington, D.C., December 17, 1948.

This official's actions and statements were so open and so frequent that they were reported by many individuals to Lewis's office. Kathryn Lewis, John L. Lewis's daughter, called Murray and insisted that the individual be dismissed. Murray expressed horror at such behavior and ordered the Chicago union official to come to Pittsburgh. There he was subjected to a blistering tongue-lashing by Murray, not about what he had done, but about the crudity of his approach. However, he was not dismissed.

Unfortunately for the Murray cohorts, they had erred in interring the king before his death. Lewis's recovery and survival were an acute disappointment and embarrassment to them. It soon became clear to everyone that a Murray machine was on the way. Murray's behavior became common knowledge. Just as in the case of a man with an unfaithful wife where everyone in town knows about it except the husband, who is the last one to find out, so it was with Lewis. Lewis not only would not believe any reports of Murray's actions, but he refused even to listen. On one occasion he ordered his daughter out of his office because she had dared to question Murray's activities and intentions.

All over the country CIO chiefs were spreading damnation against Lewis. Secretary James Carey of the CIO was particularly bitter and open in his denunciation of Lewis. Still, Lewis could not believe it. It did not make any sense. Even Murray knew that the left-wing unions "belonged" to Lewis, and between them and the United Mine Workers, Murray was inviting suicide by being party to a campaign against Lewis, which, of course, could not be true.

Then it happened. On June 22 Hitler's Nazi armies invaded the Soviet Union. The Soviet Union was at war, and within hours Lewis was to discover a large part of the forces that formerly supported him were gone with the winds of that day.

There have been many accounts of the frantic attempts by the Communist-dominated unions and the left-wingers to try to have Lewis change his foreign policy in accordance with their new line. Stories have been told that Harry Bridges and Lee Pressman, both of whom had reversed their conception of the war following June 22, had argued and pleaded with Lewis to alter his policy of isolationism.

The evidence seems to indicate the contrary. Lewis had extended his isolationist stand on foreign policy into his relationship with the CIO. He had blocked himself off from the other CIO leaders, including the left wing. Pressman stated to the writer that he and Lewis did not have discussions about Lewis's isolationism. Pressman stated, "I had only one conversation with Mr. Lewis, and that was in August, very shortly after Mr. Lewis had signed a statement with Herbert Hoover and some other people demanding that this country stay out of war. I went in to see him and said to him, 'John, I can't go along with you when the logic of the situation puts you in the kind of company that you're in when you sign that document.' Lewis didn't say anything and I walked out and I just never came back. I went with Murray." [18]

If anything, the situation seems to have bordered on the incredible in that there was no real attempt to try to bridge the gap of the foreign issue between Lewis and the left-wing leaders. One of the most prominent of the CIO left-wing officials, who was very close to Lewis, told the writer: "Right there is where the greatest error of the left wing, really a horrible, almost incomprehensible, action, took place. In fact, the cold truth of the matter is no one argued with Lewis on it. No one even bothered to talk to him about it, but you see you have to know some of the background on what happened and why this kind of incredible situation was permitted to develop without any kind of argument or discussion. First, after Lewis resigned from the presidency of the CIO and Phil Murray became president, Lewis did everything in his power to stay out of the picture and really let Phil Murray be president, in fact as well as in name. The situation became very difficult for all of the CIO chiefs who would go in to see Murray and talk to him in his office as president of the CIO and then come right downstairs to the second floor and go in to see Lewis and ask Lewis for advice and guidance and decisions. It was quite obvious that they regarded their business with Murray simply as a courteous action, but the real chief of the CIO, their chief, was John L. Lewis. Murray began to resent this, and Lewis was well aware of it and began to encourage the CIO chiefs to stay away. He would use these phrases; he would say to them, 'Stay away from me. It's

[18] Interview with Lee Pressman at his office, December 6, 1948.

Murray's job. Go see Murray, he'll decide it, but stay away from me.' With some individuals, such as myself, he actually said we should stay away because Murray just would not understand the fact that the relationship was devoid of any kind of conspiracy or malice against him. As a result, CIO chiefs, including myself, really by order of Lewis, had been staying away from him as long as three months or four before this break came. You just have to understand that in order to realize why there had not been any contact or conversation in trying to avoid this kind of dilemma, which was a real catastrophe. Whoever saw Lewis during that period was suspected by Murray, and remember how close I was to Murray at that time.

Overnight the Communist-dominated unions switched their line and their allegiances. The speed of the Communist reversal of policy and the discipline present in their ranks to implement this radical change wreaked havoc in the Lewis legions in the CIO. Now, with the exception of his own United Mine Workers, all of the CIO was behind Roosevelt's foreign policy; and, since Murray supported Roosevelt, they were for Murray. Lewis was left at the post while the entire American labor movement thundered past.

Now the left wing publicly opened the attack against Lewis, unloosing every familiar epithet from "opportunist" to "Fascist." Lewis was cornered, wounded, dazed, and bitter. He felt betrayed on every front, but he still could not bring himself to believe that in the last analysis Murray, too, would desert him. He was angry with the Communists' attacks against him and decided that now the time had come to talk to Murray and counterattack against the Communists. At this point Murray suffered a heart attack near Pittsburgh, and Lewis postponed a showdown.

The attacks against Lewis mounted daily. It was no longer the Communist-dominated unions but the officials of all non-Communist unions in the CIO who attacked him. By October, Lewis felt that the situation had become intolerable, and a meeting with Murray at Atlantic City was arranged.

For the past eight years columnists and writers have presented their interpretation and "facts" as to what took place at that fateful meeting of October 18, 1941. The only "facts" reported to date that are correct are the date and location of the meeting,

Lewis's attire (blue- and gray-checkered flannel shirt), and his closing remark to Murray, "It was nice to have known you, Phil."

The author was in Atlantic City during those two days at Lewis's invitation, stopping at the President Hotel, where Lewis, Mrs. Lewis, and their daughter, Kathryn, were also staying. He was continuously present in conversation with the Lewis family immediately before and after Lewis's visits with Murray. There had been a brief meeting the previous afternoon, and on this day there were to be two meetings between them, one in the afternoon and the other in the late evening. Lewis was extremely upset that day and recounted his conference with Murray of the day before in great detail. The writer has no question of the unvarnished validity of Lewis's statements on both the content of Murray's remarks and Murray's reactions of that day. Lewis was talking to his wife and daughter, and if ever there was a situation when one could be certain that Lewis was giving the bald facts, it was here. Immediately following these meetings with the Lewis family, the author, unknown to Lewis, retired to his room and made copious notes of what had been said, with the belief that it was important historical material.

At lunch that day Lewis reported that he had seen Murray for two hours the day before and that Murray had talked about his illness. He had found Murray distraught, his conversation disorganized, and he had kept plucking at his sleeve in a pathetic manner. He had suffered a coronary thrombosis and since that time had been having poor blood circulation and various pains.

Murray said he didn't think it would be at all possible for him to continue in office as the president of the CIO, and furthermore, he didn't want to. He also said he had recently had a visit from Henry Wallace and seemed very pleased in having that much attention.

Lewis interrupted his account of his talk. "Philip has always been that way. He just gets completely flattered when he receives any attention from any national figures, and as you know, at the White House the President will treat him like an old dirty piece of laundry and then call him in and order him as you would a puppy.

"Philip talked at random about the CIO, and he mentioned the piece that he had written on foreign policy for the convention and said he would show it to me, say about two weeks before the convention. When I told him that wasn't what I wanted to talk to him about and I wasn't particularly interested in pursuing that subject at the moment, he started talking at random again. I don't hate Mr. Murray. I recognize a simple little fact. After all, every man has his price, and Mr. Murray is no exception. . . .I didn't make any request of him concerning the CIO attacks, nor any requests whatsoever. Murray is in no condition to talk to me. Frankly, I think he is a little bit out of his mind. He talks about his place in heaven and then he talks about the CIO the next moment. I didn't ask him for any commitments."

Lewis then emphasized that his sole subject for discussion with Murray was the attacks made on Lewis by union leaders in the CIO and some of Murray's own henchmen, such as James Carey. Lewis said, "Whenever I brought up Carey's name or Van Bittner's, Phil would get very upset and tremble. He would say, 'It isn't so, Jack. It isn't so. You're hearing the wrong things.' "

Lewis then began to pace up and down the room talking alternately to his wife and his daughter. "Murray is a sick man. If I get him upset, he may have another heart attack and die—then everyone will charge me with the responsibility of Murray's death. I just can't do it. Here he is, and here am I, and here are all these attacks against me, and I can't push him or argue with him or do anything because he might have another heart attack."

Lewis was caustically reminded that Murray had shown no such consideration for him when he had his heart attack just about six months before Murray's seizure. Lewis shouted, "It doesn't matter. I still cannot do it, I cannot! I will not have a scene with him. I will not argue with him, but I know for the first time that what everyone is saying is true. Murray is against me."

After more conversation, Lewis said, "I am going out now to meet with him, and I'll try again." Then Lewis paused, and a look of wonder came over his face, and he whispered, "He believes Bittner and Carey over me. He knows Bittner as well as

I do, and Carey has just been our office boy! But Phil Murray takes their word over mine! Takes their word, when he knows and everyone knows what Bittner and Carey have tried to do to me! Well, I'll try once more, but what can I do? How can I talk when I know that excitement may kill him?" Lewis drew a deep breath. "I'm leaving, and I will see what happens. Let's all have dinner together this evening." Lewis left.

At about 4 P.M. I returned to my room, wrote up the conversation, and got to bed and took a brief nap. I was awakened by the phone. I glanced at my watch. It was 6:30. I picked up the receiver. It was Lewis. Lewis said, "Saul, could you come down and have dinner with us, say in about thirty minutes?"

"I will be down in thirty minutes," I replied.

I went down to the dining room at 7 P.M. and was immediately ushered to Lewis's table. We were the only ones in the dining room. I mentioned this to the headwaiter, who explained that cold and rainy weather as well as its being out of season accounted for the handful of guests in the hotel. The four of us—John L. Lewis, Mrs. Lewis, Kathryn, and I—started dinner.

While we were eating, Mr. Lewis reported on his conversation with Mr. Murray. He said, "Mr. Murray regards the CIO organization as being well organized today and in a very good condition. I don't. He does. Murray repudiates any maneuvers against me and says it is all untrue. I asked him if James Carey was to be renominated as the secretary of the CIO, and Murray said yes. I said, 'I am against him.' Murray got very disturbed, cried a little, and said Carey had asked him for the renomination and has assured him that what I had said about his attacking me was untrue. I reminded him of others. Murray said they weren't true. I just didn't press the issue because it would just be telling him that he was a fool or a liar or both. Probably the latter.

"Murray had been sold a line of merchandise of a preposterous nature. For example, he said that Mr. Roosevelt would resign within a few months and that Henry Wallace would succeed him as the President of the United States."

I said, "What did you say to that?"

"With a sick man there is no point in discussion." Lewis continued, "I said to Murray, 'Philip, things may get tougher and tougher and probably will. The success of the future of the organized labor movement depends on its being led by people who are prepared to fight. For example, would you be willing to go to a concentration camp for your own people?' Murray at this point became very disturbed, and he started telling me that while he was sick, he had looked at the ceiling for two months and had reconciled himself to death and the hereafter, and he just rambled along. I then said to him, 'Well, from now on Philip, you go your way and I will go mine.'

"Murray broke down and started crying and hysterically grasped at the lapels of my coat and said, 'Jack, your way is mine. It always was, and it always will be.'

"I think at that moment I could have asked him to resign and he might have, but I didn't. I don't deal that way with a man who is sick. Murray isn't a man; he is a scared puppet of those so-called advisers. I am sure that all I would have to do would be to use any pressure of any sort, and these advisers would see that the story got into the newspapers portraying me as the ogre, forcing a man who is seriously ill to reach certain decisions."

Kathryn said, "Murray calls you a liar. He is taking Carey's word against yours."

Lewis nodded and said, "Beginning now, as I told him, Murray can go his way, and I will go mine."

The latter part of the dinner was accompanied by a general silence. After the coffee, Lewis lit one of his big black cigars, leaned back and puffed for a moment, and then leaning toward me, said, "You know, Saul, things change. In many ways I guess that is the course of destiny. There are alliances and realliances of forces, not only domestic but now international, and the alignments will change tomorrow and again the day after tomorrow.

"My history in the AF of L has been illustrative of this. I have been up one year and down the next, and when I am down, they all say John L. Lewis is finished, but the next year is different. I built the United Mine Workers into the greatest and strongest union the world has ever known. Philip Murray was happy as long as I walked before him with a broadax and hewed the way for him. He was happy as long as I assumed the responsibility."

Lewis looked about the empty dining room. I realized with a shock that he was moved to the point of tears. The muscles of his face were working, and he seemed to be fighting to keep his emotions under control. Suddenly tears rolled down his cheeks. Lowering his head, he said, "This is the same hotel, this is the same dining room, and this is the same table where in 1935 a small group and myself walked out of the AF of L convention, which was a few steps away at the boardwalk, sat down here at this table, and organized the CIO." Then turning to me, Lewis continued, "Where you are sitting, Saul, David Dubinsky sat. And Mother, where you are sitting, sat Sidney Hillman, and Howard [19] sat where you are, Kathryn." Lewis then paused, clenched his fist, pushed against the edge of the table, and arising said, "Here I conceived and built the CIO, and it is here that I leave it!"

[19] Charles P. Howard, now deceased, was president of the International Typographical Union and was named secretary of the Committee for Industrial Organizations.

Chapter 11

The Break with the CIO

AFTER the break with Murray, it was only a question of time until Lewis would come to the final parting of the ways with the CIO. But there were pressing problems facing the United Mine Workers, to which Lewis had to give priority.

The most pressing of these was the relationship of the union to the steel industry's mines. These mines, known as captive mines, belonged to seven major steel companies, U.S. Steel, Weirton, Bethlehem, Republic, Wheeling, Crucible, and Youngstown. These seven pillars of the steel industry produced 70 per cent of the nation's output of steel. U.S. Steel alone was responsible for 35 per cent of the production. Since they all had more than their share of defense contracts, they were producing 80 per cent of all the steel going into war production. These captive mines, employing 53,000 miners, furnished all the coal needed by their steel-mill owners. While more than 95 per cent of the coal miners in these captive mines were union members and the union was the recognized collective-bargaining agency, Lewis nevertheless demanded a union shop.

On the surface, Lewis's position seemed to be merely that of compelling the 5 per cent or less of nonunion employees who were receiving the benefits forced from the industry by the union to join the union, since they were achieving gains without in return paying dues or making any contribution to the union.

At that time Lewis told the writer that among all the reasons for his closed-shop demand the following was probably the most important. He felt the administration had gone so far that war was inevitable, and that national policy during a war period had always been the fixing or freezing of the status quo. Lewis felt that he owed it to the mine workers union and to the entire labor movement to "batten down the hatches" and see to it that when the mine workers union was frozen, it would be with a union shop prevailing every place a man dug coal. This would protect the union through the war chaos. He also felt that it would be essential to the welfare of all labor, for Lewis had always conceived of the United Mine Workers Union as the shock troops of labor.

Actually Lewis's objective carried deep implications in the industrial world. If he could secure a union shop from this section of the steel industry, it would place Murray in the difficult and embarrassing position where he might well have to fight for the same objectives for his steel workers. Murray's union did not then possess, nor has it yet achieved, the discipline and raw strength and long traditions that have molded the United Mine Workers into the unshakable force they are. The odds would be overwhelming against Murray's being as successful as Lewis.

The steel industry recognized that if Lewis imposed the union shop in their captive mines, they might well be opening the door to considerable unrest and trouble in the balance of the industry. Steel, too, while conceding the presence and apparent inevitability of unions, still clung to the outer raiment of the traditional open shop. If Lewis had his way, even that would be lost. For these reasons the steel industry prepared to resist to the last ditch. Steel, like all other industries, recognized that the international situation had moved Roosevelt to the right and that organized labor could no longer receive the positive administration support of the mid-1930's. Industry was now in a position to resist labor demands.

Steel was adamant in its refusal to grant the union shop, and Lewis ordered a strike in September. After one week a truce was declared for thirty days, and the issue was placed in front of the National Defense Mediation Board.

October was a month of hell and fury. Everywhere the Nazi armies were triumphant. Russia, though fighting the Nazis as they had never been fought before, seemed to be going down to eventual defeat. The American Navy and German U-boats were already shooting it out, and America tensed with the knowledge that war would soon embrace its life.

In the midst of this national anxiety, on October 24, 1941, the Mediation Board announced its decision, which, first, evaded any discussion of the issue, and second, agreed to arbitrate if both parties would agree to be bound by the decision.

Lewis was furious. He felt, with cause, that thirty days had gone down the drain. Word of Lewis's determination to fight it out reached the White House. Roosevelt, acutely apprehensive of the consequences of a coal strike, immediately moved into the disintegrating scene with a call for U.S. Steel's Myron Taylor to confer and co-operate with Lewis to prevent a stoppage in coal and steel production.

The next day, Saturday, Lewis wrote the President agreeing to meet with Taylor and also castigating the Mediation Board as "casual and lackadaisical to the point of indifference." He then bitterly blamed Sidney Hillman for the decision of the Board. Lewis did not commit himself on not striking, but on the contrary implied that there would be a strike.

On Sunday, October 26, *The New York Times* front page carried a three-column headline:

LEWIS DEFIES THE PRESIDENT
ALLOWS COAL MINE STRIKE
DEFENSE STEEL THREATENED

On this Sunday, Roosevelt replied to Lewis with an unusually restrained letter in which he ignored Lewis's attacks on the Mediation Board and Hillman. Roosevelt told Lewis that arrangements were completed for Lewis to meet Taylor on the coming Wednesday morning. The President then concluded his note by appealing to Lewis and his associates "as loyal citizens to come now to the aid of your country." But the President's direct request to Lewis met a fate similar to all the others, for the President's desires found Lewis's mouth tightly shut that night and the captive coal mines shut the next morning.

Lewis's answer came the next day. He curtly told the President on Monday: "There is no question of patriotism or national security. If you would use the power of the state to restrain me as an agent of labor, then, sir, I submit, that you should use that same power to restrain my adversary in this issue, who is an agent of capital. My adversary is a rich man named Morgan, who lives in New York." He denied any interference with defense and charged that the steel mills had been storing coal and could go for an indefinite period without curtailing production. He also said that if there was any shortage the miners would later work overtime to make it up. He then reviewed his unsuccessful attempts to get Taylor to meet with him and went on, terming it a fight between J. P. Morgan and himself. He ended by telling Roosevelt that he would be glad to meet with Roosevelt and Morgan.

Within two hours Roosevelt's reply was in Lewis's hands. The President brushed away all of Lewis's arguments, including his contention that this was a fight between J. P. Morgan and the coal miners. The President told Lewis, "For the third time your government, through me, asks you and the officers of the UMW to authorize an immediate resumption of mining."

That Monday night Roosevelt in a Navy Day radio address reviewed world conditions and the imminent peril of war. Then he severely attacked Lewis, though not by name, for his refusal to stop the strike. Roosevelt had thrice pleaded with Lewis in three days, and Lewis hadn't yielded an inch on his position. The President's voice was angry and impatient as he spoke.

". . . Yes, our nation will and must speak from every assembly line—yes, from every coal mine. . . . That output cannot be hampered by the selfish obstruction of any small minority, a small but dangerous minority of industrial magnates who, perhaps, hold out for extra profits or for 'business as usual,' and it cannot be hampered by the selfish obstruction of a small but dangerous minority of labor leaders for a minute. For labor as a whole knows that a small minority is a menace to the true cause of labor itself, as well as for the nation as a whole. . . ."

Congress was now in a tempest. From Capitol Hill came the demand for Lewis's head. Congress denounced Lewis as a dictator and milled about like cattle preparing to stampede. They wanted to enact any and all kinds of anti-labor legislation. Texas was well heard from in this Congressional tumult. Senator O'Daniel shouted comparisons of "wild-eyed labor leaders" to skunks "that got our chickens back home while we were out trying to find coyotes." O'Daniel continued, "The President of the United States is being told by one of these labor leaders just where the United States should head in." From the same

state, Senator Connally charged that "John L. Lewis challenges
. . . the Government. He flouts . . . the President. I refuse to
accept the dictates and edicts of John L. Lewis. The Government of the United States cannot longer tolerate his defiance."
Missouri's Senator Truman denounced Lewis's strike as an
"outrage" and then solemnly predicted that if Roosevelt were to
appeal to the miners over Lewis's head they would all return to
work. Truman's conclusion was one-hundred-per-cent wrong,
as Roosevelt was to find out in the 1943 war strikes. Senator
George of Georgia called for the use of the Army against the
union. Senator Ellender threw the book at Lewis denouncing
him as a "traitor to American ideals . . . a menace to peace and
property . . . to the boys preparing to defend us . . . to the labor
movement . . ." and here Ellender was temporarily at a loss to
think up others whom Lewis now menaced. It should be noted
here that Ellender called Lewis a "traitor to American ideals"
during 1937, too, when Lewis was leading the charge of the CIO.
Senator Byrd of Virginia briefly spoke his piece on Lewis, "An
arrogant leader." Ohio's Senator Taft made the calmest comment of all his colleagues, "Roosevelt should do everything he
can to open the mines."

Roosevelt expressed a sympathy for the ire of Congress and
intimated that if Lewis did not stop the strike the President
would permit the wave of Congressional temper to flood into
anti-labor legislation.

Wednesday, October 29, found the Mayflower Hotel the focal
point of national interest. Here Taylor and Lewis were meeting
once again. In their previous meeting in 1937 Taylor had let
down the bars of Big Steel against the CIO. Lewis had emerged
a triumphant victor. The nation wondered what would be the
outcome of this second clash. The press pounced upon every
detail, even to the food items Taylor and Lewis ate. The conference went on for some hours, and then both Lewis and Taylor
adjourned to the White House for a meeting with the President. It was then announced that both Lewis and Taylor had
agreed to submit the issue to the Mediation Board for an opinion on the merits of Lewis's demands but that neither U.S. Steel
nor the UMW would be compelled to accept the Board's findings.

Lewis was moving up on his goal. He had a quiet understanding with Taylor that if the Board voted in his favor U.S. Steel would grant the union shop; if not, Lewis was still free to fight it out. It was a definite tactical victory for Lewis. Late Thursday morning Lewis called off the coal strike and at 2 P.M. that afternoon he notified the Board that the deadline for their decision was Saturday, November 15, or seventeen days from the moment the Board received the case. Lewis was well aware that the opening of the CIO convention was two days later, Monday, November 17. Lewis, recognizing that the CIO and AF of L would have to support him, reluctant as they might be, foresaw the tactical use of the CIO convention as a sounding board in his behalf in the event of a strike. Roosevelt would find his administration under severe attack, and Roosevelt's labor allies would be acutely embarrassed by the Government opposition to Lewis. He was now set.

On November 10, five days before the expiration of the Lewis time limit, the Board rendered its judgment against Lewis, nine to two. The two dissenters were Philip Murray and Thomas Kennedy, representing the CIO. The two AF of L representatives, William A. Calvin of the Boilermakers and George Q. Lynch, president of the Pattern Makers, voted against the union shop, although the original motion for it had been made by the AF of L members. The AF of L's behavior stunned many labor leaders. The reason given by the Board boiled down to the fact that imposition by the Government of a union shop was not democratic.

Lewis was now convinced that the Board was playing politics with himself and his union. He felt that Roosevelt had sent the word down for a decision like this. Chairman Will Davis of the Board promptly denied any influence. This same Board acting on a case almost identical with Lewis's had rendered judgment for a union shop. In the Bethlehem West Coast Ship Yards certains yards had no union shop while others had. The Board ordered the union shop in those yards so that there would be a uniform pattern for the industry. The only answer for this contradiction to Lewis and many other labor leaders was that the administration was gunning for "Big John."

Overnight Murray and Kennedy resigned from the Mediation Board, which ended it. It staggered on for a few weeks, but it was dead. Lewis ordered his policy committee to meet in Washington on Friday and rubber-stamp his now certain strike order. Lewis's labor foes were mute as they recognized Lewis's cause as the holy cause of labor. Panic gripped the administration. Roosevelt now knew that his Mediation Board had gone too far. It was possible to lean toward industry and placate or force most labor leaders, but not Lewis. Lewis was ready to ride to the end of the line. Roosevelt, bitter and angry at Lewis, tried to stop the oncoming strike by offering to write a letter over his own signature to every nonunion man working in the captive mines, explaining the benefits of unionism.

Roosevelt never knew how deeply he offended Lewis with this proposal. It was practically telling Lewis, "Well, if you can't get them to join your union, I will." Roosevelt also was not aware of the *faux pas* of writing directly to the rank and file on union business. After all, if the President could talk them into joining the union, he could also talk them into other actions that would shift power from the union chiefs to the White House. All this added to Lewis's allergy to labor's dependence upon the Government and resulted in his curt rejection of the President's offer.

Yet Lewis, in the days of the NRA, did not hesitate to use the President's name to recruit union members. In 1933 Lewis's men carried the cry of "The President wants you to join the union" to all the coal fields. It was a magic formula. Lewis then welcomed the same presidential assistance that he now rejected, but there was a fundamental difference. It was his organizers approaching the men directly and not the President. The question, however, can still be raised whether or not Lewis would have accepted the same offer from Roosevelt in 1933 which he was now spurning in 1941. The author believes that then Lewis would have leaped at the offer. When all reasons are boiled down, we reach a simple conclusion. Then he needed it; at this time he did not.

The November 10 decision of the Mediation Board kicked off a week of acute tension. This was to be the long-awaited and constantly delayed showdown between Lewis and Roosevelt. Many in the nation held their breath, and more licked their chops in anticipation of the smashing of Lewis.

Tuesday, Armistice Day, found Army Intelligence surveying the coal fields and the military setting up headquarters in Pittsburgh. Congress was in a cold rage, demanding that Roosevelt spend some time squelching "the bushy-browed Hitler at home" instead of concentrating on overseas affairs.

On Wednesday, the President ordered Lewis and the representatives of steel to meet at the White House at 11:15 Friday morning. The reason for the delay was that Roosevelt had his hands full with ensuring passage of the highly important amended Neutrality Act, which was coming up for a final vote the next day. Also the President wanted time for public opinion to generate and manifest itself.

On Thursday the House cheered as Roosevelt's message urging the passage of the amended Neutrality Act touched on the coal strike with the terse, ominous comment, "The government proposes to see this thing through." The revised Neutrality Act passed by a narrow margin. *The New York Times* emphasized in a streamer headline across the entire front page that the act was passed "After Pledge by Roosevelt to Quell Strikes."

Eleven fifteen, Friday morning, found Lewis at the White House with representatives of steel. The President spoke firmly. He ordered a settlement saying, "I'm not threatening. I don't believe in threats. . . . It is a national necessity that the production of this coal be continued without delay."

A Lewis deep in thought left the White House. It was apparent to him that, although everyone thought he was at Roosevelt's mercy, on the contrary he had the President at a disadvantage. The cost to the President's prestige abroad and to the defense program at home would be very high in the battle to destroy Lewis. The consequences could well be catastrophic on the domestic scene, with chaos resulting in the entire field of organized labor. Lewis had felt this before, but the undertone of caution in Roosevelt's militancy now convinced him that victory lay in attack. His mind was made up.

That afternoon Lewis, Murray, and mine union Secretary-Treasurer Tom Kennedy went to the Wardman Park Hotel, lunched, and conferred for four hours with U.S. Steel's Benjamin Fairless and his two colleagues representing Bethlehem Steel and Youngstown Sheet and Tube. After this affable meeting they agreed to adjourn overnight and continue these discussions on Saturday.

Saturday, November 15, Lewis sounded the call to arms. He

announced that the agreement to work expired at midnight. The strike was on. The first knowledge both Benjamin Fairless and Roosevelt had of this lightning move was from the press. Fairless gasped to *The New York Times,* "I am surprised and amazed." What Roosevelt had to say was said in the privacy of the White House. Roosevelt knew that Lewis had put all his chips down and had embarked on a one-way trip to triumph or disaster.

The first reaction of the administration reported in the press concerned hasty military conferences. Rumors flourished of fifty thousand troops about to march on the coal fields. The complete silence surrounding the White House gave birth to wild tales of horrible vengeance about to annihilate Lewis.

Monday found the strike on, and the CIO convention meeting in Detroit managed to get on the front page because the convention voted to back the strike. Lewis's timing was perfect, and the squeeze was on the President. To fight Lewis, Roosevelt would also have to fight his labor friends. Throughout the week the convention was completely overshadowed by this titanic struggle between Roosevelt and Lewis.

The public temper shot up. A Lee County, Florida, draft board shut up shop "as long as John L. Lewis dictates the labor policy of the United States." From all over the nation came howls of anger and demands for Roosevelt to crush Lewis. Even Wendell Willkie attacked Lewis. Lewis stood unmoved.

On Wednesday Roosevelt offered arbitration with one hand and with the other hand permitted stories to circulate that the Army was prepared to enter the coal fields.

Lewis's answer was to accelerate the offensive. He scorned Roosevelt's arbitration proposal, saying, "Your recent statements on this question, as the chief executive of the nation, have been so prejudicial to the claims of the mine workers as to make uncertain that an umpire could be found whose decision would not reflect your interpretations of Government policy, Congressional attitude, and public opinion."

Lewis responded to threats of the Army coming in by having miners all over the country begin to walk off their jobs. That day 175,000 miners were out, and Lewis was moving to a national strike that would halt the entire economy. Lewis dismissed the possible Army invasion, saying, "If the soldiers come, the mine workers will remain peacefully in their homes, conscious of the fact that bayonets in coal mines will not produce coal."

For two fateful days Roosevelt wrestled with the decision. His hatred of Lewis equaled Lewis's hatred of him. He passionately yearned to destroy Lewis; but the President, a master strategist, knew it would be a Pyrrhic victory.

On Saturday, November 22, the nation was shocked when Roosevelt suddenly surrendered. He named a three-man arbitration board of Fairless for steel, Lewis for the miners, and John Steelman of the U.S. Conciliation Service. Lewis promptly accepted "arbitration," for he knew as well as the President that this was not arbitration.

Steelman was a good friend of Lewis and markedly a proponent of the union shop. On this as well as many other issues, Lewis had won.

For sixteen days this arbitration panel meditated and then with great seriousness awarded the union shop in the captive mines to Lewis's union. The vote was two to one, with Fairless dissenting. The significance of the announcement was practically lost, as was our Navy at Pearl Harbor that same day. America was at war!

The issue of support for the President and his foreign policy, which had pitted the entire CIO from left to right against Lewis, disintegrated with the bombs of Pearl Harbor. The nation had been attacked and was at war. As did all American leaders, Lewis issued the following public statement:

> When the nation is attacked, every American must rally to its defense. All other considerations become insignificant. Congress and administrative government must be supported and every aid given to the men in the combat services of our country.
>
> Each true American will co-operate, and unified effort become a reality. With all other citizens I join in the support of our government to the day of its ultimate triumph over Japan and all other enemies.

The tremendous impact of sudden war seemed to act as a shock treatment on all, temporarily driving out the neurotic personal hatreds that had obsessed all leaders of labor, including Lewis and those locked in struggle with him. For the moment there was unity.

Shortly after Pearl Harbor, Roosevelt ordered a national conference of industry and labor in order to arrange for uninterrupted production for the needs of the nation in this crisis.
Basic to this conference was the setting up of procedures and
mechanisms for the peaceful and speedy solution of all labor
disputes. All were passionately agreed that there must be no
interruption of production, but rather an ever increasing flow
of everything needed for victory.

Organized labor's representatives were William Green, Matthew Woll, and George Meany for the AF of L. For the CIO
Murray appointed himself, Julius Emspak, leading left-winger
and outstanding figure of the United Electrical Workers, and
John L. Lewis.

Throughout these meetings, Lewis towered as a giant, and
both labor and industry members were soon following his lead.
Both Murray and Emspak appeared cowed and almost fright-
ened, as Lewis alternated from belligerence to expansive
humor. There are many stories told about this conference and
the ways in which Lewis captured the following not only of the
CIO and the AF of L bloc but also of the industry group. His
humor cajoled and bit and blustered, and he quickly became
the unchallenged leader of the meeting. He grasped the limelight from the moment he arose to introduce himself, when he
gravely surveyed the group and solemnly announced, "The
name is John L. Lewis of the United Mine Workers of America." Both industry and labor representatives doubled over with
laughter. Lewis grinned, and with that Lewis quickly became
the puppeteer of the conference.

The issues to be resolved soon emerged. Industry wanted to
preserve the status quo throughout the war, which would include the open shop where it then existed, and felt labor should
sheath the strike weapon for the duration. This was countered
by proposals from both the CIO and the AF of L that the new
machinery to be created be empowered to recognize the union
shop or closed shop in industries that were then open shop and
that would expand to an unprecedented extent in the war situation. Lewis spearheaded these proposals, along with demands
for joint labor-management councils, equal pay for women, and
an accepted number of working hours to make up a working

day so that there would be an unquestioned, universal rule on overtime pay.

The issue of the new machinery or board being empowered to order the union shop or closed shop in an industrial dispute stymied the conference. At this point, the President ended the conference by an executive order that practically acceded to the demands of the labor group but at the same time removed a situation from which Lewis would emerge with the increased stature of the victor. The President's executive order resulted in the creation of what later came to be called the War Labor Board. There are those who believe that Lewis's hatred for the new War Labor Board was a consequence of the President's intervention in the conference with his executive order. Those critics who make this oversimplified observation attribute to Lewis a supersensitive immature pettiness that is belied by the evidence of a lifetime.

Nineteen forty-two began with Lewis not only rid of the burden of the impossible issue of isolationism but with the recovery of considerable prestige as the result of the labor-management conferences. Lewis was now in a position to move. The peaceful aftermath of the conferences was suddenly shattered on Saturday afternoon, January 17, when Lewis called a press conference at the United Mine Workers Building and threw a bomb into the labor picture. Lewis released copies of a letter he had mailed to Murray and Green, calling for meetings between the CIO and the AF of L, looking forward to a merger and a united labor movement, or as Lewis described it, "accouplement." Addressing both Philip Murray and William Green, presidents of the CIO and AF of L respectively, Lewis wrote:

Gentlemen:
    The numerical strength of organized labor in our country is divided substantially into two great houses. . . . It is obvious that if accouplement could be achieved with unified and competent leadership, the results would be advantageous and in the public interest. . . . I address this letter to each of you in my capacity as a member of the standing negotiating committee of the Congress of Industrial Organizations, acting under the authority of its third constitutional convention. . . . If labor can compose its major internal problem, then the government will be aided in the operation of its war economy and the membership of labor

appreciably benefitted. . . . May I hope that each of you, in your official capacity, will advise me of your concurrence.

Both the AF of L and the CIO were thunderstruck. Neither desired the action proposed by Lewis, and yet it was in perfect pitch with the times, with unity for victory. If there was sentiment for this proposal, it was in the AF of L hierarchy. Green, dazed by the suddenness of Lewis's move, promptly replied, "We regard Mr. Lewis's letter as a partial response at least to the repeated appeals we have made since 1939 for the resumption of conferences to adjust differences between the CIO and the AF of L."

The press promptly recalled President Roosevelt's appeal to both conventions of the CIO and the AF of L in 1941:

"In this hour when civilization itself is in the balance, organizational rivalries and jurisdictional conflicts should be discarded. Only by united action can we turn back the Nazi threat.

"The establishment of peace between labor organizations would be a patriotic step forward of incalculable value in the creation of true national unity."

The repetition of this statement appeared to ally Roosevelt publicly with Lewis's bid for peace between the CIO and the AF of L.

The first indication of CIO reaction came the next day when Emil Rieve, a national vice-president of that organization and a stalwart leader in the Hillman faction, announced that he welcomed any proposal for peace between the AF of L and the CIO. Rieve continued by saying that he did so no matter who made the proposal.

In New York City it was reported that all leaders of left-wing CIO unions, now Lewis's most bitter enemies, were frantically caucusing to determine how the Lewis peace move might be headed off. They well knew that a merger of the CIO and the AF of L at this point would mean the death knell of the Communist-dominated unions. It was clear that in the process of a merger the jurisdiction and membership of left-wing unions would be transferred to the AF of L unions holding prior jurisdiction. For example, the left-wing State, County, and Municipal Workers Union, CIO, as it was then called, would be handed over to the AF of L's American Federation of State,

County, and Municipal Employees. The Communist-dominated unions realized the mortal consequences of the Lewis move and prepared to do all they could to avoid its fruition. There seemed to be no way to stop Lewis. They were silent and scared.

The next morning, January 19, *The New York Times* carried a front-page story signed by A. H. Raskin that more than any other single factor blew up the Lewis drive for accouplement. Raskin charged that Lewis had closed a deal with Daniel Tobin, vice-president of the AF of L and president of the International Brotherhood of Teamsters, whereby William Green was to retire from the presidency of the AF of L and receive his full annual salary of $20,000 for life; that George Meany, secretary-treasurer of the AF of L, was to be made president; and that Philip Murray would be given Meany's former job at the same salary of $18,000 a year that he was receiving as vice-president of the United Mine Workers. The presidency of the CIO carried no salary.

Raskin also pointed out that Murray had been totally ignored on all these alleged maneuvers, which were given as facts. This news article, plus its lead, which included, "Murray not consulted," was used as a basic weapon to cause Murray to react with violent anger. Murray snapped that Lewis's "so-called peace" was not so important as the contract negotiations that Murray was now entering upon with four of the companies of Little Steel. Then Murray curtly acknowledged Lewis's letter, telling him that he was presenting the proposal to the CIO executive board, which was meeting in New York City the end of that week, and invited Lewis to attend the meeting and present his point of view. Murray also "told off" Lewis in this letter, saying, "As you are well aware, all arrangements in behalf of the Congress of Industrial Organizations will necessarily have to be initiated through the office of the president of the Congress of Industrial Organizations."

Then, still wild with anger, Murray bitterly attacked Lewis, "I believe in doing things the democratic way. There have been no peace meetings in over two years, and I thought that if peace conferences should be had no Pearl Harbors should ensue."

The same day Murray was denouncing Lewis and his peace proposals, President Green of the AF of L denied in toto the Raskin story in *The New York Times* and branded it a great disservice to labor. That day David Dubinsky, president of the AF of L's International Ladies Garment Workers Union and an original wheelhorse of the CIO, told four thousand cheering members of his union that he was confident that Lewis's proposal would heal the breach between the AF of L and the CIO. Dubinsky described Lewis's letter to Green and Murray as "a document of the utmost importance and significance to the nation."

Mrs. Franklin D. Roosevelt stated at her press conference that day that she thought Lewis's peace proposal was "grand."

Her husband, the following morning, called Murray to the White House and told him that the peace conference was an attempt to drive a wedge between organized labor and the President. Roosevelt urged Murray to fight it and promised that he would support Murray to the hilt.

The confusion was not limited to the Roosevelt household, with Mrs. Roosevelt thinking it "grand" and President Roosevelt charging it as an evil plot against him, but labor leaders also were beginning to hesitate and wonder. Emil Rieve of the Hillman forces, which had always loyally supported F.D.R., had declared himself in favor of the peace plan. *The New York Times,* which had first branded it as a behind-the-scenes deal, contended that Lewis and Teamster President Daniel Tobin had been the villains in collusion. If this was true, it would make the "anti Roosevelt plot" even more fantastic, since Daniel Tobin was Roosevelt's right arm in the AF of L and practically worshiped the President. David Dubinsky, president of the AF of L's powerful Garment Workers Union, who applauded Lewis's move, was a staunch supporter of President Roosevelt.

Murray strutted out of the White House, reciting his loyalty to Lewis and demanding the return in kind, then belligerently told the press, "My manhood requires a little reciprocity and, by God, despite this feeble frame of mine, I will fight any living man to maintain my manhood."

With Murray now bellowing defiance at Lewis, both the right wing of the CIO led by Jacob Potofsky of the Amalgamated Clothing Workers Union, and the left wing led by the National Maritime Union's Joe Curran and the Transport Workers' "Red Mike" Quill, began to scream support and encouragement of Murray. Potofsky recalled Lewis's opposition to labor unity at the CIO 1940 Atlantic City convention. As for the left wing, they had been saved by the grace of Murray and Roosevelt. They extolled Murray as they had Lewis during the CIO days of 1936 to 1941.

The fact is that this was not a plot against the President. However, a merger of the two labor bodies and the de-emphasis of the power of Roosevelt's loyal followers such as Murray, Hillman, and the CIO left-wing leaders would in fact be a body blow at Roosevelt's power over the forces of labor. The CIO was utterly dominated by the President. There was no question that F.D.R.'s wish was Murray's command. From this point of view, Roosevelt was correct in feeling that Lewis's "scheme was a plot to undermine the President's standing with organized labor."

On January 22, five days after Lewis erupted with his proposal for accouplement, the President forcefully entered the picture by asking both the AF of L and the CIO to be equally represented on a six-man committee that would "consult with him frequently on matters relating to labor problems." The audacity of Roosevelt's arbitrary dismissal of a possible unification of the CIO and the AF of L with a substitute proposition of "you boys can come in and talk things over with me" will puzzle historians for years to come.

The CIO unanimously and enthusiastically accepted Roosevelt's proposal. Murray was the picture of innocent and righteous indignation as he told the CIO executive board how "astounded and hurt" he had been to learn first from the papers of Lewis's move. The AF of L accepted the President's proposal for the order that it was, and President William Green publicly expressed his deep regret "that the internal situation in the CIO" had prevented steps toward an outright reunion of the labor movement.

The CIO's public repudiation of Lewis, which was aided and abetted by Roosevelt, ensured the imminent break between Lewis and Murray and between Lewis and the CIO. Lewis's hatred of Roosevelt burned with an ever greater intensity. Roosevelt now was not fighting Lewis in the political arena but had entered Lewis's own world of trade unions. The hatred was mutual. Franklin D. Roosevelt indicated in numerous ways that he hated John L. Lewis more than any other individual on the domestic scene.

The three representatives of the CIO named by Murray were himself, R. J. Thomas of the United Automobile Workers Union, and left-winger Julius Emspak of the United Electrical Workers Union. The name of John L. Lewis was conspicuously absent.

Thus the Lewis move, carrying the momentous possibility of uniting the CIO and the AF of L into a titanic labor movement, fizzled into a "consultation committee with the President." It was one of the generation's greatest exhibitions of the mountain laboring and bringing forth a mouse.

With Roosevelt's smashing of Lewis's accouplement the labor chief retired from the public scene for one month. Then came one of the most ludicrous episodes in the life of Lewis. He set out through the ill-fated District 50 [1] of the mine workers union to organize the estimated three million dairy farmers of the nation. Reaction varied throughout the country from ridicule, as best illustrated by the famous Fitzpatrick cartoon showing a Napoleonic-attired Lewis riding a cow on his "Return from Elba," to stark panic led by New York Governor Tom Dewey. Dewey conjured up nightmares of Lewis's controlling not only three million dairy farmers and untold millions of dollars in dues but also America's supply of milk. The fantasy of one man's control of milk and coal was staggering to a large part of the press and public authorities. On the whole there was a general "viewing with alarm" as Lewis's District 50 prepared to jump and bulldoze the dairy industry. Basic to this grave concern was the reputation of Lewis's infallibility. Since 1934 he had been beaten only by Roosevelt, and that was in the political arena. In the field of labor organization Lewis was recognized as the undefeated champion. One District 50 organizer at that time told the writer, "We'll hang a union button on every udder."

Actually the implications of the objectives in this organizational campaign were enormous. If even partially successful it

[1] District 50 is a division of the United Mine Workers Union that has jurisdiction over the "by-products of coal" including gas, coke, chemicals, and, as one student of labor put it, "any human being who breathes air, for air is made of various gases."

D. R. Fitzpatrick, *St. Louis Post Dispatch*, May 4, 1942

RETURN FROM ELBA

would ally the workers and the farmers. This combination would dominate with ease the national scene. If Lewis could pull this off, it might well be a greater achievement than the building of the CIO.

But Lewis failed. He failed in this organization drive, just as he later failed in many ventures outside of his domain of coal, for one simple but conclusive reason—lack of skilled, able, and intelligent associates. In his drive for the CIO Lewis not only enlisted the finest talent in the nation, but those he did not draft volunteered. Lewis knew that basic to the creation of the CIO was the genius and devotion of the many organizers who threw themselves selflessly into the struggle, men and women fighting for a cause not a pay check. Now Lewis did not have these "believers," and since there was nothing he could do about it, he chose deliberately to strike out with subsidized organizers. Many of these alleged organizers were hired by advertisements in the UMW *Journal*. This was a fatal error—the same error that was obvious in the District 50 abortive taxicab strike in New York City, in 1949, and in countless other fiascoes.

In District 50 sat Kathryn Lewis, a daughter in many respects uncannily like her father. Talented, experienced, possessed of a resoluteness of purpose that almost equaled that of her father, she ran the organization with a tender touch, but beneath it was a hand of steel. But Kathryn Lewis was in a hopeless position. Although there were some efficient aides such as capable strategist and general counsel Alfred Kamin, by and large Kathryn Lewis was surrounded by organizers distinguished for their large whisky capacities and small mental capacities. She constantly found herself and her plans frustrated. Kathryn possessed the same passionate loyalty to a mine workers' organizer as did her father. The criterion was loyalty, and the organizers were extraordinarily long on loyalty and short on intelligence.

The writer closely observed Kathryn Lewis in operation on this venture, and there in a brand-new field for labor organization she demonstrated extraordinary facility and resourcefulness but lacked the human instruments to carry through. It was doomed from the outset by the utter lack of competent organizers. Kathryn Lewis finally left on an extended leave of absence.

From 1942 through 1945, District 50 served an invaluable function. As a constant threat to the CIO, it distracted Murray's attention and energies from an attack on the membership of the UMWA. It was a straw man. Since then the monotonous defeats of District 50 have weakened the myth of Lewis infallibility. Millions of dollars have been poured into this amorphous structure, which has long outlived even its usefulness as a threat. District 50 and defeat have become synonymous, and outside of its being a rest haven for some worn-out organizers it would have been better for Lewis if he had abandoned it.

Murray had been miraculously rescued from Lewis's drive by the Nazi invasion of the Soviet Union and the Communist flip-flop to his side. Again, when Lewis drove for "accouplement" Murray had been saved by the President of the United States. Lewis now decided to strike in a realm where he was supreme, where no one accepted any other leader or- challenged his primacy—the kingdom of the United Mine Workers of America.

When Philip Murray, still vice-president of the United Mine Workers, walked into the Mine Workers Building, he found the silent hostility suffocating. Everyone knew the break had come and that Murray would soon be a past memory in the organization. He was shunned by his colleagues as a moral leper, traitor, and Judas Iscariot. Those who still liked him were panicked with the fear that fraternization with Murray would be interpreted as being anti-Lewis. Murray sweated it out until one noon, going out of the United Mine Workers Building, he passed Lewis. He began to exchange pleasantries, at which Lewis turned on him demanding he apologize "for calling me a Jap." Murray began to expostulate that he hadn't and wouldn't say that about Lewis, but in the midst of his protest Lewis turned on his heel and stalked away.

Weeks passed, and still Lewis didn't strike. He was waiting and making absolutely certain that this time Murray would not escape. Also the cat-and-mouse game was steadily cracking the none-too-strong nerves of Murray.

The sniping soon became a steady firing under the tension of the uneasy truce. On March 14 the New York City CIO Industrial Council expelled nine locals of Lewis's Construction Workers for "nonpayment of dues."

In the same city a delegation of the CIO Transport Workers, led by its president and well-known Communist-party-line follower, "Red Mike" Quill, broke into the United Mine Workers

District 50 office, upsetting the furniture, ripping pictures of Lewis from the wall and trampling on them. District 50 organizers were physically threatened by Quill and his associates.

Ora Gasaway wrote a bitterly protesting letter to CIO President Murray, demanding he take action. This and many other letters sent to Murray by Gasaway resulted in noncommittal acknowledgments from Murray's aides. As we have seen in the previous chapter, the drive was on to build a Murray machine.

The storm intensified when on March 18 CIO received a letter from the United Mine Workers signed by its secretary-treasurer, Thomas Kennedy, requesting that the $30,000 per-month per-capita tax owed by the UMW to the CIO for February and March be deducted from the $1,665,000 owed to the UMW by the CIO.

On April 2, Ray S. Edmundson, then District 12 (Illinois) president of the UMW, resigned his other post of CIO regional director for Illinois, charging that "CIO policies . . . do not contribute to necessary labor unity within the labor movement or the nation." Two days later UMW representatives resigned from the CIO Illinois Industrial Council. The chasm between the CIO and UMW was deepening and widening by the hour.

In late April Lewis lit the oven by calling a meeting of the Mine Workers International Policy Board. The date of the meeting and the roasting of Murray was set for a month later, May 25. There was no official stated purpose or even an intimation of the reason for the meeting. Lewis is reported to have commented, "Let Murray's conscience tell him what the agenda will be."

Murray returned to Western Pennsylvania and wept before his home union local. Pleading his complete innocence, he voiced his eagerness to do anything to maintain his relationship with Lewis. On May 5 he spoke before the Pennsylvania Industrial Union Council in Pittsburgh. Murray railed that Lewis had failed to live up to his promises to support him. A state UMW aide said sarcastically that Murray should have included in Lewis's promises of support and co-operation a proviso whereby Lewis would not only sharpen the ax for his own execution by Murray, but even place his own head on the block. Murray went on excoriating the UMW request to charge off their per-capita payments against the $1,665,000 owed by the CIO to the miners as "dirty, lousy, low-life sabotage." But still Murray reiterated his immaculate innocence and willingness to do anything he could to avoid the imminent break. It was noted at that time that Murray wanted to do a lot of things to make up for something he said he had not done.

James B. Carey, national secretary of the CIO, continued the attack nine days later, when speaking in Chicago before the CIO's Department Store Employees Union, he denounced Lewis "for attempting to destroy the instrument he helped to create" (the CIO).

On Friday, May 22, Murray was elected president of the Steel Workers Union at an annual salary of $20,000. Now he had secured himself, at least financially, against the dreaded showdown that was to begin in three days.

May 25 finally arrived, and the many members of the United Mine Workers Policy Committee trooped through the portals of the United Mine Workers Building and then filed down into the basement. Behind them came a pale and shaking Philip Murray. Behind Murray Lewis relentlessly followed. Finally they were all in the basement.

The basement is the size of a large hotel lobby. Walls and posts are blanketed with the originals of the best of the hundreds of cartoons of Lewis's days with the CIO. Interspersed with the cartoons are news pictures and a painting of Lewis in some of his great moments in public crisis. In the center of one of the long sides of the basement is a small rostrum where Lewis sits. Directly behind him is a huge scroll presented to him by the entire CIO convention on the occasion of his resignation as president of the CIO in 1940. The adulations of Lewis, topping the scroll and crediting him with the formation and building of the CIO, are followed by the signature of every leader of the CIO, from Murray to Bridges to Hillman and down the line from left to right. The huge parchment has become wrinkled and folded, ominously reminiscent of the change of feeling of the CIO. Over the main entrance door hang two tremendous longhorns presented to Lewis by a grateful Packinghouse Workers Union. They lean downward, seemingly ready to impale those who are to be attacked. It has been felt by many that this basement is the control room of the

United Mine Workers Union, that it is Lewis's personal trophy room, and that here the spirit of Lewis leaps at one from every part of the room and paralyzes any resistance. A psychiatrist might reflect on the psychological significance of a leader of men from the subterranean mines building his retreat below the surface in a basement. Yet truly this basement is more than all this. It is the cathedral of Lewis's worshipers, and some of the religious services are a far cry from those of the men who pace the sidewalks above. For here Lewis is an almighty and a vengeful god.

Lewis and Murray were seated on the rostrum, and services were ready to commence. Packing the basement were the devout communicants of Lewis and the union, the UMWA policy committee.

The first day was eerie with all present sitting disinterestedly through the reading of reports of routine union affairs. Everyone knew the sole purpose of the meeting, and the basement was charged with the almost frantic restlessness of hound dogs waiting to be released after the rabbit. Time rasped Murray's nerves until adjournment found them raw and quivering. That day Murray spoke fearfully and pleadingly: "Mr. President and members of the National Policy Committee, I consider it a rare privilege to have the opportunity of addressing the members of this committee here this morning and to listen to the splendid reports with regard to the great progress that has been made by the organization during the past several years. Let me hasten to assure you that no one has a deeper sense of pride in the attainments of this organization than I have, and *that no one in the United States of America has taken greater pride in the leadership which you have than I have, and I speak with particular reference to the accomplishments of our distinguished President when I say so.*[2] And that goes for those who like it or those who don't like it. . . .

". . . And when the report is made to the members of the policy committee here this morning that we have reached the top of that mountain, the peak of that mountain to which this membership has been aspiring since the beginning of the union, I say it is a remarkable accomplishment, and *all hail to*

[2] Italics are the writer's.

the people responsible for those attainments, particularly the President of this great organization.[3]

"I understand, like a great many people do understand, that strained relationships have developed for which I accept absolutely and positively no responsibility. I should like it to be known that insofar as I am individually concerned—and I have said this repeatedly—that within this union or any other union I have never had political aspirations. I do not now, and never have had. I have loyally supported the President of this international union from the day I was a boy, and I should like to be privileged to do so as long as I live."

The next day, May 26, Lewis reached for the switch and threw it. He began by reading his letter to Murray requesting accouplement of the CIO and the AF of L, then followed with his letter to Murray rejecting the latter's demand that Lewis attend the executive board meeting to explain his move for labor peace. Lewis then continued, describing his reasons for a complete change in his previous attitude of opposing a merger with the AF of L, saying: "I believed that the war period at the present time was the psychological time for the leaders of the various groups of labor in our country to attempt to place the house of labor in order. I did not believe it could be done successfully during the formative period of the CIO. I have always believed that the peace negotiations that took place in 1937 and 1939 were harmful rather than beneficial, because they interfered with the organizing progress of the great Congress of Industrial Organizations. Field workers of that organization and its organizers continuously reported that men said to them in the industrial plants of the country, 'Why join the CIO if the CIO is going to join the American Federation of Labor?' But, at last the day came, as the letters state, when the comparative strength of the two organizations of labor was substantially equal, and bargaining could be pressed and conducted on equal terms. Previously that had not been the case. In addition to that, an emergency affected the country and imperiled the nation, and the thoughts and opinions and judgments of men were affected by that situation, because I take it for granted that in the heart and in the mind of every normal citizen of our country there is an innate desire to make a contribu-

[3] Italics are the writer's.

tion to the national being, to the success of America's war policy. . . .

". . . I thought that psychology at this time would have its powerful effect not only upon the leaders of labor, but the rank and file of labor, and upon the minds of the official staff and membership of the American Federation of Labor. . . .

". . . I believed that I was chairman of the Standing Peace-Negotiating Committee of the Congress of Industrial Organizations; I believed that because a convention had said so, and because I was present when it said so, and because I read the record in the books of the convention afterward, and the book said so, and I believed it. I believed that a standing committee with an elected personnel and a chairman with prescribed functions to perform had a right to perform those functions according to their judgment. . . .

". . . So, I wrote these letters. Again, I state that conceivably I was wrong; and, perchance, I was right. In any event, I am responsible and only responsible for my official acts to the United Mine Workers of America. And I submit this factual statement, restrained as I have made it, for the consideration of this representative body of the United Mine Workers of America. If I was wrong I could be condemned; if I was right, I should be sustained. . . ."

At this point Murray slowly arose to speak and speedily sat down as Lewis glowered, "As soon as I am through, Vice-President Murray, you may have the floor." Lewis then proceeded to present the following financial statement of the relationship between the CIO and UMW of America.

This is a joint statement by the Secretary-Treasurer of the United Mine Workers of America, and the President of the United Mine Workers of America, as follows:

From November, 1935, until June 1, 1937, the Committee for Industrial Organization had no source of revenue, except the voluntary financial assistance extended the Committee by the several unions adhering to its policies and comprising its original membership. This revenue was therefore of necessity limited to: (a) outright gifts or donations, and (b) negotiated loans. Effective June 1, 1937, the Committee received internal revenue from its affiliated membership upon a fixed monthly per-capita basis. During the period of 1936 and 1937 many of the major organizing drives of the CIO were inaugurated and effectively consummated, and collective bargaining contracts of great magnitude were negotiated with America's leading industries. By March 1, 1938, the CIO had balanced its budget and maintained itself thereafter from existing current revenues. In consequence, the financial liabilities of the CIO were substantially accumulated during the calendar years of 1936 and 1937.

The financial assistance of the United Mine Workers of America to the CIO assumed three different phases:

A. Payment of monthly per-capita tax at $30,000.00 per month up to February 1, 1942, Cash $1,680,000.00

B. Services of executives, field directors, trained organizers, attorneys, clerical help, and other incidentals paid for by the United Mine Workers from December 1, 1935, up to May 1, 1942, amounting to 3,904,303.84

C. Negotiated loans
  Cash $1,685,000.00
  Loan repaid 20,000.00

Leaving a net total of loans to the CIO of $1,665,000.00
Total services and cash $7,249,303.84

The foregoing figures clearly reveal the magnitude of the assistance rendered to the CIO by the Mine Workers of the United States and the Dominion of Canada. These figures do not include $200,000.00 donated to Mr. Sidney Hillman for the conduct of the organizing drive in the textile industry. These figures do not include cash loans of $601,000.00 furnished to SWOC for the conduct of the Little Steel strike, and which has been repaid in full. Neither do these figures include sundry donations and loans made to other struggling organizations affiliated with the CIO. No other union could have assumed the burden of financial obligation necessary to insure achievement of the aims and objectives of the working men and women of America.

It is unfortunate that the valid loans extended the CIO by the United Mine Workers of America have been questioned. . . .

Lewis then stunned even the well-calloused members of the union's policy committee by proving that through *the hectic years of 1936 and 1937 when the CIO was born and grew up the United Mine Workers Union furnished in loans 88.37 per cent of the total cost of the organization of the CIO,* while all the other unions that founded the CIO all together put up 11.63 per cent of the total expenditure. Lewis had not only conceived, built, and led the CIO but had practically completely financed it.

He pointed out that it had been requested of the CIO two months before to credit the United Mine Workers with two months of per-capita tax amounting to $60,000 and deduct it from the CIO's debt to the UMWA. Lewis then charged that the CIO answer was not only in the negative but accompanied with publicity of a malicious and hostile character. Lewis paused and then struck, "But Vice-President Murray had already called me a Jap." Murray hastily scrambled to his feet. Bellows of rage came from the delegates, which changed into a barrage of boos interspersed with cries to Murray to sit down and shut up. Lewis continued, "And another Pearl Harbor." A murmur of angry whispers could be heard all over the hall. Murray seemed on the verge of collapse. While he had schooled himself to hostility from the mine workers officials, nevertheless the spectacle of all his old friends and every ranking official and delegate of the union now shouting their hatred and telling him, who for twenty-three years had been the second ranking official of the union, to sit down and shut up was just too much. Murray gripped the table in front of him; pale and shaking, he screamed, "You big, bold, brave courageous men. I will sit down. But I want to answer this record, see, when President Lewis sits down. You big, bold courageous men that you are, paid officers of the organization, booing an officer of your organization. God forgive you." Lewis's voice lashed out like a razor, cutting Murray's legs from under him and sending Murray toppling back into his chair.

"You may talk when I am through."

Murray replied, "I will talk because you are making a nasty record."

Lewis then coldly cut the last vestige of the umbilical cord that tied Murray to him saying, "I am not a Jap, and I am just as good an American as *my former friend, Vice-President Murray*.[4] So I did not go over to the meeting, first because of the

[4] Italics are the writer's.

conditions I have told you of, and secondly, because I thought it would be absolutely hopeless and useless for me to attempt to sway the judgment of the executive board of the CIO against his position. Certainly I thought my presence there would be merely controversial, not constructive, and that no good would flow from it. I had suggested merely an idea; the idea could be accepted or rejected. It was rejected, for the reasons given here by Vice-President Murray. I do not hold that they are good reasons. I grant he has the right to have his opinion on the logic of the proposition. I do not grant the right to certain organizations in the CIO to say that there must be no peace conferences, because they don't want them for the reasons given on this record.

"I think that the well-being of labor in America and the well-being of the country should rise superior to and above those considerations. . . ." Lewis continued, demolishing any arguments that might be advanced, implying that the UMWA did not expect repayment of the loans they made to the CIO. Lewis then grimly sat down. Murray's reply is well known.

"Now, as to this constant reference that has been made about Phil Murray calling John L. Lewis a Jap, nothing could be further from the truth. I don't know how often it should become necessary for me to repeat and repeat and repeat that as a man and as a citizen and as an American I have always regarded Mr. Lewis as without a peer in the realm of America. I dislike and I resent, no matter whose mouth it flows from, the implication that I made any filthy insinuating remark concerning President Lewis's Americanism." Then Murray, pale, shaking, and badly scared, continued, "I thought as vice-president of this union and as a member of that committee, I was entitled to some conversation, and the first intimation I had of an invitation to attend peace conferences was when I read the letter in the newspapers. And I don't think that is right, and I will make manifest that kind of protest anywhere. So when the newsmen approached me in the city of New York upon my arrival there on a given Sunday afternoon, after I had read the newspapers, they asked me about the letter. The letter was given to me in the lobby of the Roosevelt Hotel several hours after I had read it in the newspapers. I thereupon said I was not going to be blitzed or Pearl Harbored into peace conferences, and the reference was not directed against Mr. Lewis and his Americanism, so much as it was the way in which the letter was directed to me. I felt I was entitled to some conversation about it, and I didn't get it. . . ."

The whining spectacle Murray had presented before the policy board caused their anger to change to pity and contempt. Murray realized this and suddenly stopped groveling. His voice raised as he began to speak with some firmness.

"President Lewis refers to me as his former friend. I regret it. However, if that is what he chooses, that is what it must be; I cannot help it. As far as I am concerned, I am not anxious to break a friendship that has lasted for a lifetime. Again, again, I have had seventeen months of this work. Again, again, I was thrust into this job against my will, thrust into it at a time when a doctor was ordering me to the hospital—and John Lewis knows that. No man knows it better than he does. I pleaded for ten days not to take the damned job, to leave me alone in my own sphere to continue my own work. I think any man who is acquainted with the facts knows that to be the truth. But I went ahead and did this work as best I knew how. Perhaps it has not met with the approval of my own union. If that is the case, then it is regrettable, because I cannot help it. I have given my union the best that is in me. I can give it no more. I have given the President of this organization, yes, almost my life in the field of loyalty, and the world knows that, and so does John Lewis. And there is nothing that makes Phil Murray feel bad about these situations more than trifling meddlers who never rendered any particular degree of service to the labor movement in their lives, indulging in their mud-slinging and their scandalizing and their maligning of men, men who have devoted their life to this work. . . ."

But this brief flash of independence was too much for Murray. He could not then, as he cannot now or ever, break away from the domination of Lewis. Lewis is the ruling force in Murray's life, whether by Murray's previous allegiance for years or by his present all-consuming hatred of Lewis. As before he acted according to Lewis's will, now he acts according to his fear of Lewis.

Murray could not take any more of the grinding of the Lewis machine. He arrived at the third day's meeting to inform Lewis that he could only stay a short time, as he had a very important meeting that morning. This was the day that full charges were to be preferred against Murray. Murray appeared that morning with a firmness and the relief of a man who had reached a decision. It was rumored that he had conferred with Roosevelt the previous evening and had absorbed self-confidence from the assurances that the President was behind him. The newly starched Murray was unveiled in the beginning of the meeting when he engaged in a sharp exchange with Lewis. Murray stood up, asking for the floor just as the charges were being presented by Michael Widman, an official of the union. Lewis then interrupted Widman, saying, "Vice-President Murray has gotten to his feet and demanded the floor while the floor was being held by Mr. Michael Widman, who is making an indictment which he is authorized to make by the Organizing Committee of District 50. . . . The indictment is voluminous in detail. Vice-President Murray arises and says he has to go to an important business meeting of affiliated organizations of the CIO and is demanding an opportunity to be heard at this time before Mr. Widman is through, after which he expects to leave.

"That is the subject of the conversation between Vice-President Murray and me. Is that a fair statement?"

Murray answered, "Yes, it is fair; I should say it is."

Lewis's voice, edged with irritation, continued, "We have no desire to take Vice-President Murray away from his regular business if that business is more important than the business of the United Mine Workers of America, which has been long deferred in consideration here. These events have been piling up over a long period of time. Vice-President Murray, to my knowledge, has made at least seven speeches attacking the United Mine Workers of America and its officers over a period of months, and this is the first time that we have had an opportunity to discuss it ourselves or to be heard on the question.

"Now, I have no desire to interfere in any way; I am simply reporting this to the conference. If Vice-President Murray insists he cannot stay this morning and must be heard right now, as far as the chair is concerned he can be heard, but the conference will be obliged to continue its discussion without his being present to learn the facts from his own organization. That is what this amounts to."

Murray calmly replied, "I understand the facts."

Lewis snapped, "You do not understand the facts that are going to be presented here."

Murray belligerently said, "Nor do you understand the facts that are to be presented to my board, the CIO board, to which I have invited you, sir, and which has jurisdiction over this problem."

Lewis, amazed at the defiant Murray, slowly said, "That is a differential—"

Murray broke in, his voice rising, "It is not a differential. You are ignoring the president of the Congress of Industrial Organizations. I am talking about these charges before the CIO board. That is where they belong; that is where they ought to be aired."

Lewis quietly retorted, "You are vice-president of the United Mine Workers of America."

Murray replied, "I understand that, sir, and I am also president of the CIO."

Lewis stared at Murray and with an authoritative tone said, "This is a conference of the United Mine Workers of America."

Murray mumbled, "I understand that."

Then the exchange began. Murray defiantly drew attention to the importance of his position in the nation, as much as to say, "All right, throw me out but I'm bigger than all this. I am much more important than just being a vice-president of the Mine Workers."

He proclaimed, "Yesterday I had to forgo a meeting with an interdepartmental committee, going to be supposedly created by the President of the United States, upon the question of wage stabilization, in order that I should sit on this platform and listen to what was going to be said about the CIO. The meeting had to be canceled yesterday, and I made arrangements to attend the meeting this morning. I also made arrangements to attend the meeting today, perhaps within the next fifteen minutes, with representatives of labor organizations from other countries who are anxious to discuss their problems with the CIO, particularly as the war affects all of us.

"I stated yesterday, and I am going to reiterate here today for this record, that I think those problems supersede any difference that this organization may have with Phil Murray, because they are problems affecting the welfare of this nation, and all of its inhabitants."

Murray then bitterly protested that he was being expected to defend himself against charges without even knowing the nature of the charges.

Lewis's answer was given with the patient paternalistic tone of a wise father reprimanding an obstreperous child. He informed Murray that District 50 of the mine workers was bringing its grievances before the International Executive Board of the union. This was the legally constitutional procedure. If these grievances resulted in charges against Vice-President Murray, then he would be duly notified and given full and adequate opportunity to refute them.

With the demolition of Murray's argument on this point he shifted to another line, demanding that any charges brought against him or any complaints should be directed to the CIO executive-board meeting and not to the mine workers board. Here Murray was overlooking the basic premise of the board meeting, which was to oust Murray as an official of the mine workers union. In this area the CIO board had no part to play or the power to play the part if it had it.

Ora Gasaway, as a member of the mine workers board and an officer of District 50, interrupted Murray's speech with a charge that Murray had goons in Washington trying to intimidate representatives of the mine workers union. Murray hotly denied this, saying, "If there is anybody around here intimidating anybody I want to know who they are."

Here Lewis intervened, telling Murray, "If you would stick around a little you would get that information."

At this Murray blew up, almost screaming, "Mr. President, I do stick around; and the point is, Mr. President, I might say I was sticking around here until you sent that letter to me last January that I read in the newspapers. I was on the third floor, Mr. President, and was out eating with you just about a week before that."

Lewis grinned, "My dear boy, you were in Florida."

Murray still shaking said, "I was, on the doctor's orders."

Lewis again coldly repeated, "I say if you stick around here I will give you the answer to that."

Murray then went into a lengthy speech repeating his feeling that he was being charged without opportunity to defend himself and that any charges should be brought before the CIO board and not the mine workers board. Lewis began to look bored and impatient. The moment Murray finished Lewis unleashed his ace card for speedy legal disposal of Murray. He coldly inquired of Murray whether it was true that he had agreed to accept the position of president of the Steel Workers Union at a salary. Murray admitted it was true, defiantly adding that he had been elected by acclamation, and then launching into an impassioned account of how Lewis, too, had held other positions. Lewis quickly disposed of this view. "Those were nonsalaried jobs. I extended my services to that organization, as did you, gratuitously, in behalf of our union, while the United Mine Workers of America paid us. Now, however, you are leaving this coal mine, according to your own words, and going over to another mine and another company to work for them. Do you expect to hold a job in both places?"

Murray knew he was caught; but he continued trying to evade the question by repeating, "John, you have held jobs in a lot of places."

Lewis cut him short. "Not paid jobs."

Murray, unable to defend the position of having two paid jobs, got off the subject and began to ramble incoherently. "Neither have I held paid jobs in a lot of places. I never did. However, again I say to you that if you are prepared to differentiate between my situation and yours, that is your privilege. You do as you please about it. Again, I say there isn't much I can do about it. That is all."

Lewis returned to the subject decisively summing up the issue: "Again the chair corrects the record and says it is not a question of what he prefers to do with relation to Vice-President Murray, in any personal sense. This is a sheer business proposition of what will be done with respect to the constitution, with respect to sound business practice of the United Mine Workers of America, as to whether or not the union will or will not have a vice-president that can carry out his constitutional duties and have some time to attend meetings of the United Mine Workers. If Vice-President Murray is going to accept a salary as president of the United Steel Workers, that is for him to decide. I have made no suggestions as to any intent or desire.

I have asked these questions merely as questions of information for the knowledge of the International Executive Board and the policy committee. That is all."

Murray, weeping, asked to be excused.

Lewis tartly replied, "You may if you wish to go, sir."

Murray's answer epitomized the conflict raging within him. He passionately yearned for the security of being enveloped in Lewis's shadow, and yet he was now obsessed with the drive for power and recognition. His answer may well be the answer of every baby leaving his mother's womb.

"I do not wish to go, I cannot help it."

Lewis looked sharply at Murray and answered with withering sarcasm, "Very well, if you don't wish to go, you may go." Then the long years of friendship momentarily welled up as Lewis gave Murray a warm pat on the back.

Murray was ashen and shaking as he stumbled up the stairs out of the union that had been his life since he was old enough to raise a pick. This time nothing, not even the President of the United States, could save Murray; for in the United Mine Workers of America the name and only name was John L. Lewis.

For some days the basement of the United Mine Workers Building became a confessional chamber. Official after official arose beating his breast and publicly proclaimed his guilt of past association with Philip Murray and of having followed and been a friend of the now perfidious, leprous Murray. It was a mass orgy of self-abnegation and personal debasement that can only be rivaled by the spectacle of highly disciplined Communist leaders beating their breasts and confessing their sins when there is a change in their national leadership and policy. All of these people were trying to show their deep loyalty to Lewis and to remove any suspicion that Lewis might have about them.

Here in an organization so highly disciplined and so compact the individual members become almost as parts of one organic entity, and if Philip Murray, long a basic part of this body, was to be vomited out, every individual part of the body would have to retch in concert with its head, John L. Lewis.

On May 28 while the country was buzzing with reports that Murray and Roosevelt were conferring on how to stop Murray's ouster from the mine workers union, Lewis suddenly struck.

Abandoning the formal preferring of charges and invoking the
constitutional power of removing officials for "just and sufficient
cause," Lewis summarily removed Murray from his vice-presidency and named a faithful old wheelhorse, John A. O'Leary,
as the new vice-president. It is interesting from a tactical point
of view that Lewis's new vice-president came from Murray's
own stronghold, Pittsburgh, Pennsylvania. This move was a
sound precaution in coping with any possible pro-Murray feeling in that region.

The reports of Murray's conferring with Roosevelt were confirmed by Murray's initial statement when told of Lewis's action. He said the mine workers union action took place while
he "was meeting with President Roosevelt at his request. . . ."
Murray expressed surprise at Lewis's quick, decisive, and final
action, as his plans, and certainly any ideas that may have been
in Roosevelt's mind, were predicated on formal charges and a
trial. In his statements to the press, Murray indicated that he
would carry the fight to the miners for vindication of his desire
to complete his term as an "unpaid" official of the United Mine
Workers. This statement is the first public record known to the
author of Murray's desire to continue his position with the
United Mine Workers in an "unpaid" capacity. There is no
mention or hint to this effect in Murray's statements before the
mine workers policy committee. As for Murray's carrying the
fight to the rank and file, he was whistling in the dark. No one
knew better than he the power of the Lewis machine, of which
Murray had once been a bulwark. Murray had seen too many
rank-and-file movements butchered, and had helped in the
butchering, to believe seriously that any rank-and-file movement he might start would meet any other fate.

On June 4, Murray addressed the meeting of the CIO executive board, which for the first time was open to the press. For
two hours he wept and excoriated Lewis. He charged Lewis as
being "hell-bent on creating national confusion and national
disunity." Murray went on, accusing Lewis of privately meeting
with him in Atlantic City on October 18, 1941,[5] and attempting
to enlist him into an alliance to "fight the foreign policies of the
United States." He said he told Lewis then, "I would not do it,
and to do so would only be regarded as an act of treason."

[5] Described in detail in preceding chapter.

Murray went on in a similar vein attacking Lewis's patriotism, completely forgetting that nine brief days before he had said, ". . . I don't know how often it should become necessary for me to repeat and repeat and repeat that as a man and as a citizen and as an American I have always regarded Mr. Lewis as without a peer in the realm of America. I dislike and I resent, no matter whose mouth it flows from, the implication that I made any filthy insinuating remark concerning President Lewis's Americanism."

This must have been in Lewis's mind as he calmly replied to Murray's denunciation, saying that Mr. Murray was probably speaking under strain of great emotion and that he had made statements "which the facts will not bear out." Lewis then made a categorical denial of every accusation of Murray, saying, "By no act or device, by no suggestion and no enterprise, have I at any time undertaken to detract by whit or jot from the services of the nation's war policies. I have sought, insofar as it was given me to participate, to make a contribution."

The facts already cited on the "private Atlantic City meeting of October, 1941," throw strong doubt on the veracity of Murray's alleged account of Lewis's attempting to influence him against Roosevelt's foreign policy. It should be borne in mind on Lewis's "influencing" Murray that he did not stop Murray's passive support of Roosevelt in the 1940 campaign.

The year 1942 had been rough for Lewis. The great labor organization he had practically created, financed, built, and led had turned on him with deadly hatred. His closest and oldest friend, Philip Murray, had betrayed him. But to Lewis all this was trivial in contrast to the crushing blow that was to come.

On September 9, his wife Myrta Edith Lewis was stricken with a brain malignancy and died. No one will ever fully realize the enormous part played by Myrta Lewis in fashioning and harnessing the talents that resulted in the well-known figure of John L. Lewis. The funeral was held in Springfield, Illinois. Those who saw the anguish and deathly pallor of Lewis marked up "finished" to Lewis's career. Those who saw Lewis and knew what Myrta Lewis had meant to him not only marked up "finished" but underscored it.

No greater demonstration of enormous inner strength and

unswerving purpose could be found than the Lewis who raged
and paced the platform three weeks later at the biennial convention of the United Mine Workers. He made only one passing mention of his so-recent bereavement, "I had a cross to
bear." He tore into the CIO and its president. He reviewed his
personal leadership and contribution in auto, steel, and all
other industries. Then reminding the delegates of the CIO
slogan that they love coal miners, but just hate Lewis, Lewis
cried out, "Why, it is a device as old as time for a destructive
critic to say, 'I don't dislike the organization, I just hate the
leader.' If you elect me to office, and your enemies succeed in
destroying public confidence in me and demonstrating that I
am one unworthy of the trust reposed in me, do you think that
you can get away scot-free, or do you think that will affect the
strength of the union, the prestige of your organization, and
the well-being of the women and children who depend on you?

"Beware of the man who comes to you with a smile on his
face and tells you that he admires you greatly, but that it is
unfortunate that your mother was a woman of ill repute.
Beware of that kind of man and answer with a blow. Then I
hear a whining from some of these miserable mediocrities in
the CIO, saying, oh, they love the United Mine Workers of
America, but they cannot stand to be in the same room with
their officers, whom they detest greatly. Love me, love my
dog . . . !

". . . I could have criticized the leadership in the CIO when
they were attempting to sell the United Mine Workers down
the river in the captive-mine fight. I could name names and
give dates and quote the text of these things, but life is too short
for me to answer the yappings of every cur that follows at my
heels. I hear the pack in my rear at times. I can turn my head
and see the lap dogs and the kept dogs and the yellow dogs in
pursuit, but I am serene in the knowledge that they won't come
too close. They are not very close now. Some of them could
have come here, but they did not come. They preferred to do
their criticizing at long distance, and that is the safer way for
them. . . .

". . . Do you want to pay dues to an organization and have
them use your money to destroy your union?

[Cries of "No," "no!"]

". . . I sometimes wonder how much abuse some of our members might take before they wake up to what their adversary is doing to kick in their ribs and stamp in their faces. I don't understand that coal miners work that way. Coal miners are not afraid of anything, because they look death in the face every time they leave their homes and go to their employment. And I am not prepared as an officer of this union and its leader to permit a perverse group who happen to hold office temporarily in a great labor movement to run amuck and defame and denounce and injure the union of men that I have the honor to represent. . . .

". . . I think this convention, in honor to itself and in honor to its officers, should adopt this committee's report. If you don't want to adopt this report, then you don't want a man like me to be your president. You will want a man with more rabbit in him than I have got. You will want a man who will lay down on his back and put his arms and legs in the air while somebody kicks him in the ribs and stomps on his face. And I am not that kind of a man . . . !

". . . So you have your views upon this question, my friends, and do with it as you wish and leave me out of your considerations. But be it known, be it known to you when you vote, that if you do not have enough pride and self-respect yourself for your own officers to sustain them in the positions they take as affecting public questions in this country on matters affecting labor, then don't expect anybody else to have any confidence, and do not expect me to carry out the rabbit policy, because, on my word of honor, there is no rabbit in me." [6]

Lewis stopped, and the vote was taken on his demand that they quit the CIO. The convention supported Lewis 2867 to 5. Lewis and his United Mine Workers had now officially broken with the CIO.

One month later the CIO convention took place in Boston. Murray opened and closed the convention by violently assailing Lewis. Lewis and the mine workers had already formally withdrawn from the CIO, but Murray could not rid himself of the ever present specter of John L. Lewis.

Many of the statements Murray made were typical of what

[6] Daily Proceedings of the 37th Constitutional Convention of the United Mine Workers of America, Cincinnati, Ohio, October 7, 1942.

he has since continuously repeated. They reveal some of the drives, fears, hostilities, and general insecurity underlying much of his behavior.

Murray has frequently attempted to explain his conflicts with analogies that pictured him in a role similar to Christ being betrayed. Addressing the convention, he cried out, "I took over the presidency against my will. I told John Lewis in Atlantic City that he would run away from me, that I was conscious of the fact that he would run away from me. I told him that in Atlantic City. I made that statement to John Lewis because I knew John Lewis. . . . But John denied me after he had held my hand and said, 'You are the president of the Congress of Industrial Organizations, and I am going to support you. I shall never deny you that right; I shall always acknowledge you as my president, the President of the CIO.' You remember that ancient story where Peter, in the course of a conversation with Christ, said that he would never deny Him, and Christ said that he would, He knew he would. And it is recorded in that incident that Peter not only denied Christ, but in his desperation to have the public know that Christ did not exist, he rushed to the home of a harlot, and standing in the midst of that den of iniquity, he denied the existence of Christ.

"And I told John Lewis in the wing of the stage in the Chelsea Hotel in Atlantic City that in all likehood he would make me go through my Garden of Gethsemane. I felt that he would. I believed that he would, I knew that he would. . . ."

It is of interest that Murray frequently adopts and articulates the position that he is being persecuted and betrayed. This pattern is again manifest in his present "holy war" against all the left-wing unions of the CIO. He had already stated that the conflict began when they "betrayed him." A leading journalist who is on close terms with Murray cynically comments, "I get tired of hearing Philip harp on his being betrayed. He's got us all now wondering whether he's trying to convince us or himself. I guess after all these years I've got to admit it's himself."

McAlister Coleman, student of the coal miners and their union for many years, who has often been critical of Lewis, states in his detailed, objective study, *Men and Coal*,[7] "In the

[7] McAlister Coleman, *Men and Coal* (New York: Farrar and Rinehart, 1943), p. 212.

meantime Murray was everywhere repeating the story of his 'betrayal' by Lewis in the manner of a victim of persecution mania. Holding his hand on his heart, the burring Scotchman would compare his betrayal with that of Jesus, with references to Gethsemane and Golgotha, and with Lewis in the role of Judas Iscariot."

Many have commented upon Murray's frequent references to himself not by the use of the conventional personal pronoun but by the use of his full name. His speeches are replete with this characteristic. For example, in the same speech in which he charged Lewis with having betrayed him, he said, ". . . In the city of Cincinnati a few weeks ago he said that Phil Murray, or he implied that Phil Murray, deserted the captive miners in the course of their great strike in the year of 1941. . . ." [8]

Psychologically illuminating are Murray's frequent references to his independence and manhood, particularly in breaking away from Lewis. At the 1940 CIO convention when he became president of the CIO, Murray, with Lewis sitting a few paces away, told the delegates, "Now perhaps what I am about to say has no particular relation to the subject already presented to this convention. Each man, I suppose, no matter who he may be, has a heart and soul and mind of his own, exercises the right to express his own convictions upon certain situations. I happen to be that kind of man. . . . That decision [referring to his candidacy for the presidency of the CIO] has been reached by me, and I imagine, I think that I have a right to make a decision once in a while in life.

". . . I think I have a conviction, I think I have a soul and a heart and a mind. And I want to let you in on something. They, with the exception, of course, of my soul, all belong to me, every one of them. . . ." [9]

We have also noted in the previous Murray and Roosevelt battle against Lewis's proposal for CIO and AF of L "accouplement" where Murray told the press, "My manhood requires a little reciprocity and, by God, despite this feeble frame of mine, I will fight any living man to maintain my manhood."

[8] Daily Proceedings of the Fifth Constitutional Convention of the Congress of Industrial Organizations, November 12, 1942, Boston, Massachusetts.

[9] Daily Proceedings of the Third Constitutional Convention of the Congress of Industrial Organizations, 1940.

This reaction reflects Murray's struggle for emancipation from a quarter of a century of complete domination by Lewis. For twenty-five years Murray's complete life grew out of, and was utterly dependent upon, the power of Lewis. Through these years he lived in a gloom darker than the coal pits—the gloom of the deep black shadow of John L. Lewis. He was a creature of Lewis's creation and beholden to him for all he possessed. Even his present presidency of the CIO was given to him by Lewis. It would have been highly improbable that Murray could have achieved either the presidency of the CIO or of the Steel Workers Union without Lewis. Lewis placed Murray in the chairmanship of the Steel Workers Organizing Committee and personally sent the union drive forward by negotiating a contract that recognized the union in U.S. Steel, thereby establishing the foundation for Murray's union.

It is characteristic of one deeply obligated to another to be possessed of a strong fundamental hatred for his benefactor. He knows that he is the creature of his creator. He resents that his patron knows what others may suspect but do not know of —his personal inadequacy and complete dependency. This is accompanied by the conviction that his benefactor is not only lacking in any respect for him as a person, but actually views him with a fundamental contempt. This reaction generates an enormous subconscious, and frequently conscious but well-guarded, hostility against the person who has given him his status, security, and actual identity, indeed, his personality and ideas. The obsessional hatred of Murray for Lewis can be understood on these grounds alone. These factors would strongly argue for a similar basic hostility toward Lewis by many of those whom he created as his satellites.

As for Murray, who for twenty-five years had chanted hallelujahs attesting to the perfection of the great god Lewis, who was now castigating this same Lewis as "loathsome," "an established national prevaricator," "diabolical mind," "a Judas," "a Hitler," it should also be remembered that Lewis in 1940 praised Philip Murray to the heavens and now was damning him to hell. Today when Lewis is informed of Murray's breast-beating and charges of betrayal, he quietly smiles and always makes the same remark, "Philip Murray is a dunghill."

Two extremely close friends for twenty-five years cannot drift apart; the ties are too many and too intimate. Such a relationship could only be broken, as it was, in an explosive upheaval.

Despite these personality traits or any other motivations that drove Murray to the break, his position in 1941 as contrasted to Lewis's stand was far more realistic on national foreign policy. On the other hand Lewis's concentration on securing a strong domestic labor movement far from being dependent upon the Government was sounder trade-union policy than Murray's actions at that time. It could be argued with merit that the foreign situation transcended the domestic scene as an American labor movement would have been decimated by a victorious Nazi Germany. The writer believes that Murray's position at that time on this point was correct. For that brief period Lewis, the great realist, was moving in a fantasy of unreality.

Chapter 12

Lewis *vs.* the People

LEWIS was alone. It was a hurt, bitter, and defiant man who faced the year 1943. He had nurtured and built the great power of the CIO, and it had turned its full strength against him. He had built up his best friend, Philip Murray, to the leadership of the CIO; and Murray had turned on him as the monster of Frankenstein. He had already broken with President Roosevelt, after helping to build him up as "the great friend of labor." The Congress of the United States was in full cry after Lewis as "a national menace." The liberals and left-wingers regarded the name of Lewis as anathema. Then came the most crushing blow of all, the death of the woman he loved. Myrta Lewis was John Lewis's private untouchable world. She was his only haven of real security and love. Myrta Lewis had been a part of his life since as a young man he had begun the long climb from the depths of an Illinois coal mine to the heights where he now stood. It angered him that she had died seeing all the betrayals of the man she adored.

A deluge of such defeat and despair could make any man desperate. A lonely, wounded Lewis could well be a force to make America beware, and Lewis was now at bay. Lewis had only the people to turn to, and in 1943 the people turned against him.

A brooding and enraged Lewis looked about him. Overseas American armed forces were successfully advancing upon the enemy, but at home American workers were in a steady retreat before the ceaseless advance of the cost of living. Enormous inflationary pressures boiling up in an economy of scarcity were tearing wide gaps through Government price control. Black markets, too, were spelling out ever mounting prices. In the race between wages and prices, the latter were soaring away, while wages were tied down. The cost of living was mounting, and by contrast the wages of the workers were frozen and fixed by what was known as the Little Steel formula or, as it later became popularly referred to by labor leaders, the Little Steel strait jacket.

The Little Steel formula was mixed and poured on July 16, 1942, when the National War Labor Board ruled on the demands of the steel workers for more pay. The Board, using the date of January 1, 1941, as a cost-of-living index, announced that from that date to May, 1942, the cost of living had increased 15 per cent, and therefore every worker was entitled to a 15 per-cent wage increase over the job rate of January 1, 1941. For example, if a given job paid $1.00 an hour on January 1, 1941, the War Labor Board tried to freeze it at $1.15 an hour for the duration of the war. This was the point where wages were anchored while prices were blowing sky-high.

This economic trap, while mangling most of labor, was nearly killing the coal miners. Most of the purchases of miners were made in company stores, where the prices were even higher than the high prices elsewhere. The miners' wives could not avail themselves of the opportunity of shopping for even slight savings in competitive stores, which were becoming less and less competitive as shortages created an extreme seller's market. It was a moot question as to how much longer the miners could take the beating of having to spend every penny of their earnings and still be "ill fed, ill housed, and ill clothed."

Since 1942, labor had been pledged to a no-strike policy for the duration of the war. Shorn of its major weapon and with its plight becoming worse daily, labor asked the big question: Was anything going to be done to remove this suffocating ceiling over the workers and if so when and how would it occur?

Lewis pondered. A strike in the midst of the war was unthinkable, and even if it was decided upon, there was the fatal question of whether the workers would follow him on this dangerous venture. Lewis knew the history of the mine workers and remembered what no one else knew: that the coal miners in 1863, unorganized, had struck in the middle of the Civil War and stuck to their guns. As Lewis grappled with the problem, his own coal miners suddenly gave him the answer. Two weeks after the New Year began, thousands of Pennsylvania anthracite miners walked out of the pits on a spontaneous strike. It was clear that this strike was unauthorized by Lewis or any of the union officials, and that the miners, although the most disciplined of union members, temporarily had broken out of union control. This was extremely significant, because it was clear that the miners had reached the breaking point of frustration and disgust with the wide disparity between their wages and the high living costs. They had had enough and in their despair expressed their protest in the only way they knew —by striking.

Stories were circulated through the country that these strikes were not bonafide stoppages against the Government but in reality were against Lewis and the union because of a recent increase of union dues. Students of the coal-mining industry and the conditions of the coal miners seriously doubted that a new, slight increase in union dues would make the coal miners, the most union-minded group in the country, strike in the midst of a war. The fact is that while there was some resentment against the increase in dues it was a rebellion primarily against the disparity between higher prices and frozen wages. Senator Harry S. Truman of Missouri made a statement in the Senate chamber that he had checked into the strike and that there was no question but that the strikers were fighting for a wage increase rather than for a decrease in union dues. Government survey after survey of mining-town, company-owned stores all fully corroborated the charges of the miners.

On January 14, it was estimated that not only were eighteen thousand Pennsylvania anthracite miners already on strike, but the strike was spreading. Six New England governors telegraphed President Roosevelt, demanding that he "use all the authority at your command to keep the mines running." At Hazleton, Pennsylvania, leaders of twenty thousand coal miners in that district announced that they were on the verge of joining the strike. The next day the National War Labor Board formally ordered the coal strike to end and demanded that all anthracite coal miners immediately return to work. The War Labor Board hinted that possibly the officers of the United Mine Workers locals were not doing everything they could to end this unofficial walk-out. Lewis replied by denouncing the strike and publicly admitting that it was beyond the discipline of the United Mine Workers Union and was an unauthorized strike. However, Lewis knew why the miners were striking and sympathized with their plight. Although they had broken union discipline, which Lewis would not long tolerate, yet he lost his temper at "outsiders" who criticized his miners. He turned on the War Labor Board with a lashing attack and ended by publicly promising the miners that they would secure a "wholesome increase" in wages when their contract expired on April 30. This was an outright defiance, not only of the War Labor Board, but also of the Little Steel formula, for other labor leaders realized that wages were pegged to this formula.

The coal miners responded to the order of the War Labor Board for the immediate termination of the strike by continuing the strike on an even larger scale. Eight thousand anthracite coal miners in the Wilkesbarre, Pennsylvania, area stopped work, walked out, and joined their fellow strikers. The National War Labor Board promptly referred the case of the coal strike to the President, stating that their "mediation efforts have failed." It is very difficult to see here just exactly what "mediation" the War Labor Board had been doing. The Board's "mediation" efforts for miners on strike against unbearable conditions resulting from their wages being frozen at the same time that prices were boiling higher was to order them to get back to work!

The next day Roosevelt officially ordered the coal strike to end. He announced he was acting as commander in chief of the armed forces and ordered all miners to "return at once to their job of producing vitally needed coal for their country." Roosevelt also warned the miners that failure to obey this order within a forty-eight-hour period would mean that "your government will take the necessary steps to protect the security of the nation against the strike, which is doing serious injury to the war effort." Roosevelt's order resulted in some six thousand miners returning to work that day, but for two days resentful miners talked it over, and on Friday, January 22, the anthracite miners of Pennsylvania grudgingly returned to the mines.

Lewis was deeply impressed by this strike. To him it spelled out two extremely important facts. First, the condition of the miners was so severe that they spontaneously struck against it, regardless of union discipline. Conditions in the coal fields were worse than they had been for years and so bad that the coal miners would strike in a war period. Second, he noted the miners' reactions during this unauthorized strike. He saw the leaderless miners of their own volition deliberately flout the authority of the National War Labor Board and even stall for two days on a direct order of the President before they finally returned to work. Lewis did not forget this lesson. He now knew that there would be no question about the coal miners' going out on strike, war or no war. He also realized that a carefully planned strike engineered by the union, with himself personally exerting the full discipline of his machine if necessary, could successfully last out against both the President and the war climate.

Saturday, January 30, was the day after the anthracite strike ended. It was also the President's birthday, but it was the day that sent rage through the coal miners of the country as well as Lewis; for that day the Office of Price Administration handed down to the western Pennsylvania soft-coal operators an increase in the price of coal of twenty-three cents a ton. The operators had complained that the working of the mines on a six-day week resulted in a higher production cost and they needed this increase in coal prices. For the coal operators to get a price increase the day after the miners had returned to the pits with the President's threat still in their ears was gall and wormwood to these miners. They were mad. Lewis knew how the miners would react. Reports flooded in of their temper, and now Lewis warily watched and waited.

Developments on related fronts were coming rapidly. On February 3, both William Green, president of the AF of L, and Philip Murray, president of the CIO, went in to see President Roosevelt, complaining that the cost of living had far outstripped the Little Steel formula, which was being used by the National War Labor Board as a measuring stick in judging whether or not workers were entitled to a wage increase. While they were in the White House complaining and asking the President to do something about it, Lewis publicly announced that he intended to ask for a two-dollar-a-day wage increase for the bituminous coal miners. This was so far above what a Little Steel formula would grant in a wage adjustment for the miners that the administration, including the National War Labor Board, just scoffed at it as a "wild statement."

Organized labor, particularly the CIO and the AF of L, continued to exert pressure on the administration to do something about just wage adjustments, and on February 6, the CIO executive board officially announced that they demanded "wage adjustment to conform with increased living costs since May, 1942." These pressures and demands of both the CIO and the AF of L were serving the purpose of relieving their own frustrations by publicly articulating their own demands and acting militantly, but they were having no effect whatsoever upon the administration or its agencies. A few days later, on February 9, the National War Labor Board denied a badly needed wage increase to the 180,000 packinghouse workers employed by the Swift, Armour, Wilson, and Cudahy meat-packing companies. The NWLB said their wages had been increased previously to meet the cost of living on December 15, 1942. It seems absurd in retrospect to think of intelligent members of a governmental agency telling workers in 1943 that they had no reason to ask for a raise in pay, because, in spite of the universally accepted fact that the cost of living had gone way up in 1943 over the cost in 1942, the same wage that had been enough to get along with a year ago was still adequate. During that time the newspapers were filled with reports of an ever growing black market.

In the midst of all these recriminations and lamenting and whining on the part of the AF of L and the CIO came the strident voice of John L. Lewis, speaking on March 5, at Scranton, Pennsylvania. That day Lewis told a tridistrict convention of the United Mine Workers that he was going to fight to get a two-dollar-a-day wage increase for the eighty thousand Pennsylvania anthracite miners as well as fighting for the same two-dollar-a-day increase for the bituminous miners.

Delegates of the coal miners' locals present at this convention unanimously voted their confidence in Lewis and his intentions. One week later the election returns came in from all over the country electing Lewis to his twelfth term as international president.

On March 10, Lewis went to the Roosevelt Hotel, New York City, and faced the Appalachian soft-coal operators across the bargaining table. The Lewis that day was a desperate, forsaken, angry man. He had been hurt to the point where there was no "beyond." He had always felt himself a part of the mine workers, but now they were his whole life, his every thought, and his every feeling. Lewis shared the suffering of his miners and their desperation to get out of the impossible impasse of the Little Steel formula.

He opened the meeting with a vitriolic attack upon the War Labor Board, charging that it "has outlived its usefulness." Then Lewis cut loose: "The War Labor Board has befouled its own nest, and the greatest contribution it could make to economic stability would be for that board to resign and not cast its black shadow in the face of Americans who want to work and live and serve their country. . . . The world knows that Mr. Davis has long had his knife out waiting to plunge it into the back of the United Mine Workers. He inserted it into its body three times in 1941 and is now waiting to do it in 1943. Well, he just isn't going to do it this time. The War Labor Board seemingly has not yet found out that the workers of this country and particularly the coal miners do not intend to eat the Little Steel formula instead of solid American food."

Scorning the labor members of the Board as "labor zombies" Lewis then flatly laid down the following demands, saying nothing more, nothing less, would suffice.

1. Improvements in working conditions and vacations with pay.
2. Retention of present basic thirty-five-hour, five-day week.
3. Amendment of present hours provision by establishing portal-to-portal practices for starting and quitting time for underground workers, time and a half for overtime, double time for Sunday.
4. Increase in vacation payments to $50 a week from existing $20 token payments.
5. Elimination of existing wage differentials within and between districts and operation of only two instead of three shifts within a given twenty-four hours as means of eliminating hazards and improving safety conditions.
6. Inclusion of 50,000 foremen, assistant foremen, and other supervisory employees of coal mines, heretofore excluded, in the new agreement.
7. Basic wage increase of $2 a day.

Lewis then spoke for four hours, attributing inflation to gigantic Government spending for war purposes.

Lewis next ripped into "the feeble control of the price-fixing instrumentality of the Government known as OPA." He then presented a carefully documented study to prove that "the average median increase in basic food prices to the miners since August, 1939, was 124.6 per cent." (Later surveys corroborated Lewis's statement.) Lewis continued, emphasizing that the miners needed meat and adequate food to do their jobs, and these could not be secured on the present wages, and that in terms of the towering costs of food in the coal towns the purchasing power of the miners' wages were so shriveled that they were now "substandard starvation wages."

Lewis paused, and fixing a cold, hostile look on the now hypnotized coal operators, he first whispered and then bellowed, smashing his fist on the table. "When mine workers' children cry for bread, they cannot be satisfied with a Little Steel formula. When illness strikes the mine workers' families, they cannot be cured with an anti-inflation dissertation. The facts of life in the mining homes of America cannot be pushed aside by the flamboyant theories of an idealistic economic philosophy. Neither can these facts be suppressed or concealed to appease employing coal corporations who smugly hope that the Government will chastise the mine worker for daring to make known the miserable facts of his existence."

Knowing Lewis as the coal operators did, they knew that anything could and would happen. Each year they would warily approach the meetings with Lewis suspicious yet fatalistic, for they were resigned to being suddenly confronted with the unexpected. This year, as always before, Lewis did not disappoint them. His demand for portal-to-portal pay came as a bolt from the blue and left the operators gasping in consternation. Here they realized was Lewis's ingenious flank attack against the Little Steel formula, which barred any significant wage increase. He was not asking for a "wage increase" but for payment for the time spent by miners from the time they entered the portals of the mine until they arrived at that part of the mine where they were to work. The time this took averaged as high as an hour and a half each day.

For two days the coal operators conferred and then rejected

every one of Lewis's proposals. Charles O'Neill, spokesman for the operators, charged that "Mr. Lewis is trying to take us over lock, stock, and barrel." Then O'Neill announced that the operators would present no counterproposals, but they would let the Government settle the issue.

Lewis still hesitated on the decision of a strike during the war. He knew full well that although he would never permit the strike to affect the prosecution of the war, nevertheless he would be charged with that by the administration and the press.

On Monday, March 15, Lewis made his decision, and in a joint meeting with the Appalachian soft-coal operators he flatly stated he was prepared to strike unless he got a satisfactory wage agreement for the coal miners. While Lewis's threat to strike was regarded by the Government as just belligerent talk, it was not taken as such by the coal operators, who knew Lewis well. While there were few certainties in this complicated situation, one thing they knew was that Lewis did not make threats any more lightly than he would break his word. This does not necessarily mean that when Lewis makes an initial demand and backs it up by a threat of a strike that he will strike unless given that full demand. It is assumed in bargaining that one always asks for more than one finally settles for. The coal operators knew from Lewis's statement that he was willing to strike in the middle of a war and also was not too concerned about the no-strike agreement of labor with the administration.

The first reaction of the administration came when OPA administration chief, Prentiss Brown, announced in Milwaukee that, if the mine workers got their demands, the AF of L and CIO would then try to do the same thing, and the attempt to fight inflation would be defeated.

Negotiations continued for a week which were in actuality mere conversations, for the coal operators now felt that their initial reaction, that Lewis would really dare to strike, was completely wrong. They believed that for the first time in years their position was almost invulnerable and that if Lewis struck it would mean his end, that no labor leader, not even John L. Lewis, could lead a nationwide strike on such a basic and essential wartime commodity as coal and survive the inevitable volcano of national wrath. They felt that even if he dared to strike, he could not last long or even begin to cope with the executive powers possessed by the President during time of war. Because of this, the coal operators turned a bold, deaf ear to Lewis. Throughout this week of negotiation Lewis continued to press his proposals. He felt as though he were talking to deaf mutes as the coal operators blandly sat, not commenting upon any of his proposals and not advancing counterpropositions. The operators were doing what their spokesman had told Lewis they would do—they were not negotiating or intending to bargain in any way. This was their time and opportunity to smash both Lewis and the United Mine Workers Union. Here was their chance, for if Lewis went so berserk, in their eyes, as to lead a nationwide strike, he and his union would be certain to be smashed. They knew of the President's burning hatred for Lewis and realized that this time they would have the powerful support of the administration.

The scorn of the coal operators toward proposed portal-to-portal pay vanished with a decision of the United States District Court of Appeals of the Fifth District upholding the rights of iron-ore workers to be paid for travel time while underground in the mines.

The press printed reams about Lewis's "arrogance" in attempting to bargain as though there were no war and no War Labor Board. No one credited Lewis with striving to save organized labor's independence, its freedom to use its only weapon, the strike. With rare exception all America denounced Lewis, and liberal magazines drew little if any distinction between Lewis and Hitler. Lewis replied to the attacks of the press, which he pointed out were drawing enormous revenue from the lavish war advertisements of industry, which would charge its advertisements up to "morale" and cost of production.

Despite Lewis's repudiation of the press he felt the impact of public opinion and retaliated with full-page advertisements in fifty-eight newspapers pointing out that the miners were getting seven hours' pay for eight and one-half hours of work. The public was informed that the vast majority of miners had to travel long distances underground to get to their working site. The advertisement presented a study of sixty Kentucky coal mines showing that miners spent an average of one hour and forty-eight minutes going and coming to and from their job. The advertisement continued:

> We American coal miners are doing our part in the war effort. We don't mind hard work. If we did, we wouldn't be in a coal mine. We know we could go to war plants and get a lot more money for much easier work. We also know somebody has to mine coal—the prime mover of American industry. Because of our years of experience in the coal industry, we know we are serving our country best by remaining there. We are proud of our war-time production record.
>
> We are asking that an injustice be corrected. We are not asking to be paid for the time we spend getting our tools and necessary equipment. We are not asking that the company give us the powder we now pay for, nor to stand other charges which are rightfully theirs. We do ask that we be paid for the most dangerous part of our day's work, the time we spend in travel into the mine in the morning and coming out again at night. This is portal-to-portal pay as now paid to the miners in the country's metal mines and other industries.

On March 26, Lewis was served a summons to appear before a hostile Truman Senate War Investigating Committee, after he had already told them he would voluntarily appear. When Lewis arrived, the committee was questioning AF of L official John P. Frey. As the questioning continued, it became evident that the senators had deliberately decided to make Lewis wait. They were going to cut down this arrogant giant to size. He would sit and cool his heels until it suited the convenience of the senators. It was apparent that the senators anticipated a Roman holiday. Lewis would be machine-gunned with questions until he would appear ridiculous to the point of absurdity. The senators were hungry for the kill, and they had Lewis in their own stamping grounds.

Lewis quietly waited his turn and with the calling of his name solemnly walked to the witness chair. What happened then will never be forgotten by the audience or the senators. The lamb to be slaughtered suddenly became the wolf and turned on the senators. He slyly punctured their pompousness, exposed the fallacy of their arguments, baited them, trapped them, and left a group of senators minus their hides.

It began with Lewis leaning back in his chair. Senator Truman opened the hearing by telling him that the Senate committee was interested to learn what the Lewis thoughts were on the problem of absenteeism among war workers. Lewis in a low, calm voice advanced the proposition that absenteeism is determined by a great number of factors, including the worker's physical ability, that add up to the general human equation basic to the problem. After completing a succint discussion on this point, he paused, calmly looked over each senator, and then in a very soft voice put the committee back on its heels, where it remained through the balance of the hearing, with the statement: "As for absenteeism I have been told that absenteeism is higher in Congress than in industry. I do not know. I know that absenteeism prevails on this committee this morning. I do not know why some of the senators aren't here, but I am sure they are away for perfectly competent reasons."

Guffaws and loud laughs from many members of the audience reddened the senators' faces. Lewis then launched into a critical appraisal of the prevailing economic conditions. He pointed out that the current type of cost-plus contract under which industry was working for the Government was providing not only complete security but enormous profits. He confessed that he felt at a loss trying to reconcile these ever increasing profits for industry while at the same time the wages of labor were frozen. He accused the Government of aiding and abetting inflation with its cost-plus contracts. He then paused in his lengthy exposition. Senator Ralph Brewster of Maine, who was showing by both gesture and facial expression strong disagreement and opposition, impatiently broke in with, "Under the existing tax legislation and proposed tax legislation and under renegotiation . . . we will hope that the rich will not get richer out of this war."

Lewis's answer came back edged with sarcasm, "We all hope with you, but hope deferred maketh the heart sick."

Brewster flushed and in a rising voice said, "If we had waited to work out reasonable prices Hitler would have been on our shores."

Lewis wheeled on the witness chair and grimly asked, "Do you mean to imply that American industry wouldn't provide essential war goods to a nation that needed them unless guaranteed profits first?"

Brewster was staggered by this thrust and blurted, "I mean it was impossible for a governmental agency to negotiate fair contracts."

Lewis with a wry look on his face quietly answered, "The Government has awarded to industry forty-nine billions in contracts, and assuming ten per cent of that was profit, I assert that all of those profits are inflationary." Lewis then followed through with an explanation of why no wars had ever been fought without inflation.

Brewster defensively replied, "It is possible that out of this war may come a new deal."

Lewis interrupted, laughing, "I thought we already had one."

By this time Senator Brewster, groggy from Lewis's crushing retorts, inquired in an almost pleading tone if Lewis were willing to "help hold the dike against inflation."

Lewis replied coyly, with a satirical Horatio-at-the-bridge gesture, "Oh, my dear Senator, I will do anything I can to hold the dike."

Senator Truman, chairman of the committee, looked bewildered as the room rocked with raucous guffaws. His embarrassed appeals for order added to the merriment.

Brewster, desperately trying to regain his lost dignity, made one last attempt, "Now, Mr. Lewis, you aren't under any illusions that we are prejudiced in favor of United States Steel after what happened here last Tuesday?" (Brewster was referring to the committee's examination of employees of the Carnegie Illinois Steel Corporation, a subsidiary of U.S. Steel, in which it was admitted that 5 per cent of the steel plate manufactured for the Navy was faked to circumvent specifications.)

Lewis's reply crushed Brewster for the balance of that hearing. With a twinkle in his eye Lewis remarked, "I have no illusions on that, sir, but I couldn't think until I came here that you even knew about it, because otherwise I would have heard your golden voice denouncing it. . . . Congress can't condone a policy in this country that fattens industry and starves labor, and then call upon labor to starve patriotically."

Laughter swept the audience. Brewster, in almost an apoplectic rage at having been cut down at every point by Lewis, tried a final attack of name-calling. His voice rose sharply as he accused Lewis, saying, "You have been a disciple of discontent all your life."

Lewis gazed at Brewster for almost a minute and then slowly answered, "That is a misapprehension on your part, sir."

Senator Joseph Ball of Minnesota, having witnessed the debacle of his associate from Maine, was intelligent enough to avoid getting into a logical discussion of issues with Lewis. Instead Ball flew to the attack with name-calling.

Ball barked at Lewis, "Mr. Lewis, you are not seriously trying to tell the committee that any large number of workers in the United States don't get enough to eat? That is demagoguery, pure and simple, and you know it."

For the first time Lewis looked angered. Glaring at Ball he said, "You make your asseverations before you wait for a reply. If you have an opinion that I am a demagogue, then you do not need an answer."

Ball began to back off, replying, "All right, how many of your mine workers are hungry?"

Lewis, still angry, snarled, "If you ask the question, I will answer it. But when you call me a demagogue before you give me a chance to reply, I hurl it back in your face, sir."

Lewis then portrayed the conditions of the coal miners, claiming that when he talked about starvation he was referring to "a dietary deficiency" because it was impossible for the miners to purchase enough of the proper kind of food with their earnings.

"Hunger is a relative term. I said the coal miners are hungry —they suffer from a dietary insufficiency of foodstuffs. . . . That is what is happening to the coal miners . . . and when you call me a demagogue, I say to you that you are less than a proper representative of the people."

Senator Truman quickly arose and demanded that there be order at the hearing. He told Lewis he would not tolerate "any sassy remarks to the committee."

Lewis irately roared back at Truman, "Who cast the first stone?"

Truman looked around the room nervously and said, "Well, I'm stopping it right now. We must leave personalities out of the picture." Then glancing at Senator Ball, he continued, "That goes for both sides."

Lewis then put the finishing touches to the melee by almost purring, "I shall try to follow the lead of the distinguished senators on matters of courtesy."

Lewis then continued explaining that the miners ". . . were not getting enough to eat in the sense that it maintains their strength. The coal mine burns a man out pretty fast." Lewis then cited the outrageous prices prevailing in all coal towns.

Then suddenly Lewis began flattering the committee. He narrated some of his problems and in a very confidential, almost appealing manner suggested he would be most appreciative of any advice that could be given to him by the committee or by such people as Senator Brewster, ". . . having a very alert, capable mind on these things." Having spread the committee with honey, Lewis then poured on the vinegar as he charged that "the War Labor Board breached its contract with labor and with industry when it adopted the Little Steel formula as an arbitrary formula to fix wages and threw equity out the door."

This statement by Lewis resulted in his being bombarded with questions from members of the committee as to whether he implied that breaking of this pact meant that neither he nor his union felt that they were any longer bound by the no-strike pledge. Lewis then began a long series of identical answers· "Not necessarily."

An example of the quizzing is to be found in the questioning of Senator Ferguson of Michigan, a former prosecuting attorney and an expert cross-examiner, who decided that he would try his hand at eliciting information. Ferguson began saying, "Therefore, the agreement not to strike is not binding, according to what has been said, Mr. Lewis."

Lewis coolly replied, "Not necessarily binding."

Ferguson came back, "We are coming back again to the words 'not necessarily.' "

The Senator kept plying him with question after question, but Lewis would not budge. The members of the committee began to look more and more frustrated. Notes were exchanged, and heads were bent together trying to figure out how to force Lewis out of his position of "not necessarily binding," but it was hopeless. Just before Lewis was excused, Senator Burton provided the opportunity for a final *coup de grâce* to this hearing.

He said to Lewis, "We want to help to make sure we don't start off inflation from this corner."

Lewis replied with, "Do you mind first inflating the stomachs of some of my members?"

Burton, looking very uncomfortable, answered, "If we restrain industry and finance, are you willing to work on holding down the wages?"

Lewis almost sneered in the Senator's face. As he was getting up from the stand, he looked at Senator Burton, saying, "My dear Senator, whenever you have restrained industry and finance, just call me on the telephone and let me know."

Within a few days after Lewis's warning to the Truman Committee that if necessary he would strike for a satisfactory wage, Roosevelt entered the arena. He requested by telegram that the operation of the mines continue after the contract expiration date of April 1. Roosevelt also made a bid to Lewis by stating that the ultimate wage agreement would be made retroactive to April 1. At the same time he made an overture to the operators by suggesting that if necessary there would be revisions of the coal prices in order to permit satisfactory wage readjustments. With this soft approach to both Lewis and the coal operators went a firm reiteration that the ultimate power of decision over wages rested in the hands of the War Labor Board. While Lewis was reading the wire, he was informed that at that moment the NWLB had just rejected a petition by the AF of L that the Little Steel formula be abandoned.

The coal operators accepted the President's offer, and Lewis temporarily stalled until notified that his ally of the captive-mine strike and other crises, Dr. John Steelman, U.S. Conciliation Service director, was assigned to participate in the negotiations as Roosevelt's personal representative.

On March 29, the coal truce was approved. It was agreed that negotiations would continue for an additional month. Immediately after this agreement the administration began to show its hand with a rapid series of moves against Lewis.

It was becoming obvious even to those labor critics who were hostile to Lewis that the administration intended to use its full wartime political power to stop and, if necessary, destroy Lewis. The coal operators, fully aware of the political implications of the coal crisis, adopted the policy of refusing to engage in any kind of collective bargaining with the union and sitting it out. They believed that by waiting they would provoke Lewis into making a move that would result in a deadly battle between him and Roosevelt. This time, however, all of the odds would be on Roosevelt's side. The operators hoped to profit by the administration's uncompromising hatred of Lewis.

Certainly the circumstances were such that any aggressive strike action by Lewis would result in his being branded a traitor in the eyes of the American people. Public rage supporting the full power of the United States Government might well mean the finish of Lewis as a labor leader. In many quarters the word had spread that Roosevelt had been waiting for a long time to even scores and that the time had finally arrived. The War Labor Board's hatred for Lewis was common knowledge. Too many members of the Board had commented on Lewis, and their opinions were well known. If Lewis could be prevented by the administration from getting any kind of increase for his people, it would cost him his reputation among the miners as their infallible leader; and, because of the terrific economic squeeze that the miners were now suffering, almost anything might happen. In short, it was becoming pretty clear that the President was out to reduce the great man of coal to ashes.

On April 2, the Truman Committee, which in Lewis's presence on March 26 had become chastened, doubtful, and finally ridiculous, suddenly gathered its courage and issued a report denouncing Lewis for his statement that his no-strike promise to the President was "not necessarily binding."

Lewis, while not responding to this attack by the committee, was reported to have informed one of his close associates that "the hand of Roosevelt is creeping into the picture, and we shall soon see his fist." The presidential fist came six days later when Roosevelt in a comprehensive executive order designed to "hold the lines" re-emphasized the imperative necessity of "freezing wages and prices." Lewis was meeting with the coal operators in New York when he was informed of Roosevelt's order. He bitterly replied, "The President's order freezing wages left the coal miners resentful in having their demands for bread made a political pawn." Lewis was now convinced that the President by various means was discouraging the coal operators from negotiating any kind of settlement, to the end that Lewis eventually would be forced upon the "mercy" of the War Labor Board and the President. It was certain that the coal operators were committed to this objective, as they steadfastly refused to entertain any offers made by Lewis while for days they abstained from offering any kind of counterproposal. There was no collective bargaining.

. Lewis now became desperate. He did not want a showdown with Roosevelt at this time. He wanted a settlement with the coal operators that would avoid a wartime strike and its possible fatal consequences. He offered to "revise" his two-dollar-a-day wage increase if the coal miners would be guaranteed the six-day week throughout the year. It is reported that the Lewis offer for a guaranteed six-day week throughout the year came about in the following way: During the negotiations the coal operators presented a detailed chart that analyzed the wages of the coal miners through the year of 1942. The coal operators presented a professional statistician who lectured for some time on this chart, ending with the conclusion that the average wage of the coal miner in the year of 1942 had been $2,450 a year. Once this statement was made, Ezra Van Horn, chairman of the Appalachian Joint Conference and one of the leading coal operators, turned to Lewis and snapped, "And not even you, Mr. Lewis, can say that $2,450 is a substandard starvation wage." [1]

Lewis chewed on his cigar for a few moments, and then looking at Van Horn, softly drawled, "Mr. Van Horn, disregarding for the moment the question of the validity of your figure, you and your fellow associates appear to be concerned with the inflationary results of any wage increase which the coal miners might receive. You say this to me, you say it to the public in the form of large paid newspaper advertisements which your association has taken out and the cost of which is charged to the Government as part of your operating expenses, a Government

---

[1] It should be remembered that during Mr. Lewis's testimony before the Truman Committee, as well as in statements made previously, he had referred to the wages of the miners as substandard starvation wages.

cost which the coal miners pay for in taxes. In these advertisements you emphasize that one of the reasons you do not wish to have the coal miners receive any increase in wages is that it would increase the danger of inflation in this nation. An inflation which in fact is here.

"The President of the United States has also stated that he wishes to 'hold the line,' and therefore he chooses to freeze wages. He says that he does this purely for the good of the nation, purely because of his deep patriotism to preserve this nation from the horrors of inflation. You gentlemen profess the same *pure* motive. Let it never be said that John L. Lewis is not as patriotic as you are or as Franklin Delano Roosevelt. I herewith withdraw all my wage demands. I am prepared to sign a contract right here and now for no increase whatsoever as long as you will guarantee the coal miners six days' work each week throughout the year of the contract." Lewis's demands, which were actually for a guaranteed annual wage, caused the coal operators to huddle in a panic. After a brief conference, they decided to terminate the meeting for that day and began to leave. As they were walking out, Lewis barked, "Make me an offer."

One of them turned at the door, snarling, "We won't negotiate with you on anything for anything. Our only offer is to see you in front of the War Labor Board. That's where this is going to be settled."

John Steelman, of the Federal Conciliation Service, officially backed Lewis's proposal for a six-day week, which the operators had already rejected. Steelman disappeared from the "negotiations" at that point. It was reported that Frances Perkins was in favor of a $1.50 wage increase for the union, but she also eased out of the picture and little more was heard from her. The administration was discouraging any official approval of any of Lewis's proposals. Stories were rampant throughout the country that both Steelman and Perkins had been pulled out of the case by the President in order to ensure that there would not be a settlement and that the administration's plans to get Lewis before the NWLB would not be foiled.

On April 22, Frances Perkins certified the dispute to the NWLB. Lewis refused to recognize the NWLB, and the first meeting of the Board turned out to be nothing more than a

conference with the bituminous coal operators. Lewis had
ignored his invitation. The NWLB immediately ordered that
the operators and the miners of the Appalachian region continue "the uninterrupted production of coal." The miners'
answer came within a few hours as seven thousand miners
failed to report in the Birmingham area and two thousand
miners in western Pennsylvania went on strike. An exasperated
and worried NWLB promptly set up a three-man coal panel,
and NWLB Chairman Davis asked Lewis to name one of the
members. The request went unanswered, as did Davis's appeal
of the next day that Lewis halt the strikes, which were now
affecting sixteen thousand coal miners of Pennsylvania, Kentucky, and Alabama.

The next day Lewis broke his silence and electrified the nation as he told the press that the 450,000 bituminous coal
miners of the U.S. would not "trespass" upon coal property
after May 1, in the absence of any kind of a wage contract. This
was strike! No one doubted now that Lewis would go through
with it. The shock of Lewis's statement had not worn off when
in a few hours he declared war on the NWLB in a letter from
the union policy committee to Secretary of Labor Frances
Perkins. He denounced the War Labor Board as a kangaroo
court and curtly refused to have anything to do with it. The
union went on charging that the coal operators were trying to
hide behind the War Labor Board. Lewis declared that any
hope of a settlement rested in the resumption of meetings between the coal operators and the union, provided the operators
would engage in genuine collective bargaining. The union requested that the Government order the operators to negotiate
in fact, not just in form.

In the short time that it took for the policy committee's message to be delivered to Secretary of Labor Perkins's office, ten
thousand more coal miners walked off their jobs.

Concrete evidence in support of Lewis's contention that the
coal operators would not negotiate came on April 28, when
John R. Steelman reported to Roosevelt that the blame for the
collapse of negotiations rested on the coal operators, who had
consistently refused to engage in collective bargaining. Steelman's report was ignored by the President.

Madame Perkins promptly replied, rejecting the union's demand that the Government order the operators to meet again with the union and really negotiate. She closed her message with a personal plea that the union stop spreading stoppages.

The press reported that labor's deadly enemies, Representative Howard Smith of Virginia and Senator Tom Connally of Texas, had joined forces to put through a bill that would imprison anyone who so much as dared to "encourage" a strike. They practically did this in their Smith-Connally Act, which a panicked Congress was soon to pass.

On Thursday, April 29, the administration began to move. Roosevelt telegraphed Lewis threatening to "use all the powers vested in me as President and Commander-in-Chief of the Army and Navy . . . if the United Mine Workers soft-coal strikes continue after 10 A.M., May 1." He bitterly assailed Lewis and the walkouts of the miners "as strikes against the United States Government itself," which actually "have the same effect on the course of the war as a crippling defeat in the field."

The first reaction came from Ohio, the State of Presidents, when 9,700 miners laid down their tools and walked out of the mines. Roosevelt was to learn the bitter lesson that he could order all strikers, as he did 52,000 rubber workers who struck on May 26, to get back on their jobs "by noon tomorrow" and the union's officials to order them back "without delay." But he could not expect the same reaction from the coal miners, who did not care what the President said when it came to sticking by the union.

The next day was "Black Friday" in the nation as Lewis coldly rejected the President's order and threats, charging the mine operators with blocking negotiations and the War Labor Board with having prejudiced the case.

That night the nation churned with terrific tension. For the moment Hitler, Hirohito, and Mussolini were pushed off the front page. The common enemy had now been defined by President Roosevelt as John L. Lewis. All talk of beachheads, landings, precision bombings, and D Days turned to the number-one target, John L. Lewis. Stories were crackling all over the nation, hysterical ones that Lewis was to be arrested for treason, that he would be inducted into the armed services and then drawn and quartered by them. Then there were conjectures that Roosevelt would draft the strikers into the army, and as soldiers they would be assigned to mine coal, or there would be legal prosecution of Lewis, or a court injunction would be sought. That night, just as on another night in 1937 in Detroit, Lewis went to bed.

The first edition of the Saturday morning *New York Times* appeared on the newsstands late that Friday night with glaring headlines:

COAL MINES CLOSING, DEFYING ROOSEVELT ORDER
PRESIDENT READY TO SEIZE PITS THIS MORNING
LEWIS IS UNSHAKEN

On Saturday morning, May 1, 10 A.M. came and went with the miners immovably on strike. It had happened! Nearly a half-million American coal miners were defying their Government and their national commander-in-chief in the midst of war. It was insurrection bordering on revolution. As the nation held its breath, Roosevelt seized the coal mines and ordered Solid Fuels Administrator for War, Harold L. Ickes, to take over and direct operation of all coal mines closed by strike, which meant practically all of them.

Ickes promptly telegraphed all mine operators and managers, notifying them that they were to administer their coal mines as Government employees and that the American flag was to be flown at every mine. Then Ickes issued a call to striking coal miners to return at once and work for their Government. The miners watched the flags appear over the mines, then turned to Lewis awaiting instructions. They would do as Lewis told them, and what Lewis would tell them only Lewis knew.

Lewis was silent, but Americans everywhere shouted and railed against him. Motion-picture theaters showing newsreel pictures of Lewis were deafened with hisses, booes, and jeers. High-school boys picketed Lewis's Alexandria, Virginia, home with signs of "John L. Lewis—Hitler's helper."

The press mirrored the berserk rage of the people. From every subway, commuters' train, bus, trolley car, and street corner poured the anger of the people. Lewis was caricatured in cartoons as stabbing the American soldier in the back, and even the liberal *St. Louis Post-Dispatch* cartoonist, Fitzpatrick, portrayed Lewis as a second Huey Long. The name of Lewis came to be used as a profane adjective. Liberal Senator Claude Pepper of Florida attacked Lewis as a leader of a "rebellion!" He was publicly convicted in the American mind as an arch traitor. The public maelstrom embraced all creeds and politics, from the Communists, to the Old Guard Republicans, to Willkieites, to the Southern and Northern Democrats.

From the forces of organized labor Lewis received thousands of cheering letters, from CIO auto workers, rubber workers, and other rank-and-file members. From the CIO officials came vilification. Typical was CIO United Automobile Workers Union President R. J. Thomas's declaration that Lewis had called "a political strike against the President." Other labor leaders refrained from any comment. The AF of L officers shook in a scared silence. Lewis was alone. By all except his beloved miners and thousands of rank-and-file workers he was looked upon as a leper.

From overseas came the first reaction of the armed forces—a reaction that was ultimately to build up Lewis in the serviceman's mind as "the worst menace back home." The service paper, *Stars and Stripes,* printed on their front page, "Speaking for the American soldier, John L. Lewis, damn your coal black soul!" From every theater of war came the rage of American troops denouncing Lewis as a saboteur, as a traitor. War correspondents and columnists were later to comment frequently on the deep burning hatred for Lewis held by the armed forces.

The strike captured the world's attention. From Berlin came reports that it was "a protest against war." The Tokyo radio announced that the strike signified the date when the inevitable collapse of the American machine became apparent. The Battle of Coal had transcended every other conflict on the globe.

Then came word from the White House. The President of the United States would address the nation and the striking miners in a special radio speech at 10 P.M. the next night. Speculation was rife as to what the President would do and how far he would go.

In Washington that day Lewis was clamlike. He refused to comment on anything. Lewis was not concerned about the extent to which Roosevelt would go in a personal attack. He never worried about that because the attacks through the years had calloused him almost to the point of imperviousness. Lewis was never perturbed by Roosevelt, because he knew too much Roosevelt would not want publicly aired, as it would be if Roosevelt attacked Lewis to the point where they began to trade blows.

But Lewis was worried about the strike. He knew the supply of surplus coal above ground was so large that a short strike here and there would not affect the prosecution of the war. He knew the facts, even if the President, the Congress, the War Labor Board, and the press were telling the American people just the contrary. Lewis knew a long strike was absolutely taboo, as it would interfere with the war, and this Lewis would not do. He could not, his own patriotism aside, assume personal guilt for the loss of American lives and battles. Only a complete madman would do that, and in all the castigation hurled at Lewis through the years there had never been the slightest insinuation of madness.

In addition, Lewis was fully aware of the impossibility of cracking the Little Steel formula by a long strike. The nation would never permit it, and the ever mounting pressure might well destroy both the union and himself. His strategy would have to be of the hit-and-run type, short strikes with interludes of unbearable tension between. In this war of nerves he believed that the administration would of necessity have to break first. Lewis was well aware of the President's concern with innumerable problems of war, all requiring intense concentration. Lewis was fighting a one-front war while the administration was involved on innumerable fronts. He also knew that coal was related to the majority of the Government's operations, and as the latter's importance became more acute, the Government would sooner or later make concessions in order to settle the issue so that the question of coal supply would no longer be in doubt.

Sunday morning found Ickes and Lewis conferring behind closed doors. He and Ickes always had a mutual affection and respect for each other's integrity. Ickes, as the new administrator of coal mines, became the new employer of the miners. Both of them agreed to try to bargain on wage adjustments and other demands of the miners. Since this would take some time, Lewis agreed to end the strike for fifteen days, during which time of truce both Lewis and Ickes would try to work out a mutually satisfactory arrangement.

Lewis told Ickes that the truce would have to be approved by the mine workers policy board, which was still in New York City, where they had originally assembled for the negotiations with the coal operators. He told Ickes that he would recommend the truce, which meant that its formal approval by the union's policy committee was a routine rubber stamp, as it is and has been on every matter. Both men acted and spoke seriously about the policy committee. Lewis left for New York City that afternoon, after promising to phone Ickes the instant a decision was reached. Ickes arranged for a telephone wire to be kept open from his office to Lewis's hotel room in New York City.

In the meantime, it was reported that at the White House the President's speech writers had prepared two talks: a soft one if the union called off the strike during the day, which would praise the miners union for its patriotism and co-operation as an example of an America united—a hard one, if the strike continued, a blistering, vitriolic attack upon the officials of the United Mine Workers Union.

That evening the strike was ended on a weird and dramatic note. A half hour before Roosevelt was to go on the air, Lewis called a press conference behind locked doors. There Lewis leisurely announced that the union's policy committee had ratified a two-week truce for the reasons that:

"The mine workers recognize that they have a new employer who has not yet had time to appraise the immediate problems facing the industry. It is our desire to co-operate with the Government and to relieve the country from the confusion and stress of the existing situation.

"I salute you, coal miners! Your hearts are of oak and your patriotism can never be challenged."

The doors were opened at sixteen minutes to ten, and the reporters stampeded for the telephones. In five minutes all radio programs were being interrupted for the flash of the truce.

Roosevelt's radio address a few minutes later was an enormous anticlimax. A great many citizens felt sorry for him, thinking that he did not know of the settlement and that "somebody should tell the President." Others felt sorry for him, believing that he did know but had had no time to change his speech. But all were agreed that Lewis's timing was diabolically perfect, in terms of his hostility for the President. It was a masterful demonstration of his tactics of surprise and shock in the war of nerves.

The fact is that Roosevelt did know of the settlement before the broadcast and could have used his soft speech, but his anger with, and hatred for, Lewis were so strong that he lashed out at Lewis with, "Coal will be mined no matter what any individual thinks about it," and dismissed the strike as an action that would "involve a gamble with the lives of American soldiers and sailors and the future security of our whole people. . . ." Then Roosevelt's voice shook with anger as he struck again, placing responsibility "squarely on these national officers of the United Mine Workers."

The President's speech was hailed by the press and particularly the Republican conservative papers, which gloated over his words. The *New York Herald Tribune* editorialized:

> . . . Whatever governmental errors lie behind the present crisis—and they are many—the fact remains that now the President is right and John L. Lewis and all who support him are wrong. . . . The flag that will fly over the mines is the same that was raised in the dawn at Midway when the whole Pacific battlefront hung in the balance and Americans died for the things that flag represented. If the miners are worthy of the sacrifices which fighting men have made and are making for them, they will find in the flag the strongest argument against their irresponsible leadership. It places the United States in one camp; John L. Lewis in another. He is not alone in his camp: he has company there that any American with a shred of patriotism would shun as he shuns the most virulent plague. The miners of America can no longer have any illusions about the significance of their choice.

But the *Herald Tribune* and the other papers were wrong. The miners who might have read the editorial would have agreed with the last line; but the person about whom they would "no longer have any illusions" would have been Roosevelt and not Lewis.

With that radio speech the President shattered irreparably

among the miners the myth of Rooseveltian infallibility they had maintained for so long. They knew that Roosevelt was wrong in placing the full blame upon the union but, worse, that he knew and deliberately lied. To them it was unforgivable. They may have voted again for him in 1944 in preference to Dewey, but he was no longer their legendary champion.

Monday morning the miners were surly and resentful over the bitter national attacks against their union and themselves. They were disheartened by Roosevelt's actions. He had issued strong demands, given out executive orders, and made a radio speech—all against them. They were pleading that he permit their wages to be raised, and instead he raised the American flag. He had not raised a finger to help them, but had done all he could to encourage the wave of unparalleled attack upon the miners. Maybe the "old man" had been right about Roosevelt.

Never before had the miners felt further removed from Roosevelt or closer to Lewis than they did that year. Roosevelt's actions, and the avalanche of criticism and attacks from everywhere, united the miners into a more cohesive body than they had been for years. Even Lewis's critics and enemies among the miners were driven to side with him by the vehemence of the public storm. If ever Lewis had represented and articulated the needs and temper of his miners, he was doing it now. A local leader of the United Mine Workers told a *New York Times* reporter, "When John L. Lewis tells us to go back to work we'll go back, not before. We have gotten a pretty raw deal on the wage-negotiation proposition." [2] Similarly *The New York Times* quoted President Norman, of the United Mine Workers local at Sommer No. 4 Mine near Belle Vernon, as saying, "If President Roosevelt himself came down to the patch and told these men to go back to work without an agreement, without something in the way of an increase, they would say to him, 'You go back and get an order from John L. Lewis. Then we'll go back to work.' " [3] Every man of them would now follow Lewis through hell. Lewis was their leader, and they swore by him as passionately as they did at the administration and everything else.

[2] *The New York Times*, April 30, 1943.
[3] *Ibid.*

With the miners now back at work, Lewis set out to negotiate the union's demands with their new employer, the United States Government, via Harold Ickes. That day the chief announced that the miners would continue to insist upon portal-to-portal pay as well as increased wages. Lewis's appraisal of Ickes showed a number of favorable items. First, enough statements by Ickes were on record to indicate a positive distrust and dislike of the coal operators on his part. He resented their lobbying activities and refusal to grant the miners a guaranteed six-day week. Lewis also knew that Ickes, both by temperament and by lack of patience, was contemptuous of intrigue. Furthermore he hated the White House "Palace Guard" led by Lewis's bitter enemy, the prime adviser to the President, Harry Hopkins. Lewis believed that Ickes was honest and strong and that, lastly, he was more concerned with securing uninterrupted production of coal than with Little Steel formulas or War Labor Board plans.

The next day Ickes ordered all coal mines to be operated on a six-day week and then explicitly denied any commitments or deals with Lewis as "payment" for the strike truce. He went on to say that any demands of Lewis would have to be negotiated with the coal operators and must be approved by the War Labor Board.

It came as a shock to the coal miners, who could not comprehend Ickes's statement that the union must "negotiate" with the coal operators. Had not the Government seized the mines and wasn't it now supposed to be technically operating them? Had not President Roosevelt stated that week that "the coal miners are employees of the Government"? And yet here were their new employers telling them to go bargain with their old employers. The situation exposed "Government seizure" for the utter farce it was.

The union promptly denounced the entire maneuver as the most colossal trick in history and began to gird itself for another strike. If Roosevelt thought the miners would accept this extraordinarily distorted interpretation of Government seizure, he was to learn a bitter lesson.

The temper of the miners steadily rose as they saw examples of evidence verifying Lewis's position filter through the mass attack and the administration's vilification of the justness of their claim for higher wages. While the War Labor Board righteously held the line against wage increases in order "to stave off inflation," its chairman, William H. Davis, reported to Vice-President Henry Wallace that wage adjustments "have had a microscopic effect on prices." That week the War Labor Board resumed its hearings on the soft-coal dispute with no representative of the miners present. Lewis was boycotting the Board.

Lewis was now moving slowly. He knew Ickes's statement was the result of a White House order and that the latter actually resented and opposed both the Hopkins influence and the War Labor Board. If Ickes would become more responsive to the needs of the miners as well as uninterrupted coal production, it would mean a split in the administration forces that could be exploited for the benefit of the miners.

Lewis was also becoming increasingly aware of the Congress. On May 5, the Senate passed the Connally bill, which expanded the President's power of seizure of strike-bound plants and made instigation of any slowdown or strikes in those plants punishable by imprisonment. The stage seemed to be set for a struggle involving the fundamental liberties and rights of the entire labor movement. For this battle he would need vast support.

Lewis looked about for alliances. He rejected the CIO as a lackey of the President. The CIO would do anything Roosevelt desired. The left-wing unions at this point were vociferously and aggressively waiving many of labor's rights including that of the strike. As if to punctuate Lewis's convictions, the CIO executive committee, meeting in Cleveland on May 15, attacked Lewis for "jeopardizing the just demands of the miners" because of his hatred and "personal vendetta" against Roosevelt. It was clear that in the eyes of the CIO anyone who opposed Roosevelt was doing it for personal reasons. It would have been of interest to see what suggestions the CIO could have offered Lewis to help secure these "just demands." Certainly nothing was being done by either the CIO or the AF of L to win the "just demands" of their membership.

However, there was no other place Lewis could look for allies except to the American Federation of Labor; and on May 20, a highly excited and pleased William Green, squealing, "Isn't it wonderful," announced that he had just received Lewis's application for affiliation of the United Mine Workers with the AF of L. The application was accompanied by a check for the first year's dues of $60,000.

Lewis's move confounded his opposition. CIO leaders, always attributing a sinister motive to Lewis's every move, charged that he was trying to dragoon organized labor into the Republican camp. If not, then he was trying to organize all the dissident groups in the country for some malevolent purpose. Lewis told the writer once, "The utter lack of integrity, morals, and motivation of the CIO high command is always exposed by the fact that they attribute that to me as my purposes or reasons. Just as Murray always accuses me of betrayal, they take that which is in them and attribute it to those whom they oppose. Petty-minded, treacherous mentalities can only think in those terms. They know what they have done, and what they are, and for that reason not one of them trusts the other."

But Lewis had immediate business at hand that could not wait. The strike truce was expiring, and nothing had happened. The ever present War Labor Board was haunting the footsteps of both Lewis and Ickes. Now the Board ordered Lewis either to appear or to be represented at a special coal hearing to be held the next day. Lewis spurned the order, charging that the jurisdiction of the coal issue rested between Ickes and himself. He then flayed the Board for hampering and obstructing a wage agreement, ending by accusing them of "malignancy." The same day Lewis announced the extension of the truce until May 31.

The next day Ickes responded to White House pressure by informing Lewis he did not have the power to force the operators to negotiate, and that, at any rate, any contract must have the War Labor Board approval.

Lewis kept his silence. He knew of the pressure operating on Ickes and felt that if Ickes's sympathetic attitude was backed up by strike action, the ranks of the administration opposition might be broken. He continued his silence as the War Labor Board issued a fact-finding report against a wage increase for the miners, although they did not completely close the door on the issue of the six-day week or portal-to-portal pay.

The few days left of the truce were passing and five days

before the expiration date Lewis offered to drop his demand for portal-to-portal pay in exchange for a straight two-dollar-a-day wage increase. The operators greeted this as they had everything from the first day when negotiations began by saying, "No!" Again Lewis asked for a counterproposal, and again the answer was silence.

With one day to go before the deadline the operators continued to sit silent and adamant. Ickes frantically wired both Lewis and the operators, demanding that they negotiate a settlement. The answer was a complete breakdown of any negotiations.

Tuesday, June 1, found Roosevelt in a fury as 530,000 coal miners all over the country, contemptuously ignoring his statement, "The coal miners are employees of the Government and have no right to strike," went on strike. Ickes promptly announced that the strike was a strike against the Government, and then losing his temper, angrily denounced "a few powerful operators who from the beginning have deliberately opposed any compromise."

The strike was on again, and again the nation was beginning to work itself into a frenzy. The War Labor Board ordered all negotiations between the operators and Lewis, which had blown up the day before, to be stopped until the miners returned to work. Lewis laughed when he was notified of this action, and is reported to have said, "If this august Labor Board read the papers they would have known that there were no negotiations to be 'ended.' They seem to have known as little about this as they do about the condition of the coal miners."

The next day the spotlight switched to the White House, as Roosevelt called an emergency conference of Secretary of the Interior Ickes, War Mobilization Director James E. Byrnes, and eight members of the War Labor Board. As the chief officers of the administration met, they knew that Government seizure or raising the flag over the mines no longer meant anything to the miners, who believed that this was an administration mask to conceal their real employers, the coal-mine operators themselves. Lewis watched and waited for the results of this meeting. He also watched the Congress as the House voted 211 to 163 to call up the Smith-Connally bill for immediate consideration.

The storm began to build up. The War Labor Board publicly charged Lewis with having repudiated "at each step" the no-strike agreement and that John L. Lewis "challenges the Government of the United States in time of war." From far-off San Francisco came the voice of left-wing Longshoremen's Union President Harry Bridges denouncing Lewis as a "traitor" and "agent of the Fascist powers." Not only Lewis but the public generally was becoming bored with these left-wing clichés, which were shot out at the drop of a word, such as "*provocateur*," "disruptionist," "obstructionist," and "Fascist agent."

With Ickes putting on the pressure, the coal operators and Lewis again sat down to attempt to negotiate an agreement. For the first time the operators listened, and then for the first time they made counterproposals. For the first time, therefore, negotiations really began. The coal operators were stripped of their previous stubborn self-assurance. They had been totally wrong. Lewis not only had dared strike in the midst of war, but he had already struck twice. They thought the miners would respond to Roosevelt's appeal over Lewis's head, and the miners did not. Now that even Government seizure had not stopped Lewis, the operators were scared and wanted to settle.

Lewis proposed a formula that he credited to Ickes which would solve the portal-to-portal issue. He asked that the miners receive $1.50 a day as travel pay until a commission of operators and miners could survey the whole problem and report their findings within thirty days. The operators practically accepted the offer but held off because of the fact that a commission's findings might result in considerably more than the $1.50. Coal-operator spokesman O'Neill claimed that the commission's judgment might well exceed the $1.50 daily rate and "constitute a contingent liability which was not a stabilizing force for the industry."

Lewis again held up his banner of the "empty bellies and stomachs" as he rumbled, "We want stabilization of the mine workers' stomachs."

Thursday, June 3, the negotiations continued and the miners stayed on strike—all oblivious of Roosevelt's angered "order" that the miners "return to work." No longer was the President referring to "my friends, the miners." Now he was hostile and hurt. The people had always responded to his call, but now the miners were ignoring him. Roosevelt found that although to the nation he was the commander-in-chief, to the miners, when it involved their union, he was not; John L. Lewis was their commander-in-chief.

As the coal operators bargained with Lewis, it began to appear that an agreement was in the offing. Suddenly, the War Labor Board ordered the cessation of all negotiations as long as the miners were on strike. Lewis fumed that this was a "malicious interfering, illegal action" and then lashed out at the War Labor Board, charging, "These little strutting men have sought to place upon the miners the responsibility for this work stoppage, which rests actually upon their smug shoulders. Fearful lest a solution be reached under auspices not compatible with the self-importance of the War Labor Board, that body maliciously commanded that these negotiations cease."

The coal operators, now sick of the sorry mess, realizing that Lewis was going to worry Roosevelt ragged with his jolting stoppages, and wanting their mines back, added to Lewis's attacks against the administration.

Lewis was now splitting up his opposition. He had cracked the unholy alliance of the coal operators with the Government, and he had Ickes leaning toward him and away from the White House. Again he renewed his war of nerves using his union policy committee as a front. The policy committee contemptuously slapped back at both the President's and the War Labor Board's orders for an immediate return to work, announcing that the strike was being called off not immediately but four days later. The President smarted under this flouting of his will, but as the nation took a deep breath of relief Lewis struck again, knocking the wind out of everyone. He announced another deadline thirteen days away, June 20.

Negotiations began again, and the second day Lewis and the operators announced an oral agreement on the portal-to-portal issue of $1.30 a day as travel allowance for each miner. With a settlement seemingly reached, Ickes responded to pressure from the administration by fining 450,000 soft-coal miners $5.00 a man for their five-day strike, June 1–5. The avalanche of curses from the miners and their threats to quit sent Ickes reeling back, and for one of the few times in his career the Secretary of the Department of the Interior retreated. Ickes quickly announced that all fines could be appealed, which was a polite way of saying, "Forget all about what I said."

Lewis unemotionally watched the House of Representatives pass the Smith-Connally bill vesting statutory powers in the War Labor Board. This authority included the right to subpoena witnesses, which would force Lewis to appear before them. It provided imprisonment for any leader promoting a strike in a Government-seized industry, but Lewis knew that it would not be enforced. He knew that Roosevelt knew that locking up Lewis meant locking up the coal mines.

On Friday, June 18, the War Labor Board, flushed with confidence because of their new power under the Smith-Connally bill, rejected the agreement between Lewis and the operators of $1.30 travel time as well as the union's demand for a flat $2.00-a-day wage increase.

Lacking representation, depositions, or testimony from the miners, the Board's findings of necessity were predicated upon the figures presented by the coal operators. They stated, "With the provision for a six-day week and the wartime demand for bituminous coal, the mine workers, in March, 1943, were able to secure an average weekly take-home pay of $42.97 for a work week of 38.3 hours, which is 65.3 per cent greater than their average weekly take-home in January, 1941, when they averaged 29.7 hours per week. . . ."

The three-cent hourly increase recommended by the Board would have amounted to an approximate wage increase of $1.14, making the coal miners take-home pay a total of $44.11. It is important to bear this in mind, as a guide to the extent of Lewis's success in his drive for more money for the coal miners.

It is significant to note that the four labor members, while dissenting with the Board's decision, still recommended only 80¢ temporary travel time, pending a survey, instead of $1.30 a day. These labor leaders were caught in the trap of their own failings. They knew that if Lewis won his demands they would be vulnerable to attack by their own followers for their failure to have secured similar gains for them.

These same labor leaders then attacked Lewis by saying, "The labor members of the War Labor Board, representing the overwhelming majority of organized labor in America, are just as firmly convinced that the no-strike pledge we made to the

American people through the President of the United States must be carried out today as on the day we made it."

Two of the signers were ex-UMW officials, Van A. Bittner and John Brophy. For days they were cursed by the miners as traitors.

As quickly as the news spread, so quickly did the miners start the exodus out of the pits. On Friday, a full day before the deadline, 58,000 miners quit, and on Saturday, June 20, 530,000 miners stopped. For the third time in seven weeks the miners were on strike.

Chairman Will Davis of the War Labor Board announced that the contract approved by the Board called for a three- to four-cent-an-hour increase over the 1941 contract, which he quoted the *United Mine Workers Journal* as having boasted was the greatest contract ever achieved. Discounting the fact that the *United Mine Workers Journal* is inclined to grandiose statements and frequently reflects more accurately the opinions of its editor, K. C. Adams, than those of Lewis, the fact remains that Davis's reasoning was unsound. After all, in the saga of labor, there were many contracts in years past that many unions proclaimed their "best contract," but it was a "best contract" for those days and definitely not a model for a later time and different circumstances.

The union indignantly spurned the Labor Board's contract as a "yellow-dog contract," and then Lewis uncorked a flanking maneuver that acutely embarrassed the administration and almost gave apoplexy to the War Labor Board. He announced that the mine workers were willing "to work and continue the production of coal for the Government itself under the direction of the custodian of mines. The mine workers have no favor to grant the coal operators nor the members of the War Labor Board, who have dishonored their trust, but will make any sacrifice for the Government, the well-being of its citizens, the upholding of our flag, and for the triumph of our war effort. Accordingly the executive officers of the United Mine Workers of America are hereby instructed to hold themselves in readiness to confer with the Secretary of the Interior, who by Presidential Executive Order of May 1, 1943, is instructed and empowered to do all things necessary for or incidental to the production, sale, and distribution of coal."

Lewis's strategy was to set up a situation where the operators would get panic-stricken and become his firm allies in order to regain possession of the coal mines. Also by flattering Ickes by their announced willingness to work under him, the mine workers would drive another wedge between Ickes and the Labor Board. Now there was fertile ground for the breeding of suspicion and hostilities between the Labor Board and Ickes. Lewis was still pounding away on his basic strategy of "divide and conquer."

The War Labor Board began to certify the case to the President, and the President began to get ready to attack when suddenly the strike was off. Roosevelt, all primed to attack, could not stop the momentum of his hostility; and, although the miners were back at work, he denounced the actions of the officials of the union as "intolerable" and went on to announce he had already taken steps "to set up the machinery" to induct the strikers into the army so that they would be ordered to dig coal as soldiers.

With this statement of the President, Lewis felt assured of victory. He knew now that the strain had told on Roosevelt. He knew that the induction of the miners into the service as a method of strike-breaking would end Roosevelt with the entire organized labor movement. He knew, too, that even if Roosevelt did take this action, more than a half a million "service miners" could still refuse to work and that there was nothing the President could do. Could he shoot or imprison a half a million men? This was a threat that could only enter when good judgment left, and Lewis knew his war of nerves was winning.

The President's threat resulted in 40 per cent of the miners indignantly refusing to return to the mines. Now the President had lost all his influence with them and they were beginning to be bitter and resentful toward him.

The U.S. Steel Corporation announced that ten of its blast furnaces would be closed down by the next day. This was the result of lack of coal at hand. Similar announcements in other cases of this kind have always been one of the obstacles that Lewis has had to fight constantly in his campaigns. These statements by industry act as incendiary torches to ignite public opinion against the miners. In many cases there have been needless acts deliberately designed to incite reaction against a coal strike. It should be noted here that *on the occasion of each strike the Bureau of Mines reports showed that sufficient coal had been mined and was above ground to satisfy all the demands of industry for at least a month.* Lewis kept an eagle eye on these reports, as he would never permit the slightest interference with the war effort. For this reason he was unruffled by the mad hysteria accusing him of sabotaging the war.

The next day, Friday, June 5, the President vetoed the Smith-Connally Act, and two hours and fifteen minutes later Congress overrode the veto. Roosevelt's veto message did ask the Congress for an act enabling the military draft of strikers. Despite this, both AF of L's William Green and CIO's Philip Murray praised the veto message. Senator Harry S. Truman accurately appraised the situation when he opposed the President's request saying, "I am neither for a military dictatorship nor for drafting labor."

In the meantime Lewis announced that the miners would work if Government operation of the mines was a genuine operation and not a masquerade. Then Lewis slammed across another deadline of October 31. This was a strategic date falling at the very height of the forthcoming political elections.

Roosevelt in a white heat lunged back, telling a press conference that he would not recognize this deadline or any other deadlines of Lewis. Roosevelt then told the coal operators that their investments and rights would be protected. The War Labor Board, almost hysterical, demanded that War Mobilization Director James F. Byrnes force the mine workers to sign the Labor Board contract.

The miners, as before, retaliated against administration threats. Their answer came on the same day as 20,000 Pennsylvania miners walked off their jobs. The next day 210,000 more decided that they were going to stay home.

The press at home and abroad, along with the armed services, went berserk. The Army newspaper, *Stars and Stripes,* ran the following editorial:

> A soldier in the Middle East, who once was a successful artist, drew a cartoon for "Stars and Stripes." We didn't print the cartoon, because soldiers are not supposed to get involved in matters that would be termed political: but we'll tell you what

the cartoon portrayed. John Lewis, in miner's dress, was throwing dirt with a coal shovel upon the freshly marked grave of some kid in Africa. It's a grim bitter piece of work and God knows it expressed the attitude of the overwhelming majority of the soldiers in this and any other theatre. We are telling you what that cartoon was about because we believe that the activities of John Lewis have transcended the realm of politics and legitimate unionism and have entered the realm of treason.

Nor is John L. Lewis a traitor to his government alone. He has betrayed by his excesses the cause of union labor with which he has so long been identified. He has betrayed the spirit of democracy which gives him the right to move against the welfare and will of America's millions. He has betrayed the belief of the American soldier that this would be a war in which the individual's gain and the individual's interest would be sublimated to the common purpose. Speaking for the American soldier, John L. Lewis, damn your coal black soul!

The War Labor Board, now armed with the power given it by the passage of the Smith-Connally Act and filled with hatred of Lewis, vindictively attacked him and the mine workers union. The Board demanded that President Roosevelt order Lewis to sign the approved War Labor Board contract and implement this order with authority to use sheer force such as seizing the treasury of the United Mine Workers of America, which involved about six million dollars. Furthermore, with the Government now operating the mines, they could cancel the established check-off of union dues. Still thirsting for vengeance, the Board then followed through with a personal attack against Lewis, urging either civil or criminal prosecution or both.

Lewis was unperturbed by these threats, knowing that the administration realized that in the last analysis the coal miners could always walk off the job and no power except his could send them back to work. The miners were now recipients of every type of abuse, insult, and attack that could be made, and took striking during the war as a matter of course. The net result of Roosevelt's denunciations, the violent attacks by the press, and the towering anger of public opinion had been simply to solidify the forces. Lewis now knew he had well-disciplined seasoned veterans with whom to carry on the campaign.

Secretary of the Interior Harold L. Ickes began arrangements
for the operation of the coal mines during the period of truce.
He appointed Carl Elbridge Newton, the forty-five-year-old
president of the Chesapeake and Ohio Railroad Company, to
be the director of mine operations for the federal Government.
He was in charge of operation of all coal mines seized by it.
Along with this appointment Ickes also attempted to allay the
growing fears in the country that the Government was planning
to nationalize the coal industry by announcing that the Government had no plans to this effect.

The coal miners, smarting under the impact of the President's threats as well as those of the War Labor Board and the
Congress, were still keeping away from the coal pits. As late as
Wednesday, June 30, Secretary Ickes announced that approximately 130,000 coal miners were still out on strike. Ickes
made a special broadcast from Washington, appealing to the
miners to return to work and pointing out that there must be
"continuous mining of coal whether there is or is not a contract
between the miners and the operators." It took five days, but on
July 5, the coal miners came back, and for the first time it was
reported that bituminous production was nearly normal and
the anthracite output was 15 per cent above normal.

On Friday, July 9, President Roosevelt, during a press conference, was quizzed as to what he intended to do about the
War Labor Board's demands that the President force Lewis to
sign the contract they approved. Roosevelt admitted "that he
could not force John L. Lewis to sign a War Labor Board approved contract." He pointed out that although the Government could seize property, it could not seize a labor union. It
was now obvious that Roosevelt was beginning to realize the
desperate character of his previous statements and threats, such
as demanding the drafting of all strikers, and was backing away
from such tactics. It is reported he turned to the newsmen and
inquired in a sarcastic tone of voice whether they would suggest that he send Lewis a social invitation inscribed on pink
paper politely pleading, "Dear Mr. Lewis, I hope you will sign
the contract."

By the end of the week, on Saturday, July 10, the coal
operators ran up the white flag, with Edward R. Burke and
R. L. Ireland, Jr., both spokesmen for the operators, publicly

admitting to War Mobilization Director James F. Byrnes that from their point of view Lewis had won the battle and that they might just as well give in and capitulate. They dejectedly reminded Byrnes that President Roosevelt's admission to a press conference of his inability to force Lewis to sign a War Labor Board contract was "proof that Mr. Lewis, through his defiance of the Government had gained his point."

With the coal operators now in a state of complete surrender, Lewis struck from another quarter. With brilliant generalship and his flair for always launching a perfectly timed surprise attack at the first break in the opposition's ranks, Lewis hit at the operators and broke through. He announced that the union had just signed a two-year contract with the Illinois Coal Operators Association involving 30,500 miners. This contract provided that the Illinois Coal Operators Association would pay miners $1.25 a day for portal-to-portal travel time, effective as of April 1, 1943, and that 50 per cent of this amount should be made retroactive to October 24, 1938, at which date the Fair Labor Standards Act became law. The agreement also provided that the seven-hour day be increased to eight hours and that the miners should receive time and a half or $1.50 for this extra hour. With this went 25¢ a day for vacation pay and a no-strike agreement. The actual terms of this contract provided approximately $3.00 a day extra in the pay check of every coal miner instead of the original $2.00-a-day wage increase. It involved simply extra work plus payment for portal-to-portal travel time. From Lewis's point of view, he was now in a very solid position. Here was a contract that had been arrived at through normal collective bargaining, agreed upon by the operators as well as the union.

August 3 was a red-letter day for the War Labor Board, as Lewis, for the first time, not only acknowledged them but personally appeared before them to argue for and request the approval of the Board for the Illinois contract. If the War Labor Board believed that Lewis had weakened and was giving in to them, they were as wrong as the operators had originally been when they thought that Lewis would never dare to strike in the midst of a war.

Lewis's tactics were now to discredit the Board so that it would be rendered ineffective. If the Board approved the

Illinois contract, everyone would know that Lewis had not only won and smashed to smithereens the Little Steel formula, but had actually gained more than he had originally demanded.

If the Board rejected the contract, then every coal miner in the country would curse and defy the Labor Board forever. To the miners the unalterable picture would be that Lewis and the operators had agreed on a contract that would give the miners what they so badly needed, and had been overruled by this infamous, infernal Government Board.

So a calm Lewis entered the Labor Board's den. There he confronted the members of the Board, whom he had publicly cursed so eloquently and so fervently for these long months. Facing him sat these men filled with mingled hate and fear of this incorrigible rebel. Lewis was quiet, calm, and courteous. His arguments were marked with dignity. It was difficult to believe that this was the same man whose bellows and roars had occupied the Board members' every waking hour and given most of them nightmares of "little strutting men."

Outside the Board's chamber, Lewis's henchmen were unsheathing the sword with threats that a War Labor Board rejection of the Illinois contract would mean "widespread dissatisfaction, turmoil, and strife in the coal fields." There were whispered threats of wholesale lawsuits against all the operators for portal-to-portal back pay going back to October 24, 1938.

On August 16, Roosevelt reinforced the War Labor Board with an executive order empowering it to withhold dues of unions not complying with its decision and also to cancel draft deferments of the strikers. Now the stage was set for the Board to hand down an adverse decision and to have the power to back it up. It came on Wednesday, August 25, when the National War Labor Board rejected the United Mine Workers contract with the Illinois Coal Operators Association, charging that the portal-to-portal travel payment was nothing more than a concealed wage increase.

Lewis hesitated, recognizing that here was a situation that required cautious maneuvering. He realized that the War Labor Board was anxious to hurl the full impact of the power of Roosevelt's executive order against him, withholding the union's check-off dues and otherwise striking at the heart of the financial structure of the mine workers union.

Negotiations between the mine workers union and the Illinois Coal Operators Association were resumed at once, with a quick agreement on a revised contract that provided for an eight-and-a-half-hour working day with a wage increase amounting to two dollars a day for a five-day week. The issue of portal-to-portal pay was omitted from the contract. The wage increase came in the time and a half for overtime after five days plus holidays. Two days after the union and the Illinois Coal Operators Association reached this agreement on a revised contract, Harold Ickes announced that all coal mines were now being returned to their private owners.

Ickes's action set off a series of violent explosions in the coal fields. The coal miners furiously watched the return of the mines back to the coal operators while they still had no contract. In Alabama 22,000 coal miners refused to return to work. The next day 3,500 coal miners in Indiana struck. The National War Labor Board joined with Lewis in ordering the striking coal miners in Alabama and Indiana to return to work. Lewis indicated to the miners that the War Labor Board would soon reach a conclusion on the revised contract with the Illinois Operators Association and strongly intimated the decision would be favorable. In spite of Lewis's statement, most of Alabama's 22,000 coal miners refused to return to the pits, despite the apparent efforts of mine workers officials. In other parts of the country wildcat strikes were breaking out like measles. Kentucky, Arkansas, Illinois, Indiana, Ohio, and Pennsylvania were showing big rashes. Ickes announced that these wildcat strikes had cost about eighty thousand tons of coal for the week of October 16.

On October 26, the National War Labor Board rejected the revised contract between the mine workers union and the Illinois Coal Operators Association, but this time the Board offered a compromise that was pretty close to what Lewis was asking. The spreading wildcat strikes were beginning to tell on the War Labor Board. Here was a condition for which the union disclaimed all responsibility and with which it would be difficult to deal. The basic daily wage in the contract of $8.50 was cut down by the War Labor Board to $8.12½. The Labor

Board also warned Lewis that it was going to refer the wildcat strikes now taking place in seven states to President Roosevelt "for appropriate action," if the miners were not back at work within two days.

As had been the case throughout the year, the miners turned a deaf ear to the threats of the War Labor Board and stayed out on strike two days longer. By November 1, every miner was out—530,000 men refusing to work without a contract. Lewis's November 1 deadline coincided with the opening of the national CIO convention, which was meeting in Philadelphia, where its president, Philip Murray, spent the day bitterly denouncing labor leaders who were encouraging strikes in war industries.

There was considerable suspicion as to the genuineness of these wildcat strikes and of Lewis's alleged inability to bring them to a halt. Certainly they did not fit into the pattern of the almost perfect discipline that these miners had demonstrated in response to Lewis's will. Lewis's order to the union to return to work was taken by them simply as a tongue-in-cheek measure that they could openly defy still leaving Lewis free from any charge of violating the War Labor Board's decision and the consequences of having union dues sequestered.

Roosevelt, now confronted with the fourth general strike since March 15, had no alternative but again to order immediate Government seizure of the coal mines by Ickes. A frustrated and harried administration acceded and permitted Lewis to negotiate a contract with Ickes. Two days later came the settlement; the wage contract between Lewis and Ickes gave the miners a wage rate of $8.50 a day, which was an actual $1.50 more daily pay for the miners. The mine workers had previously demanded a $2.00-a-day wage increase for seven hours of work. The net result of this contract was that the coal miners, who had previously received a wage of approximately $45.50 for a 42-hour week, were to earn $56.74 for a 48-hour week. After Lewis had got the wage increase of approximately $1.50 a day, the War Labor Board finally approved the contract after scaling down the wage increase to $1.12½ an hour. Ickes then agreed to make up the 37½¢ in return for a so-called face-saving agreement with the union whereby the miners would ostensibly take a fifteen-minute reduction in their lunch period.

Wayne L. Morse, later United States senator, a public member of the Board, strongly opposed the approval, charging that negotiations should not have been carried on as long as the miners were on strike. Bitter and angry voices were heard coming from Congress. Virginia's Senator Harry F. Byrd attacked the Government for "coddling" Lewis and demanded that the President stamp Lewis as a "traitor" and invoke the Smith-Connally Act against him. The press of the nation carried banner headlines grudgingly acknowledging Lewis's ultimate victory. Lewis, flushed with triumph at having broken through the Little Steel formula, was receiving acclaim of all his miners throughout the country.

That the miners were going to exploit every part of the contract favorable to them and not permit exploitation against them was apparent the following week as thousands of coal miners struck on Armistice Day, complaining that it was not one of the holidays President Roosevelt had designated for time-and-a-half pay. The War Labor Board began to fume, attacked the UMWA, and urged Congress to pass legislation that would "require responsibility of the union" and would also give the nation protection "against those who misuse the power presently permitted."

The final decision of the National War Labor Board was handed down on Saturday, November 20, and it contained a number of minor revisions, one of which cut 30½¢ from the basic weekly wage of the coal miners as it existed in the contract, and left it finally at $57.07. The operators promptly signed this contract with Lewis and also put up a sum amounting to $40 for each miner, which was to serve as a per-capita retroactive payment for all underground travel time. Lewis had clearly won, regardless of how some of his critics might try to disparage his victory. The battle had lasted eight and a half months before Roosevelt succumbed to Lewis's sharp, unceasing, jabbing attacks in the war of nerves.

Moreover, the President announced the month after he abandoned the struggle with Lewis that he was abandoning the New Deal. He told a press conference, on December 28, that the program had to be adapted to the times "no matter who runs the Government," and pointed out that the New Deal had outlived its usefulness.

In Lewis's entire lifetime he had never embarked upon and fought through a campaign as bitter as the one just ended. Never before had the miners answered the union's call to arms with such unswerving loyalty, discipline, and devotion to the UMWA and John L. Lewis. Completely alone, they had withstood the annihilating impact of the attack on all fronts—from the President, the Congress, the press, and the people. They had stood it unflinching and unyielding. Nowhere but in their own ranks had even a voice or hand been raised in their behalf. The organized labor movement, both AF of L and CIO, had sat it out in terror lest the tidal wave of public wrath breaking over Lewis engulf them.

There was sufficient evidence for Lewis reasonably to believe that Roosevelt was interested in exploiting the situation to the end of destroying Lewis. It would be difficult to explain the coal operators' refusal to bargain in any way for the first months of alleged "negotiations" unless they had been so advised and encouraged. It should be pointed out, however, that any fair analysis of the situation must take into consideration the fact that Roosevelt, in 1943, was planning the groundwork for the second front in the war in Europe. Lewis's attacks at home during this crucial year were exasperating to the point of utter distraction.

Not even in the most torrid periods of the CIO organizing drive had Lewis been subjected to such unanimous vilification and attack. It told on him as it would on any man. The end of 1943 found Lewis's natural pallor touched with grayness, and the rugged lines of his face were drawn. The war had taken its physical and nervous toll of Lewis, too, as he carried the victory back to his miners. Though triumphant, he was utterly exhausted.

Chapter 13

Imbroglio

LEWIS reaped the whirlwind of the 1943 war strikes. Throughout the country he was damned as a Benedict Arnold. Even Lewis recoiled before this nationwide condemnation and felt constrained to issue a personal statement in his own defense. In an article called "Not Guilty," which he wrote for *Collier's*,[1] he opened bitterly with: "For a year and more, I have been branded Public Enemy No. 1, and the 600,-000 members of the United Mine Workers have been stigmatized as malcontents who put mean greeds above the welfare of their country."

Then, smarting under Roosevelt's tarring of his patriotism, he continued, slashing at the President, "Political malignity, springing from a determination to destroy all who cannot be controlled, has conducted an organized campaign to stir a fury of rage against us, both at home and on the firing lines abroad. . . . Countless strikes, many for reasons shocking in their essential triviality, have disrupted and are disrupting the nation's war effort, but neither leaders nor strikers have been named and pilloried. *No clarion from the White House*[2] starts the hue and cry against them by accusations of disloyalty and sabotage. Miners alone, for pressing just demands have been singled out for hate and obloquy . . ."

Lewis carried his vendetta against Roosevelt everywhere he went. He told his miners that "Roosevelt kicked every coal miner in the face." When the AF of L stalled on an application for readmission because of Lewis's insistence that it include his "catch-all" District 50, he flayed their executive council for

---

[1] John L. Lewis, "Not Guilty," *Colliers*, June 15, 1944.
[2] Italics the author's.

"characteristic servility to the Roosevelt administration."
When one of his own minor officials made a brief, hopeless attempt to challenge Lewis's position, he was denounced as being
"the candidate of Hillman, Browder,[3] and Roosevelt." This was
an election year, and again Lewis opposed Roosevelt in every
way he knew, and again Roosevelt swept to victory. Lewis wearily resigned himself to another four years of uncompromising
war with his hated enemy.

In the coal fields, the year was comparatively quiet. Lewis
had demanded and received a payment from the operators of
forty dollars to every miner as a settlement for retroactive
claims of portal-to-portal wages. An estimated eighteen million
dollars was involved in this transaction.

In Congress, a substitute bill for the Guffey Coal Act designed to prevent profiteering and fixed maximum and minimum prices was passed with the support of both the miners and
the operators.

After the Allied forces crossed the British Channel in June,
the attack in Europe mounted as the American and British
troops began closing in on Germany. There was a desperate
need for more and more coal. The situation was rendered more
pressing by the coal demands of the liberated territories.

A nationwide dimout ushered in 1945, as the Government
took steps to conserve fuel. As the restrictions on the use of coal
began to pile up, Lewis suddenly filed formal notice [4] of a possible strike. The public realized with a shock that the UMWA's
bituminous contract would expire on April 1, 1945. It seemed
that the coal crises were interminable, and that the settling of
one merely opened the door to the next.

Lewis tried to temper public reaction by pointing out that
the miners were very anxious not to strike, as above all they did
not wish "any interruption of coal production . . . so vital to the
prosecution of the war."

On March 1, Lewis met the coal operators at a conference in
Washington with a number of demands, foremost of which was
one for a health and welfare fund, to be financed by a royalty
of ten cents for each ton of coal mined. The purpose of the fund
would be to extend services and insurance to the miners.

[3] Then chief of the Communist party, U.S.A.
[4] In accordance with the requirements of the Smith-Connally Act.

The operators rejected Lewis's proposals, and the now familiar pattern began to unfold and repeat itself. Secretary of Labor Frances Perkins tried to get both sides to compromise, and Lewis started his war of nerves with the Government, the operators, and the public. At the last minute, Sunday, April 1, before the miners were to strike, he announced a thirty-day extension of the prevailing contract to permit time for more negotiations. During this "extension" period of "no strike," 40 per cent of the soft-coal miners stayed away from the pits. Lewis again was negotiating with a cocked pistol. On Wednesday, April 11, he won a contract involving pay increases for travel and lunch which amounted to $6.44 for a six-day week. Lewis also got time and a half for work over thirty-five hours per week and $75.00 annual vacation pay. This contract included a no-strike clause.

Just as Lewis's victory in the captive-mine strike of December 7, 1941, had been completely blanketed by the news of Pearl Harbor, so did this victory pass unnoticed as a shocked and dazed nation was plunged into mourning. America wept at the sudden death of Franklin Delano Roosevelt on Thursday, April 12, at Warm Springs, Georgia. Rarely has a public leader been so revered and loved by the vast majority of the American people as was Franklin Delano Roosevelt.

With approval by the War Labor Board of his new contract for the bituminous coal industry, Lewis made the same demand upon the anthracite operators. Here he refused to agree to a similar thirty-day contract extension, saying, "We see no reason for procrastination." On Tuesday, May 1, seventy-two thousand anthracite miners walked off the job. Again came the usual commotion in the nation's capital with the War Labor Board issuing various "back-to-work" orders, and "threatening silences" were reported in the White House.

For the first time, Lewis was to square off against the new President, Harry S. Truman. Truman's first move was to order Solid Fuels Administrator Harold Ickes to seize the mines. Lewis responded with "no comment." Now Lewis began to test Truman with the nerve-wearing tactics that had worn Roosevelt ragged. Lewis's "no comment" was translated by 10,000 anthracite miners into "no work" as they flouted the Government's order.

On Monday, May 7, Lewis received unexpected reinforcement when the United States Supreme Court upheld portal-to-portal pay for the bituminous-coal miners. The decision was celebrated that day, to the Government's consternation, by a strike of all of the anthracite miners. Seventy-two thousand anthracite miners stood in open defiance of an aghast Government. The next day was VE Day, and as America celebrated victory, Lewis continued steadily to tighten the screws on the anthracite operators. Within ten days they surrendered and agreed to portal-to-portal pay of an additional $1.37½ a day among other concessions. Lewis ordered the strike to end on May 21. He had won the first round with Truman. But this was a Truman completely preoccupied with the closing phase of World War II in Europe.

The balance of the year saw a demand for coal never equaled before in this country. Eight million tons of bituminous coal were to be exported to Europe. The price of coal steadily rose as the OPA ceilings were continuously adjusted upward. Released from the pressure of the war emergency, Lewis attempted to exploit the drastic demand for coal by using the situation to strengthen further his union to include in its membership the supervisory mine personnel.

He sought a meeting with the bituminous-coal operators on October 1 to negotiate his demands for UMWA representation of their foremen and supervisors. The operators' refusal to yield was branded as "insolent" by Lewis, and again trouble began.

In October, about one fourth of the miners struck, and the strike spread to 200,000 miners. On October 17, Lewis ordered the strike to end on October 22 "in the public interest." His demands that supervisory mine personnel be permitted to join the union were dismissed with the comment that negotiations "have been discontinued temporarily."

On October 31, 1945, Truman called a labor-management conference. Lewis was one of eight labor representatives in attendance. Here Lewis passionately defended the unrestricted right of labor to strike, and resisted any pattern of action that would restrict labor's right to use its own strength to get as much as possible for its people. He assailed a resolution introduced by Murray, charging that it was "innocuous." He declared he was completely opposed to this proposal which would

place "limitations" around collective bargaining by tying it to
the "cost of living" formula. Lewis has always opposed tying
wages to any formula, including cost of living. He has felt this
would anchor the worker to an economic level that he could
not improve. Similarly, his hostility against Government participation was displayed when, before the House Labor Committee on December 10, he attacked Truman's proposal of
"some impartial machinery for reaching a decision" in the
field of labor as "the first step toward an absolutist state to regulate the liberties of all citizens." He charged that the right to
strike was the very cornerstone of freedom.

Nineteen forty-six found Lewis back in the AF of L, fraternizing with his former enemies. Lewis felt that this move was a
step in the direction of ultimate amalgamation of the AF of L
with the CIO. He believed that the AF of L could serve as the
platform from which he could make moves in that direction.
Before he could begin a new drive for "organic labor unity,"
the expiration dates of the coal contracts approached.

On March 2, he issued his thirty-day strike warning, and
again developments followed the usual routine: the balking of
the operators and the national strike on April 1. After a month-
long strike, Lewis unleased his second weapon with a thirty-
day warning of an anthracite strike.

In the midst of the strike, President Truman expressed his
doubts of the legality of Lewis's demand that a welfare fund be
financed by royalties on each ton of coal. Lewis is reported to
have snorted to one of his intimates, "Truman doubts the legality of our demands? What does Truman know about the
legality of anything?"

The long strike began to exact its toll on American economy.
The Government ordered a dimout over twenty-two Eastern
states to conserve the fast-fading stockpiles of coal. This was
of little avail as the railroads laid off 51,000 workers and the
Ford Motor Company, with its 110,000 employees, began to
close down. New Jersey declared a "state of emergency" and as
a national crisis seemed more and more imminent, Lewis suddenly sent the miners back on a two-week truce. This was
typical of Lewis's tactics, retreating just as an infuriated nation
was preparing to retaliate drastically. It was, again, another
demonstration of Lewis's jabbing campaign.

The operators and Lewis, however, remained deadlocked. When Truman's proposal of arbitration was rejected by both sides, he ordered Julius A. Krug, his new Secretary of the Interior, to seize the mines.

The expiration date of the truce, Saturday, May 25, found Krug appealing to the miners to keep on working while Lewis rejected a further deferring of the strike. The miners, calloused with repeated Government seizures of the past years, ignored Krug and struck.

Four days later Lewis triumphed over Krug, and the fifty-nine-day strike ended with the miners winning from the Government a "welfare and retirement fund" to be financed by a royalty payment of five cents for every ton of coal mined. The administration of the fund was to be in the hands of three trustees, one from the union, one from the Government, and a third to be mutually acceptable. Furthermore, the miners received in addition a wage increase of 18½ cents an hour which, with overtime, meant a daily boost of $1.85; $100 vacation pay, a guaranteed work week of five nine-hour days, with overtime pay after the seventh hour; and actual enforcement of a revised Federal Mine Safety Code.

One week later, the anthracite miners received almost the identical terms, and two weeks later the price of soft coal went up 40½ cents a ton and anthracite went up 91 cents a ton. Within a month another price increase took place, with soft coal going up another 18 cents a ton and hard coal another 30 cents a ton. With the public paying the bill for peace in the coal fields, the miners worked uninterruptedly through the summer.

September 27 found Lewis undergoing an appendectomy and three weeks later preparing to operate on the Government with a charge that the latter had broken the contract.

Then began the struggle that was to end in the unprecedented three-and-a-half-million-dollar fine against the United Mine Workers of America. Secretary Krug met with Lewis on October 19 and was unmoved by Lewis's demands for adjustments on the issues of both vacation pay and the Welfare Fund.

Two days later, Lewis charged Krug with breaking the contract by his "unilateral misinterpretations." Krug promptly denied Lewis's statement, pointing out that the contract "covers wages, hours and working conditions during the period of Government operations," with no provisions for any reopening on either wages or hours. Lewis hotly replied that Krug's answer was another breach of the contract and threatened to end the contract if Krug maintained this attitude.

On October 29, U.S. Attorney General Tom Clark [5] announced that Lewis was within his rights in requesting a reopening of negotiations. This ruling irked the coal operators and they launched verbal broadsides against decisions made "without consulting the owners of the mines."

With Krug absent on a Western tour, his subordinate Captain Collison held a series of fruitless meetings, November 1 to November 7, with representatives of the miners. Both sides finally agreed to recess their meeting until Krug's return on November 11.

Lewis felt that his hand was strengthened when on November 9 the President, by executive order, abolished all wartime controls on wages and coal policies. Now he could operate unencumbered by official wartime restrictions.

Finally Krug returned to Washington, and after hearing Lewis's proposals he conferred with the coal operators. On November 14, Krug wrote Lewis that his proposals were of such a "fundamental nature" that they were outside the jurisdiction of the Government, which was an "interim custodian" of the coal mines. He told Lewis to begin negotiating directly with the operators and then warned him that if no agreement was reached by the end of two months, the mines would be returned to the owners and "normal operation of economic forces would then prevail."

Lewis angrily repudiated Krug's statement as "a sixty-day freeze," and reminded him that he had a contract with the Government and not with the operators, "who have no status under the contract." He forced Krug's hand by serving formal notice that the contract would end in five days, on November 20.

Krug answered, citing a new opinion from the Attorney General, "which rules that you (Lewis) are without power to terminate the contract with the Government."

---

[5] Nominated to the Supreme Court of the United States on July 28, 1949, to fill the vacancy caused by the death of Justice Frank Murphy.

Lewis remained silent as the strike date approached. The press reported a long night conference at the White House and the country fatalistically awaited the coming of the inevitable strike. Suddenly, on November 17, the President announced his order to the Attorney General to "fight John L. Lewis on all fronts," and the Government began to move.

The next day, November 18, Attorney General Clark requested a restraining order against Lewis from Judge T. Alan Goldsborough of the Federal District Court in the District of Columbia. Judge Goldsborough issued a temporary court order restraining Lewis and other union officials from breaching the Krug-Lewis agreement provision against striking during the contract term.

The entire American organized labor movement denounced the resurgence of the dreaded injunction in labor disputes. William Green, AF of L president, blasted Truman's action, saying, "Neither troops with bayonets, nor court injunctions, nor incarceration of miners or their representatives in jail can serve to produce one single ton of coal."

But Truman was indifferent to labor's threats, and in the midst of the uproar departed for a Florida vacation. When he left, the War Department announced that "upon call of the Federal Coal Administrator, the War Department is prepared to cooperate fully in meeting the requirements set."

Lewis continued his silence. The morning of the twenty-first found every coal mine closed. Truman returned from his Florida vacation on November 23, and immediately went into a conference with his advisors: Attorney General Tom Clark, Secretary of the Interior Julius A. Krug, Secretary of Labor Lewis B. Schwellenbach, Reconversion Director John R. Steelman, and special counsel Clark M. Clifford. The meeting ended with the decision to press the fight against Lewis.

Two days after this meeting, Judge Goldsborough ordered Lewis and the United Mine Workers of America to appear in court on November 27 to answer charges of contempt of court. Almost immediately Government officials began behind-the-scenes maneuvering to try to get Lewis and the operators together to settle the strike. At the same time the story leaked out that Secretary Krug wanted the court action to be followed through, regardless of any possible settlement. Krug was soon to feel the full wrath of Lewis.

On December 3 it was reported that both Lewis and the operators were "very close to settlement," and Lewis was prepared to call the miners back to work the next morning. Word, however, came from the White House that the President opposed a settlement until Lewis had been "slapped down" in court. Judge Goldsborough found both Lewis and his union guilty of civil and criminal contempt of court.

The next day Judge Goldsborough fined the union $3,500,-000, and Lewis, personally, $10,000. The union promptly gave notice of appeal and the Government requested the Supreme Court to review the case at once.

On December 7, Lewis called off the strike and ordered the miners to work under the Krug-Lewis agreement until March 31, 1947. Lewis had been beaten in battle. He and all other labor leaders had assumed that Government injunctions in labor disputes had ended with the passage of the Norris-La-Guardia Act. He discovered that Truman thought otherwise.

There were many who believed that Truman conceived labor battles as military campaigns and wielded the power of the Government to crush the "enemy." His strong-arm conduct during the 1946 railroad dispute indicated this. It caused A. F. Whitney, president of the Brotherhood of Railroad Trainmen, to charge Truman with acting in behalf of the "vested interests" against the welfare of the people.

Lewis was so accustomed to dealing with a subtle, brilliant, wary Roosevelt that he could not anticipate the directness of a politically insensitive Truman.

Nineteen forty-seven began with both sides awaiting the decision of the Supreme Court. The miners were back at work and Lewis was studying the terrain and weighing his next move. Defensive fighting was strange to Lewis, who was impatient to counterattack. On March 6, the Supreme Court by a vote of seven to two upheld the conviction for contempt of court of Lewis and the mine workers union, but reduced the $3,500,000 fine to $700,000 on the condition that the union withdraw its notice of termination of the Krug-Lewis agreement within five days. Justices Murphy and Rutledge sharply dissented. Murphy flatly accused the majority decision of casting "a dark cloud over the future of labor relations in the United States." Both Rutledge and Murphy held that Goldsborough's injunction had been invalidated by the Norris-LaGuardia Act. Lewis abided by the Court's decision and withdrew his notice to Krug of the ending of their contract.

The Government's complete control of Lewis and the union blew up on March 25 in the dust of the explosion of the Centralia Coal Company's Mine No. 5 at Centralia, Illinois. Out of 141 miners, 111 were killed in this horrible catastrophe. Four days afterward, Lewis defied the Supreme Court and the President by proclaiming a six-day Holy Week as a memorial to the Centralia dead. Cessation of work was to begin on March 29. Lewis knew that under the circumstances public opinion would not brook the interference of any authority.

Both the House of Representatives and the Senate appointed investigating committees to determine if there had been any federal negligence. April 17 found a violently angry Lewis testifying before the Senate committee. He venomously attacked Secretary Krug. From the witness stand Lewis charged, "Now, as a matter of fact, when this inspector's report was filed with him [Krug] in the month of November, it showed that the mine was not rockdusted . . . There was no air in that mine. It was filled with explosive dust. That was a mechanized mine, with the roar of machinery, the stirring up of dust from the machines was constant. Any little pocket of gas could have ignited the dust, or any blown-out shot, or flame, could cause an explosion, and in addition to that, the inspector showed that they were violating the law of the state in permitting the men to be underground while those shots were being fired. . . . yet Mr. Krug, in his defense to the Senate committee, said that there was no danger imminent. . . .

". . . This great modern Hercules, with a No. 12 shoe and a No. 5 hat, by the imposition of his magnificent genius of administration has reduced the deaths in coal mines from 95 a month to 85 a month, and then he rests from his labors, he stops saving any more then. He goes to Japan in a Government bomber at $120 an hour and his department pays the War Department; he visits around the Pacific Islands; he goes to

Palm Springs; he goes to the Waldorf and the Mayflower suites, and Sea Island, Georgia, resting at Government expense.

"After his magnificent labors, under his administration, the deaths are now only 85 a month, and they used to be 95 a month under that *damnable Ickes*. What a defense for a sensible man. . . .

". . . I might suggest that he might stay away a little longer from Sea Island and Palm Springs and do some of this work.

". . . I reiterate that J. A. Krug did not affirmatively kill those men. He just permitted them to die by negligence in action and by a dishonorable violation of his own agreement made with the United Mine Workers of America, his promise given to the coal miners and American people.

"That is all he has done, and in so doing I think he has dishonored his office. I think he has brutalized the mine workers and I think he has brought confusion and bitterness and economic loss to the American people.

"You may think he is worthy of the trust imposed in him, but I think he is dishonorable and without a moral conscience on his side; a friend to the coal operators, a scheming, a designing politician, unfaithful to his trust . . .

"And, O God! what a grotesque, monstrous mistake he is in the position he is occupying."

As Lewis fought Truman and the courts, Congress, obsessed with its hatred for Lewis, began to move in with harsh anti-labor legislation. They were fortified by public opinion and other work stoppages such as the telephone workers' strike. The Eightieth Congress capitalized on Truman's anti-labor statements and actions of the previous year, his use of the injunction against Lewis, and his threat of military induction against the railroad workers. It cannot be gainsaid that Truman also helped pave the way for the Taft-Hartley Act.

The Taft-Hartley Act of 1947 was the most extensive enactment dealing exclusively with labor-management relations ever passed by any Congress. It amended or modified in almost every major detail the Wagner Act of 1935. The earlier law placed restrictions only upon employer conduct which might interfere with, restrain, or coerce employees in the exercise of their "right to self-organization, to form, join or assist labor organizations, to bargain collectively through representatives of their own choosing, and to engage in concerted activities, for the purpose of collective bargaining or other mutual aid or protection."

The Taft-Hartley Act declared a new "right" for American workers—"the right to refrain from any or all" of the pro-union activities listed. The 1947 statute set up elaborate governmental machinery to aid those workers who were believed by the Congress to resent the very concept of union organization.

The Taft-Hartley Act undertook to regulate and restrict the gamut of orthodox union activity. Closed-shop and union-shop contracts in their traditional form were outlawed. Union security contracts of a limited degree might be negotiated only after a tedious Labor Board authorization election.

The federal courts were opened to suits by employers against unions for breach of any collective-bargaining agreement, "without respect to the amount in controversy or without regard to the citizenship of the parties."

The judicial injunction was reintroduced to American labor relations after their virtual ban for fifteen years under the Hoover-approved Norris-LaGuardia Act.

Whatever rights a labor organization might wish to assert under what the Eightieth Congress left of the Wagner Act were contingent upon the filing of elaborate reports concerning union financial transactions and annual tender of affidavits executed by every single union officer disavowing Communist party membership or belief in "the overthrow of the United States Government by force or by any illegal or unconstitutional methods."

The uproar of indignation from all labor unions caused Truman to veto the bill. Congress speedily passed it over his veto and the Taft-Hartley bill became law. After its enactment, the 1947 labor law became a major issue of contention between Congress and the organized labor movement. It was the principal campaign issue of the 1948 presidential election. Eventually all major labor unions,[6] after snarling and shouting bold, defiant slogans of "last-ditch fights," "never giving in to the

[6] Such last hold-out CIO unions as the United Steel Workers of America or the United Electrical Workers of America have already expressed their intention to submit and sign the affidavits.

labor slave law," and many other militant statements, were to surrender tamely—all but Lewis, who alone defied the law.

At the time of its passage, Lewis was not unduly concerned about the effects of this law, for he believed it would collapse under a boycott of organized labor. He assumed that every labor leader possessed enough integrity and intelligence to agree with his simple solution.

He dramatically ignored the law, as almost at the moment when the vote was cast to override the presidential veto, 300,000 miners went out on wildcat strikes. Within a few days, he signed a new contract with the coal operators for a pay raise of 44⅜¢ an hour and enraged Congress by circumventing the employer lawsuit provisions of the Taft-Hartley Law with a clause providing that the miners would work only when they were "able and willing." No stoppage could legally be called a strike in violation of the contract if the miners were "unable and unwilling to work."

With the coal fields at peace, Lewis went to Chicago on September 9. There he won over the AF of L executive council to a fighting stand and an agreement to boycott the Taft-Hartley Law by refusal to comply with the reporting and affidavit provisions. A month later, at the AF of L convention in San Francisco, the AF of L heads reversed their Chicago position and voted to comply. But before the final vote, the high command of the Federation was subjected to what will be a long-remembered, unparalleled, merciless excoriation by Lewis.

" 'Thou shalt not muzzle the ox that treadeth out the corn.' So runs the scripture. But the Congress of the United States designated 15,000,000 workers in this country, organized into one form or another, of unions, as being cattle that treadeth out the economic corn of our country, and the Congress placed an economic muzzle on each of you. What are you going to do about it? Oh, I see. You are going to change our Constitution. God help us!

"The Taft-Hartley statute is the first ugly, savage thrust of fascism in America. . . .

". . . When this statute is enacted, some seventy-three pages in length in the printed copy, containing only two lines that say labor has the right to organize and thirty-three pages of other additional restrictions that dare labor to organize, when that comes to pass, the welkin is filled with the outcries and the lamentations of our great leaders of labor in this country calling upon high heaven to witness that all indeed is lost unless they can grovel on their bellies and come under this infamous act.

"I am one of those who do not think that all is lost. I represent an organization whose members believe they pay their officers to fight for them, not to deliver them into slavery. . . .

". . . And is it true that the leaders of our movement are to be the first of our mighty hosts of 8,000,000 members to put their tails between their legs and run like cravens before the threat of the Taft-Hartley bill? I am reminded of the Biblical parable, 'Lions led by asses.'

". . . This mighty host of 8,000,000 workers in the American Federation of Labor, each filled with enthusiasm and ambition, each having responsibilities and dreams for himself and his family, each looking forward to the realization of a substance that will carry him through the evil days that must come to every man, . . . I think of that mighty host trying to advance across the plains of America, led and flanked and having their thinking done for them by intellectually fat and stately asses.

"I think you should think about these things. God knows, you are all paid enough for thinking. I am, too, but I do try to shut my mouth occasionally and think once in a while, and that is what the American Federation of Labor should do. . . .

". . . As far as that is concerned, on this particular issue, I don't think that the Federation has a head. I think its neck has just grown up and haired over." [7]

Lewis left the convention indignant and alone. The clear, simple course he had recommended to upset the Taft-Hartley Act had been rejected.

Repudiation by the AF of L was too much for Lewis. On December 12, he contemptuously wrote to Green, using a blue crayon on a half-torn, rumpled sheet of paper:

> Green.
> We disaffiliate.
> Lewis.

So 1947 ended with Lewis and his miners again out of the American Federation of Labor.

[7] Speech by John L. Lewis in opposition to the Taft-Hartley Statute, delivered before the AF of L convention, October 14, 1947, San Francisco, California.

Nineteen forty-eight coupled a fateful Ides of March with Lewis's perpetual war. On March 12, he demanded that the Welfare Fund pay a pension of one hundred dollars a month to all miners more than sixty years of age, with twenty years of service. The operators' refusal involved their obstinacy in agreeing to the selection of the third trustee, essential to the operation of the Fund, thereby creating a stalemate that made it impossible for Lewis to secure his demand for the hundred-a-month pension. This stand of the operators caused Lewis to announce that the contract had been dishonored. Because of this fact, the Fund's administration was rendered completely inactive.

A startled nation wondered whether Lewis would strike in the face of the Taft-Hartley Law, a hostile administration, and an expectant court. The answer came with Lewis's suggestion that all union locals "discuss" the matter. On March 15, 360,000 miners were still "discussing" and 90 per cent of the coal mines were idle.

Truman waited for nine days and then appointed a three-man fact-finding board consisting of U.S. Circuit Judge Sherman Minton,[8] of New Albany, Indiana, Mark F. Ethridge, the publisher of the Louisville, Kentucky, *Courier-Journal*, and Professor George W. Taylor, of the University of Pennsylvania, former chairman of the National War Labor Board. With instructions from the President to complete and report their investigation by April 5, this board promptly invited Lewis to appear before them.

Lewis at first ignored the request and then on March 29 wrote his sarcastic "imbroglio" letter.

Hon. Sherman Minton
Room 3422, Department of Labor
Washington, D. C.
Sir:
    My disinclination to attend falls substantially into two categories:
    1. The law:
    No action has been taken by this writer or the United Mine Workers of America, as such, which would fall within the pur-

---

[8] Named by Truman on September 16, 1949, to the vacancy on the Supreme Court caused by the death of Justice Wiley B. Rutledge.

view of the oppressive statute under which you seek to function. Without indulging in analysis, it is a logical assumption that the cavilings of the bar and bench in their attempts to explicate this infamous enactment will consume a tedious time:

2. Prejudice:

Two members of your board are biased and prejudiced and in honor should not serve. They are Ethridge and Taylor. Since the inception of this imbroglio, Ethridge has published biased and prejudicial editorials and special articles deleterious to this union and this writer in a newspaper controlled by him.

Taylor for years has been an administrative hanger-on in Washington, and he has never lost an opportunity to harass and persecute this union and this writer. He is inherently incapable of determining the distinction between a fact and a scruple.

In attendance is Ching, a truly remarkable man, who sees through the eyes of United States Rubber.

Yours truly,

JOHN L. LEWIS[9]

The New York Times's Arthur Krock's interpretation of the letter on Thursday, April 1, 1948, attracted considerable attention.

A pundit simplified:

Lewis: My disinclination to attend falls substantially into two categories.

Translation: I have decided not to attend for two reasons.

Lewis: 1. The law.

Translation: (Same.)

Lewis: No action has been taken by this writer or the United Mine Workers of America, as such, which would fall within the purview of the oppressive statute under which you seek to function.

Translation: Neither this writer nor the United Mine Workers of America, as such, has done anything prohibited by the tyrannical Taft-Hartley Act, the source of the authority you claim.

Lewis: Without indulging in analysis, it is a logical assumption that the cavilings of the bar and bench in their attempts

---

[9] Lewis's use of the term "imbroglio" was regarded as his latest colorful noun and excited considerable newspaper comment. It is interesting to note that in a mine workers union convention in the early twenties Lewis foiled an attack from his opposition by constantly shouting about the "imbroglio." The delegates rallied behind him suddenly both in confusion and admiration for the man who could use a word that no one understood.

to explicate this infamous enactment will consume a tedious time.

Translation: Your hearing will be tedious and a waste of time, during which judges and lawyers will mouth about what this infamous law means.

Lewis: 2. Prejudice.

Translation: (Same.)

Lewis: Two members of your board are biased and prejudiced and in honor should not serve. They are Ethridge and Taylor. Since the inception of this imbroglio Ethridge has published biased and prejudicial editorials and special articles deleterious to this union and this writer in a newspaper controlled by him.

Taylor for five years has been an administrative hanger-on in Washington, and he has never lost an opportunity to harass and persecute this union and this writer. He is inherently incapable of determining the distinction between a fact and a scruple.

In attendance is Ching, a truly remarkable man, who sees through the eyes of United States Rubber.

Translation: Two of your board members, Ethridge and Taylor, are so biased against this union and me that they cannot honorably serve. Ethridge has filled the newspaper he publishes with prejudiced editorials and articles ever since this controversy began.

Taylor, in the five years he has clung to government jobs, showed his bias against me and the union whenever and in any way he could. Also he is fundamentally unable to tell a fact from an allegation.

Ching, the odd character who attends your meetings, still sees labor problems from the viewpoint of an executive of the United States Rubber Company.

Again Lewis became the subject of headlines and lead editorials, and with rare journalistic exception he was again described as a national villain. April 3 found Lewis facing the mandate of court injunction to call off the strike. Suddenly he executed a totally unlooked-for maneuver. House Speaker Joseph Martin was brought into the dispute and promptly announced a settlement whereby New Hampshire's Republican U.S. Senator Styles Bridges was named the third trustee for the Welfare Fund. The Fund could now commence operations.

Martin may have sought favorable publicity in a national emergency labor dispute as a stimulus to his presidential ambitions. In any event, he quickly overcame the objections of Ezra Van Horn, the hitherto obstinate operator's representative.

Forty-eight hours later, Lewis won his pension plans when Senator Bridges voted in favor of the UMWA proposal. Everything had worked according to plan. Lewis then dispatched a telegram to the miners, carefully phrased, to the effect that he was calling off a strike which he had never called.

The miners had finished their "discussion" strike. Lewis now had to appear before Judge Goldsborough to discuss a strike that continued despite the court's restraining order. Lewis's denial that he had called the strike evoked a withering response from Judge Goldsborough. He pointed out that Lewis's telegram to the miners saying that the contract had been "dishonored" was the equivalent of a strike order. Goldsborough continued lashing Lewis, saying, ". . . If a nod, or a wink, or a code was used in place of the word 'strike,' it was just as much of a strike as though the word 'strike' had been used. The miners walked out when told the agreement was dishonored; they came back when told it was honored. Now, what else can that be but a code? . . ."

Goldsborough then set legal precedent by finding that "as long as a union functions as a union, it must be held responsible for the mass actions of its members."

Again Goldsborough levied fines of $20,000 against Lewis personally and $1,400,000 against the UMWA. Thousands of miners walked off the job in protest. Goldsborough met this by promptly issuing a preliminary Taft-Hartley injunction against a coal strike. Lewis, bitterly knowing his Goldsborough, hurriedly ordered the miners back to work and appealed the fines.

The coal operators, certain that Goldsborough would fail Lewis at every turn, brought suit for an injunction to block the pension plan of the new Welfare Fund of one hundred dollars a month for retired miners of sixty-two (later lowered to sixty) years of age or older.

On June 22, the coal operators, completely confident of victory, appeared before Goldsborough. Lewis was there, glum, resigned now and convinced that Judge Goldsborough was the unplacable enemy of the union. The operators were aghast when Goldsborough denied their application for an injunction and scored the operators with, ". . . it is meager enough, and it offers the miners a little something for their old age. It gives them just enough to hold their heads up . . ."

Lewis's face was a study of shocked surprise as he stared unbelievingly at Goldsborough.

Peace in the coal fields was interrupted on July 6, when the steel industries refused to sign another contract for their captive mines. They charged that the union demand for the union shop was illegal.[10] Immediately, Robert N. Denham, general counsel of the National Labor Relations Board, petitioned Judge Goldsborough for a Taft-Hartley injunction to restrain Lewis from demanding the union shop.

The miners struck for one week. On July 13, their strike was settled with the help of Judge Goldsborough. The terms of the contract included a wage increase of a dollar a day plus a royalty of twenty cents on every ton of coal mined to be paid into the Welfare Fund. The next day Goldsborough dismissed Denham's petition for an injunction. Lewis began to revise his opinion of Goldsborough as the Judge continued to deal justice in successive cases involving other labor unions.

No further rumbles were heard from Lewis and the UMWA in the summer and fall of 1948. October found the United Mine Workers assembling in Cincinnati for their convention. It was a month before the national elections. Lewis spent an hour telling the delegates his opinion of the Democratic party's candidate, the incumbent President, Harry S. Truman. His voice snapped out sharply: ". . . He is a man totally unfitted for the position. His principles are elastic, and he is careless with the truth. He has no special knowledge on any subject, and he is a malignant, scheming sort of an individual who is dangerous not only to the United Mine Workers, but dangerous to the United States of America . . ."

While Lewis did not mention Truman's opponent, the Republican standard-bearer, Thomas E. Dewey, the convention signified a weak preference for Dewey as the better of two bad choices. However, Lewis also unleashed a tirade against Dewey. The miners' leader showed little active interest in the 1948 presidential election, but the district UMWA organizations

[10] According to the Taft-Hartley Law.

joined with other labor groups in opposing senators and congressmen who had voted for the Taft-Hartley Law.

The convention doubled Lewis's salary to $50,000 a year. Lewis is reported to have told one of his intimates that he wanted the salary increase in order to be able to leave his children some inheritance. The two other union officials, Vice-President Kennedy and Secretary-Treasurer John Owens, were boosted from $18,000 to $40,000 a year.

Throughout the proceedings of the convention, Lewis and the delegates manifested a deep pride in their hard-won Welfare Fund. There was almost a spiritual satisfaction in their achievement.

This reaction can be understood when one realizes that men work not only to pay for the immediate cost of living, but also for security for their family and themselves. Over the heads of nine-tenths of America's families hang the fears and worries of an impoverished old age, of lack of earning power in the event of physical disability, of the obliteration of even life-long savings by the medical and hospital expenses arising out of family illness and a host of the perils so common to a worker's quest for even a shadow of security.

The condition of the miners was the poorest in the poor lot of all the workers. The toll of blood, broken backs, and loss of life inside the earth was appalling. In thirty-five years, from 1910 to 1945 inclusive, the mines mangled more than 2,000,000 men of whom 68,842 were killed outright.

Today Lewis, through the United Mine Workers Welfare and Retirement Fund, has singlehandedly given his miners a security beyond that of any industrial group.

The breadth and scope of this fund is such that it far transcends not only any other known union program, but even Great Britain's "Cradle to Grave" Social Security. The fund is often referred to as the "before the womb and after the tomb" program. Miners' wives get free medical and hospital care with free choice of physician, including specialists and unlimited periods of hospitalization. If a miner is disabled for any reason he receives cash benefits as well as the prescribed medical care. If he retires at the age of sixty he receives a monthly pension for life of one hundred dollars. When he dies his widow or surviving dependents receive a cash payment of one thousand dollars.

There is no time limit on these aids and men injured thirty-five years ago as well as widows of men caught in mine disasters as long as thirty years ago are now receiving real help.

The Mine Workers Welfare and Retirement Fund is aimed at every human need of the mining population. It will be recorded as one of Lewis's greatest achievements, not only for the welfare of the miners, but as a model for all other unions. This, for Lewis, is his monument to the miners of America.

But Lewis's victory was not without its price. The Welfare Fund is dependent upon coal production, and stoppage of the latter also means the cessation of payments to the fund. The Fund has partially put the miners into the coal business, and now a strike against the operators, is also against themselves. This has been the dilemma of 1949 for Lewis, and presents a problem that must be solved.

Chapter 14

Something of a Man

F OR thirty long years, the storms of public passion have swirled about Lewis. For thirty years, Lewis has been interminably battered by unparalleled attacks from the public, the press, and the Government. And yet for these thirty years he has stubbornly held to his course. From 1919 to 1949 the newspapers have regularly bannered the headline, "U.S. ACTS TO STOP LEWIS"; and with rare exception Lewis has not been stopped. During these same thirty years, millions of Americans have developed a fierce hatred for this public menace who defies all constitutional authorities, ignores an outraged citizenry, and is impervious to the violence of a hostile press. It has been said that no man in our history has been so hated for so long a period. It must be remembered that few have held power uninterruptedly for a generation and a half.

Every American today has grown up with Lewis and his coal strikes. These never ceasing eruptions have become a fixed part of our lives. To this generation Lewis's regular coal strikes have long since supplanted the robin red breast as the harbinger of spring. He has been accepted as a necessary evil in our national scene. His unusual face, an ideal subject for cartoonists and artists, has been caricatured until today thousands of cartoons and drawings have acquired those stylized Neanderthal characteristics that fit the image in the public mind. He has been made into America's bogey man and during the 1943 war strikes mothers would threaten insubordinate children with the name of Lewis. It is significant that a public-relations firm, hired by the mine workers union Welfare Fund to interpret Lewis to the public as a human being, in a brief biographical sketch had to go to the length of saying that Lewis ". . . feels at home with children and knows how to please them."

This widespread hatred carries with it the corrollary fact that Lewis is known to practically every American. Many a citizen would have great difficulty naming the chief justice of the United States Supreme Court or any past vice-president of the United States; but any American, any place, will unhesitatingly spit out the name of the ruler of the coal miners. Not only does everyone know his name, but everyone has a definite, positive opinion about "that man Lewis." And yet accompanying that almost unanimous hatred of Lewis, there is quite commonly an undertone of grudging admiration for his audacity and willingness to carry on the fight against all odds. In the writer's survey he continually encountered a reaction along the following pattern: "That John L. Lewis, who does he think he is? Imagine telling the President where to get off! Well, you got to hand it to him, he always gets away with it." With rare exceptions, too, a common response is that Lewis has taken good care of his miners but at the expense of the public.

He has fought the people in every quarter. Within his own world of organized labor he challenged and fought the founder and president of the AF of L, Samuel Gompers. He fought the AF of L and almost destroyed it. He built the CIO and later fought it. He fought American industry. He has infuriated the press with his apparent lack of concern for their increasing barrage of vitriolic attacks, which have often bordered on hysteria. His standard answer to the press has been a cryptic "no comment."

The Congress has assailed him with every possible charge, and at times their sessions on Lewis have transformed this deliberate legislative body into a veritable lynch mob whipping up its every passion. Every piece of anti-labor legislation passed by the Congress has been aimed and fired primarily at Lewis. The name of Lewis sends congressmen into a frenzy, not only because of their resentment of his silent contempt for them, but because of their bitter knowledge that he usually ends up by having his way.

His public fights with American Presidents past and present are known to all. Roosevelt hated Lewis more than any other individual in this nation and practically charged him with treason. Lewis fought Roosevelt and was beaten by him but later beat the President in 1941 and again in 1943. It was maddening to the Chief Executive to be helpless as Lewis ignored, insulted him, and then went on to win.

He has been portrayed and accepted as being devoid of human emotion or humor. To America as a whole, John Llewellyn Lewis is a power-mad egomaniac who recognizes no higher authority than himself. He is an absolute dictator of the coal miners union and is driven by an insatiable appetite for power. He plays God and unleashes strikes much as Zeus hurled his thunderbolts. His florid histrionics are crude and deliberate attempts at self-dramatization. He is a brooding, frustrated, angry man. He sulks unless he has his own way. He has no friends because people to him are simply instruments to be used in his violent quest for power. He is callous and as brutal as his pugnacious face. He is a thug who knows no law or interest save his own perverse will.

These opinions and charges, as well as others, will be examined here as we attempt to arrive at an understanding of John Lewis, the man.

It is commonly believed and charged that Lewis administers his union with the iron hand of a dictator, that Lewis has machine control over the union and brooks no dissent, and that within the union his whim is law.

This popular conception of Lewis's role in the union is reflected in the many anecdotes told about him. While many of these are myths, rumors, and half-truths, they are important because behind these fantasies and tales lies a psychological process whereby people invent or shape an anecdote or story for the purpose of dramatically expressing their beliefs. These anecdotes and tales, many bordering on the grotesque, therefore, are actually verbal caricatures of specific facets of the subject. The following two anecdotes commonly told and retold about Lewis and accepted as facts are examples of this. Both of these stories have been carefully checked, and no evidence has been produced attesting to their validity; and Lewis categorically denied both to the writer. Actually, the only "facts" in these cases are the facts of the popular will to believe.

One story aimed at Lewis's machine control is a tale supposed to have as its locale the coal fields of southern Ohio.

Here Lewis was confronted with a bitter hostility on the part of a large group of miners who were illiterate Italian immigrants. Lewis, allegedly always obsessed with the urge to have an almost unanimous vote for re-election to the presidency of the union, ordered his field representatives to roll up a huge vote of those illiterate miners.

In order to satisfy their boss, the union representatives approached these immigrant miners as they came out of the pits saying, "Hello Tony. Today is election day. This piece of paper I've got in my hand is the union ballot. You want me to help you vote?" The illiterate miner would nod consent and the union representative would then point to the top name, saying, "This name is John L. Lewis. You don't like him, do you?" The miner would spit vehemently and say, "I hate him." The organizer would reply, "All right, I'll tell you what we'll do. You see this box next to his name, Tony? We scratch him out, O.K.?" Wherewith the organizer would put a big X in the square. Lewis carried the district without exception.

Another anecdote for which there is no evidence and which would be difficult to surpass as a reflection of public opinion of Lewis's alleged egotism concerns a tourist bus filled with visitors coming down Orinoco Street in Alexandria, Virginia. It stopped before the home of John L. Lewis; and the guide began a speech, pointing out that this house was a historic landmark, that it had been occupied by Richard "Light Horse Harry" Lee, that Washington had frequently visited there, and that now it was the residence of that nationally known (here the guide grimaced) labor leader, John L. Lewis. Just then Lewis, with one of his henchmen, came down the stairs of his house, and every passenger on the tourist bus craned his neck for a look at this incredible villain. Lewis turned down the sidewalk, walked a few paces, and with his back to the bus stopped and bent to tie a loosened shoe lace. As he bent over his companion whispered, "Mr. Lewis, they are all staring at you." Lewis straightened up, looked at his companion, and said, "Of course, even the behind of John L. Lewis is of national interest."

There are many of these stories, and they all add up to the public's belief that John L. Lewis is arrogant and a dictator who commands his union as a Caesar.

There is no question that Lewis runs the union with a strong, dictatorial hand. His union policy committee is a mere rubber stamp as is everyone else in the union. Lewis once made the statement to the writer, "I work harder than anyone else in this union, and I know more about the problems of the miners than anyone else. Therefore, I should think that my decisions would mean more than those of anyone else." And Lewis's decisions not only mean more, but they actually mean everything; for, when Lewis makes a "recommendation," it is an order. And no one knows that better than those who surround him. Occasionally they will be given the thrill of a free debate and decision on an issue, but only when the issue is so minor and so unimportant that the democratically arrived at decision is also unimportant. Even so, they find themselves in a strange and terrifying situation, for their initiative is so atrophied through disuse they find it difficult to make any kind of a decision. Their servility is reflected in the unhealthy awe that permeates every cranny and every stone of the UMW building in Washington, from its outside step to the ceiling of its sixth floor, and to that great Holy of Holies, where the union God abides.

Here one does not take the Lord's name in vain, nor does anyone dare to utter a light or frivolous comment on the God of Coal. One day the writer humorously referred to the many resolutions that flow in from different districts demanding that Congress declare February 12 a national holiday not only because it was Abraham Lincoln's birthday but also the birth date of that great champion of labor, John L. Lewis. The writer's laugh was cut short by the sober expressions of those listening. It was as if the United Mine Workers Building had been defiled by blasphemy. Finally one spoke up, "In many ways he is far greater than Lincoln."

However, instead of halting our inquiry on this point, with the label of "dictator" or "machine control," it is important that we inquire into the nature of this autocracy, both as to why it came about and what have been its results.

We have surveyed the period of the bloody twenties when Lewis built his machine to dominate completely the life of the mine workers union. He chose this course to unify a weak, loose, quarreling structure into a solid force of great power.

Lacking this unity, the union might well have followed the pattern of the past and disintegrated. From the writer's point of view, it is impossible to draw a dichotomy of Lewis's motivations of both thirst for personal power and desire to build a strong union. It would be naïve to hold that Lewis had operated and does operate on a completely altruistic basis, and it would be just as naïve to define all of his actions as motivated by a personal hunger for power.

Criticism has been raised that many of the means employed by Lewis were not and could not be justified by the end he was seeking. In the arena of power politics, the question of the ethics of means and ends can only be relegated to an academic arena.

However, the experience of the past has emphasized the thesis that evil means beget evil ends. For means and ends are part and parcel of a continuous process; and in the space of time, dimensions, proportions, and objectives alter and change so that it becomes difficult to tell where a means ends and where an end begins.

The means employed by Lewis in the building of his union certainly involved tactics that were based on the prime consideration of victory, with ethical considerations being an afterthought, if thought about at all. A perfect example would be Lewis's statement on his mysterious possession of the contract between Farrington and the Peabody Coal Company that was supposedly in the coal company's safe. He said, "It is enough that I have it." Lewis's defense would be the same as that of any leader in a similar situation, and that is, "You have to fight fire with fire."

Basic also to Lewis's building a machine were the psychological factors earlier discussed, such as his reaction to the Lucas, Iowa, strike of 1892 against the White Breast Fuel Company, where the men returned to work despite the blacklisting of one of their leaders, the father of John L. Lewis. This experience had engendered a cautious suspicion on the part of Lewis against depending upon personal gratitude as a base for allegiance and support. Furthermore, he knew that poverty was not inevitably the partner of nobility, gratitude, and loyalty. Lewis was also mindful of the fact that the terms of his predecessors were unusually short and that many a mine worker president had been ousted from office after he had given his very life's blood in the service of the organization. It was true that the mine workers' delegates made sentimental protestations of their affection for the incumbents, but nevertheless they kicked them out of office. This, also, to Lewis, was not a demonstration to encourage his trust in the miners purely on the basis of their appreciation. Lewis knew that the history of the union presidents had been one of having to devote as much time to their struggle to maintain office as in carrying out union policies.

Today, John L. Lewis has served as president of the United Mine Workers longer than all his predecessors taken together.

As to the tactics of the machine, one of the UMW executive board members is reliably reported to have made the drunken statement, "It doesn't matter how the miners vote. It only matters how we count them." Possibly such tactics were necessary in the past, but for the last fifteen years the miners would have overwhelmingly re-elected him against any candidate.

Lewis's operation of his union involves an extremely unusual personnel policy: He demands unreserved loyalty, and in return he gives full loyalty.

He recognizes the limitations of many of his associates; but, when they are assigned to a job, he grants them full discretionary powers. Most administrators would supervise their subordinates on particularly important issues or on levels of operation where there would be a question as to the ability of these individuals to carry on alone. Lewis, however, from the moment he places a man on a job, gives him his full support and trust, permitting him to operate on his own regardless of his ability. When the subordinate fails or muffs his job pretty badly, Lewis never reprimands him. As long as the man is loyal to him, Lewis will stand completely behind him. No case is known where he has either publicly or privately reprimanded a loyal subordinate. Lewis will listen to him and make suggestions for future activities, but he will not intervene, even though he may see his subordinate acting in error.

A typical example of this is the case involving a letter sent by Earl Houck, legal director for the United Mine Workers of America, to the Federal Wage-Hour Administrator. This letter, sent in 1940, was approved by Philip Murray during a period when Lewis was seriously ill. It informed the Administrator that the union rejected the premise of portal-to-portal pay as unreal and unworkable.

Three years later, when John Lewis spearheaded the union's campaign for a wage increase based on the principle of portal to portal, the operators publicly released this letter to Lewis's acute embarrassment. Lewis repudiated the letter, saying that neither Houck nor any other employee of the United Mine Workers Union was authorized to speak for the policy, program, principles, or purposes of the organization. As we know, Lewis then proceeded to strike and litigate successfully and win an agreement for portal-to-portal pay.

From a very reliable source the writer learned that Houck was never reprimanded, punished, or embarrassed in any way. In any other organization there would have been serious repercussions. The writer checked this fact with Lewis, who replied, "Earl Houck has been a long-term, devoted, and loyal follower of the United Mine Workers of America. He made a mistake, and I know that because of his loyalty he has inwardly suffered. As for my reprimanding him, does anyone think I would discount all those years of service and loyalty just because Earl Houck made one error? I have never rebuked him in any way because I know that Earl Houck will never repeat that error."

Lewis feels toward the union as a parent does toward his children, handling them in many ways with the same affectionate concern. His paternalistic conception of his own role in the union is indicated by a portion of a speech he made on behalf of his mother before the 1942 miners convention. He mentioned the ever present demand for autonomy, saying:

"Mother reared six sons and two daughters, and when those sons were growing boys at home and they began to demand autonomy, Mother never had any difficulty at any time in putting down autonomous uprisings. When one of the boys would come home and tell the others that in some of the neighbors' houses the sons had more autonomy than we had in our house, and we would hold a caucus on it, we used to get along fine until Mother intervened and made the decision. In the light of the greater knowledge that comes with increasing years, as one of the sons, I can look back now and see that Mother was right every time, although at that time I was convinced that she did not properly understand the situation."

Lewis's machine domination of his union has always been castigated as an evil practice. Few have understood that Lewis could not have embarked upon the organization of the CIO or any other major action unless he possessed complete security within his own organization. It would have been impossible for two reasons: first, because most of his time would of necessity have been occupied in strengthening his own position to insure his re-election to the union presidency. An insecure leader dares not venture too far afield, fearing the machinations of his rivals while his back is turned. Second, such a leader would be blocked by his fears, feeling that if his ventures proved disastrous they would arm his rivals in their campaign to unseat him.

Lewis's absolute control of the union emancipated him from any of these barriers. He was free to give his undivided attention to the CIO and move as he chose. Lewis's freedom of operations in all areas is the result of the security his machine control of his union gives him. Lacking this complete domination of the union, Lewis would have had a different life.

Lewis has welded the United Mine Workers Union into the most powerful single striking force in our national economic structure. On his order, nearly half a million miners now go into or out of action with a breath-taking precision and discipline. Once on a strike, this immovable object cannot be budged by all the power of the state. Everything has been tried, and everything has failed. Franklin Delano Roosevelt's record is ample testimony to this effect. The miners, tough, fatalistic, and always ready for a fight, view even a quarrel with the Army with contempt, saying, "You can't dig coal with bayonets."

If you couple this kind of disciplined army to the greatest tactical genius in the history of American labor, and add to these the fact that coal is the major foundation of our industrial economy, you have the makings of an upheaval. And an upheaval it has been, regular convulsive twistings of our economy until Lewis got what he wanted. Lewis once made a statement to the writer that is vividly revealing of both his appreciation of the indispensable role of coal in our economy and his understanding of how to exploit that fact. This remark is the key to his grand strategy in all coal strikes.

"When we control the production of coal we hold the vitals

What John L. Lewis Has Won For His Miners Since 1940

1940 ▼   **NOW** ▼

HOURLY PAY

85.7¢ (NORTH) 80¢ (SOUTH)	$1.63

TRAVEL-TIME PAY

NONE	1 HOUR A DAY

VACATION PAY

NONE	$100 A YEAR

LUNCH-TIME PAY

NONE	81.5¢ A DAY

EXTRA NIGHT PAY

NONE	4¢ AN HOUR, 2nd SHIFT 6¢ AN HOUR, 3rd SHIFT

WELFARE FUND

NONE	$50,000,000 A YEAR

TOOLS & EQUIPMENT

SUPPLIED BY MINER	SUPPLIED BY COMPANY

SAFETY RULES

ON STATE BASIS	FEDERAL RULES ENFORCED BY OPERATOR-UNION COMMITTEE

STATE COMPENSATION FOR MINE ACCIDENTS

NOT MANDATORY IN SOME STATES	APPLIES IN ALL STATES

PAY DIFFERENTIAL

5.7¢ AN HOUR LOWER IN SOUTHERN STATES	SAME RATES, NORTH & SOUTH

TAKE-HOME PAY

$30 (NORTH) } $28 (SOUTH) } 35 HOURS	$84.82 FOR 48 HOURS

of our society right in our hands. I can squeeze, twist, and pull until we get the inevitable victory. Whenever we strike, time is always on our side, for coal is basic to our economy.

"There are not huge profits in the coal industry, but there are enormous profits in steel, autos, rubber, and other industries. Stop coal and you stop steel. Stop steel and you stop autos and then tires and every part of our economy. Therefore, as a strike progresses, the hostility of the press and the Government begins to build up pressure against us; but on the other hand the pressures for profits in steel and autos also develop and increase. The industrialists of autos and steel begin to apply pressure on the coal operators to accede to our demands, so that their own fabulous profits will not be interrupted. Thus we become the immovable anvil, with the operators lying on us being hammered into surrender by the pounding blows of steel, autos [here Lewis laughed], and all our other industrial allies accomplices, if you will."

With this fact of coal as the prime source of energy of our economy, and with the complete unification of the miners to a degree where they act as one man in carrying out the orders of their chief, it was inevitable that the miners should finally dig themselves out from the serfdom that engulfed them as late as 1920. Let us glance at the record.

A listing of the fifteen major basic industries such as steel, automobiles, all manufacturing, printing, shipbuilding, meat packing, etc., on the average wage of 1935–39 showed the coal miners third from the bottom with a weekly wage of $22.16. By January, 1949, John Lewis had through successive successful strikes increased the coal miners' wage by 246.8 per cent and brought that weekly $22.16 wage up to $76.84! The coal miners' wages now lead the list of average earnings of these fifteen basic industries.

Lewis's drive for high wages for the miners was marked by a series of victories, but his real triumph came in the Welfare and Retirement Fund. Here with one sweep he wrested for his half-million miners that complete security that suddenly made life free from fear and filled with all the essentials for the pursuit of happiness.

Much has been talked and written concerning the resentment of the coal miners toward their "dictator," John L. Lewis. All the evidence is completely to the contrary. Lewis is almost revered by his followers.

One of the first miners to receive his pension check from the union Welfare Fund looked at Lewis and then stammered, "Mr. Lewis, this is the greatest thing since Jesus Christ."

Fortune in March, 1947,* featured a study of a typical coal miner named John Allshouse. *Fortune* stated, "John Allshouse is completely loyal to the United Mine Workers. John L. Lewis, he says, has won for the miners everything they've ever got. 'He earns his $25,000 a year.'" The discussion of Allshouse's feelings on Lewis continued with "He [Allshouse] knows that every time wages go up prices go up. 'Somebody's got to quit sometimes. Somebody's got to put things in balance. People say John L. Lewis ought to be shot or strung up, but it wouldn't surprise me if he turned out to be the one to balance things.'"

John Martin, reporting in the lead story of January 15, 1949, of the *Saturday Evening Post* on "What the Coal Miners Say about John L. Lewis," writes:

> Late that night some of them sat drinking beer in a circular booth at Steve Oravecz's clean tavern. Hoot Croyle, recording secretary of Local 3648, United Mine Workers of America, an earnest, intense young man with a thin face and pale arms, was saying, "Hell, the miners are proud of their union. It's a part of their lives. And they're proud of Lewis. He can take 'em all on, the whole world. He can meet with Senators and hold his 'ead up. . . .
>
> ". . . When I started in the mine there wasn't no union here. Our fathers worked without air. We've got portal to portal; we've got this and that. But the Health and Welfare Fund is the best thing the miners ever got. It protects the miner from the cradle to the grave. And if John L. Lewis didn't do another thing in this world, there should be a monument to the man."

Martin further reports:

> . . . He walked down the road and climbed a stony path. On a broad L-shaped porch overlooking the valley, sat Sam Osewalt, a round sad man in an undershirt. He sat in a wheel chair where he had sat since rock fell on him in the mine seventeen years ago. He had been twenty then. His industrial compensation award, the maximum, had amounted to fifteen dollars a week for about ten years. After that, except for $655 in donations from the local

* Reprinted from *Fortune*, March, 1947, by special permission of the editors. Copyright, Time, Inc.

union there had been nothing till Lewis won the Health and Welfare Fund. It pays him sixty dollars a month for life. He said bitterly but quietly, "The company never even bought me adhesive tape, and, buddy, when you buy a roll of tape now, it's eighty-five cents at the company store. They thought I'd be dead in a few weeks." Osewalt, nervous, wheeled himself to and fro.

Hoot held out a thumb-worn copy of the UMWA *Journal*. "This is what I come to see you about," he said, and pointed to a headline: REHABILITATION PROGRAM OF WELFARE FUND STARTS PARALYTICS ON ROAD TO NEW LIFE.

Osewalt nodded, "I seen it."

Hoot said, "Does that give you new hope, Sam?"

"Yeah. They have some way of fixing their backs up, I don't know."

"Well, I'm gonna write in about you and I need your papers." Osewalt smiled hopefully. "Yeah?"

They talked about fishing, about the new wash house, about the union. And what did Sam Osewalt think of John L. Lewis? He said, "What do you think I think of John L. Lewis?"

These two reports from national publications certainly not prejudiced in favor of Lewis are a sample of the vast majority of all surveys.

Frequently the miners' adulation of their chief expresses itself in mawkish verse such as:

> It takes courage to fight injustice,
>   To champion decency,
> To replace gloom with light and cheer
>   In the hearts of the needy.
>
> John L. Lewis, may God bless you,
>   You have put up a noble fight.
> The aged miners and the widows
>   Send their blessings day and night.[1]

Reams of this kind of eulogizing flow into the mine workers headquarters and are regularly featured in the mine workers *Journal*. They have their counterpart in the frequent reports that in the homes of many miners there are two pictures in the parlor, one of the Virgin Mary and the other of John L. Lewis.

Another outstanding example of the relationship between Lewis and his union is indicated by a statement of UMW Vice-

[1] *United Mine Workers Journal*, July 1, 1949.

President Thomas Kennedy, a devout Catholic, before the 1948 UMW convention in Cincinnati. Here, after Kennedy had delivered a vitriolic attack against the Government's attempts to divide Lewis from his miners, he ended, saying, ". . . Well, I think that is simply the application of the old adage of 'divide and conquer,' and if they think they can separate the membership of the United Mine Workers of America from its president, John L. Lewis, then they certainly have a ridiculous situation in mind. It would be about as reasonable to expect to separate His Holiness, the Pope, from the Catholic Church in the world. . . ."

This unanimity of feeling of the miners could not have been achieved just by machine power. Today even Lewis's severest critics admit the complete allegiance of his miners.

It should be noted here that Lewis not only organized his union as he did but also organized the coal industry. By means of legislation such as the Guffey Coal Act and by strikes Lewis introduced order and control to an industry dying of its own chaos. Lewis knew that the organization of the coal industry was almost as essential to the welfare of the miners as the organization of the union; for high wages could not be secured unless the industry could afford them. The coal operators today will be the first to admit that Lewis is the final authority on facts and figures and everything pertaining to coal.

He knows that to stabilize the coal industry and to stabilize his miners, his lone weapon is power. Lewis now is a disciple of power. He knows that an agreement is valid just so long as there is the power to enforce it. He knows that an advance in the living conditions of the miners will be permanent so long as there is the power to maintain it.

John Lewis once wrote in a letter, "My greatest error was to believe too long that the innate fairness and sense of honor of the leaders of finance and industry would cause them to voluntarily work with labor for the solution of our great economic questions and problems of industrial relationship."

Lewis rarely repeats his errors.

Lewis's battle for the miners recognized no barriers, whether they were coal operators or the President of the United States. His defiance of all official authorities resulted in a public picture of him as a mad egotist, driven by a lust for power so consuming that he refused to recognize or tolerate any interference or restraint upon his actions. Yet here, in this thirty-year, one-man war that Lewis has unabatedly waged against Presidents and Congresses, lies one of his greatest contributions to the American way of life.

It is important, as an essential ingredient in the leavening process of democracy, that every so often at least one individual, maybe just one in each generation, arise on his hind legs, look at the President of the United States, at the Congress of the United States, and in many cases the courts of America, and graphically and loudly condemn them to perdition, simultaneously challenging them to do their worst. Without this kind of one-man rebellion by a person with sufficient power to give meaning to the rebellion, there is always the danger that the executive, legislative, and judicial parts of our democratic government may become embalmed in their own prestige and feelings of self-importance and infallibility. Lewis's defiance and conflict have repeatedly pricked the growing bubble of inflationary self-importance on the part of the Congress and the President. His rebellion has shaken their acceptance of expected supine obedience from all before the altar of the "duly constituted authorities." Even when he has been wrong, his actions have contributed to this end. It is also very evident that Lewis still firmly believes in a principle that has been abandoned by the vast majority of American citizens, that publicly elected American officials are "servants of the people." Therefore to Lewis, the flaying of a senator or of a President is not insolence or disrespect but rather an American citizen telling his "servant" what to do. In a very significant sense, this is a fundamental contribution to the American scene; for being an American citizen should carry with it a dignity, a sense of mastery, as well as a clear recognition that public officials are and should be looked upon as servants of the people.

A graph depicting the political pattern of John Lewis would be expressed in a zigzag line fluctuating from left to right above a base of opportunism for organized labor. As Lewis changed, his politics followed suit. It was a long road from the Lewis of 1919 who declared that "we cannot fight our Government" to the Lewis of the past decade who has defied the Government at every turn. It was the same Lewis who almost daily denounced

communism in Russia and in the United States from 1920 to
1934 and who in 1935 replied to a question about Russia, "Russia? I don't care what Russia or the Russians are doing; that
is their business; but I do know that if this country needs and
wants a Russian system—or a Scandinavian system or a Chinese
system or any other kind of a system—then I am for it. To
determine . . . what is actually taking place in Russia is quite
impossible—at least for me. I think we will solve our own difficulties in our own way." [2]

We have seen Lewis desert the Republican party and march
up the hill to be a leading New Dealer, then turn around and
march down again to the Republican Old Guard. As late as
1932 Lewis was a Republican stalwart, wholeheartedly supporting Hoover against Roosevelt. As Lewis blossomed under and
gave support to the New Deal, many wondered how he possibly could have supported Hoover so shortly before.

There was good reason for Lewis's decision at that time. As
a life-long Republican, Lewis had an old personal friendship
with Hoover dating back to the days when Hoover had been
Secretary of Commerce and had helped Lewis in connection
with the Jacksonville agreement in 1924. Lewis felt that his personal relationship with Hoover would provide a base for some
concessions to the miners and broad pro-labor legislation along
the lines of what later became Section 7A of NRA. Also, Lewis
had concrete evidence that Hoover was tending in this direction since it was under Hoover's administration that the Norris-
LaGuardia Act was passed, containing many of the elements
of Section 7A. Furthermore, Lewis was so strong within the
Republican party that important segments of it had boomed
him as a candidate for the vice-presidency on the Hoover ticket.
The fact that there were forces in the Republican party that
thought of him in those terms made Lewis more hopeful of
wringing concessions from the Republicans than from the
Democrats. It should be noted as a postscript that Roosevelt's
campaign speeches in 1932 gave little clue of what was to come.

Lewis has always been a political maverick. Fundamentally
he is possessed of contempt for most political leaders and has
a deep distrust of their motivations and character and is not too
impressed by them, knowing that they are here today and usu-

[2] Selden Rodman, "Labor Leader No. 1," *Common Sense*, January, 1936.

ally gone with the counting of the ballots of the next election.

Much more complicated than his politics, and much more fascinating to the public, is Lewis's personality.

The grim, forbidding austerity and the slow deliberate gesture and manner of speech are suddenly adopted by Lewis as he steps out on the public stage. This conscious acting is absent in his personal relationships. Among his intimates he is warm, extraordinarily sympathetic, very expressive, filled with good humor, and a great raconteur. He enjoys a good story to the hilt, laughing until he shakes. Frequently, when narrating a humorous tale, he punctuates the story by prodding his listener with his finger. He has a very well-developed sense of humor, laughing as heartily at those jokes of which he is the butt as he does at others. In telling stories he will not only re-enact the roles of various individuals including himself but at times come close to an uproarious burlesque of the incident. In his family life, he would frequently tell his children, "He that tooteth not his own horn, the same shall not be tooted," and Lewis takes his own advice. Personally he is the antithesis of the appearance he presents to the public.

In the spring of 1943 the writer was conversing with Lewis in a New York restaurant. Lewis, as always in public places, was the center of attention, his physiognomy and eyebrows demanding and receiving immediate recognition, which the diners at various tables accorded by stopping and gaping. On this particular occasion, the writer mentioned to Lewis that there must be drawbacks to the lack of privacy and to being the cynosure of all eyes; that while it might be satisfying to the ego that people popularly attributed to him, nevertheless any person would want a certain degree of privacy and anonymity. The writer then gestured about saying, "Just as all these people around here are staring at you at this table. Doesn't it ever become rather embarrassing?"

Lewis laughed and said, "Well, it just happens that the other night I had an embarrassing experience. As you know, I am in New York negotiating with the operators; and the papers as usual are trying to lynch me with their headlines. Well, I was retiring about ten o'clock the other evening, and I walked into the hotel elevator. The car was empty, and I stepped to the back and faced front. Just before the elevator started to go up, a couple attired in formal dress entered the car. I could see by the expression on the man's face that he recognized me. The woman had not even glanced at me. They turned around facing forward so that their backs were toward me. As we started up, the woman turned to her escort saying, 'Say, it just occurred to me. I read in the papers that this is the hotel where that horrible John L. Lewis is stopping.'

"The man, somewhat agitated, nudged her, at the same time hissing, 'Shush.'

"The woman, somewhat startled, turned to him, saying, 'I don't know why you are trying to hush me up. Maybe you just didn't hear what I said. I said that this is the hotel where that terrible John L. Lewis is staying.'

"The man repeated the performance except this time much more agitated. It seems that his reaction irritated the good woman and she burst out with, 'I certainly cannot understand it. You seem to be afraid of my even mentioning his name. Well, all I can tell you is that you and everybody else, including the President of the United States, might be afraid of this monster, John L. Lewis, but if I ever saw him I would tell him a thing or two.' "

Lewis then chuckled and continued, "I brushed my eyebrows upward a little more and stepped forward in front of her saying, 'Yes, madam, what is it you wished to tell me?' She screamed and fainted. The operator stopped the car at the next floor, and we all helped to carry her out. While the operator was fetching some water, her escort was kneeling alongside of her slapping her wrists and calling her name. I tapped him on the shoulder saying, 'I beg your pardon but may I be of any assistance?'

"The man looked up at me and in a complete panic shouted, 'Yes, for God's sake go away, and I'll tell her she had a nightmare!' "

Lewis's body shook with laughter as he ended the story.

Lewis regards with great humor many of the motivations that are popularly attributed to him. It is generally believed, certainly by the press, that many of the obnoxiously antisocial editorials of the *United Mine Workers Journal* accurately reflect Lewis's opinions.

One day, during a discussion between Lewis and the writer,

the latter was critical of certain editorials appearing in the *Journal*.

Lewis replied, "Well, I can't comment on that because I don't get around to read much of what goes in that paper."

And yet many organizations and people promptly begin to develop ideas of Lewis's attitudes and forthcoming plans from these editorials, which are unfortunately more revealing of the thinking and attitudes of the editor of the magazine than they are of Lewis. This has been frequently true in the past, and should be borne in mind when the press constantly reports on Lewis's plans and thinking and position drawn from *United Mine Workers Journal* editorials. It is pertinent to point out here that the scurrilous nature of many of these editorials is most unlike Lewis.

Lewis's personal habits are not unusual except for his reading. He is devoted to the classics and has read a vast part of the so-called great books. He is extremely interested in detailed accounts of military campaigns such as the Napoleonic wars, the history of the Peloponnesian wars and military strategy during the Civil War. The Bible and Shakespeare are his prime sources for quotations. Although an inveterate reader of the classics he shifts over to sensational detective stories for relaxation.

His drinking is confined to an occasional highball; and he is rarely seen without his cigar, either lit or unlit. He does not gamble and has very few hobbies. He became interested in the collection of Americana his wife and daughter began some years ago. It is significant that one of the largest pieces of early American furniture in his home is a cabinet that once belonged to John Brown. For certainly Lewis is the modern prototype of "God's Angry Man."

One of the secrets of John Lewis's amazing energy is his ability suddenly to relax and rest. He is able to dismiss the most pressing controversy from his mind and concentrate on some minor point. The story is often told that, at the height of the sit-down strikes in General Motors with every newspaper screaming that the country was on the verge of a revolution and that John L. Lewis was the arch revolutionary, Lewis suddenly was incommunicado in his office. Speculations ran rampant in the nation as to what Lewis was doing and why he refused to see anyone. It later developed that he was closeted

with one of his associates, calling up various furnace r
places in Washington since the coal furnace in Lewis's home
in Virginia had gone out of order. During that brief time
Lewis was able to forget completely about the sit-down strike
in Detroit and the tension throughout the country and concentrate on this one domestic matter.

Contrary to public opinion, Lewis does not nurse grudges
and plot vendettas. Even with his bitterness toward Murray, he
does not operate on the basis of revenge. True that if the opportunity presents itself, he will hit Murray with all of his
power, but Lewis is not intent upon creating the opportunity.
Lewis's past history is indicative of this fact. He has made alliances with men whom he had bitterly fought on various issues,
such as Brophy, Hapgood, Germer, Hutcheson, Green, Dubinsky, Woll, Haywood, Edmundson, and a host of others. Lewis
once told the writer, "He who seeks vengeance ultimately
destroys himself."

Lewis loves to pose as an all-knowing modern version of the
mythological oracle. Although professing a disdain for gossip
and stories, he absorbs them like a human sponge. He will never
give the slightest indication about his knowledge to the person
involved in the tale. However, each bit of information is carefully stored away and suddenly brought forward when it is
needed. His timely use of this information transforms it from
interesting gossip to a humiliating weapon against its victim.

Lewis once gave a dramatic taste of his "oracle" role to a
prominent labor leader whom he resented for remaining in the
AF of L after professing allegiance to the CIO.

These were the circumstances: During the summer of 1936
the AF of L executive council met at the Hamilton Hotel at
Fourteenth and R Streets, Washington, D.C. The CIO offices
at that time were across the street in the Tower Building.
The main business of this AF of L executive board meeting concerned a review of the activities of the CIO and consideration of
measures to be taken against the CIO with specific reference
to the disbanding of the Steel Workers Organizing Committee.
Because of the dramatic sensation of the CIO, this particular meeting of the AF of L found itself the center of attention by the press. The AF of L's threat against the very life
of the CIO was then front-page news. The AF of L itself was

not news, but its impending struggle with the CIO made it of national interest. The press room outside of the board meeting was jammed with reporters. As the meeting continued through the hours, the waiting reporters became more and more restless. Finally one of them left the press room to go to the bathroom down the hall on the same floor. In the bathroom he suddenly began to "hear voices." After a momentary panic he reassured himself of his sanity and began a careful investigation of his surroundings. The "voices" continued, and he recognized the voices of Green, Woll, Frey, Hutcheson, Dubinsky, and others. He soon stumbled across the explanation: a ventilating shaft ran directly from the room where the AF of L board meeting was being held to the bathroom.

The reporter listened intently for some time, then left the building, crossed the street, and told Lewis what he had heard. This reporter was well known for his strong sympathy for the CIO.

Fifteen minutes later the AF of L board meeting adjourned. The union leader in question hurriedly left the Hamilton Hotel, raced across the street to the Tower Building, and ran into Lewis's office breathless, with his necktie awry, his face flushed, and generally giving the appearance of a loyal Lewis partisan who had rushed as quickly as he could to inform his "ally" of what the enemy was plotting. He stood breathlessly before Lewis's desk holding out his hand in a gesture of. "Just give me a moment until I can catch my breath and then I will tell you."

While he stood there, Lewis suddenly arose and speaking slowly and deliberately with an accusing tone said, "When they attacked me, why did you agree with them? When Frey charged what he did against the Steel Workers Organizing Committee and the CIO and I repeat [Lewis then repeated Frey's verbatim statement], why did you agree and say, and I repeat verbatim what you said [Lewis then repeated the leader's statement verbatim]? Why do you agree with me here in the CIO office and agree with those in the AF of L board meeting across the street? I ask you, why?"

Speechless and covered with confusion, the flabbergasted intriguer fearfully left Lewis's office.

But for Lewis, the role of the oracle is an infrequent one.

He revels in the battle of the word and of the wit, for here his ability to think incredibly fast on his feet and his keen wit are able to confound those who square off against him. He has the invariable knack of swinging a verbal smash at the right time. He possesses an extraordinary faculty for epithets. He has been able to excoriate individuals with insulting appellations that have clung to them for years, and in some cases, have destroyed their public careers. Former Vice-President John Nance Garner will always carry Lewis's brand of a "poker playing, whisky drinking, labor baiting, evil old man."

The enigma of Lewis has baffled all who have tried to understand the extraordinary combination of extreme contradictions that is fused into his personality. His radical stand on certain issues and his conservative position on others have confounded both his critics and his allies.

No one could have been more radical and stubborn to the point of self-destruction than was Lewis in the late 1920's when he refused to yield to the Jim Crow of the South. When mine workers union organizers went below the Mason-Dixon line to unionize the coal mines, they faced the full prejudice of a South unleavened by the New Deal or CIO or much of an AF of L. Lewis was deluged by requests and petitions from his own organizers and the union locals themselves that they be segregated into white and Negro locals. He was warned that if he barred segregation he might destroy his own union in the South. Lewis refused to budge and the nonsegregated union locals of the miners union were labor's first big denting of the South's Jim Crow practice. It has never received the publicity it has deserved; and now the Southern locals are almost half white and half Negro.

Just as Lewis refused to retreat before the pressure of these forces, so did he in a contradictory fashion stubbornly ally himself with the isolationists in this country during the time when Hitler made his bid to Jim-Crow every non-German. Here, Lewis refused to analyze logically and act on the dynamics of the situation, and stuck to his position though it cost him his own creation—the CIO.

It is the writer's conviction that the key to the understanding of Lewis's personality is to be found in his extraordinary tenacity of purpose. Lewis is stiff-necked in his stubbornness. He continues to cling to a position regardless of world change. He will obstinately stand fast on a policy even after he has developed along avenues running at cross-purposes to his previous, but still held, opinions. Inconsistencies or contradictions create no conflict in Lewis.

A vivid demonstration of this obliviousness to inconsistencies occurred once in late 1935 when Lewis, then a crusading New Dealer in support of the economic planning that was the core of the New Deal, was queried about his book, *The Miners Fight for American Standards,* which espoused the "free play of natural economic laws," then blasphemy to the New Deal. Lewis replied, "Would that mine enemy had written a book!" and then went on to say that he more or less still agreed with the thesis of his book.

The recognition of this fact illuminates Lewis's answer to Britain's Harold Laski when, during the height of the CIO drive, he questioned Lewis, asking, "Tell me, Mr. Lewis, how do you explain your present progressive actions, radical political policies, and being the great leader and hero of the liberal and progressive movements, as well as of the CIO, in the light of your past reactionary labor leadership and red baiting?"

Lewis stolidly replied, "I am still the kind of man I have always been, contrary to your previous estimates."

It is possible that Lewis absorbed the slogan he shouted from 1920 to 1930, "No Backward Step." His mulish refusal to budge from a position, regardless of the intensity of the attack, is one of the outstanding characteristics of his personality. Certainly the building of his own union and later the CIO and his incessant battle throughout this period with every institution in the country would not have been possible without his indomitable, unyielding stubbornness.

And yet, as is common in persons and nations, his greatest strength proved also to be his greatest weakness. Lewis's inflexibility in the face of the changing tides of time placed him in the position of an embattled Don Quixote. His adamant, almost blind stubbornness kept Lewis from reaching to the stars. He could have changed the destiny of his nation and with it the world. America today might well have been ruled by an American labor party. Destiny was at Lewis's feet, but he refused to stoop even slightly to conquer. Facts are stubborn, but Lewis tried to be more stubborn than the facts, and so, refusing to bend with the times, he fell from power in the CIO.

In his own life Lewis had already been conceded the position of the greatest and most dynamic leader of labor in the history of the United States. Even his critics bitterly admit to his historic place.

Harold Laski states: "Looking over the history of American trade-unionism, it is difficult not to admit that, despite his illimitable vanity, his ruthlessness, and, what was no doubt its main source, his vast appetite for power, Mr. Lewis has been, thus far, the most dynamic figure in its record." [3]

Professor Selig Perlman, foremost American authority on the theory and history of the American labor movement, discussing the period of Roosevelt's New Deal, told the writer: "Of those that kept their eyes open, and with the 'will to organize,' John L. Lewis was the only one who possessed the indispensable capacity to dramatize in his own person that 'the hour of labor's redemption has arrived.' By the early months of 1937 when the auto workers 'sat down,' Lewis was the 'George Washington of American labor.' Not many of the contemporaries will forget how the press and the radio issued bulletins on his journey to Detroit to meet the top men of General Motors. It is hard to conceive of the rise of American mass production unionism without the confidence of victory radiating from his personality and self-assurance.

"Gompers and Lewis both faced the realities in their land— the one excelling in the art of persuasion within his own camp and of advocacy to the public at large, the other believing in power, the appearance no less than the substance. It looks as though the latter has missed becoming the acknowledged ancestor of the 'new nation' because of too much concern with being a crowned personage." [4]

The late Powers Hapgood, one of Lewis's leading foes through the twenties, stated to the writer, "I fought against him and fought with him. There never was a leader of his stature and ability. He is a great leader. The other so-called

[3] Harold Laski, *The American Democracy* (New York: The Viking Press, 1948), p. 243.
[4] Interview with Professor Selig Perlman, July 8, 1949, Madison, Wis.

labor leaders I have worked under are like children compared to John. He can set you afire, he is the greatest of them all. There is no comparison." [5]

Even his greatest adversary, Franklin Delano Roosevelt, during his fierce war with Lewis in 1943 grudgingly acknowledged, "Well, you have to admit Lewis has done a lot for his miners." [6]

Today Lewis is as content as he ever can be with the progress of the coal miners. Impatient of national planning and politicking, he has fought and won social security for his miners. Since 1932 he has, without exception, steadily boosted the earnings of the miners until now they are close to being the highest-paid working segment of our population.

But Lewis glowers at the national scene. From his point of view, he sees the American labor movement almost servile in its dependence upon the political administration. For a bit of promised help here and there, such as investigating panels and other devices, he feels organized labor has bartered its independence. To Lewis, the labor movement should be independent and strong enough to force the Government to respond to its will, rather than that labor should respond to the desires of the Government. Labor's abject capitulation to the Taft-Hartley Law shocked Lewis, who advocated that by the one simple tactic of the AF of L and the CIO not signing the affidavits the entire Taft-Hartley Law would have been wrecked. He pleaded for this course of action, but the labor movement had lost the will to fight.

Lewis, in action and thought far younger than his years, appears at his prime. But Lewis is restless. He is accustomed to far more *lebensraum* than the area of the mine workers union. There are stories loose in the land that the politically left unions of the CIO would like to forsake it for the building of a third labor movement. But another labor movement today could be successful only if led by Lewis. For only Lewis, who towers over all other labor leaders as a giant over pygmies, could provide the genius, the strategy, and the dramatic leadership necessary for such a vast venture. The left wing is prayerful that Lewis will take the challenge, but it is dubious that he is

[5] Interview with Powers Hapgood, January 12, 1949, Indianapolis, Ind.
[6] Frances Perkins, *The Roosevelt I Knew* (New York: Viking Press, 1946), p. 327.

willing or feels able to try to repeat the great drive of the CIO. He will never forget his desertion by the left-wing leaders after the Nazi invasion of the Soviet Union on June 22, 1941. It is impossible that he would again ally himself with a group for which he now harbors such deep distrust and contempt.

What will Lewis do now? He is, as he always has been and will be, planning and attacking. There will still be sudden shocking moves, for Lewis has never backed away from an all-or-nothing gamble. Everything in Lewis's past points to his careful planning for the future. He is restless within the confines of coal. About him he sees a labor movement that he is convinced has become so dependent upon political power that it has lost its independence and strength. Lewis has always viewed his mine workers union as the "shock troops of organized labor," and it is probable that the shock troops will again be hurled into the arena. It is fairly certain that Lewis is preparing a general offensive to break this dependency of labor upon the Government. However, the future is as utterly unpredictable as is John L. Lewis.

As this is written, John L. Lewis stands on the threshold of three score and ten years. No ingenious maneuvering, no grand strategy, no force of the single undivided discipline of nearly one half a million miners, no human element can avail itself against the inevitable, which casts its dark shadow of finis on the life of Lewis. The active years ahead are by all universal laws drastically limited, but just as definite is the fact that they will be years of tempest; for Lewis is a man of strife.

One gloomy late afternoon, during a meeting with Lewis, the writer referred to certain parts of Lewis's life with the remark that if Lewis had acted differently in a number of crises or if certain factors, both international and domestic, had not impinged as and when they did, the history of our nation would have been radically changed, that a third major political party would have emerged in a climate of revolution.

Lewis's answer came slowly as he almost seemed to weigh each word, "The doors of history swing on tiny hinges. Nothing is more barren and futile than speculation on what might have been." His head sank further, and for some moments there was silence as his eyes were fixed on the floor. Suddenly he tossed his head back; his face seemed to light up as he spoke. "I care not what might have been. I care only for today and the wonder of life itself, the sunrise of tomorrow and the new dawn. For this and in this I live." And for this and in this Lewis has lived. He will go on leading his miners until death will take him— as quickly as his miners answer his call to strike.

Conflict, defiance, rage, dreams of fire, bold maneuvering, and cold calculation are some of the characteristics that spell out the drama of the life of Lewis.

His passing will mean the end of an era. It will be greeted with curses and the feelings of deliverance from a life-long plague. People will no longer be concerned about coal strikes occurring every spring. No longer will the President of the United States be defied, insulted, and publicly humiliated. No longer will Congress be treated as a lackey and challenged to a match of power. No longer will the constant national crises and the turbulent doings of this dramatic outlaw crowd nearly everything else off the front pages of the press.

America will sigh with relief, and yet America will sorely miss him. We shall miss those perennial strikes, his unbearable insolence to all authorities, the grimness of his unparalleled, stiff-necked determination, and his colorful epithets. We will miss cursing, ridiculing, fuming over him, and giving that grudging admiration for his doing what so many people would like to do: openly and successfully defy the political as well as the economic royalists. We shall realize that his defiance of every power was a note of reassurance for the security of the democratic idea, that his dissonance was part of our national music. For all these things have been indelibly woven into the fabric of the past thirty years of America and have become part of the tradition of America. But until that time, today, as before, and to the end, Lewis will continue as the incredible earth-quake beneath our economy. The years of thunder in the earth will roar on as Lewis lives on, for he is, as he has bellowed at his miners, "something of a man."

Index

Epilogue to the Vintage Edition

The years have passed and the world has changed drastically. The C.I.O. merged with the A.F.L. and the labor movement receded from its former position of being the nation's spearhead of realistic radicalism to becoming increasingly conservative politically and economically. With the rare exception of labor leaders such as the late Walter Reuther and Ralph Helstein, the organized labor movement was noticeably absent in the militant vanguard of the civil-rights battles of the 1960's. On Vietnam the rich establishment of organized labor was aligned with the hawks. The A.F.L.–C.I.O. had become middle-class and in many ways part of the establishment.

A few labor leaders dreamed of a resurgence and an organizing drive among the poor, but this was a romantic fantasy. It was a nostalgia reflection of the turbulent days of the 1930's. What was overlooked by these few labor leaders was that the leaders who organized the C.I.O. were fiery young radicals fighting all forms of social injustice; they were men and women immersed in the battles against fascism, against evictions of sharecroppers in the country and the unemployed in the cities, fighting for the recognition of organized labor by the mass corporate structure of America; in itself a revolutionary idea. They were concerned about civil rights, about the New Deal, public housing (which was a radical idea in those days), the International Brigade in Spain and a myriad of revolutionary ideas, and to them the C.I.O. and its labor-organizing activities were simply the most pragmatic vehicle for carrying on these multiple activities. The labor union organizer of today is generally a college graduate who has majored in economics, accounting, labor relations and is a professional encysted in his own little world of welfare funds, automation, escalator clauses and the straight bread-and-butter economics of his organization. The kind of radicals that built the C.I.O. are not present today in the labor movement, and their closest facsimiles are in many of the more realistic campus activists, not to be confused with the pathetically sick Weathermen or their neuro-types.

Through this period the coal industry steadily deteriorated and so did the union. In the interim John L. Lewis resigned in the late 1950's. Kathryn, his daughter, and a central figure in his life, had died. Her death to a significant extent was the death of a large part of the heart and will of John L. Lewis. She was the one member of his family who realized her father's place in history.

Following his retirement he would visit his private offices on the sixth floor of the Mineworkers Building from time to time and there were occasional phone calls and a couple of visits between us. These were regrettably few, as my own life and activities found me rarely in Washington. He was always informed about my doings, and that beautiful sense of humor so characteristic of him was always there. With all, I found myself still learning from a John L. Lewis of an advanced age.

On his sense of humor he once growled at me, "I've kept up on your doings and I want you to know that I resent the fact that you are more hated in Rochester, New York, than I ever was," and then he would break up with laughter.

On his teaching me, I remember one day, just a couple of years ago, when I stopped in and he said to me, "How old are you, Saul?" I replied, "Fifty-six, going on fifty-eight." He said, "That's very interesting. You're exactly the same age that I was when I really organized the C.I.O." I stared at him and then said, "Oh, you must be putting me on." He snorted, "What are you talking about? You ought to know. You wrote my biography." I thought quickly to myself, "Let's see, he was born February 12, 1880, the C.I.O. was really rolling in 1937–38—why, yes, he was fifty-seven or fifty-eight at the height of the C.I.O." Lewis broke into my thoughts, "Your trouble is that you are another victim of the Kennedy brainwash. You see, before Jack Kennedy and the 1960 presidential campaign, no one was deemed to have reached his prime of vigor and ability until he was around sixty, and until his early sixties one was not even seriously considered as a senator or presidential candidate. But by the time the Kennedys got through with their propaganda, anyone past the age of forty-five was ready to go to a mortuary or junkyard or drop dead." He was right, and it was an important lesson to learn in these days when chronological "youth" has become a fetish.

Lewis' absences from the union office became greater as he began to suffer health problems. But almost to the end his mind was alert and competent to a degree rarely found at that age.

The year following his death found the union beset with closing coal mines, factionalism, internecine warfare and the highly pub-

licized killing of Joseph Yablonski. Public hostility, press and governmental coolness and criticism mounted in proportion as the power of
the union waned. Lewis' physical presence was no longer there as a
central bulwark.

In June, 1969, he died.

History is written in the enigma of the paradox. To survive physically the time of life itself—the years of passion, adventure, creation,
conflict and the changing of the world—is in itself tragic. It can be
fatal to one's place in history. Gandhi came perilously close to cross-
ing that chronological threshold when already his *Satygraha* was
being undermined by his approval of the armed invasion of Kashmir.
He knew the importance of his last words to his assassin: "You are
late."

John L. survived his life by a full generation. If he had died in
1939 or 1940, history would have recorded him as the great champion
of the oppressed, our folklore would have included the saying, "If
the great John L. Lewis had not died, this would never have happened." Lewis was idolized by the oppressed and the have-nots of
the world. In South America his name was revered by the peons
and peasants, feared and hated by the establishment. He was the
battling, invincible gladiator fighting for all the workers. *Unfortunately*—and I choose the word carefully, for I loved him not only as
my teacher, my close friend but literally my political father—unfortunately he survived his life. He survived his life and that of his enemies, and with few exceptions, his friends, his allies and, in a
significant sense, his union, and the world he had known. It is sad
that John L. Lewis physically left at a time when his enemies were
not here to exult or his friends to grieve, and when the younger
generation was saying, "We thought he died years ago." And because
of this he is bound to suffer historically. It is the paradox that history
has great difficulty making a valid judgment if one physically goes
on too long. One's place in history is decided not only by *when* one
dies but by *how* one dies, so in a real way the assassin becomes the
friend and historical ally of the gladiator. The inner unspoken
prayer of the gladiator in the arena is that he will die in battle and
that his very physical act of dying will carry a meaning and a force
to the eternal struggle.

Of course, the John L. Lewis I knew was different in human
quality from the towering grim, belligerent, pontifical public figure
whom the public saw. He loved life, loved the laughter and the joy
and the danger of it. He had a habit with his personal friends of
punctuating humorous anecdotes by jabbing you in the stomach
with his forefinger, and many a time late at night I would ruefully

look at the bruises on my stomach and ribs and then break up in laughter, recalling the stories. When he laughed, he laughed with every part of his body.

I remember his anger and hurt when we left the White House after the stormy bedroom scene with Franklin Delano Roosevelt which came to a climax when Lewis wheeled on the President and said, "No one can call John L. Lewis a liar, and least of all, F.D.R.!" There was fire between us as Lewis stormed out of the White House muttering, "Plague on both their houses," and I insisted that if he was not going to support my political hero, F.D.R., he would have to declare for Willkie. He could not stay neutral without playing into the hands of complete Communist domination of the then C.I.O. He could not strengthen the claim of the American Communist Party that Roosevelt was a warmonger and Willkie "a barefoot Wall Street boy," that it was an imperialist war and the hell with both of them. There was that moment when Lewis charged me with being more with F.D.R. than with him. But then he knew that it was not being more with F.D.R. than with John L., but being totally against Adolf Hitler which transcended every other consideration, and so our friendship continued.

If I speak here in personal terms it is because it is the best way to see and understand that man John L. Lewis. There was an afternoon a few weeks after I had experienced a shattering personal tragedy and was in deep mourning. I went to Washington and did what I had done every place else—walked alone. As I passed the White House the gate swung open and a big Cadillac came out. It braked to a sudden stop and out came Lewis. He had just left the President and suddenly saw his friend and knew of the ordeal. Without a word he put his arm through mine, and we walked for some hours in utter silence except for the frequent reassuring squeeze from the hand of that man. Tenderness he possessed and compassion and love. One had to dig for it as though he were a deep mine, but the deposits were rich and beautiful.

He cared and felt deeply beneath the impassive mask of seemingly cold unapproachable ruthlessness. I saw him weep at the plight of others.

Human to the inner atom, a master of power on a mass base, he would constantly make the mistake in his personal life of not abiding by the lessons of power he so brilliantly formulated and propounded. When I would criticize him for permitting personal relationships to confuse and cloud his own understanding of power, he would grin and say, "Sometime you'll understand." In later years I found myself making the same mistakes. Of all my teachers in power and mass organization, he was the greatest.

What else is there for me to say except to quote from the last page of this biography: "The doors of history swing on tiny hinges. Nothing is more barren and futile than speculation on what might have been. I care not what might have been...I care only for today and the wonder of life itself, the sunrise of tomorrow and the new dawn. For this and in this I live."

His defiance of every power from the White House out was a note of reassurance for the security of the democratic idea, that his dissonance was part of our national music. He was and will always be to me—as history will eventually make him to all men—in the words which he had bellowed at his miners, "Something of a man."

S.D.A.

1970

About the Author

SAUL ALINSKY was born in Chicago in 1909, and educated first in the streets of that city and then in its university. Graduate work at the University of Chicago in criminology introduced him to the Capone gang, and later to Joliet State Prison, where he studied prison life.

He founded what is known today as the Alinsky ideology and Alinsky concepts of mass organization for power. His work in organizing the poor to fight for their rights as citizens has been internationally recognized. In the late 1930's he organized the Back of the Yards area in Chicago (Upton Sinclair's *Jungle*). Subsequently, through the Industrial Areas Foundation which he began in 1940, Mr. Alinsky and his staff have helped to organize communities not only in Chicago but throughout the country, from the black ghetto of Rochester, New York, to the Mexican American barrios of California. Today Mr. Alinsky's organizing attention has turned to the middle class, and he and his associates have a Training Institute for organizers. Mr. Alinsky's early organizing efforts resulted in his being arrested and jailed from time to time, and it was on such occasions that he wrote most of *Reveille for Radicals*, available in Vintage Books.

A free catalogue of VINTAGE BOOKS *will be sent at your request. Write to* Vintage Books, 457 Madison Avenue, New York, New York 10022.

VINTAGE HISTORY—AMERICAN

A free catalogue of VINTAGE BOOKS *will be sent at your request. Write to* Vintage Books, 457 Madison Avenue, New York, New York 10022.

VINTAGE BIOGRAPHY AND AUTOBIOGRAPHY

A free catalogue of VINTAGE BOOKS *will be sent at your request. Write to* Vintage Books, 457 Madison Avenue, New York, New York 10022.

GLASSBORO STATE COLLEGE